GLOBAL FORESTS

ISSUES FOR SIX BILLION PEOPLE

McGraw-Hill Series in Forest Resources

Avery and Burkhart: Forest Measurements
Brockman and Merriam: Recreational Use of Wild Lands
Brown and Davis: Forest Fire: Control and Use
Dana and Fairfax: Forest and Range Policy
Daniel, Helms, and Baker: Principles of Silviculture
Davis: Land Use
Davis and Johnson: Forest Management
Dykstra: Mathematical Programming for Natural Resource Management
Ellefson: Forest Resource Policy: Process, Participants, and Programs
Harlow, Harrar, Hardin, and White: Textbook of Dendrology
Heady: Rangeland Management
Knight and Heikkenen: Principles of Forest Entomology
Laarman and Sedjo: Global Forests: Issues for Six Billion People
Panshin and De Zeeuw: Textbook of Wood Technology
Panshin, Harrar, Bethel, and Baker: Forest Products
Sharpe, Hendee, and Sharpe: Introduction to Forestry
Shirley: Forestry and Its Career Opportunities
Sinclair: Forest Products Marketing
Stoddart, Smith, and Box: Range Management

Walter Mulford was Consulting Editor of this series from its inception in 1931 until January 1, 1952.

Henry J. Vaux was Consulting Editor of this series from January 1, 1952, until July 1, 1976.

Paul V. Ellefson, University of Minnesota, is currently our Consulting Editor.

GLOBAL FORESTS

ISSUES FOR SIX BILLION PEOPLE

Jan G. Laarman
Professor, Department of Forestry
North Carolina State University

Roger A. Sedjo
Director, Forest Economics
and Policy
Resources for the Future

McGRAW-HILL, INC.

New York St. Louis San Francisco Auckland Bogotá
Caracas Hamburg Lisbon London Madrid Mexico Milan Montreal
New Delhi Paris San Juan São Paulo Singapore Sydney Tokyo Toronto

This book was set in Times Roman by Publication Services.
The editors were Anne C. Duffy and John M. Morriss;
the production supervisor was Denise L. Puryear.
The cover was designed by David Romanoff;
cover photo by Carlos Wilson.
Project supervision was done by Publication Services.
R. R. Donnelley & Sons Company was printer and binder.

Cover Photo
Rainforests, like this one in Costa Rica, are the subject of widespread international controversy on which to preserve and which to open for economic development. Courtesy of Carlos Wilson.

GLOBAL FORESTS
Issues for Six Billion People

1 2 3 4 5 6 7 8 9 0 DOC DOC 9 0 9 8 7 6 5 4 3 2 1

ISBN 0-07-035702-1

Library of Congress Cataloging-in-Publication Data

Laarman, Jan G.
    Global forests: issues for six billion people / Jan G. Laarman, Roger A. Sedjo.
        p.   cm.—(McGraw-Hill series in forest resources)
    Includes bibliographic references.
    ISBN 0-07-035702-1
    1. Forests and forestry.   2. Forest management.   3. Forests and forestry—economic
aspects.   4. Forest products industry.   5. Forests and forestry—International cooperation.
I. Sedjo, Roger A.   II. Title.   III. Series.
    SD373.L33   1992
    333.75—dc20
                                                                                      91-15182

ABOUT THE AUTHORS

JAN G. LAARMAN is Professor in the Department of Forestry, North Carolina State University. His interests are the role of forests in regional economic development with emphasis on employment, forest products trade, forestry policy reform, and forestry project design and evaluation. He was recently a Fulbright Fellow in Central America, and for 15 years has served as advisor or consultant to various international agencies and development banks. Professor Laarman's B.S. degree in forestry is from the University of Michigan, and he holds his Ph. D. in wildlands policy and economics from the University of California, Berkeley.

ROGER A. SEDJO is a Senior Fellow and Director of the Forest Economics and Policy Program at Resources for the Future, Washington, D.C. Dr. Sedjo has considerable international experience, having been formerly employed by the United States Agency for International Development, and having done considerable international consulting. He is the author and editor of several books, and has written extensively on international forest resource and environmental issues. Dr. Sedjo received his Ph.D. from the University of Washington, and his B.S. and M.S. from the University of Illinois.

To those among you, our readers, with the curiosity and determination to learn as much as possible about the forests of the world and the people who need them. May your journey for understanding be rewarded, and may you blaze a path where others will follow.

ACKNOWLEDGMENTS

This book has lived in the hearts and minds of several persons for a number of years. We thank all those who had a hand in its conceptualization, many reformulations, and eventual production. In particular, we want to acknowledge the substantial contributions of Prof. Robert Healy, Duke University, for his critiques of the first few chapters of the book, and for his direct input to early drafts of Chapter 7. To him goes much of the credit for defining the book's direction.

We also express our appreciation to numerous colleagues and reviewers who have attempted to keep us on the track of factual accuracy and interpretive objectivity. Among the individuals who made suggestions at one stage or another are Clark S. Binkley, University of British Columbia; William Burch, Yale University; Dennis Dykstra, Northern Arizona University; Paul Ellefson, University of Minnesota; John C. Gordon, Yale University; Hans Gregersen, University of Minnesota; David Harcharik, U.S. Department of Agriculture; William Hyde, U.S. Department of Agriculture; William McKillop, University of California–Berkeley; Gerald Schreuder, University of Washington; and Harold Wisdom, VPI & SU. Additionally, we are indebted to 14 graduate students in the class of FOR 512 at North Carolina State University (Fall 1990) for their evaluations of substantial portions of the manuscript. We realize that we have not met every expectation of our reviewers, and we alone stand responsible for the book's remaining deficiencies.

Finally, we express appreciation to the many individuals who contributed to the production aspects of this book. For their gracious help in directing us to photos, we thank Stephen Dembner, Guiditta Dolci-Favi, Yosef Hadar, Cheryl Oakes, Jonas Palm, and Pete Steen. John Abbott, librarian at North Carolina State University, was exceptionally helpful in locating references. We are pleased to have worked with John Zumerchik, Scott Spoolman, and especially Anne Duffy in their able coordination of manuscript reviews and other production tasks at McGraw-Hill. We likewise thank J.C. Morgan and staff at Publication Services for capable management of copyediting and page production. Paul Ellefson, consulting editor to McGraw-Hill for this series of forestry texts, maintained an abiding faith in our ability to write this book. To each of these individuals, and to others not mentioned by name, we are deeply grateful.

Jan G. Laarman

Roger A. Sedjo

PREFACE

Demographers estimate that the world's human population will reach six billion around the year 2000. These six billion persons will live in about 170 countries, a number that continues to fluctuate with shifting political alignments. The 170 separate countries and territories will divide or share—according to the observer's perspective—over five billion hectares of forests, open woodlands, and shrublands. This is about 40 percent of the earth's terrestrial surface. Six billion people will depend on these five billion hectares for material, cultural, and life-support needs.

Importantly, the way forests are managed in any of the 170 countries and territories affects the welfare of people living in the other 169. These effects may be small or large, economic or environmental, intended or unintended. Recognition of connections across national borders affirms the premise that the world is a "global village."

In the global village, forest clearing in Brazil alarms environmental groups in London and Washington. Emissions from fossil fuel combustion in the USA provoke political speeches alleging damage to forest ecosystems in Canada. New Zealand's exports of forest products to East Asia compete with exports from Chile, Canada, and the USA. Development assistance from Japan supports forestry projects in Thailand and the Philippines. The list of examples could be extended and amplified, but its central point is that issues of forest protection and management are defined by events and possibilities beyond national borders.

This observation is neither original nor revolutionary. Millennia ago, reconnaissance expeditions left Mediterranean ports in search of ship timbers from distant shores. Medieval Flanders supported a thriving international trade in timber and wood. Norway's wood exports developed considerably in the thirteenth and fourteenth centuries. From these early origins has developed an even wider and more complex international trade in forest products.

Besides international commerce, a second set of connections across countries is much more recent but at least as complex. This refers to the rise of environmentalism and the growing "Green Movements" nationally and internationally, particularly since 1970. The environmental agenda, in turn, is conceptually linked with a whole series of major problems defined at a world level. Not least among these are population pressures, numerous and bitter regional wars, huge "North-South" economic gaps, deficient institutional structures to manage international affairs, and disturbing crises of political priorities.

In seeking a way out of this distress, strategists urge us to think in terms of one small planet and one common future. The imperatives to manage the planetary environment and to reduce mass poverty on a global scale loom large among the grand challenges posed by contemporary societies. These and related concerns should be drawing us outward. The view must be outward towards allied professional and scientific disciplines concerned with many of these same issues. It must be outward towards new interest groups and voluntary organizations deeply concerned about these problems. Moreover, it must be outward towards professional colleagues around the world separated from each other by accidents of geography and language, but united by bonds of genuine good will.

The one-world ideal seriously challenges conventional approaches in professional education. A common tendency has been to study forests and forestry in a domestic setting, treating international aspects separately or as a footnote. The consequence is to produce perspectives which are narrower, less creative, and ultimately less relevant than they could be. The view that "international forestry" is an interesting but subsidiary area of study fails to acknowledge the conceptual wholeness of economic, social, and biological systems which link across political boundaries. It fails to connect national problems with a supranational context. It fails to enable foresters and other land managers to practice the first part of the familiar instruction, "think globally, act locally."

This book is not a solution to those problems. However, it does attempt to enlarge the context in which forests are studied. This context is less one of world forest geography than of identifying policy and management issues which cut across national borders.

The first three chapters constitute an introduction to the book's central theme of forests for human development. Chapter 1 presents a framework of forest products, services, and values within a one-world context. This context is both the same as and different from worlds which existed previously. Chapter 2 provides a broad overview of world forest areas, deforestation dynamics, and key transitions from deforestation to forest renewal. Chapter 3 then connects forests and forestry with the goals and complexities of economic development in different settings and against different constraints.

The second part of the book (Chapters 4–7) addresses leading issues in policy and management at a global level. Chapter 4 describes world production and consumption of forest products, together with varying perspectives on the role and appropriateness of forest industries in regional development. This is followed in Chapter 5 by the patterns, determinants, and institutional arrangements governing international trade in forest products.

Chapter 6 considers the principles and limitations of tree growing on farms and in local communities. Our preference is for the term "farm and community forestry" (using agroforestry technologies), although this is largely synonymous with "social forestry" as these meanings have come to be understood since the 1970s.

Chapter 7 takes up the highly complex links between forests and environmental management of the biosphere. These are issues dominated by immense scientific uncertainties and challenging valuation problems. Protection of the environmental services of forests has a rich international history, leading in recent years to a variety of innovative approaches to the management of forests.

The concluding chapters (Chapters 8–9) focus on cooperation and learning. Chapter 8 looks at the prospects and problems of international cooperation in development assistance for forestry, collaboration in forest science and technology, and international agreements affecting forestry. The final chapter argues that future progress in forest management depends on a deliberate learning process guided by an optimistic vision of the future, and the management of surprises.

Each chapter ends with "Issues for Discussion and Investigation." This is to provide questions that will generate discussion in the classroom. Some issues could be selected to become the core of homework assignments or undergraduate term papers. Other issues may lead graduate students in the direction of possible research projects. Still others may stimulate both students and practicing professionals to pursue individual reading along particular paths of inquiry.

We cannot hope to present within this single volume the vast body of descriptive material on world forest types, deforestation causes and consequences, shifting international patterns in the production and trade of forest products, development assistance for forestry, forests in relation to global environment, new and emerging agroforestry systems, and other expansive topics. The growth of literature in these subjects is exceptionally rapid, and its origins are more diverse every year. Rather, we attempt to offer a basic frame of reference, holding readers responsible for pursuing additional materials from outside sources. The references cited in the text and listed at the back of each chapter make a good beginning.

CONTENTS

LIST OF FIGURES

LIST OF TABLES

LIST OF ABBREVIATIONS AND ACRONYMS

AID	Agency for International Development (of USA)
CAMCORE	Central America and Mexico Coniferous Resources Cooperative
CARE	Caring Americans for Relief Everywhere
CATIE	Centro Agronómico Tropical de Investigación y Enseñanza (Tropical Agricultural Research and Training Center)
CCCE	Caisse Central de Coopération Economique (of France)
CFCs	Chlorofluorocarbons
CIDA	Canadian International Development Agency
CITES	Convention on International Trade in Endangered Species of Wild Fauna and Flora
CTMP	Chemi-Thermomechanical Pulp
DANIDA	Danish International Development Agency
EC	European Community
ECE	Economic Commission for Europe
EEC	European Economic Community
FAO	Food and Agriculture Organization (of the United Nations)
F/FRED	Forestry/Fuelwood Research and Development Project
FINNIDA	Finnish International Development Agency
FTA	Free Trade Agreement (between the USA and Canada)
GATT	General Agreement on Tariffs and Trade
GEMS	Global Environmental Monitoring System (Program of UNEP)
GDP	Gross Domestic Product (a measure of national income)
GNP	Gross National Product (a measure of national income)
GSFP	Gujarat Social Forestry Project (in India)
GTZ	Gesellschaft für Technische Zusammenarbeit (German Agency for Technical Cooperation)

IBPGR	International Board for Plant Genetic Resources
ICIHI	International Commission on International Humanitarian Issues
ICRAF	International Council for Research in Agroforestry
IIASA	International Institute of Applied Systems Analysis
IIED	International Institute for Environment and Development
IITA	International Institute for Tropical Agriculture
IJC	International Joint Council (between USA and Canada)
ILO	International Labor Organization
ITTA	International Timber Trade Agreement
ITTO	International Tropical Timber Organization
IUCN	International Union for Conservation of Nature and Natural Resources
IUFRO	International Union of Forestry Research Organizations
JICA	Japanese International Cooperation Agency
MAB	Man and the Biosphere (program of UNESCO)
MPTS	Multipurpose Tree Species Research Network
NAPAP	National Acid Precipitation Assessment Program (of USA)
NAS	National Academy of Sciences (of USA)
NFTA	Nitrogen-Fixing Tree Association
NGO	Non-Governmental Organization
ODA	Overseas Development Administration (of UK)
OECD	Organization for Economic Cooperation and Development
OTS	Organization for Tropical Studies
PADF	Pan American Development Foundation
PICOP	Paper Industries Corporation of the Philippines
SIDA	Swedish International Development Authority
TFAP	Tropical Forestry Action Plan
TMP	Thermomechanical Pulp
UK	United Kingdom (of Great Britain and Northern Ireland)
UNCTAD	United Nations Conference on Trade and Development
UNDP	United Nations Development Program
UNEP	United Nations Environment Program
UNESCO	United Nations Educational, Scientific, and Cultural Organization
UNIDO	United Nations Industrial Development Organization
UNSO	United Nations Sudano-Sahelian Office
USA	United States of America
USSR	Union of Soviet Socialist Republics
WCED	World Commission on Environment and Development (the "Brundtland Commission")
WFP	World Food Program
WWF	World Wide Fund for Nature (Known as World Wildlife Fund in the USA, Canada, and Australia)
WRI	World Resources Institute

GLOBAL FORESTS

ISSUES FOR SIX BILLION PEOPLE

THINKING ABOUT ONE-WORLD FORESTS

In July 1947, the Food and Agriculture Organization (FAO) of the United Nations issued its first number of a forestry publication later to achieve global circulation. The publication was *Unasylva*, meaning "one forest" for one world (Orr 1947). Upon reflection, the name was well chosen. The word lends itself to imagery of the earth's forests as one great biophysical system, with transitions connecting temperate and tropical, wet and dry, fertile and infertile, highland and lowland. At the same time, we are given an implicit philosophy which aims at world scope and global mission. A name which calls attention to the unity of forests inspires grand achievements, and reminds us of present shortcomings. It challenges us with an intellectual framework whose dimensions are temperate world and tropical world, rich world and poor world, industrialized world and wilderness world. In sum, reference to one-world forests furnishes a good basis for thinking about old and traditional uses of forests side by side with new and radical ideas about their benefits, purposes, and management.

FOREST PRODUCTS, SERVICES, AND VALUES

Forest resources in the narrow sense are the products, services, and values derived from vegetation complexes dominated by trees. A wider concept includes brushlands, open woodlands, and other wildlands in a largely natural state. Forest resources also embrace manmade plantings of trees in large or small blocks, in linear strips, or interspersed with agricultural and pastoral activities. Arboriculture and horticulture may be considered to provide forest resources in certain contexts. A universal definition of forest resources is neither possible nor desirable. The concept must be kept open and flexible to correspond with perceptual differences across societies and historical periods.

The frequent allusion to "forest development" is more correctly "the place of forests in human development." This refers to the ways and means by which forest products, services, and values do and do not satisfy human needs. It is generally agreed that physical human needs—such as basic needs for defense, food, shelter, and clothing—must be satisfied before other needs are felt. Complexity is added by differences among "needs," "wants," and "demands," particularly as these concepts vary across societies and languages.

Forest management is a process of deliberate and guided intervention to manipulate the complex biotic and human components of forests in order to satisfy the needs of particular beneficiaries. The matter is summed up succinctly in the two-part question raised by economist Marion Clawson (1975): forests for whom and for what?

This question is equivalent to a choice of policy goals. Goals, in turn, convey values about the structures of particular societies, and about the power and status of different individuals in them. The response to "for whom and for what" is inherently political, in turn raising other questions which are philosophical, ideological, ethical, and historical in their origins.

The products, services, and values of forests are numerous, complex, and not easily assigned to exclusive and exhaustive categories. Figure 1-1 presents a classification according to five domains of human welfare. The protective services and influences often are referred to as life-support functions, but human welfare would be decidedly more barren without the other categories, as well. To a greater or lesser extent, all five groups contribute to basic life support.

Protective Services and Influences

Forest ecosystems provide a broad range of environmental services, some of them necessary for the operation of the system itself, and some directly useful to humans. Some benefits, e.g., microclimatic influences, are strictly local, while others are regional and global in their significance.

That forests protect water catchments, reduce flooding, and regulate streamflow has been known for millennia. The use of trees to stabilize sand dunes, reclaim degraded lands, lessen wind erosion, and maintain agricultural productivity also has ancient foundations. Although these influences are understood in a general way, serious gaps in science and technology characterize many individual practices.

Other protective influences are the provision of wildlife habitat, the cycling of nutrients, the maintenance of biological diversity, and climate regulation. Biological diversity may be disaggregated into issues of genetic diversity, species diversity, and ecosystem diversity, with a broad spectrum of direct and indirect human benefits stemming from conservation at each level (McNeely et al. 1990). Climatic influences likewise are divided into several categories, including maintenance of global carbon balances, cycling of water, removal of particulate and gaseous matter, and effects on patterns of temperature and rainfall. Many if not

FIGURE 1-1
Role of forests in five domains of human welfare.

Protective services and influences
- Climate regulation
- Regulation of atmospheric composition
- Stabilization of slopes, streambanks, water catchments, and sand dunes
- Shelterbelts, soil moisture retention
- Streamflow regulation, flood reduction
- Land reclamation
- Buffer against spread of pests and diseases
- Nutrient storage, distribution, and cycling
- Wildlife habitat
- Conservation of biological diversity

Educational and scientific services
- Research on ecosystems and organisms
- Zones to monitor ecological changes
- Specimens for museums, zoos, botanical gardens
- Wild stocks for foods, chemicals, biological control agents
- Environmental education

Psychophysiological influences
- Recreation, tourism, sports
- Sense of stewardship, peace, harmony with nature
- Inspiration for art, literature, music, myth, religion, and philosophy
- Historic sites and values

Consumption of plants, animals, and derivatives
- Timber: logs, pulpwood, posts, poles
- Fuelwood: firewood and charcoal
- Food products: fish, game, fruits, nuts, berries, seeds, mushrooms, spices, eggs, larvae, honey, syrups, teas, other beverages
- Herbs, flowers, medicinal plants, pharmaceuticals
- Gums, resins, lacs, oils, tannin, waxes, distillates
- Livestock fodder (grass, leaves)
- Thatch, ropes and string, weaving materials, silk
- Non-wood structural materials (e.g., bamboo, rattan)
- Skins, feathers, teeth, bones, horns
- House plants and pets

Source of land and living space
- New lands for cropping and grazing
- Habitat of indigenous (aboriginal) peoples

most of these climatic influences are poorly understood, conjectural, and hence highly controversial.

Educational and Scientific Values

The use of forests in science and education includes research and teaching to obtain and transmit basic knowledge. Some forested areas represent undisturbed samples of ecosystems, enabling scientific investigation of natural processes. Undisturbed

The protective services of trees include their use to stabilize sand dunes, reclaim degraded lands, and lessen wind erosion. Here men and women plant *Casuarina equisetifolia* to prevent sand dune formation south of Da Nang, Vietnam. (*Photo courtesy of FAO.*)

forests may be used as standards and monitoring zones against which outside changes, e.g., species dynamics, can be measured and evaluated. Among the fruits of applied forest research are new sources of plant and animal strains, genetically improved seedlings, and biological control agents.

Moreover, students and other members of the public visit forests to educate themselves about their environment. The benefits of science are not for scientists alone, but also for persons who want to fully appreciate forest fauna, flora, and landscapes. No one properly sees the redwood forests of California or the birds of Central America without minimal knowledge of how natural systems operate.

Psychophysiological Influences

Forests penetrate deeply into psychological and spiritual realms, where connections between natural systems and the human condition are broad, intricate, intangible, and often mystical. Forests provide aesthetic satisfaction, religious symbolism and practice, and creative endeavors in writing, music, and art. It has been argued that the character of forests is able to shape the character of individuals and entire cultures (e.g., Reunala and Virtanen 1987; Sullivan 1987).

The educational and scientific values of forests are not for scientists alone, but also for persons who want to fully appreciate forest fauna, flora, and landscapes. *(Photo courtesy of Forest History Society.)*

Tree planting and forest conservation are acts of peace and good will. Planting and caring for trees is a demonstration of faith in the future, and an expression of self-help. If the work is done cooperatively, it promotes working relationships. If it is done by volunteers, it is a tribute to sharing and community. If it restores degraded lands and protects wildlife and streams, it heals the earth. These are real but elusive contributions of forests and forest practice in human culture. In many cases, the physical accomplishment in field and forest is less significant for human welfare than is the satisfaction created by a sense of stewardship.

Various forest plants, animals, firewood, and other products are prized for spiritual significance, prestige, and symbolism. The Koran discusses the sacredness of trees (Ahmed 1984), and the Bible refers to the tree of knowledge of good and evil. Ceremonies draw inspiration from the forest, and also depend on the forest for materials and mood. Traditional folk cures using medicinal plants and animals have psychological as well as physiological content (Prescott-Allen 1982). The importance of trees and forests for symbolism, ritual, and spiritual fulfillment varies across countries, but surely exists in all of them.

However, the psychophysiological influences of forests are individualistic. The Greeks and Romans consecrated holy groves, while the Biblical Jews and Christian popes eradicated these symbols of paganism. The Russians prize birch juice as a health tonic and the Argentines drink Paraguay tea (*Ilex paraguayensis*). Yet neither beverage has achieved wide acceptance elsewhere. As symbols of Christmas celebrations in many parts of the world, mistletoe and the Christmas tree have cultural significance descending from the ancient Greeks, Druids, Norsemen, and Teutons. Completely different antecedents must be found to trace the cultural significance of *Ficus religiosa* in India, the ginkgo tree in East Asia, and the baobab tree (*Adansonia digitata*) in the African bushlands. On the one hand, these examples demonstrate a universality of respect and even sacredness for forest plants and trees. On the other, they reflect the uniqueness of different intersections of history, forest biology, and legends about man, god, and nature.

The importance of trees and forests for symbolism, ritual, and spiritual fulfillment varies across countries. *(Photos courtesy of World Bank [African tree burner] and Forest History Society [Boy Scouts].)*

In the African savanna, the baobab tree *(Adansonia digitata)* can attain large size and an age of 300 years. Its leaves are used for traditional medicines, fibers of its bark are woven to make cord and rope, and the juice of its fruit reduces acidity in other foods. The baobab has spiritual significance for certain ethnic groups, who bury their dead at the base of the tree. *(Photo courtesy of FAO.)*

Extraction of Plants, Animals, and Derivative Products

This is the domain best known in traditional forest practice, where management aims to produce tangible products for removal. Timber and its derivatives belong in this category, as do numerous plant and animal products for fuel, food, fiber, and forage. Extracted products can be grouped in various combinations according to whether they are (1) consumed on-site or off-site, (2) produced and consumed by industry or for subsistence, (3) marketable or nonmarketable, (4) easy or difficult to deplete, and (5) end products or intermediate products.

As indicated in Table 1-1, FAO's statistics report that over half of the world's consumption of roundwood (i.e., unprocessed primary wood) is for fuel (firewood and charcoal). The proportion of total roundwood which is fuelwood reaches 80–95 percent in some groups of developing countries. The usefulness of these statistics is limited by measurement inaccuracies, and by the complication that fuelwood is obtained from both forest and non-forest sources. Neither organized markets nor monetary prices exist for the bulk of fuelwood consumption. Despite these and other problems with quantification, there can be little doubt that fuelwood is one of the world's principal forest products, and that most fuelwood is consumed by the world's poorest households.

TABLE 1-1
Fuelwood as a proportion of roundwood consumption by world regions in 1986, and projections for 1990 and 2000

	Year		
	1986	1990	2000
	(fuelwood as a percent)		
Industrialized regions	18	17	15
USA and Canada	17	17	15
USSR	24	23	20
Europe	16	15	12
Japan	1	1	1
Australia and New Zealand	13	13	11
Developing regions	80	77	73
Asia (excluding Japan)	79	77	73
Africa	91	92	92
Latin America and Caribbean	72	69	61
Oceania (excluding Australia and New Zealand)	86	86	82
World	52	52	49

Source: FAO (1988).

Firewood and charcoal constitute over half of the world's wood consumption. This woman in Myanmar (formerly Burma) cooks on an open fire in a rural household. While estimates of fuelwood consumption are difficult to make, a family of five may consume five tons of fuelwood per year. *(Photo courtesy of FAO.)*

TABLE 1-2
Production of industrial roundwood
by world regions, late 1980s

Country or region	Percentage of total
USA and Canada	36.5
Europe	18.4
USSR	17.9
China	6.1
Brazil	4.1
Japan	1.9
All Other	15.1
Total	100.0

Source: FAO (1989).

Table 1-2 shows that roughly three-fourths of the world's industrial roundwood (sawlogs, pulpwood, chips and particles, and wood residues) is produced in a relatively small number of supplying regions in the northern hemisphere. The share of industrial roundwood produced from the world's tropical forests is small, well under 15 percent.

So-called "minor" forest products (i.e., non-timber products) are in reality major in numerous countries. Japan's "special forest products" (mainly mushrooms) accounted for 22 percent of the value of that country's forest

Three-fourths of the world's industrial roundwood is produced in a few countries of the northern hemisphere. *(Photo courtesy of Jonas Palm.)*

Gums and resins are among the non-timber forest products of significance for low-income, mainly subsistence populations. *(Photo courtesy of Yosef Hadar and World Bank.)*

output in the mid-1980s (Kumazaki 1988). Europe's non-timber products include naval stores (i.e., turpentine, pitch, and resins), decorative lichens, mosses, cork, Christmas trees, meat and skins from wild animals, and fodder for livestock (ECE/FAO 1986). The USSR's forests are important in national food policy, contributing significantly to the production of fruits and berries, nuts, honey, mushrooms, medicinal herbs, and fodder for livestock (Barr and Braden 1988).

Non-timber forest products achieve their greatest relative importance for low-income, mainly subsistence populations. Hence the minor forest products of India include fuelwood and charcoal, fibers and flosses, grasses, bamboos and canes, several essential oils, nonedible oil seeds, tanning bark and dyes, gums and resins, lac and lac products, flowers, tasar silk, tendu leaves, drugs and spices, and medicinal plants and herbs. This is in addition to dozens of food products, both vegetable and animal (Pant 1984). Even though each of these products is tangible and theoretically measurable, production is grossly underestimated because of statistical gaps and the fact that most such products pass through no market. Thus even products which in principle are relatively straightforward to record and value go underrecorded and undervalued. This underreporting of non-timber products in India is not an isolated case, but rather represents a common situation where sizable rural populations live in or close to forests.

Land and Living Space

Forested lands are being converted to cropland, pastures, roads, and residential and industrial sites in both industrialized and developing countries. Rates of conversion, and the forces which drive them, are highly variable. However, a unifying factor worldwide is that the forested areas being opened and cleared were lands nobody wanted for developed (i.e., non-forest) uses up until now.

Particularly in densely populated countries of the tropics, forest conversion to cropping and grazing continues to be a main forest "use." This refers to land clearing by commercial as well as subsistence users, the latter often practicing forms of shifting ("slash and burn") cultivation (Peters and Neuenschwander 1989).

Although now joined in some regions by immigrant peasants from elsewhere, traditional forest farmers are mainly tribal (i.e., indigenous or aboriginal) people. These groups vary greatly in their ethnic, social, and economic composition. Yet a common element is use of forests and associated wildlands for living space and cultural survival (ICIHI 1986; Clay 1988).

LIVING WITH CONSTANCY AND CHANGE

One of the great complexities of forest management in the late twentieth century is the simultaneous existence of all states of material and industrial development superimposed upon each other. Hence persons whose subsistence depends on shifting forest cultivation live only a few hundred kilometers or less from persons dedicated to space exploration and weekend backpacking.

The first population includes billions who search for wood to make cooking fires, while the second comprises millions who like to see a few fireplace logs as an aesthetic complement to coffee and brandy. One population accepts game meat, nuts, berries, wild honey, and mushrooms as subsistence fare. The other regards them as gourmet foods. Both populations depend on forests for water supply, but through sharply contrasting technologies and delivery systems. Both appreciate forests for spiritual and aesthetic reasons, but may perceive the forest's mysteries and beauties very differently. Both are affected by the relation of deforestation to conjectured atmospheric warming, but only the second is aware of the problem, and is able to make it an issue.

This odd and often incongruous mixture of old and new societal values can be observed within some countries, but is even more salient when looking across them. The old and new demands on forests are not easily harmonized, and the big picture of human interaction with forests is not easily comprehended. It is a world of competing values, conflicting needs, enormous complexity, and simultaneous constancy and change.

In the first quarter of this century, McGraw-Hill Book Company published a two-volume account of the forests of the world (Zon and Sparhawk 1923). That historical perspective illuminates both old and new themes for the 1990s and beyond. Even in the 1920s, the authors recognized that "under present conditions no civilized country is entirely independent economically of other countries" (p. 1). Several other comparisons with the present age are worth noting:

• *Forest destruction*—In the early part of the century, forest area was decreasing as the result of land settlement, destruction by fire, and excessive cutting. The central "world problem" in forestry was defined as making available timber supplies keep pace with rising demand for wood (p. viii).

• *Inadequate statistics and measurements*—The authors lamented the poor statistics on forest resources, the lack of a useful definition of forest land, and the absence of universally accepted units to measure standing and felled timber (pp. xi–xiv).

• *International timber supplies*—Due to depletion of high-grade hardwoods in many temperate regions, forest industries in Europe and North America were looking towards the tropics, Siberia, and other regions for potentially new sources of supply. Main problems, then as now, were geographical inaccessibility and difficulties with wood utilization (p. vii).

• *Need for international collaboration*—The work by Zon and Sparhawk constituted one of the first comprehensive inventories of world forests. To the extent permitted by the crudeness of the information, the inventory included attention to the "vast undeveloped tropical forests." The authors hoped that their efforts would lead to international policies for forest protection and management (p. viii).

• *Perceptions of a small world*—The first part of the century was described as an age of steel, electricity, and cheap transportation. The world had been made smaller by a constantly enlarging network of highways, railroads, canals, and steamship lines. After the First World War, expanded international transportation enabled countries like China and South Africa to import large quantities of sawnwood from North America and northern Europe, respectively (p. 68).

These themes in Zon and Sparhawk reveal a great deal of sameness about leading perspectives on forests and forestry from the beginning through the end of this century: (1) forests are disappearing, (2) our data about them are poor, (3) knowledge of international timber supplies is critical for decision making, (4) we need international collaboration to formulate intelligent forest policies, and (5) the world is small and interdependent. Each of these five themes finds continuation, to a remarkable degree, into present thinking. Perhaps this is not surprising of a sector which, forced to take a long-term perspective because of lengthy biological processes, has been decidedly conservative in outlook and practice.

Yet departures from the world of Zon and Sparhawk are just as striking in their significance. Virtually the entire focus of their analysis was production, consumption, and trade of timber and wood products. A few environmental issues (e.g., the effect of forests on water supply and agriculture) were given passing reference. However, other environmental issues high on today's global agenda were not widely recognized as issues then. In the first years of this century, the implicit possibility of timber scarcity was the clear and compelling reason for the world forest inventory.

Technically, socially, and politically, we live in a vastly changed world from that of Zon and Sparhawk. Jet aircraft, satellite telecommunications, and computers lay well into the future. Over 100 new countries were to emerge from colonial rule after 1945. The world had yet to experience the profound and widespread social learning from the Great Depression, the Third Reich, the Marshall Plan, the Cold War, and the softening of European communism.

The United Nations and all of its special agencies did not exist. Official development assistance to so-called "backward economies" was limited to occasional disaster relief in the colonial empires. There was no World Bank, and no official foreign aid. Metaphors such as "global village" and "spaceship Earth" were unknown. Also unknown were terms like "Third World," "Green Revolution," "New International Economic Order," "East-West conflict," "North-South dialogue," and other ways of looking at the world originating mainly after the Second World War.

Moreover, Zon and Sparhawk long preceded contemporary attempts to redefine the role of forests and forestry in developing countries. The industrial forestry of central concern to Zon and Sparhawk has since been joined by themes on village

The industrial forestry of central concern in the first half of this century has since been joined by themes on village forest projects. Villagers in the highlands of Ecuador prepare for afforestation with *Pinus radiata*. This work is carried out through the traditional system of voluntary labor known as "mingas." *(Photo courtesy of FAO.)*

forest projects, forest management by indigenous tribes, forests for household food security, and other conceptual directions arising mainly since 1970. It is increasingly understood that forestry for local populations implies moving the locus of tree-growing from the forests to farms and communities. This represents a distinct break with most forestry tradition.

Finally, Zon and Sparhawk could not have anticipated the recent scientific and popular preoccupation with global environmental threats. Nor could they have foreseen that governments are beginning to work together to mitigate shared economic and environmental problems through an increasing array of international institutions.

DYNAMICS SHAPING THE FUTURE

The world of forest management is filled with surprises and discontinuities. Assuming that surprises continue, the historical path from past to present offers few guidelines for the projection of present into future. Yet, in a general way, the future is defined in relation to shifting populations, shifting economic power, diffusion of science and technology, and the rise of world environmentalism.

Growing and Shifting Populations

Feelings of global interdependence are heightened by the uneasy prospect of dividing scarce natural resources among huge and still swelling populations. A familiar and acrimonious debate pits faith in the expansion of technology and human ingenuity against various notions of finite carrying capacity (Simon and Kahn 1984). The school of thought which argues "limits to growth" commands a sufficient following to reinforce the perspective of human crowding on a small planet (Meadows et al. 1972).

Significantly, 90 percent of today's babies are born in the developing countries. The developing countries will have eight of the world's ten largest cities by the year 2000, compared with only three in 1950. These population shifts, combined with deforestation in some countries and intensified forest management in others, imply dramatic demand and supply changes for industrial wood and fiber.

The broad perspective in many of the industrialized countries is expanding supply potential, but falling or steady demand for many classes of wood and paper products. In contrast, a number of the developing countries see steady or declining supplies accompanied by rising demands. Thus most of the industrialized world has largely solved its wood consumption problem through production and trade, while much of the developing world continues to struggle with scarcity.

Regarding the link between forests and environment, shifting population growth has consequences for deforestation rates and locations. In many developing countries, increased population density reduces forest area as a proportion of total land area. Hence the origins and movements of population growth affect strategies for forest protection, especially where population movements are related to inadequate government policies.

Approximately 90 percent of today's babies are born in the developing countries. Pictured is a rural household in the Philippines, where fertility rates are 3.9 births per woman. This is well below 6.8 births per woman 25–30 years ago, but still sufficiently high to strain the country's capacity to feed and house its growing population. *(Photo courtesy of World Bank.)*

Shifting Economic Power

An increasing international presence in domestic economies is driven by rapid technological innovation and diverse forms of transnational organization. The rise and fall of different economic powers is closely watched. At issue is a sweeping and turbulent redistribution of production and consumption at a global level.

The changing economic power of nations affects forests and forestry in many ways. It is their wealth which enables the European Community, Japan, and the USA to import large quantities of forest products. Growth or depression in these economies has worldwide implications for forest products markets.

Economic changes elsewhere also can be significant, as when a severe economic depression in Latin America during the early 1980s dramatically reduced that region's imports of paper. Yet indebtedness also was the primary factor in "debt-for-nature swaps" to cancel foreign debt in exchange for nature conservation (Prestemon and Lampman 1990). Hence a major economic adjustment can have multiple, complex, and sometimes unexpected results.

Changes in wealth affect mixtures of demanded forest goods and services. This is illustrated by Taiwan's evolution from timber production towards timber imports and non-commodity forest uses during a period which corresponded with rapidly rising national income (Ku et al. 1989). More broadly, the increasing wealth of countries shifts expectations of forest management increasingly towards environmental and amenity values. On the other hand, countries unable to break loose from the bonds of mass poverty face an entirely different set of goals and constraints.

Diffusion of Science and Technology

In forest management, experience and knowledge at scientific and technical levels are by no means confined to just a few countries. Classical silviculture achieves its fullest expression in central Europe, while expertise in fire management has developed in California and Australia. Forest mechanization is well advanced in the Nordic countries, the USSR, and Canada, while labor-intensive methods fit the realities of heavily populated regions of Asia and Africa. Fast-growing industrial forest plantations are found in numerous countries, both industrialized and developing. Likewise, energy plantations are found in regions of both high and low income (e.g., Sweden, Hawaii, Philippines, and Brazil).

Achievements are being realized in regions and countries not previously considered leaders in forest science and technology. Substantial and rapid increases in biological productivity of forest plantations in various countries of the southern hemisphere are explained by sound strategies of genetic selection and other tree improvement technologies (Zobel et al. 1987). The company

The company Aracruz Florestal of Brazil has been able to develop eucalyptus plantations which are possibly the world's most productive industrial forests. The photo shows two test clones. *(Photo courtesy of William Dvorak.)*

Aracruz Florestal of Brazil has been able to develop eucalyptus plantations which are possibly the world's most productive industrial forests. Not only Brazil, but also other countries of the southern hemisphere, show promise of substantial gains in plantation forestry. At issue is the extent to which this diffusion of tree-growing technologies will alter patterns of world competitiveness in production and trade of industrial wood products (Sedjo 1983).

Not all advances depend on new and improved biological technologies. Other achievements take place in the "soft technologies" of organization and management. For example, village forest associations in the Republic of Korea reforested and afforested more than one million hectares in just five years during the 1970s, attesting to highly efficient organization and effective public-private coordination. Moreover, some of the developing countries of Asia seem likely to become world

Village forest associations in the Republic of Korea reforested and afforested more than one million hectares during the 1970s. This old man joins younger workers in Jun Seong Village. *(Photo courtesy of FAO.)*

leaders in extension methods in farm and community forestry. This increasingly diffuse base of forestry knowledge and practice suggests simultaneous strategies of international competition in some areas, and cooperation in others.

Rise of Environmentalism

Threats to the environment command serious attention not only among scientists, but also now among world opinion leaders. The incredible rise of scientific and social interest in tropical deforestation is one manifestation of concern. A second is public attention to the perplexing decline of forests in Europe and North America because of atmospheric contaminants. The extinction of wild species, particularly in tropical forests, arouses both moral indignation and pragmatic (i.e., mainly economic) sentiments for their protection. A few political leaders, as well as officials responsible for development assistance, propose large-scale reforestation as a necessary if insufficient strategy to alleviate Africa's food shortages (Harrison 1987). Avoidance of global warming in its more extreme scenarios is portrayed as a matter of economic and political self-preservation (Mintzer 1987).

This focus on forests and other wildlands for their environmental attributes commands a relatively new and high position on the global agenda. By "global agenda" is meant the top-priority issues which force their way into the minds of the world's intelligentsia, opinion makers, and political leaders. Traditionally, elite

These denuded mountains in Madagascar were once forested. Threats of tropical deforestation command serious attention not only among scientists, but also now among many of the world's opinion leaders. *(Photo courtesy of FAO.)*

decisionmakers in world politics concentrate on the "high politics" of peace and security. Natural resources and other matters of economic welfare are subsumed within "low politics," managed at subordinate levels (Kegley and Wittkopf 1984).

However, beginning in the 1970s a number of influential papers and speeches have elevated several natural resource issues—including forest issues—to the higher status of security problems. Environmental stress, poverty, and security are closely interrelated. Hence the gloomy prospect of large-scale and severe environmental dysfunction is construed as a threat to human survival. When viewed as a security issue, management of the world's forests claims considerable attention in "high politics."

UNASYLVA: TOWARDS AN UNDERSTANDING

The one world of forests does not necessarily point to world government, but it does rationalize strong international understanding. Most simply and accurately stated, the one world of forests is a way of thinking in contexts both geographical and historical. In the introduction to the revised edition of his classic book on forestry history, Bernhard Fernow contends that world experience and the historical approach are nowhere more useful than in the study of forests. This is due to the closely related but not equivalent observations that forest management is still a developing technical art, and that forest change demands considerable time to provide learning experiences (Fernow 1911).

To the extent that the history of forests and forestry has been repeating itself, contemporary goals and policies to conserve and develop forests are often echoes of goals and policies propounded elsewhere and earlier. It stands to reason that policy analysis is barren and even errant without considering lessons learned by looking internationally and farther back in time. This provides a practical motive for comparing human uses of forests between the ancients and the moderns, between industrialized and agricultural societies, and between temperate and tropical regions.

The one-world view can be presented in terms of transition factors, linking factors, and differentiating factors. The idea of common transitions points forest policy and management towards similar strategic transitions all around the globe (Figure 1-2). At issue are (1) whether these transitions are worthwhile as social goals, (2) their varying applicability in different parts of the world, (3) internal contradictions which may be present among them, (4) political and cultural limits to their feasibility, and (5) alternative social goals that may have to be sacrificed in order to achieve them. Actions towards making any of the transitions possible have unintended consequences, since the view ahead is blurred by rapid social and economic changes. For the same reason, predictions of gains and losses between and within countries are vulnerable to many uncertainties.

Linking factors refer to direct and indirect connections among countries. The first link, the commercial connection, is international investment and trade in forest products, mainly but not exclusively in wood products (Chapters 4 and 5). A second link is environmental, referring to complicated political and economic questions of managing environmental services from forests, and of devising means

FIGURE 1-2
Desirable transitions in forest management at local and global levels.

Transition 1:	to slowing of deforestation and forest degradation, accompanied by efficient and socially progressive investments for reforestation and forest rehabilitation.
Transition 2:	to increased efficiency in industrial forestry leading to economic gains for forested regions.
Transition 3:	to increased economic and social gains from expanded international trade of forest products.
Transition 4:	to expanded interest and capability in tree growing by communities, farmers, and other nonindustrial landowners.
Transition 5:	to improved management of forests for environmental protection at local, regional, and global levels.
Transition 6:	to more effective international cooperation in development assistance, forest science, and technology transfer in order to facilitate the preceding transitions.

to protect and enhance these services (Chapter 7). A third link is international cooperation, mainly but not entirely in the form of international development assistance, together with international collaboration in forest science and technology (Chapter 8). Much of this assistance and collaboration is directed to farm and community forestry, especially in developing countries (Chapter 6).

The common transitions and linking factors lead us in the philosophical direction that the world is a unified and well-connected system. Closer examination shows that this is not true. Hence differentiating factors reveal major international differences in combinations of forest endowment, level of economic development, cultural and social functions of forests, political significance of forests, and distribution of property rights in forests. It is still one world, but a world where these crucial differences must be identified and comprehended if there is to be intelligent forest management.

ISSUES FOR DISCUSSION AND INVESTIGATION

1 In 1987, the World Commission on Environment and Development released its report, *Our Common Future* (WCED 1987). The first chapter opens as follows: "The Earth is one, but the world is not." (i) What does this mean? (ii) What is the significance of the statement for forests and forestry?
2 Explain each of the following concepts: (i) forests for human development, (ii) protective services of forests, (iii) psychophysiological benefits of forests, (iv) educational and scientific benefits of forests, (v) extractive products from forests, (vi) minor forest products, and (vii) use of forests for land and living space.
3 What factors explain the different mixes of forest products, services, and values from one country to another?
4 Suppose that the global village consists of 100 families (Baum 1988). Ninety do not speak English, and 65 cannot read. Only seven families own 60 percent of the land, and only seven consume 80 percent of available energy. Some 80 families have no members who have flown on airplanes, and only one family

has a member with a university education. (i) How many families burn firewood or charcoal for household energy? (ii) How many read a newspaper? (iii) How many have drinking water at home? (iv) How many have visited a national park? (v) In the global village, why is it impossible to separate issues of forest management from issues of income distribution?

5 In forestry, science and technology are widely diffused. What reasons account for this, and in what ways is it important?

6 The world's population is increasingly shifting towards the developing countries. Consider how this does and does not change the mix of issues in forest management.

7 The crucial issues affecting forests in "today's world" are defined only in relation to "today" and the scope of "world." Search for perspectives on "today's world" when yesterday was today, and the world was in some ways different. Potential sources are Marsh (1864), Fernow (1911), Thomas (1956), Glacken (1967), Hughes (1975), Thirgood (1981), Perlin (1989), Totman (1989), and Bechmann (1990). (i) What forestry issues are common to the worlds of yesterday and today? (ii) What issues are truly new today? Explain and defend.

REFERENCES

Ahmed, Salahuddin. 1984. "The holy Quran and vegetation," *Pakistan Journal of Forestry* 34(1):49–52.

Barr, Brenton M. and Kathleen E. Braden. 1988. *The Disappearing Russian Forest: A Dilemma in Soviet Resource Management.* Rowman and Littlefield, Totowa, NJ.

Baum, Julian A. 1988. "A glimpse of life in the global village," *Christian Science Monitor*, April 25, p. 11.

Bechmann, Roland. 1990. *Trees and Man: The Forest in the Middle Ages.* Paragon House, New York.

Clawson, Marion. 1975. *Forests for Whom and for What?* Johns Hopkins University Press, Baltimore.

Clay, Jason W. 1988. *Indigenous Peoples and Tropical Forests: Models of Land Use and Management from Latin America.* Cultural Survival Report 27, Cambridge, MA.

ECE/FAO (Economic Commission for Europe; Food and Agriculture Organization). 1986. *European Timber Trends and Prospects to the Year 2000 and Beyond*, Vol. I. United Nations, New York.

FAO (Food and Agriculture Organization). 1988. *Forest Products: World Outlook Projections.* FAO Forestry Paper 84, FAO, Rome.

FAO. *1989. Yearbook of Forest Products, 1976–1987.* FAO, Rome.

Fernow, Bernhard E. 1911. *A Brief History of Forestry in Europe, the United States, and Other Countries*, 2nd edition. University of Toronto Press, Toronto, Canada.

Glacken, Clarence J. 1967. *Traces on the Rhodian Shore: Nature and Culture in Western Thought from Ancient Times to the End of the Eighteenth Century.* University of California. Press, Berkeley.

Harrison, Paul. 1987. *The Greening of Africa.* Penguin Books, New York.

Hughes, J. D. 1975. *Ecology in Ancient Civilizations.* University of New Mexico Press, Albuquerque.

ICIHI (International Commission on International Humanitarian Issues). 1986. *The Vanishing Forest: The Human Consequences of Deforestation.* ICIHI, Geneva, Switzerland.

Kegley, Charles W., Jr. and Eugene R. Wittkopf (eds.). 1984. *The Global Agenda*, 2nd edition. Random House, New York.

Ku, Timothy, James M. Guldin, and R. Scott Beasley. 1989. "Management shift embraces nontimber values," *Journal of Forestry* 87(6):16-18.

Kumazaki, Minoru. 1988. "Japanese economic development and forestry," pp. 1-15 in R. Handa (ed.), *Forest Policy in Japan*. Nippon Ringyo Chosakai, Tokyo, Japan.

Marsh, George Perkins. 1864. *Man and Nature* (David Lowenthal, ed., 1965). Harvard University Press, Cambridge.

McNeely, Jeffrey A., Kenton R. Miller, Walter V. Reid, Russell A. Mittermeier, and Timothy B. Werner. 1990. *Conserving the World's Biological Diversity*. International Union for Conservation of Nature and Natural Resources, World Resources Institute, Conservation International, World Wildlife Fund-US, and World Bank. Gland, Switzerland, and Washington, DC.

Meadows, D. H., D. L. Meadows, J. Randers, and W. W. Behrens III. 1972. *The Limits to Growth: A Report for the Club of Rome's Project on the Predicament of Mankind*. Universe Books, New York.

Mintzer, Irving M. 1987. *A Matter of Degrees: The Potential for Controlling the Greenhouse Effect*. World Resources Institute, Washington, DC.

Orr, John Boyd. 1947. "One world, one forest," *Unasylva* 1(1):2-4.

Pant, Madan M. 1984. *Forestry for Economic Development*. Medhawi Publishers, Dehra Dun, India.

Perlin, John. 1989. *A Forest Journey: The Role of Wood in the Development of Civilization*. W W Norton, New York.

Peters, William J. and Leon F. Neuenschwander. 1989. *Slash and Burn: Farming in the Third World Forest*. University of Idaho Press, Moscow, ID.

Prescott-Allen, Robert and Christine. 1982. *What's Wildlife Worth?* Russell Press, Nottingham, England.

Prestemon, Jeffrey and Scott Lampman. 1990. "Third World debt: Are there opportunities for forestry?" *Journal of Forestry* 88(2):12–16.

Reunala, A. and P. Virtanen (eds.). 1987. ["The forest as a Finnish cultural entity,"] *Silva Fennica* 21(4):315–480. In Finnish, English summaries.

Sedjo, Roger. 1983. *The Comparative Economics of Plantation Forestry: A Global Assessment*. Resources for the Future, Washington, DC.

Simon, Julian L. and Herbert Kahn. 1984. *The Resourceful Earth: A Response to Global 2000*. Basil Blackwell, Oxford, England.

Sullivan, Rosemary. 1987. "The dark pines of the mind: The symbol of the forest in Canadian literature," *Canadian Studies* 23:173–182.

Thirgood, J. Vincent. 1981. *Man and the Mediterranean Forest: A History of Resource Depletion*. Academic Press, London and New York.

Thomas, William L., Jr. (ed.). 1956. *Man's Role in Changing the Face of the Earth*. University of Chicago Press, Chicago.

Totman, Conrad. 1989. *The Green Archipelago: Forestry in Pre-Industrial Japan*. University of California Press, Berkeley.

WCED (World Commission on Environment and Development). 1987. *Our Common Future*. Oxford University Press, Oxford, England, and New York.

Zobel, Bruce J., G. Van Wyk, and P. Stahl. 1987. *Growing Exotic Forests*. John Wiley and Sons, New York.

Zon, Raphael and William N. Sparhawk. 1923. *Forest Resources of the World*, Vols. I and II. McGraw-Hill Book Company, New York.

GLOBAL FOREST COVER AND TRENDS

Despite the historical and contemporary importance of forests for human civilization, systematic knowledge of their extent and condition is sorely inadequate. Assessment of forests in the cross-country context is hampered by differences in terminology and classification, and continuously changing assessment purposes. In the 1970s, one commentator noted that modern science has produced better assessments of the moon's craters than of the world's forests (Persson 1977). Although global forest assessments have improved considerably since the 1970s, Persson's observation may continue to be valid for some time.

FOREST CLASSIFICATION AND ASSESSMENT

The world's forests can be described and mapped within a variety of ecological, socioeconomic, and political frameworks. Ecological classification and typing must take account of several complex gradients (Figure 2-1). The lack of distinct climatic and biogeographical boundaries suggests the problems which arise when separating forest from non-forest lands, and drawing lines between one forest type and another.

World Forest Formations

The world's forest vegetation is classified according to blends of two main approaches. The geographical-climate classification conventionally recognizes four world vegetation zones: (1) boreal and north temperate zones, (2) paleotropical, or Old World tropics, (3) neotropical, or American tropics, and (4) southern oceanic and subantarctic, or south temperate zones. On the basis of broad floristic differences these four zones are subdivided into large geographical

A. Increasing aridity, rainforest to desert (South America)

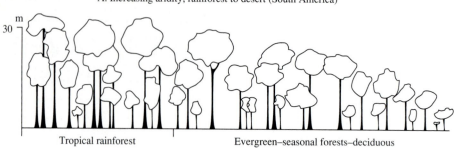

B. Increasing elevation, rainforest to paramo (South America)

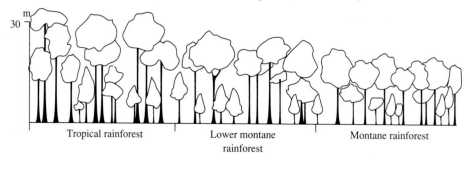

C. Increasing latitude, equator to poles

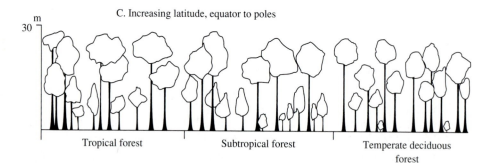

FIGURE 2-1
Gradients of forest cover by precipitation, elevation, and latitude. *(Reprinted with permission of Macmillan Publishing Company from* Communities and Ecosystems, *2nd ed., by Robert H. Whittaker, pp. 164–165. Copyright © 1970, 1975 by Robert H. Whittaker.)*

regions. Geographical regions are disaggregated into sectors, and sectors into districts. The greater the degree of disaggregation, the more vehement the disagreement on classification.

The alternative for classifying world vegetation is the physiognomic-structural approach. This method considers the appearance of the vegetation (e.g., closed

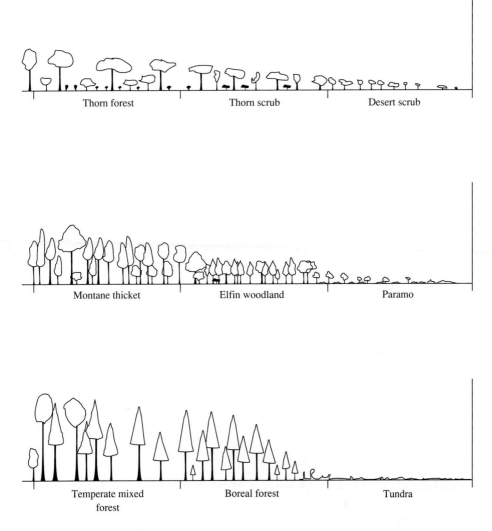

Thorn forest   Thorn scrub   Desert scrub

Montane thicket   Elfin woodland   Paramo

Temperate mixed   Boreal forest   Tundra
forest

FIGURE 2-1 *(continued)*

forest, open woodland), together with its structural features (e.g., evergreen forest, deciduous forest, thorn forest). Further classification takes place according to environmental factors, especially temperature and precipitation. Classification based on structural data is appropriate on a broad level, but also can be used on a smaller scale. Advantages are the ability to collect data rapidly, and the fact that inexperienced personnel can be trained to do the work. The approach has advantages where flora are not well known, explaining its adoption in many tropical forest assessments.

No single approach for classifying world vegetation has achieved widespread recognition and use (UNESCO 1973). This is explained by the unique history of each geographical area, the particular geographical distributions of each genus and species, and the consequent inability to define mutually exclusive compartments. The number of alternative geographical, ecological, and floristic classifications expands as more countries and hence more ecosystems are included (Udvardy 1975). Additionally, classification is done by professionals who differ in language, technical training, and historic schools of thought. At least four schools of classifying plant communities have arisen in western Europe; at least two have developed in northern Europe and the USSR; and at least seven exist for vegetation in the tropics.

Several conceptual models of world forest vegetation are illustrated in Figure 2-2. The alternative schema reveal considerable variation in the number and choice of descriptive categories. Classification is mainly geographical-climatic, although modified in some cases by the inclusion of physiognomic units (e.g., conifers, mangrove forests, etc.).

A classification developed by FAO in the 1970s recognizes a few broad forest formations (Figure 2-3). These formations are described briefly (Sommer 1976):

• *Cool coniferous forests*—An extensive circumpolar belt of boreal forests reaches across northern latitudes in North America, the Nordic countries, and

An extensive circumpolar belt of boreal forests reaches across northern latitudes in North America, the Nordic countries, and the USSR. Here forest technicians gather data for Finland's national forest survey. *(Photo courtesy of Erkki Oksanen and Finnish Forest Research Institute.)*

FIGURE 2-2
Selected conceptual views of world forest vegetation.

Camp (1956)	Sommer (1976)
Coniferous	Cool coniferous
Mixed broadleaved–coniferous	Temperate mixed
Tropical rainforest	Warm temperate moist
Light tropical forest	Tropical moist evergreen
Undifferentiated montane forest	Tropical moist deciduous
Thorn forest and scrub	Dry forest
Transition forest	
Xeric scrub and woodland	
Gallery forest and groves	
Savanna	
Prairie	

Duffield (1982)	Spurr and Barnes (1980)
Northern coniferous forest	Tropical forests
Pacific coniferous forest	Swamp forests
Central broadleaved forest	Salt water
Southern mixed forest	Fresh water
Mediterranean	Rainforest
Coastal California and Chile	Lowland
Coastal Australia	Montane and cloud
Tropical rainforest	Monsoon forest
Drought-deciduous forest	Dry forest
Mangrove forest	Closed
Temperate rainforest	Savanna and woodland
	Temperate forests
	Boreal forest taxa
	Spruces
	Firs
	Larches
	Birches and aspens
	Temperate forest taxa
	Pines
	Oaks
	Beeches and maples
	Miscellaneous hardwoods
	Miscellaneous conifers

the USSR. These boreal forests occur between tundra to the north and temperate mixed forests to the south. They also are found at high altitudes in temperate zones. Characteristic forest types are the spruces (*Picea*), firs (*Abies*), larches (*Larix*), birches (*Betula*), and aspens (*Populus*). Larch forests (mainly *L. siberica*) occupy about 40 percent of the total forested area of the USSR. Spruce-fir, larch, and birch-aspen forests share common physiognomy and ecological relationships everywhere. The southern hemisphere has no equivalent of boreal forests.

• *Temperate mixed forests*—A mix of many different and separate temperate tree populations is found south of the cool coniferous forests but north of the tropical forests over large areas of the northern hemisphere (e.g., southern Canada, the USA, non-Nordic Europe, much of the USSR, Japan, China, and elsewhere

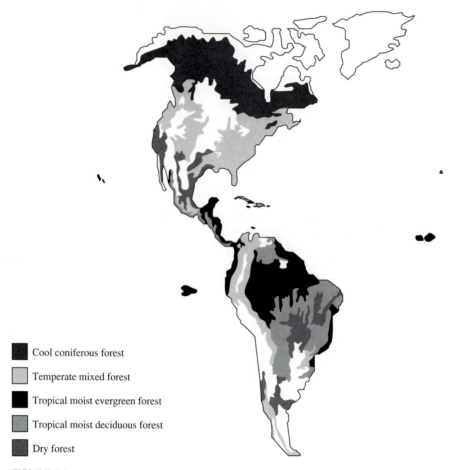

Cool coniferous forest

Temperate mixed forest

Tropical moist evergreen forest

Tropical moist deciduous forest

Dry forest

FIGURE 2-3
The world's main forest formations. *(Sommer, 1976; used with permission of the Food and Agriculture Organization of the United Nations, adapted from map between pages 20–21 in Unasylva 28 (112–113), 1976.)*

in East Asia). Temperate forests also occur in the southern hemisphere south of the tropics (e.g., parts of Chile, Argentina, New Zealand, and Australia), although they tend to be sparse and restricted. Principal forest genera include pines (*Pinus*), oaks (*Quercus*), beeches (*Fagus*), maples (*Acer*), elms (*Ulmus*), ashes (*Fraxinus*), walnuts (*Juglans*), hornbeams (*Carpinus*), chestnuts (*Castanea*), sycamores (*Platanus*), willows (*Salix*), and alders (*Alnus*). Temperate forest trees of the southern hemisphere include southern beech (*Nothofagus*) and several hundred species of eucalypts (*Eucalyptus*).

• *Tropical moist evergreens*—Evergreen rainforests characterize tropical regions where annual precipitation is high (greater than 2000 mm) and evenly distributed through the year (greater than 100 mm per month). The world's three major rainforest regions are (1) Amazonia, together with adjacent northern South Amer-

FIGURE 2-3 *(Continued)*

ica and the Atlantic coast of Central America and southern Mexico, (2) the Congo Basin and adjacent western equatorial Africa, and (3) the Indo-Malayan region, including the west coast of India, much of Southeast Asia, Papua New Guinea and other Pacific islands, and northeast coastal Australia. Forest composition and structure vary with distance from the ocean, distance from rivers, changing altitude, and changing geographical position. As altitude increases, rainforests grade into montane rainforests (i.e., cloud forests) which are shorter, floristically simpler, and more heavily laden with epiphytes (e.g., mosses and lichens) than lowland rainforests.

• *Tropical moist deciduous forests*—In tropical regions where annual precipitation is 1000 to 2000 mm, and a dry season occurs for one month or more, some dominant trees lose their leaves towards the end of the dry period. Monsoon forest refers to particular deciduous and semi-deciduous forests in South and Southeast Asia, where a very dry period of 2–6 months is followed by heavy rains. The Asian tropical deciduous forests include timber groups significant for industrial

Evergreen rainforests, such as these in West Africa, characterize tropical regions where annual precipitation is high and evenly distributed. *(Photo courtesy of World Bank.)*

forestry, especially the dipterocarps (lauan, Philippine mahogany, meranti, etc.), teak (*Tectona grandis*), and sal (*Shorea robusta*).

• *Dry forests*—In both temperate and tropical zones, low and simply structured wooded areas are found where annual precipitation is less than 1000 mm. These dry forests vary along climatic gradients from structured closed forests to open woodlands, thornlands, shrublands, savannas, and other short and sparse woody vegetation. Dry forests occur over most of sub-Saharan Africa not occupied by equatorial rainforests. They also occur over large expanses of India, Australia, South and Central America, Mexico and southwestern North America, parts of the Caribbean Basin, and most of the Mediterranean Basin. Some areas of dry forest represent the result of repeated burning over thousands of years. Representative dry forest types include oaks (*Quercus*), mesquite (*Prosopis*), pinon-juniper (in North America), maquis (Mediterranean), and *Acacia* (tropics).

World Forest Assessments

While the mix of forest goods and services changes continuously, much of the rationale for learning about them in a global context remains more or less the same in every age. Three principal driving forces for world forest assessments are international commerce, national political strategy (including national defense), and science. Moreover, international forest assessments now play an important role

Dry forests vary along climatic gradients from structured closed forests to open woodlands, thornlands, shrublands, savannas, and other short and sparse woody vegetation. *(Photo courtesy of Yosef Hadar and World Bank.)*

in guiding the direction of development assistance, and in global environmental planning.

A number of studies attempt to systematically describe and evaluate forest resources at the level of the world and major world regions. Emphasis is on forest areas and types, forest conditions and uses, and human alterations of forests (i.e., deforestation and forest degradation). The task to produce classifications and definitions suitable for multiple world regions and countries is highly demanding in terms of conceptualization, methodology, and integration. The process requires extensive planning, discussion, and compromise.

Purposes and Background   Estimates of forest areas and conditions at regional scales have little application for forest management on the ground. Rather the value of forest data at high levels of aggregation is principally to help furnish a mental geography of forest distribution, establishing the general importance of forests as a proportion of land area and in relation to human population. This can have political significance, potentially aiding top levels of planning and policy.

In this century, the two-volume survey of world forests by Zon and Sparhawk (1923) served as the standard reference until the Second World War. FAO's first World Forest Inventory was carried out in 1947–1948 and published in 1950. Subsequent studies were published periodically during the 1950s and 1960s. This series was discontinued, followed by studies in the mid-1970s for individual major regions.

Beginning in the late 1970s, forest assessments increasingly emphasized the tropical countries. Assessments of tropical forests from the 1970s onward aim to fill information gaps about deforestation, a subject barely touched in earlier assessments except in highly qualitative terms. Early efforts to assemble data on areas and conditions of tropical forests were frustrated by confusing and incomplete reports dispersed across many countries. Furthermore, data were applicable for only limited forest areas.

In light of these problems, a comprehensive effort to measure tropical deforestation was initiated in 1979–1981 by FAO with financial assistance from the United Nations Environmental Program (UNEP). The project, named GEMS (Global Environmental Monitoring System), attempted to apply consistent definitions of forest area and forest clearing across 76 tropical countries for the base year 1980 (Lanly 1982). The GEMS initiative represented a major advance by incorporating remote sensing surveys where available, explicitly reporting dates and judgments about the reliability of measurements for each country or subregion, and improving the system of defining and classifying forest areas. The assessment has since expanded from 76 to 129 countries, and was recently repeated for the base year 1990.

The assessment for 1990 improves upon the 1980 study by integrating a tropical assessment with a temperate assessment in a global synthesis. Moreover, the 1990 tropical assessment provides new information items on forest biomass, forest formations by ecological zones, and risks of forest degradation. Very importantly for farm and community forestry, the 1990 work estimates certain categories of tree cover on non-forest lands. Despite continuing organizational and technological advances permitting improved capability, global forest assessments are inherently constrained by a series of limitations, as follows.

Limitations   Under ordinary circumstances, forest assessments are difficult. Difficulties multiply considerably when adding an international dimension. Not surprisingly, most global assessments in the forestry sector have been defined from the perspective of industrial timber. This is reflected in the following pairs of adjectives to describe forests at the general level: closed or open, coniferous (softwood) or broadleaved (hardwood), natural forest or plantation, productive (capable of growing timber) or nonproductive, and exploitable (accessible) or unexploitable. The geopolitical context may be phrased in terms of industrialized country or developing country, and market economy or centrally planned economy.

These descriptors can be subjective. Hence the separation of closed forests, open woodlands, and non-forests is a highly creative exercise when considering gradients of forest cover. Moreover, the meaning of productive forests is not the same in different countries. Finally, the classification of countries as industrialized or developing, or as market economies or planned economies, is problematic for intermediate cases.

Even when matters of terminology and economic context can be resolved, this leaves the very difficult task of evaluating a country's forests for their many resource values. Hence in the late 1970s, the fuelwood problem in the developing countries suddenly commanded worldwide attention. This found FAO with only sparse data on fuelwood across countries. Forest inventories had excluded vast areas of open shrublands and bush savannas in arid and semiarid regions. This can be appreciated by reviewing remarkably different estimates of open woodlands, as shown in Figure 2-4. Compared with closed forests, these sparsely wooded areas implicitly had been considered "wastelands."

A second issue of recent global importance is the conservation of biological diversity (Wilson 1988). Various areas of tropical moist forest have negligible or negative commercial value because of species heterogeneity and inaccessible location. Often, these are precisely the vegetative complexes of most significance for biological diversity. Thus the areas historically classified and inventoried with the greatest amount of detail for commercial timber leave critical voids in

Forest or not forest? The separation of closed forests, open woodlands, and non-forests is a highly creative exercise when considering gradients of forest cover. *(Photo courtesy of World Bank.)*

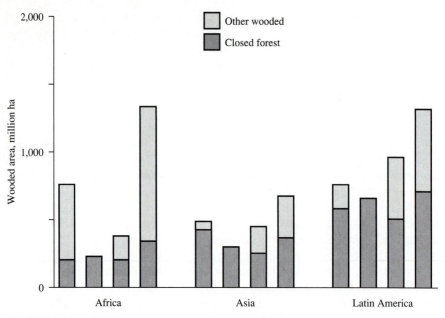

FIGURE 2-4
Four estimates of wooded areas in Africa, Asia, and Latin America during the 1970s and 1980s.
(Sources: Sedjo and Clawson (1984, p. 159); FAO (1988, Table 1a).)

information when considering this more recent issue. Moreover, outlooks for supply and demand of timber may not clearly inform public policy when other major
questions of the day are release of carbon dioxide into the atmosphere (e.g., due
to deforestation), distributions of rare fish and wildlife, and the extent of shifting
cultivation in forested regions.

Extent and Characteristics of Forest Cover

In view of the constraints outlined in previous sections, the extent, condition,
and trend of global forest cover cannot be described in detail or with precision.
Common sense must prevail in subjectively weighing the quality of information
presently available. Knowledge is more complete and reliable for temperate zones
than for the tropics, for Europe and Japan than for Africa and China, and for
closed forests than for open woodlands. This does not invalidate cross-country
comparisons, but cautions healthy skepticism.

Natural Forests and Woodlands Table 2-1 shows the extent of forest cover
by broad world regions. When considering all wooded areas (i.e., including open
woodlands, shrublands, and forest fallow), the world is about 40 percent forested.
When limiting the view to the 3.6 billion hectares of closed forests alone (i.e.,
excluding "other wooded area"), this falls to 27 percent. The difference between
all forms of woodland and closed forests is most pronounced in regions with large

TABLE 2-1
Global forest cover around 1980, by major world regions

	Forested area (million ha)			Other wooded area (million ha)	Total wooded	
	Productive for timber	Legally protected	Other		Area	% of land
Africa	340	51	319	630	1339	45
South America	657	19	196	253	1125	64
USSR	483	20	237	190	930	42
USA and Canada	410	36	44	244	734	40
Asia	363	26	103	177	669	25
Europe	126	2	9	42	178	38
Caribbean*	44	4	28	94	167	56
Pacific Islands	55	8	28	67	158	19
World	2478	162	964	1696	5300	40

* Includes Mexico and Central America
Source: FAO 1988 (Table 1a).

expanses of arid zones, shifting cultivation, or both, e.g., much of Africa, the Mediterranean Basin, Australia, China, India, Mexico, and northeastern Brazil.

Figure 2-5 shows the wide range in previous estimates of global forest cover. Note that figures have varied from 2.5 billion to more than 6.0 billion hectares. Discrepancies should be attributed to revised definitions of forest cover, variations in total geographical coverage, the existence of newer generations of forest surveys, and other factors which together constitute "better information." The comparison aptly illustrates the high risk of uncritically comparing forest data at different points in time, and of accepting deforestation rates derived from questionable figures on the forest base.

Despite known data deficiencies, statistics at the international level support a few general observations. The first is highly uneven forest distribution for reasons of climate and soils, agricultural history, and human population patterns. Figure 2-6 shows that seven countries account for about 60 percent of the world's closed forests. Approximately half of the closed tropical forests are located within Brazil, Zaire, and Indonesia. The USSR, Canada, and the USA account for roughly 80 percent of the world's coniferous forests, a major factor explaining why they also account for approximately half of the world's annual harvests of industrial timber.

Countries can be arrayed by closed forest area as a proportion of total land area (Table 2-2). Individual percentages, country by country, are inaccurate and not worthy of detailed attention. Yet there can be little doubt concerning pronounced unevenness across countries. Guyana and Suriname represent one extreme, and Saudi Arabia and Yemen another. Only three industrialized (i.e., high-income) countries are over half forested, and only four are less than 10 percent forested. That most industrialized countries are not at the extremes of either high or low forest cover is worth pondering as both a result of their wealth, and possibly also as a partial explanation for it.

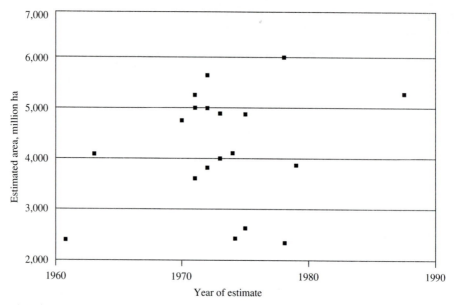

FIGURE 2-5
Varying estimates of global forest cover. *(Sources: Sedjo and Clawson (1984, p. 158); FAO (1988, Table 1a).)*

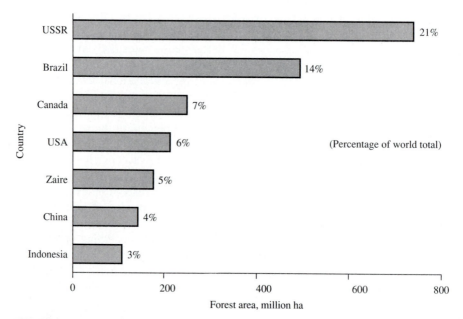

FIGURE 2-6
Countries with the largest forested areas. *(Source: FAO (1988, Table 1a).)*

TABLE 2-2
Closed forests as a proportion of land area, most-forested and least-forested countries

I. 50% or more forest cover (percent forested in parentheses)

31 Developing Countries		3 Industrialized Countries
Guyana (95)		Finland (65)
Suriname (93)	Brunei (61)	Japan (64)
French Guiana (90)	Laos (59)	Sweden (59)
Solomon Islands (89)	Central African Republic (58)	
Papua New Guinea (85)	São Tome-Principe (58)	
Gabon (80)	Senegal (58)	
Zaire (78)	Botswana (57)	
Guinea-Bissau (75)	Cameroon (55)	
Kampuchea (72)	Dominica (55)	
Indonesia (66)	Panama (55)	
Republic of Korea (66)	Peru (55)	
Malaysia (64)	Ecuador (53)	
Belize (63)	Guadeloupe (53)	
Republic of Congo (63)	Zimbabwe (51)	
Bolivia (62)	Colombia (50)	
Brazil (61)	Paraguay (50)	

II. 10% or less forest cover (percent forested in parenthesis)

32 Developing Countries		4 Industrialized Countries
Bangladesh (8)	Afghanistan (2)	Netherlands (9)
Comoros (8)	Burundi (2)	United Kingdom (8)
Mauritius (8)	Haiti (2)	Australia (6)
Morocco (8)	Iran (2)	Ireland (5)
El Salvador (7)	Niger (2)	
Jamaica (7)	Algeria (1)	
Mali (6)	Cape Verde (1)	
Mongolia (6)	South Africa (1)	
Kenya (5)	Syria (1)	
Israel (4)	Egypt (<1)	
Lebanon (4)	Jordan (<1)	
Uruguay (4)	Lesotho (<1)	
Djibouti (3)	Libya (<1)	
Iraq (3)	Mauritania (<1)	
Pakistan (3)	Saudi Arabia (<1)	
Tunisia (3)	Yemen (<1)	

Source: FAO (1988, Table 1a).

The definition of forest management varies among countries and contexts. By almost any definition, a substantial amount of the world's area of natural forests is under no kind of management. In the 1950s, one informed estimate put the amount of forest under management in northwestern Europe at about 65–75 million hectares. An optimistic guess assumed an equal amount outside of Europe, for a total managed area of just under 150 million hectares. This led to the conjecture that only 3–5 percent of the world's forest lands were under reasonably good management (Rostlund 1956).

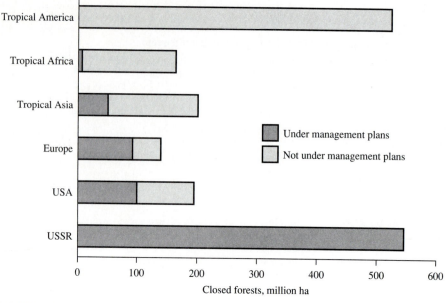

FIGURE 2-7
Closed productive forests under management, selected world regions. *(Source: IIED and WRI (1987, p. 60).)*

Although the amount of forest land coming under management appears to be increasing rapidly, this increase is on a small base. Perhaps three-fourths of all world forests are still unmanaged (IIED and WRI 1987). Figure 2-7 shows the extent to which forest under management plans is greater in temperate regions than in the tropics. The forest management applied in the USSR is sometimes more theoretical than actual (Barr and Braden 1988). Important large countries (e.g., Canada, China, and others) are not represented in the data. Despite these qualifications, there should be little doubt that most forest management occurs in the industrialized countries. The proportion of forests under management in the developing countries is likely below five percent (FAO 1988).

Manmade Forests A manmade forest refers to trees established artificially. Biologically and perhaps also philosophically, manmade forests can be difficult to define. Thus in some European forests dominated by centuries of human influence, only experts can tell the difference between natural and manmade stands, and sometimes only with great difficulty.

Man makes forests by seeding, by planting seedlings, and by assisting natural regeneration. Afforestation of bare land is distinguished in terminology, purpose, and technology from reforestation of previously forested areas. A subjective and simplified classification of manmade forests according to purpose may recognize (1) industrial plantations for production of sawtimber, veneer logs, pulpwood, and

Most forest management occurs in the industrialized countries. This equipment thins a stand of Norway spruce (*Picea abies*) in Finland. *(Photo courtesy of Erkki Oksanen and Finnish Forest Research Institute.)*

Man makes forests by seeding, by planting seedlings, and by assisting natural regeneration. This plantation of *Pinus silvestris* in Sweden has wide spacing for production of high-quality industrial wood. *(Photo courtesy of Jonas Palm.)*

Much tree planting for soil and water protection takes place in the context of government conservation projects like this one near Lumaco, Chile. *(Photo courtesy of FAO.)*

other industrial wood; (2) tree planting for soil and water protection, often in the context of government conservation projects; and (3) individual and collective tree planting on farms and communal lands.

These categories are not mutually exclusive. Objectives often are overlapping, blurred, and unclear. Many plantings are for multiple uses, and many are for uses which are undefined at the time of establishment. Also, division by subsectors or socioeconomic modes is not necessarily practical or possible. Thus plantings for fuelwood include highly industrialized operations at one extreme (e.g., by some of Brazil's iron and steel industries), and plantings by millions of individual peasant households at the other.

The areas and economic significance of manmade forests in a global context are important only in recent times. While tree planting took place in parts of the Mediterranean Basin, China, and Europe well before the twentieth century, most of the world's artificial regeneration through reforestation and afforestation has occurred since the Second World War, particularly after 1960. The dramatic upturn in planting over the last few decades responds to a complex mixture of market, technological, biological, and policy factors.

Statistics on the extent and condition of manmade forests are not trustworthy. In many countries, planted areas have been increasing rapidly, while statistical re-

Tree planting on farms often takes the form of rows, small plots, irregular patches, and even individual trees—as shown here in the Dominican Republic. Areal extent of dispersed tree cover is difficult to estimate, and possibly meaningless to interpret. *(Photo courtesy of FAO.)*

porting lags far behind. Planned forest establishment often exceeds realized planting, even though statistics confuse the two. Where realized planting has occurred, the trees may be eliminated because of fires, pests, and human occupancy. Finally, much of tree planting on farms and in conservation projects takes the form of rows, small plots, irregular patches, and even individual trees. Measures of areal extent are difficult if not impossible to make, and possibly meaningless to interpret.

These precautions apply to Table 2-3, showing estimates of planted areas in the mid-1980s. The world total of about 100 million hectares includes planted forests for industrial timber, fuelwood, soil and water protection, and all other uses. It is doubtful that the table captures non-forest trees planted on farms, communal lands, and in small aggregations elsewhere.

About one-third of the world's manmade forests in 1985 were located in the USSR and China. Data for China are unreliable (Evans 1982), and data for the USSR sometimes include assisted natural regeneration within a total for forest restoration and afforestation (Barr and Braden 1988). The other largest shares of manmade forests are in western Europe, the USA, and Japan. Hence the leading plantation regions in terms of area established are predominantly temperate or subtropical.

TABLE 2-3
Global area of forest plantations around 1985,
by major countries or world regions

	Plantation area (thousand ha)
Industrialized countries	
USSR	21,900
Western Europe	13,000
USA	12,100
Japan	9,600
Canada	1,500
New Zealand	1,100
Australia	800
Subtotal	60,000
Developing countries	
China	12,700
Brazil	6,100
India	3,100
Indonesia	2,600
Republic of Korea	2,000
Chile	1,200
Argentina	800
Others	7,400
Subtotal	35,900

Source: FAO (1988, Table 5); Postel and Heise (1988, p. 28)

DYNAMICS OF DEFORESTATION

The current extent, location, and condition of the world's forests mirror thousands of years of increasing human impact and influence. Global forest area may be about one-half to two-thirds of its extent in preagricultural times. Even before sedentary agriculture, indigenous hunters and food gatherers annually set fires that regularly pushed back tree cover over vast areas of both temperate and tropical regions. The subsequent advance of the agricultural frontier led to piecemeal and frequently indiscriminate clearing of forested tracts to obtain fuel and timber, and to make room for cropland, pastures, human settlements, and infrastructure.

Historical forest clearing and conversion responded to widespread cross-cultural notions of Western human progress as taming the wilderness and opening the forest for settlement and civilization. To the Roman Empire, forests symbolized wilderness and the hostility of nature. The Romans regarded regions north of the Alps as forbidding and barbarous because of the forests and woodlands there, and because of the tribal groups which inhabited them (Sartorius and Henle 1968). Even George Perkins Marsh, nineteenth century pioneer in ecological studies who stressed the considerable damage which man often inflicts on nature, saluted Vermont farmers at an agricultural fair in 1847 for "filling with light and life, the dark and silent recesses of our aboriginal forests" (Marsh 1864, p. xvii).

Deforestation in the industrialized countries of Europe and North America stabilized and then reversed itself, but continues in many of the developing countries. Forest degradation and conversion in both humid and dry regions of these countries are driven by a complex interaction of continued demand for new lands, complex tree and land tenure systems, technical difficulties of managing tropical forests, and effects of government policies.

Forests as Land Frontiers: Historical Context

Historical accounts of forest areas evolve by piecing together studies of land-use changes in local regions in particular historical periods. Cross-regional comparisons are used to discern broader trends and furnish synthesis. Some approaches relate changing forest areas to successive changes in world markets, population, and political relationships. Others examine changes in forest areas resulting from the diffusion of the steel plow, steam power and railroads, iron-hulled ships, control of malaria and other diseases, agricultural plant breeding, and other technological innovations. Climatic changes, volcanic activity, and related natural causes affect forest advance and retreat over truly long periods, but human activity unquestionably has been the principal agent in forest contraction and expansion.

Pollen analyses and surveys of vegetative remains indicate that virtually all of western and central Europe, together with extensive regions of southern and eastern Europe, was covered with forests at the beginning of the Neolithic Period (Darby 1956). Analysts also surmise that forests were very abundant in India and China before the spread of sedentary agriculture. Forest cover is now about 12–13 percent of land area in China, and less than 20 percent of land area in Europe and India. The principal factor in the removal of these vast forests undoubtedly was to provide land for food production.

Since 1700 and particularly since the mid-1800s, the expansion of cropland and pasture by pioneer frontier settlement has been a worldwide and large-scale phenomenon. Forests and woodlands stand as an impediment to sedentary farming and related settlement. The most useful timber and fuelwood are extracted before the remaining forest vegetation is removed by girdling, bark stripping, cutting, and burning. In aspects of both technology and motivation, the advance of the pioneer settler to convert forested land for crops and livestock bears remarkable similarities across societies and through the centuries (Richards 1986).

Central Europe more or less completed its conversion of large forest areas into agricultural lands during the twelfth and thirteenth centuries. This was followed by grazing pressures on the remaining forests, together with rising fuelwood demands when medieval industrialization began to grow. Ore smelting and glassmaking, whose development in central Europe began in the fourteenth century, relied entirely on wood for energy. By the end of the sixteenth century, entire mountain ranges in the Alps had been deforested to provide wood for blast furnaces. This was followed somewhat later by Alpine torrents and enormous damage from landslides, violent flooding, extreme soil erosion, and disruption of adjacent agriculture (Sartorius and Henle 1968).

By the seventeenth century, forest clearing for wheat production extended into peripheral areas that are now part of eastern Europe. In the eighteenth century, the demand for land and wood led to transatlantic clearing in North America, Brazil, and sugar-producing islands of the Caribbean region. A wave of forest clearing in the early nineteenth century affected major areas of India and the midwestern USA. By the middle of that century, rapid forest clearing had expanded to large parts of the British empire (Himalayan India, Australia, Southeast Asia, South Africa), as well as to Manchuria and Taiwan in East Asia. The late nineteenth century witnessed further expansion into sub-Saharan Africa, the western USA, and Siberia. In the current century, especially after the Second World War, zones of forest clearance for agricultural settlement have been particularly widespread and intensive in what are now considered the developing countries (Tucker and Richards 1983; Richards and Tucker 1988).

Dramatic increases in cultivated land date from about the middle of the nineteenth century. While the data are crude, the world's cultivated land appears to have more than doubled since 1860 (Figure 2-8).

The concept of forest clearing in the wake of European expansion is not appropriate everywhere. Much forest removal was largely autonomous, not linked with Western colonial settlement or influences. Historically, a considerable amount of deforestation was caused by internal wars and post-feudal invasion of newly

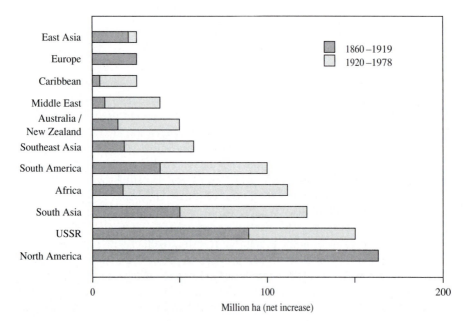

FIGURE 2-8
Expansion of world land areas under regular cropping, 1860-1978. *(Source: Richards (1986, p. 55).)*

ownerless forest tracts, such as following the French Revolution and Russia's abolishment of serfdom. In the Togo Gap of West Africa, deforestation for iron smelting had been occurring for centuries, long predating European arrival (Goucher 1988). In premodern Japan, rapid deforestation took place in the absence of either industrialization or Western colonization (Osako 1983).

Contemporary Deforestation in Developing Countries

Analyses of contemporary deforestation focus primarily on the degradation and removal of forest cover in mainly tropical and subtropical regions. The pace of deforestation in the tropics alarms scientists, captures the imagination of the news media, and ultimately influences the thinking and pronouncements of numerous political leaders. The voluminous and often emotional writings and speeches on tropical deforestation, mainly since 1980, constitute an important historical development of the late twentieth century.

Numerous analyses consider the amount of tropical deforestation taking place, its geographical distribution, and projections of remaining areas of tropical forest at various points in the future. This requires one or more definitions of deforestation.

Deforestation in the tropics alarms scientists, captures the imagination of the news media, and ultimately influences the thinking and pronouncements of numerous political leaders. Here new agricultural land is opened in Sumatra, Indonesia. *(Photo courtesy of FAO.)*

It assumes that the amount of deforestation in different regions can be measured, and that the numbers of hectares so deforested can be aggregated in a meaningful manner. Finally, it requires one or more methods of forecasting future forest and non-forest areas from past and current deforestation rates and patterns. As should be clear from the problems of forest statistics at a global level, the analytical demands of this exercise run far ahead of the limited and weak information actually available (Grainger 1984).

The rate at which tropical forests are converted to other land uses is graphically illustrated with a few examples. Perhaps two-thirds of all forest clearing in Central America since the onset of European settlement has occurred since 1950 (Leonard 1987). Thus Figure 2-9 shows the pronounced shrinking of forest area in Costa Rica. In a recent year, Brazil's remote sensing program tallied as many as 5000 daily fires for forest clearance in the Brazilian Amazon (Worldwatch Institute 1989). Madagascar's forest area in 1985 was only half of what it had been in 1950. Hundreds of other anecdotes and individual statistics could be assembled, which together portray a composite picture of spotty but often rapid and locally severe deforestation in the tropics.

Various attempts have been made to scale the magnitudes of tropical deforestation at a global level. These have produced widely varying estimates. This is explained by varying concepts and classifications of forests, by substantially differing definitions of deforestation, by suspect estimation methods, and by serious weaknesses in the validity of the primary data. Within the limits of available data, tropical deforestation was estimated at about 17 million hectares annually for 1981–1990 (Table 2-4). The rate of deforestation was approximately one percent per year. This is apart from additional millions of hectares logged annually, but not deforested.

Deforestation rates across countries vary by factors of 100 and more. Many deforestation problems are most severe in countries with limited forest in relation to population (e.g., Rwanda, Haiti, Nepal), even if the absolute amount of deforestation is much less than in Brazil, Indonesia, Zaire, and other large countries. This is one reason why deforestation data at a global level are meaningless for most kinds of decisions in forest policy and management. Rather, deforestation rates and impacts usually are best defined at the levels of subnational and local regions. Moreover, cross-country comparisons of high and low deforestation rates are valid for no more than one or two decades at most, given that pockets of deforestation shift from zone to zone and country to country.

Deforestation estimates have been challenged on both conceptual and empirical grounds. In the Forest Resources Assessment for 1990, deforestation is defined as the conversion of forests to land uses that have a tree cover of less than 10 percent, and are not actively regenerating. Excluded is forest degradation where logging, fuelwood extraction, forest grazing, and other modification processes reduce productive potential on lands which continue to be classified as forest. Thus most useful timber, wildlife, medicinal plants, etc., can be depleted from an area, but the area is not considered deforested so long as forest cover remains on 10 percent of it.

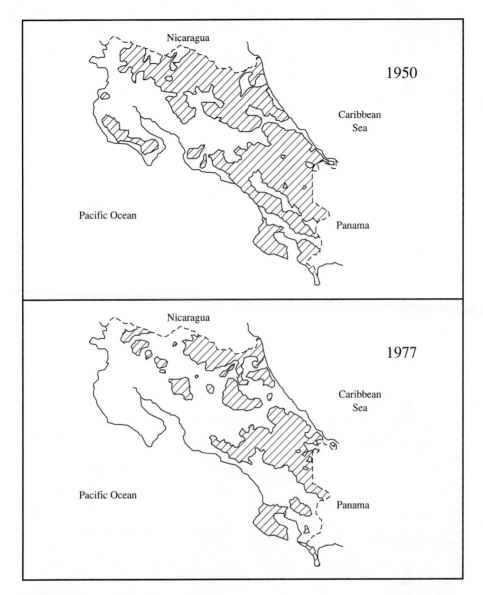

FIGURE 2-9
Contraction of forest area in Costa Rica, 1950–1977. *(Source: Tropical Science Center (1982, p. 29). Used with permission of Tropical Science Center.)*

Yet gradual and cumulative degradation, not outright deforestation, is the true nature of the resource problem in the pine forests of Central America, over vast areas of dry woodlands, and over extensive subregions of tropical moist forests. In general, the conventional concept of deforestation is physical rather than economic, even though progress towards the latter might be far more useful for policy and management.

TABLE 2-4
Areas and rates of deforestation in the tropics, 1981–1990

	Forest area (million ha)	Annual deforestation (million ha)	Deforestation rate (percent per yr)
Moist tropics	840	8.5	1.0
Dry tropics	860	8.6	1.0
Total	1,700	17.1	1.0

Source: FAO, Forest Resources Assessment 1990 (preliminary data).

Deforestation Causes

To fix blame for tropical deforestation on a cause or causes invites a diversity of viewpoints. There is no accepted and unifying theoretical explanation of deforestation, even though observers easily identify groups of factors which explain why deforestation is progressing (Palo and Salmi 1987; Palo and Mery 1990).

A first issue is to separate deforestation determinants from agents. Primary reasons for deforestation are poverty, highly unequal political power, and institutional failures such as landlessness which follow from these circumstances. Lack of well-defined property rights frequently results in deforestation, since those en-

Gradual and cumulative degradation, not outright deforestation, is the true nature of the resource problem over vast areas of dry woodlands, such as these in Kenya. *(Photo courtesy of FAO.)*

gaged in forest clearing have no incentive to protect and manage forests if competing claimants later will appropriate them. Additionally, governments ambivalent about deforestation often promote agricultural settlements and other developments in forested zones, even while praising the virtues of forest conservation.

Underneath these policies lies conflict among social classes. Still deeper are corruption and other moral issues. To explain deforestation in these terms is to slice through multiple layers of a cake, with the most fundamental causes as bottom layers upon which rest the more visible layers at the top (Guppy 1984).

The top and most easily observed layer reveals only the active deforestation agents. This refers to enterprises and persons observed to be physical instruments in the conversion process. It is sometimes convenient to separate purely subsistence agents (e.g., shifting cultivators, nomadic pastoralists, and fuelwood gatherers) from commercial agents such as forest industries and cattle ranchers. In many cases, these agents are competing for the same forested lands in the absence of clear ownership rights to them. In other cases, the rights are nominally provided, but are largely unenforceable.

Very important are cross-regional differences in the nature of the forest converter and conversion process. Deforestation agents in tropical dry forests include an important component of fuelwood collectors and animal herders, as in the African Sahel, dry regions of Haiti, and arid woodlands of South Asia. These same components are often present in sparsely wooded, high-elevation zones.

Cattle ranching has been an important deforestation agent in Central America and Brazil. *(Photo courtesy of World Bank.)*

In comparison, fuelwood extraction and pastoral herding are rarely cited as factors explaining deforestation in Amazonia. Cattle ranching has been an important deforestation agent in Central America and Brazil (Shane 1986), while commercial logging plays an equivalent role in parts of humid West Africa and Southeast Asia. Hence the role and intensity of the human factors vary greatly by region.

The various deforestation agents rarely operate independently. They can be closely linked, as when lands fallowed after shifting agriculture in humid zones of Latin America are consolidated and then cleared for cattle raising. Often shifting cultivation appears as a secondary rather than primary agent of deforestation when road construction opens new areas to either spontaneous or directed occupation. Many other interactions and sequences exist, especially along the penetration of new transportation routes. This makes it difficult, if not also misleading, to isolate individual deforestation agents (Myers 1980). On the other hand, it serves no end to ascribe deforestation to society at large without identifying at least a few specific explanations, as follows.

Demand for Land   Prominent among the interrelated reasons for tropical deforestation is the demand for agricultural soil. This is the contemporary manifestation of continued agricultural extensification. Traditional shifting agriculture by indigenous tribal groups is only one form of forest conversion for food crops. Other forms include encroachments by smallholder peasants of nonindigenous backgrounds, and land settlement by various groups of colonizers and squatters. Still other demands for land are felt through expansion of modern agribusiness, with forest clearing making way for oil palm, rubber, fruit orchards, ornamental plants, beef cattle, and other enterprises. Each of these forms, in turn, has numerous typologies within it.

These typologies are essential for an adequate understanding of land-use practices and their impact on deforestation. For example, it is generally assumed that indigenous shifting agriculturalists practice cropping methods which have evolved over many generations, and which are sustainable in the long run if not disturbed by outside influences. In contrast, pioneer fronts of peasants from nonindigenous groups may be new to a particular forested zone, insecure in their claim to the land, and uninformed of good agricultural practices in their new setting. As a result, their encroachment leaves in its wake unsustainable land use and a mosaic of degraded lands. This differential impact between indigenous cultivators versus immigrant peasants represents a dangerous generalization subject to more investigation, but reveals a leading theme in much current thinking.

Almost half of all tropical deforestation occurs through shifting agriculture in its many variations (variously known as slash-and-burn, swidden, milpa, ladang, kaingin, and other terms). Its share in total deforestation is believed to be about 70 percent in tropical Africa, 50 percent in tropical Asia, and 35 percent in tropical America (Lanly 1982). Because the extent of shifting agriculture is extremely difficult to ascertain, these magnitudes are merely indicative. Yet they suggest overall importance and regional differences.

The area occupied by shifting agriculture and forest fallows is roughly one-fifth of total forest area in the tropical world. Forest fallow, or land which has been cleared for shifting cultivation and then left for regeneration into woody vegetation, exceeds the area of remaining closed forest in several countries, particularly in subregions of West Africa and Southeast Asia. The number of persons living from shifting agriculture might be 500 million, or almost 10 percent of world population. This is not a precise estimate, but indicates order of magnitude (Lanly 1985).

Tree and Land Tenure   The ownership of trees and the land on which they grow is a complex arrangement. Variations in property rights are determined by different patterns of land settlement, sociocultural traditions, and legal and political systems. Through the centuries, the passage of forests from strictly common property to various claims of individual and collective ownership has produced a worldwide diversity of tenure conditions. Abrupt changes in these conditions, or insecurity about them, are prominent among forces which give rise to deforestation (Fortmann and Bruce 1988).

Tenure (from the Latin word for "to hold") is the possession of the different rights to trees and land as they are divided among individuals, communities, and the state (i.e., represented by national governments). The different tenure types rarely exist in pure form. Thus individual and family holdings can be found in regions of predominantly communal tenure. Conversely, traditional community rights of access to specific forest goods and services are common in regions otherwise dominated by state and private ownership. Legal (de jure) ownership of trees and land is not necessarily the same as effective (de facto) possession. Nor are tree rights and land rights always vested in the same persons. This complicated picture of rights and lack of rights in trees and land explains a great deal about where and why deforestation occurs.

There is no current inventory of forest ownership at a world level, although a few generalizations are possible using FAO data from the 1960s (FAO 1963). Those data cover about three-fourths of global forest area, and no sweeping shifts in ownership status have occurred since then. Hence about three decades ago, 77 percent of global forest area was "public" and 23 percent was "private." This is a crude and highly simplistic division when considering the complexities of property rights noted previously. Most public forest is state-owned, meaning that only a small share is owned by municipalities, cantons, and other public entities below national level. Given the particular countries missing from the FAO study of the 1960s, reported figures underestimate state ownership in the global total. Conceivably, state ownership could encompass 90 percent or more of the world's forests (Stewart 1985).

Ironically with respect to a long-standing doctrine that state ownership protects the public interest in forests, it is on state lands where the bulk of the world's deforestation takes place. While the state as forest owner has legitimate nonmarket and long-term interests to defend, in practice it frequently lacks the ability and resources to do so. Two distinct situations can be recognized, passive possession and active exclusion.

Passive possession is nominal state ownership of sparsely populated lands, which are claimed by indigenous tribes, shifting agriculturalists, and other subsistence groups. However, ample documentation indicates that land rights by these peoples are frequently forgotten, ignored, or compromised in the face of encroachment pressures by new claimants. Deforestation occurs when traditional tenure arrangements break down due to the strife and insecurity provoked by the encroachments, and when there is little if any government presence to clarify and enforce ownership disputes. The state is little more than an absentee landlord, or "invisible owner" (Stewart 1985). Thus while theoretically in state possession, lands and forests in practice are common property. The "tragedy of the commons" is the lack of rationale for users to individually or collectively husband natural resources because of well-founded beliefs that competing claimants will appropriate them first (Hardin 1968).

Active exclusion refers to the next stage in the progression, when the state acts to protect land tenure now assertively claimed by itself or by newly arrived claimants. The origins of the forester are traced to this role. For at least a thousand years, the forester has been employed by governments and private landowners to evict and later exclude indigenous groups and peasants from lands formerly used by them. As early as the eighth century, kings and barons in central and western Europe attempted to prevent tribal hunters and pig herders from trespassing on newly proclaimed hunting reserves. *Forestarii* and *forestmasters* were appointed to police these royal *banforests*. The steady disappearance of communal land as the kings claimed more and more *banforests* was one of the contributions to rebellions in which apparently hundreds of thousands of peasants were killed (Fernow 1911).

Even when indigenous and peasant populations have coexisted with imposed settlement, Western concepts of land and tree ownership radically restrict traditional access to forests and wildlands. Examples in the early years of this century include British attempts to exclude villagers and their livestock from declared forest reserves in India, attempts by British settlers to evict native Kikuyus from the forested slopes of Mount Kenya, and French policies to have West Africans produce export crops over extensive Sahelian bushlands (Richards and Tucker 1988). These are just a few documented cases among hundreds which have no written record. They have left a bitter legacy and a mistrust of purposes persisting into the present era.

That some national governments claim ownership of all trees for the state is yet another factor contributing to deforestation, lack of tree planting, or both. The policy supposedly protects trees, but in effect it denies individuals property rights to trees they might otherwise take care of or establish. A tree-planting program in Haiti confronted the problem that tree cutting is illegal unless special governmental permission is obtained and a tax paid, even for trees on peasant plots. In Panama the state's legal claim to trees has been an obstacle to initiating industrial reforestation on private lands. Nepal, which had nationalized all forests in 1956, later handed forests back to local communities (i.e., *panchayats*) as a policy to improve their management. Survival rates in China's tree planting are reported to be much improved following the country's policy to allow peasants to own the trees they plant. In summary, the state's claim to tree tenure frequently can be counterproductive to intended objectives (Postel and Heise 1988).

Property rights to trees are determined by patterns of land settlement, sociocultural traditions, and legal and political systems. In Haiti, tree cutting is illegal unless special government permission is obtained and a tax paid, even for trees on peasant plots. *(Photo courtesy of FAO.)*

In some countries, freehold ("private") tenure is established by deforesting government lands and thus "improving" them. This is relatively widespread across a variety of cultures and biogeographical contexts. Thus while natural forest is communal property in Zaire, individuals claim exclusive land rights by forest clearing (Lumpungu 1977). Complicated tenure laws in Costa Rica have in the past allowed squatters on forest lands to petition for land titles after a period of demonstrated occupation. The planting of perennial crops helps establish a recognized permanence.

This leads to yet another dimension of property rights, the observation that trees create tenure (Bruce et al. 1985). Private property can be obtained by forest clearing, but it also can be obtained by tree planting, particularly in open and fallow areas. Often these lands are in communal ownership, with the consequence that tree planting is resisted by traditional users who stand to lose access. The predictable response is antagonism towards forest plantation projects perceived to restrict or eliminate traditional use rights. Other responses are sabotage of woodlots, fences, and other government investments for similar reasons.

Technologies for Forest Management   Regarding methods to manage tropical forests, the adequacy of science and technology is highly disputed. This applies especially with respect to the humid tropics. The constraints are species heterogeneity, disputed issues regarding soil fertility after tree removal, and large gaps in knowledge relative to forest regeneration and silvicultural treatment. Here it is important to distinguish between forests which are unmanageable versus those which are simply unmanaged. Biological complexity in the natural world intersects with limited experience in the managerial world, creating argument as to the true limit of constraints.

One school of thought calls attention to how few tropical forest species are actually utilized or even identified. Huge gaps remain in knowledge regarding fruiting, flowering, flora and fauna variation, and other puzzles in basic forest biology and ecology (Gomez-Pompa et al. 1972; Reid and Miller 1989). The other opinion contends that methods to manage tropical forests are workable if not perfect, but that application has been all too sparse, sporadic, and discontinuous (Schmidt 1987; Poore et al. 1989; Buschbacher 1990).

Government Policies   Sometimes purposely, sometimes inadvertently, government policies aggravate the deforestation problem. Comprehensive analyses argue that government policies contribute to forest depletion and economic and fiscal losses, even while espousing protection and wise use (Repetto and Gillis 1988). The problem is most extreme in some of the developing countries, but is shared to a greater or lesser extent around the world, especially in countries where forest areas are still large. For example, until recently government subsidies encouraged conversion of bottomland hardwood forests in the southeastern USA into soybean fields, even during periods of agricultural overproduction.

Key policies affecting forest cutting in market economies are those which prescribe how private buyers, lease holders, and concessionaires contract rights to extract timber and other goods and services from public lands. This refers to contract terms and prices, together with regulations and incentives regarding logging methods and forest regeneration. External to the forestry sector are policies which affect wood processing as a specific branch of national industrialization, and policies which affect international trade in logs and wood products.

Figure 2-10 links deficient forest policies, weak public forest administration, and negative consequences for forest conservation and use. Weak forest administration results in inadequately conceived and enforced forest policies. Poor policies, in turn, lead to unmanageable pressures on the forests, and to meager generation of public revenues from timber royalties and other forest charges. Both of these unfortunate results hurt the image and morale of public agencies responsible for forest administration. Their ineffectiveness keeps them low in national funding and political priorities. Simultaneously, the timber concessionaires—often wealthy and politically powerful—ensure that government forestry agencies listen carefully to their point of view. This is made easier by low salaries throughout the civil service.

Policies outside the forestry sector can tip the balance decidedly to the negative. This happens when other government agencies (e.g., those connected with agrarian reform and land development) regard forested regions primarily as "empty lands" to accommodate expanded infrastructure projects, plantation crops, annual

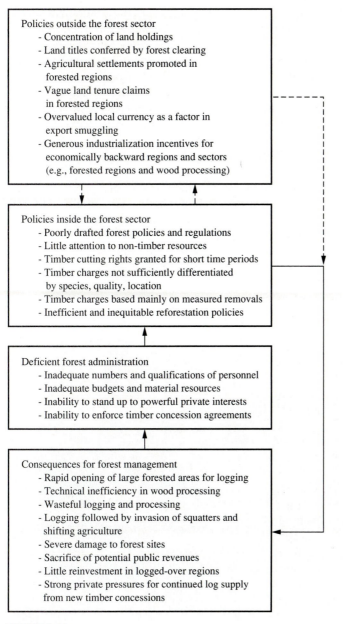

FIGURE 2-10
Vicious circles of deficient forest policies, forest administration, and forest management. *(Source: Repetto and Gillis (1988).)*

crops, pastures, and colonization schemes. Pressures for colonization are exacerbated by implicit policies which protect concentrated agricultural land holdings relative to the number of farmers and landless farmers. New penetrations into the forest are facilitated by vague or unrecognized tenure claims, as described earlier.

Two immense and frequently criticized schemes are Brazil's Trans-Amazon highway construction to open the Amazon region for settlement, and Indonesia's Transmigration Program to relocate millions of land-hungry Javanese to the Outer Islands (Ascher and Healy 1990). Yet colonization schemes to "develop" tropical forested lands are by no means limited to Brazil and Indonesia. Among other reasons, governments favor resettlement projects because the opening of new agricultural lands entails considerably less political discomfort than the redistribution of existing lands. Additionally, the filling of "empty lands" may increase a sense of national security for countries concerned about possible territorial claims with neighbors. In an earlier era, the filling of an "empty" frontier had been important policy in North America for similar reasons.

Many conversions of forested areas could not proceed as rapidly or at all except for very heavy government expenditures to support them. This takes the form of land titling, government-provided infrastructure, subsidies and tax benefits, price

The government of Bolivia moved this family from the country's altiplano to the more sparsely populated tropical lowlands. Governments favor resettlement projects because the opening of new agricultural lands entails considerably less political discomfort than redistribution of existing lands. *(Photo courtesy of FAO.)*

controls, credit policy, export promotion policy, and protection from imports. For example, direct and indirect subsidies to cattle ranching and timber extraction in the Brazilian Amazon have been extraordinarily generous, leading to virulent land speculation and subsequent deforestation (Hecht et al. 1988; Mahar 1989).

All of these policies reinforce the uncertainty and general disorder of property rights in forests, hastening the pace to obtain and harvest timber concessions before such lands are taken for other uses. As logging opens up more new areas, squatters and shifting cultivators follow the roads and other access routes. This makes forest administration that much more difficult, and forest policies that less useful and enforceable.

The terms of timber concession agreements frequently are inimical to forest management, even though alternative systems are known in principle. In the developing countries, timber licenses and concessions traditionally have short duration. Licenses can be as short as 1–2 years. Some concessions may not extend beyond 10 years. Under these circumstances, careful forest management and measures to ensure forest regeneration are neither technically possible nor in the financial interests of the concession holder.

Negative consequences of short concessions are compounded by greatly understated timber fees, royalties, taxes, and other forest charges. These generous terms provide great stimulus for private operators to obtain timber concessions and extract the timber, capturing high profits or cushioning high costs. Moreover, forest charges typically are insufficiently differentiated by species, log qualities, and location. In Belize, for instance, government timber royalties are not differentiated by difficulty of extraction, giving timber operators an incentive to harvest only the most accessible trees. This leads to high-grading of the forest, extensive forest exploitation across wide areas, and loss of potential government revenues. These problems are accentuated when timber fees are based on volume actually removed rather than volume theoretically available. Also, the focus on timber removed creates a potential for graft and corruption in timber scaling.

Various industrialization policies affect the numbers, technologies, and efficiencies of wood-processing facilities. Not surprisingly, a combination of log export bans and generous incentives to encourage local processing industries often results in inefficient enterprises. This translates into low physical utilization of timber and logs, increased demand for logs to satisfy capacity, increased logging expansion, excessive costs, and loss of badly needed government revenue. Once processing plants are in place, governments may feel obligated to keep log supplies flowing, even if this means uneconomic practices. This phenomenon transcends developing countries to also include the USA, for example (Boyd and Hyde 1989).

Why do these policies remain in place if they do not promote rational forest protection and management? A number of answers can be offered. The first is simple failure to understand and appreciate the economic, social, and humanitarian impacts of policies. The full consequences of a number of forest policies have not been thought through in their entirety. Figure 2-11 summarizes key misunderstandings revealed by studies of the forestry sector in highly diverse countries. Note that errors of perception and judgment are not those of foresters alone, but extend through all layers of policy beyond the sector itself.

FIGURE 2-11
Common errors of perception and judgment regarding the rational use of forests.
(Source: Repetto and Gillis (1988).)

Undervaluation of natural forests left intact
- Neglect of forest's protective services
- Neglect of non-timber products
- Underestimation of psychophysiological benefits

Overestimation of net benefits from utilization
- Exaggerated employment, income, and revenue effects
- Overlooked dissipation of taxes and foreign exchange due to heavy subsidies
- Exaggerated cropping and grazing potentials of forestlands and uncounted costs of habitat destruction
- Overlooked disturbance of indigenous communities
- Ignored costs of "boom town" infrastructure
- Unanticipated damages to soils and watersheds

Insufficient biological, economic, and policy knowledge
- Ignored consequences of sparse information on ecosystems and forest regeneration, particularly in tropics
- Inadequate study and application of land-use capabilities

Unsuccesful attempts to use forestlands to solve problems elsewhere in society
- Migration to forested regions as "escape valve" to resolve landlessness and overcrowding in developing countries
- Timber revenue as substitute for reformed taxation

Reluctance to invest public resources in forest management
- Underfunded research on forest ecology and management
- Inadequate investment in economics and policy expertise
- Inadequate investment in forest management and enforcement

Underestimated importance of local governance
- Ignored products and services of local benefit
- Omission of local communities in program planning
- Overlooked opportunities for community forest management

A second answer is inadequacy of institutional structure. Understanding exists, but resources do not. An example is the structure of fees and other charges on tropical timbers. Forest services know that more revenue should be collected, that each tract of timber should be appraised and charges set accordingly, and that policies should encourage greater utilization per hectare. However, they lack personnel and budgets to accomplish these tasks on the ground. From a distance, policies seem simplistic and wrong. Yet a closer look shows that better policies cannot be initiated without the necessary inputs. Vicious circles continue indefinitely unless broken from the outside.

A third answer adds an ingredient of malevolence to the first two. This refers to corruptive influences where wealth and power are able to bend forest policies for personal gain. In the preceding example, the forest service knows how to improve its system of timber charges, but the private concessionaires know why new policies should not be pursued. The magnitude of this problem is impossible to assess, but should not be ignored or disguised.

Deforestation Consequences

Because the extent and causes of deforestation are highly variable, consequences likewise are variable. Impacts occur along multiple dimensions. Ecological and social effects may be difficult to separate, and often are two sides of the same coin. Some impacts are immediate while others are delayed, and some are local while others are distant or generalized. Finally, the severity of impacts is highly controversial. Some perspectives call attention to prospects for imminent catastrophes, while others challenge the evidence for doomsday predictions. Perceptual and attitudinal differences combine with enormous scientific uncertainty to produce conjecture and controversy.

The severity of forest alteration ranges from only slight disturbance to complete clearing (i.e., deforestation), with all intermediate stages present in one place or another. The sequence from slight disturbance to severe degradation to total conversion can be rapid or gradual. Some impacts reflect discrete events (e.g., natural disasters or one-time logging), while others mirror persistent and chronic land-use pressures. Not all initial disturbance is driven to final conversion, since degraded forests recover some of their attributes if pressures on them are relaxed.

In some places, deforestation is socially, economically, and politically desirable. The circumstances of desirability hinge on scientific and technical arguments regarding soil fertility and other bases of ecological and social sustainability. This is a vast and much debated theme, especially for huge and still sparsely populated forest regions like Amazonia. Perspectives range from environmental apocalypse (Goodland and Irwin 1975) to faith in managed agronomic systems (Sanchez et al. 1982).

Partly because of these complexities, the consequences of deforestation are not easily defined and organized. Figure 2-12 identifies seven broad categories of impacts in light of current knowledge and opinion. Various categories are interrelated, although the mixture of consequences is highly variable by country and local regions:

• *Loss of potential commodities and services*—Deforestation and severe forest degradation result in gross underutilization of timber, food plants and animals, extractives, and other tangible products and services potentially available from the site. In tropical moist forests, the amount of timber felled and simply burned or left to rot in the path of expanding agriculture, road construction, and other penetrations can be enormous. Potential resources are not always economically viable at the time deforestation occurs, but many would have use value in the future if they could be conserved. In this sense, deforestation entails opportunity costs and the elimination of future options.

• *Decreased fuelwood availability*—Fuelwood is noted separately because its decreased availability implies particular hardships on the very poor, and because its scarcity often reflects wood depletion in open woodlands and other areas of scant vegetation outside of closed forests. A study by FAO in the early 1980s estimated that over 100 million people in 26 low-income regions face acute fuelwood scarcity (De Montalembert and Clement 1983). Regions seriously affected are Sahelian

FIGURE 2-12
Known and speculated consequences of deforestation

Loss of potential commodities and services
- Industrial timber
- Wide assortment of non-timber products and services

Decreased fuelwood availability
- Increased time and money costs of obtention
- Negative effects on health and nutrition
- Lessened cropping productivity by diverting crop residues and animal manure for fuel

Impacts on agriculture
- Erosion and soil compaction reduce on-site productivity
- Irregular water flow jeopardizes lowlands irrigation
- Desertification pushes back cropping and grazing

Impacts on downstream infrastructure and human life
- Sedimentation fills irrigation systems, canals, reservoirs
- Floods and landslides damage roads, bridges, buildings, crops, and fishing
- Floods claim personal property and human lives

Impacts on natural habitats and biological resources
- Reductions and extinctions of genetic resources
- Threats to domesticated plant and animal breeding
- Lessened opportunities for research and education

Negative impacts on indigenous cultures
- Loss of lands for hunting, fishing, gathering, farming
- Vulnerability to diseases and human rights abuses
- Loss of traditional ecological knowledge

Impacts on climate
- Release of carbon into atmosphere
- Changes in local and regional precipitation patterns

Africa, eastern and southeastern Africa, Himalayan zones of Asia, the Andean plateau of South America, northeastern Brazil, and densely inhabited subregions of the Caribbean Basin and Central America. These are not the geographical limits of the problem, since fuelwood scarcity is a localized phenomenon which can be present even in countries which are heavily forested as a whole.

• *Impacts on agriculture*—The links between deforestation and reduced agricultural productivity are many and complex. Substitution of agricultural wastes for fuelwood has become extreme in some cases, but not by preference. Because many of these wastes would otherwise be used as mulches and fertilizer, this substitution is associated with reductions in crop productivity. Besides the relationship with fuelwood scarcity, other effects of deforestation are direct soil erosion and alteration of water flows. The areas available for farming in mountainous uplands are reduced where slope erosion is severe, as in Madagascar and the Himalayas. At the same time, slope erosion in uplands catchments may negatively affect the quality and timing of water downstream. However, the physical relationship between alteration of tree cover and resulting impact on water flow is often misunderstood (Ives 1987). In the world's arid zones, the problem is desertification following the progressive deterioration of sparse vegetation (FAO 1989).

In tropical moist forests, the amount of timber felled and simply burned or left to rot in the path of expanding agriculture and road construction can be enormous. *(Photo by Jan Laarman.)*

Fuelwood scarcity often reflects wood depletion in areas of scant vegetation outside of closed forests. *(Photo courtesy of World Bank.)*

• *Impacts on infrastructure and human life*—Deforestation of upland water-sheds has been blamed for advanced sedimentation of costly infrastructure down-stream, particularly irrigation systems, canals, and hydroelectric basins. Land-slides due to slope erosion result in expensive road building, maintenance, and repair. Floods damage crops and carry silt into mangrove forests, with the possibility of adversely affecting coastal fishing. Finally, floods are a factor in loss of personal property and human life. That the losses are great is not disputed. More controversial is the extent to which deforestation explains the problems (Hamilton 1987). At issue is the separation of natural hydrological events and processes from the direct impacts of forest clearing.

• *Impacts on natural habitats and biological resources*—The elimination or severe alteration of forest habitats can have negative consequences for plant and animal breeding stocks, including potential loss of genetic resources. Also at issue are lessened opportunities for research, education, and nature-oriented tourism. Only some of these consequences have monetary values, and very few have been estimated (McNeely 1988).

• *Impacts on indigenous cultures*—A by-product of deforestation is the conflict of cultures when groups with different traditions, values, and needs meet in the forest. Some indigenous groups have adapted reasonably well to contact with outside societies. Elsewhere, tribal groups are vulnerable to introduced infectious diseases and only partial or maladaptive acculturation (World Bank 1982). There is much concern that the disappearance and acculturation of tribal groups is closing off traditional ecological knowledge (Posey 1985). This knowledge, much of it still unfamiliar to Western science, offers possibilities for gains in medicine and management of tropical ecological systems (Schultes 1979). Issues concern the extent to which this knowledge can be saved before it fades away through the social change implicit in forest conversion.

• *Impacts on climate*—The role of deforestation in altering regional and global climate is highly controversial. The elimination of biomass through the cutting and burning of forests releases carbon dioxide and other "greenhouse gases" into the atmosphere. The debated scientific question is then the extent to which this contributes to long-term atmospheric warming (Chapter 7). A second question is the extent to which regional precipitation will shift if deforestation alters evapo-transpiration patterns, e.g., for large vegetation masses in Amazonia (Salati and Vose 1984).

FORESTS IN TRANSITION

The managerial response to past and present deforestation is reforestation, af-forestation, and intensification of forest protection and management. As forests and their products and services become scarcer and thus more costly, societies invest to manage them more intensively than when forests appeared limitless and an obstacle to alternative land uses. The passage from forest removal to forest stewardship and finally to forest management is occurring very unevenly around the world, but with significant and sometimes outstanding achievements in view in many countries.

All of this leads to the theme of "forests in transition," as previous centuries of casual and often careless forest exploitation are offset by policies and investments to reestablish or expand forests, improve their productivity, and extend protection. Four leading developments are (1) stabilized or increasing net forest area over vast regions of temperate forests, (2) increased cropping of industrial timber through forest plantations, (3) increased interest in agroforestry systems to integrate tree culture and agriculture, and (4) increased reservation of forest areas for national parks, ecological reserves, and other protection status. Each of these trends is made possible by the others, and the four together represent deliberate choices to break with past histories of forest depletion.

Regions of Forest Reversion and Stabilization

Following centuries of forest removal for agriculture and other land uses, net forest area in the world's temperate zones appears to have more or less stabilized (Sedjo and Clawson 1984). With regional and local exceptions, the prevailing pattern is one of forest conversions compensated or exceeded by forest replacements. This has occurred through manmade reforestation and afforestation, plus natural forest regeneration on lands formerly under cropping, grazing, and other non-forest

In most of the world's temperate zones, forest conversions are compensated or exceeded by forest replacements. *(Photo courtesy of Jonas Palm.)*

uses. These developments demonstrate the lack of inevitability in extrapolating deforestation trends.

Most likely the minimum of Europe's forest area was reached one or two centuries ago (Thirgood 1989). Upturns might have begun about the middle of the nineteenth century in central Europe (e.g., Figure 2-13 for France), and several decades later in Britain. By the early 1900s, Europe's forest cover was gradually increasing through migration of rural population to the cities, reforestation of former agricultural lands, intensification of agriculture, and major conversion to non-wood energy. Importantly for the recovery of forest area, western Europe has been importing large quantities of agricultural commodities, food, paper, and wood products from other regions. Furthermore, the region has made enormous progress since 1950 in recycling waste paper and using wood residues formerly burned or wasted.

Recent statistics by the United Nations show increasing areas of closed forests and timber growing stock over most of Europe (Table 2-5). Through a combination of tree-planting programs and other factors, some increases are dramatic. Thus in the decade from 1970 to 1980 alone, areas of exploitable closed forests in the UK and Ireland expanded by roughly 30 percent. Other countries like Spain, the Netherlands, and Hungary also recorded large gains. Substantial increases in growing stock attest to the building of timber inventories, although the statistics do not incorporate the post-1980 assessments of forest damage due to air pollution (Chapter 7).

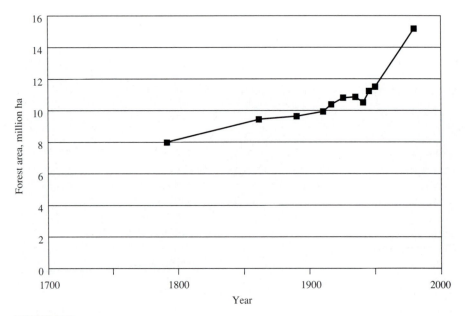

FIGURE 2-13
Expansion of forest area in France since the late eighteenth century. *(Sources: Lowenthal (1956, p. 272); ECE/FAO (1986, p. 34).)*

TABLE 2-5
Expansion of productive closed forests in Europe,
1970–1980

	(Percent Increase or Decrease)	
	Area of closed forests	Timber growing stock
Finland	+3.6	+7.8
Norway	+1.5	+11.4
Sweden	+0.2	+5.1
Denmark	−1.3	+7.9
France	+1.7	+29.1
Ireland	+29.5	+80.0
Netherlands	+7.8	+10.0
United Kingdom	+32.6	+50.4
Austria	−2.0	+6.1
Switzerland		+18.4
Cyprus	−14.2	+1.3
Spain	+9.2	+6.1
Czechoslovakia	−1.5	+15.3
Hungary	+8.9	+17.7
Poland	+0.4	+9.8
Total (15 countries)	+2.5	+12.3

Source: ECE/FAO (1986, p. 46).

The USSR is the world's leader in terms of forested area within its borders. While forests in Soviet Europe are subject to severe local pressures, forested areas east of the Ural Mountains are still vast and often inaccessible in view of the current state of transportation infrastructure. Like Europe, the USSR's forest area and timber growing stock have been increasing over the last several decades. From 738 million hectares in 1961, forest area in 1984 was 811 million hectares (Holowacz 1985).

Like western Europe, Japan in this century has been able to import a very large share of its industrial wood, especially after 1960. Japan's forest cover is extensive, covering roughly two-thirds of the country, despite severe forest depletion a century ago. Japanese forests are costly to manage and harvest for industrial timber, and Japan has been importing logs and forest products from around the Pacific Basin at less cost than it can produce them domestically.

After a substantial decline from 1800 onward, forests in the USA have steadily increased in extent since around 1920 (Williams 1988). Small fluctuations in forest areas since then are relatively inconsequential, and the overall perspective is one of stabilization (Clawson 1979). In the southern region, lands which were once under cotton and tobacco now support pine and mixed hardwoods. Forest cover in New England was less than 50 percent in the mid-1800s, but today is over 80 percent. Pine stands logged a century ago in the Great Lakes states have since regenerated into second-growth forests. Net increase in forest area is explained by large-scale abandonment of farmland and subsequent forest succession and regrowth. Other and related factors include major advances in fire suppression, large and successful tree-planting programs, vigorous biological growth of the regenerated forests, and falling per capita consumption of timber products. In addition to forest reestablishment, the USA joins western Europe and Japan as a large net importer of forest products.

The main temperate regions which have reversed the decline of forest cover have been transformed from predominantly agrarian populations into highly industrialized and urban societies. For over a century, farm families have been leaving the rural areas for employment and residence in the cities. Although the trends are not universal, the agriculture which remains important in the industrialized countries has increased output more through improved yield per hectare than through continued expansion into forested areas. Also, national income in the industrialized regions has risen to levels sufficient to import large quantities of food and forest products. Declining rural populations and affordability of food and wood imports sharply contrast with low-income developing countries struggling with growing rural populations, and whose wealth is inadequate to purchase agricultural and forest products from elsewhere.

Yet the margin held by forests against competing land uses in the temperate regions is by no means permanent. The apparent reversion and stabilization of forest area implicitly assumes an ability to continue to pay for imports of food and wood, and continued ability and willingness of exporting regions to supply them. These assumptions require constant updating in light of changing circumstances.

Moreover, the margin to and from forests shifts back and forth as national economies and domestic policies continue to change. Especially important in the industrialized countries are policies on food self-sufficiency, subsidies to farmers, soil and water conservation, and outdoor recreation. Future urban expansion and attendant infrastructure are not easily forecasted, nor are land-use impacts of potentially new agricultural technologies. Agricultural intensification, together with the reservation of new lands for recreation, suggests an enlarging forest area. On the other hand, urban expansion suggests contractions. Nobody can yet accurately foretell the land-use consequences of global climate change (Chapter 7). In sum, the present outline of forest area in the "stabilized regions" should be regarded as a stage to possibly yet another configuration, especially if the outlook is for a century rather than a decade or two.

From Old-Growth Towards Timber Cropping

Forestry is experiencing a transition similar to that which occurred in agriculture centuries earlier, which is from shifting and extensive extraction to settled and intensive cropping. Increasing shares of industrial timber are being obtained from forest plantations and managed second-growth forests rather than from previously uncut forests (i.e., virgin old-growth). This shift reflects reductions in the remain-

ing areas of old-growth forests, and environmental concerns to protect these relatively undisturbed forests. Improved tree-growing and wood-utilizing technologies
make timber cropping increasingly feasible. From the viewpoint of forest industries, manmade forests shorten time horizons, simplify biological management,
simplify and increase wood utilization, increase land productivity, and place raw
material in desirable locations (Zobel et al. 1987).

The dramatically increased pace of forest planting in the last three decades
is explained by several factors. In light of shifting world supply and demand for
wood and paper products, many countries have had to reevaluate timber adequacy.
This applies particularly to countries lacking large supplies of long-fiber conifers
for pulp and paper production. It also applies where remaining old-growth forests
are increasingly allocated for environmental, aesthetic, and recreational functions.
Furthermore, improved worldwide integration of markets and transportation permits plantation wood to be produced in formerly non-forested regions and then
transported to consuming regions.

Plantations in the temperate northern hemisphere commonly substitute for
forests which have been recently logged. The species planted may be the same
as that harvested, e.g., Douglas-fir (*Pseudotsuga menziesii*) in the northwestern
USA, and scots pine (*P. silvestris*) in the Nordic countries. Alternatively, exotic
(i.e., nonnative) species may be introduced to increase growth and broaden the
species base, e.g., Douglas-fir and lodgepole pine (*P. contorta*) in central and
northern Europe, respectively. Much planting is occurring on lands not forested
in centuries, such as on the moorlands of Scotland and the barren hills of China.

In recent years increased attention has been focused on manmade forests in
the tropics and especially subtropics. Reasons include land availability, low-cost
labor, and high biological productivity. Productivity comparisons are illustrated
in Table 2-6. These substantial differences in biological growth, combined with
rapid expansion in areas planted, explain why a number of "emerging regions"
will account for increasing shares of the world's industrial timber. The large global
share of industrial timber traditionally produced by North America, the USSR,
and the Nordic countries will continue to stay large. Yet some gradual reduction
of that share is virtually assured by investments already made in these emerging
regions.

TABLE 2-6
Representative timber growth in natural forests and plantations,
southern USA compared with Latin America.

	Natural forests (Hardwoods)	Plantations	
		Pines	Eucalypts
	(m^3/hectare/year)		
Southern USA	3	10	10
Latin America	3–5	15–25	40–60

Source: Kellison (1988).

Between 1965 and 1980, the area of tropical plantations more than doubled (Evans 1982). Lanly and Clement (1979) projected a tripling of area under industrial plantations in the tropics and subtropics between 1975 and the year 2000. Policies and programs in many tropical and subtropical regions indicate intentions for major increases in new plantations, even in countries where almost no plantations exist presently. This accelerated plantation activity, now including countries having little prior experience with manmade forests, is a logical and perhaps unavoidable response to scarcity.

Some of the key emerging regions are Brazil and Chile in Latin America, New Zealand and Australia in the Pacific Basin, Spain and Portugal in the Mediterranean Basin, South Africa and Zimbabwe in southern Africa, and a host of other plantation-growing countries around the world. The dominant species are exotics, especially tropical pines, North American pines, and eucalypts. The majority of plantations appear to have been established on lands which have not been forested in recent times.

The impact of manmade plantations on industrial timber supply is particularly dramatic in Latin America. While less than one percent of Latin America's forests are industrial plantations, they supplied roughly one-third of the region's industrial timber during the 1980s. As increasing areas are planted and harvested, it is expected that one-half or more of the expanding timber harvest will derive from plantations by the year 2000 (McGaughey and Gregersen 1983).

Through its recent establishment of vast areas of forest plantations, Brazil will account for an increasing share of the world's industrial timber. Here in southern Brazil, loblolly pine (*P. taeda*) is planted as an exotic (nonnative) species. *(Photo by Jan Laarman.)*

The trend towards timber production in plantations and intensively managed second-growth forests has important implications for land use. Under reasonable assumptions about plantation yields and land availability, a modest 5–10 percent of the world's productive forest area could conceivably meet total world demand for industrial timber (Sedjo 1983). This is a theoretical benchmark which leaves out constraints presented by investment costs, transportation costs, and various risk factors. Lamentably, plantation establishment is too slow and uneven to effectively supply industrial needs in most developing countries in the near future. For example, plantation sources will account for no more than a tiny proportion of high-quality tropical sawtimber by the year 2000 (Grainger 1988). Also, a substantial amount of planting in the developing countries is nonindustrial because of low productivity or designation for purposes other than wood products (Table 2-7).

Nevertheless, the main point is that relatively small areas of intensively-managed timber will continue to displace timber extractions from old-growth natural forests in many world regions. This is the concept of plantations as compensatory forests, or replacement forests (Zobel et al. 1987).

The World Bank uses Kenya and Zambia as examples of two countries which, during the last three decades, shifted from almost complete dependence on logging of natural forests to new log supply from plantations of cypress (*Cupressus lusitanica*) and pine. The plantations occupy only 10 percent of productive forest area, permitting the reservation of large areas of natural forest for national parks and nature reserves (Spears 1988).

TABLE 2-7
Nonindustrial component of forest plantations in developing countries and territories around 1985.

	Nonindustrial component (percent)
Africa	
North Africa and Sahel	79
Insular Africa	53
Southern Africa	38
West and Central Africa	19
Asia (except China)	
Middle East	100
Southeast Asia	43
South Asia	28
Latin America	
Tropical South America	47
Central America and Mexico	43
Southern Cone	6
Caribbean	3
Pacific Islands	6
All Developing Countries and Territories	24

Source: FAO(1988, Table 5).

Integration of Tree Growing with Agriculture

A third transition in response to widespread and often serious loss of tree cover in many parts of the world is agroforestry. This is the deliberate integration of trees, shrubs, and other woody perennials on the same land with agricultural crops, livestock, or both (Nair 1985). Like plantation forestry, agroforestry normally represents an intensification of land use and an emphasis on cropping. In this light, agroforestry stands with plantation forestry as a strategy to mitigate scarcity by improving land productivity.

Agroforestry practices encompass an enormous variety of biological components, management objectives, and agro-ecological settings. Examples of commercial agroforestry are livestock grazing and pine growing; plantation crops of coffee, tea, and cacao under overstory shade trees; and combinations of food crops and domestic animals under oil palm, coconuts, and rubber. Many of these enterprises are operated by governments and agribusiness companies, sometimes on a large scale.

Yet agroforestry proponents often stress production modes which are small, dispersed, and useful to a rural peasantry. In this context, agroforestry refers to a variety of technologies intended to serve goals and aspirations in "social forestry."

Agroforestry proponents often stress production modes which are small, dispersed, and useful to a rural peasantry. Here trees of nitrogen-fixing *Acacia albida* ("gao" in the Hausa language) have been planted in a millet field in eastern Niger. Where soils are deficient in nitrogen, gao trees can dramatically raise yields of millet and sorghum. *(Photo courtesy of FAO.)*

By this is meant tree planting by or for small farmers and the landless at the level of farms, villages, and communities (Chapter 6).

While the concept and practice of agroforestry are relevant in industrialized countries, most current professional interest concentrates on the tropics and subtropics. It is in these regions where agroforestry is often viewed as both a technical approach to upgrade land use and a development vehicle to address socioeconomic imbalances.

The impact of agroforestry on global forest cover is at once trivial and profound. Agroforestry makes a trivial contribution to the area of closed forests, but has a potentially profound contribution towards alleviating some of the social and economic pressures for clearing them. Moreover, the growing professional interest in agroforestry enlarges the relevant scope of tree cover to include not only timber trees but also bamboo groves, rubber trees, palms, shrubs, and so on.

Some of the most intensive forms of agroforestry are found in South and Southeast Asia, typically where populations are densest in relation to the productive land base. Thus various types of multiproduct tree gardens on the Indonesian island of Java occupy perhaps 20 percent of the arable land (Wiersum 1982). In the Philippines and elsewhere, multipurpose species like *Leucaena leucocephala* have been widely established for subsistence needs, protective purposes, and harvests for cash sales. Farm and community forestry in India is characterized by trees in shelterbelts, along field boundaries, around buildings and wells, along transportation corridors, and on village commons and government wastelands.

Because of its challenge to feed over one billion mouths from limited areas of fertile lands, China is perhaps the world's most graphic example of integrating tree culture with agriculture. Massive programs of afforestation and forest rehabilitation began after 1949, supported strongly at top political levels. A major emphasis was "four around" tree planting around roadsides, around canals and riversides, around houses, and around villages. Additionally, China's shelterbelts are the world's most extensive. One of them, the "Great Green Wall," extends 6000 km along the Gobi Desert, covering a land area of 1.6 million hectares. Tree planting has been used extensively to stabilize sand dunes, slow gully erosion, form coastal windbreaks, stabilize agricultural terraces, reforest denuded watersheds, and augment scarce fuelwood. Documented cases suggest that agricultural yields sometimes have risen dramatically, with clear links to restored tree cover. Although not precise, China's data indicate that tree cover expanded by 26 million hectares between 1949 and 1980 (FAO 1982). This was possible despite huge population growth and only modest reductions in mass poverty.

Reservation of Protected Areas

Growth in the number, extent, and variety of the world's protected natural areas is yet another response to scarcity, the scarcity of wildness after centuries of taming frontiers to make room for development. The concept of wild areas, especially wilderness, must be flexible to fit highly diverse situations from country to country.

For example, the concept of wilderness as it evolved in the USA refers to wild areas which are remote, large, pristine, uninhabited by humans, and designated "wilderness" by legislation. Only a few other countries (Canada, Australia, New Zealand, and South Africa) formally recognize wilderness through legislation. Everywhere else, wilderness is defined in a de facto sense but not a legal one. Also, the remoteness and size of wilderness areas in North America, the USSR, Australia, Greenland, and Africa are not possible to achieve in small regions and countries.

Furthermore, the phrase in the USA's Wilderness Act of 1964 that "man is a visitor who does not remain" is inappropriate and often socially repugnant in countries where indigenous groups are still part of the natural world. Not only indigenous groups, but also other subsistence populations, live on lands which otherwise have the characteristics of wild areas. Hence a broad concept of wilderness for use in an international setting is as follows (Eidsvik 1989, p. 58): "Wilderness is an area where natural processes dominate and people may co-exist as long as their technology and their impacts do not endure." This definition is unlikely to settle the matter completely, since definitions and criteria for classifying wild areas have been debated for decades.

What is the extent of the world's wild areas, and where are they located? Because of incomplete information and problems with international comparisons, these questions are not easily resolved. One study used military data to identify global land units with a minimum size of 400 thousand hectares having no roads, buildings, transportation infrastructure, power lines, pipelines, mines, dams, canals, aqueducts, reservoirs, or oil wells (McCloskey and Spalding 1989). As shown in Table 2-8, this revealed nearly five billion hectares of undeveloped ("wilderness") lands, equivalent to about one-third of global terrestrial area. Some 60 percent of the wilderness total is tundra, deserts,

TABLE 2-8
Extent of wild area in the world, by major regions.

	"Wild Area"* (thousand km²)	As proportion of total land (percent)
Antarctica	13,210	100
Africa	8,230	27
USSR	7,520	34
North America	6,850	37
Asia (excluding USSR)	3,780	14
Latin America	3,750	21
Australia and Oceania	2,370	28
Greenland	2,170	99
Europe (excluding USSR and Greenland)	140	3
World	48,020	32

* "Wild Area": Land units with a minimum size of 400,000 hectares having no roads, buildings, transportation infrastructure, power lines, pipelines, mines, dams, canals, aqueducts, reservoirs, or oil wells.
Source: McCloskey and Spalding (1989, pp. 222, 226).

and other lands of very low biological productivity. Forests of all kinds constitute another 30 percent, or 1.5 billion hectares, mainly in cool coniferous and tropical moist forests. These results have been challenged on grounds of deficient data and inability to identify impacts from all logging and agricultural activities (Dearden 1989).

Yet there can be little doubt about two key conclusions: (1) a substantial proportion of the earth's land area, including its forested area, remains in a largely wild condition, and (2) lands in a largely wild condition occupy a significant share of total area in all major world regions except Europe. At an aggregate level, the evidence indicates that wild areas are still numerous and often extensive.

Many, if not most, wild areas exist by default because they are not wanted for alternative uses. Not all wild areas are protected, nor are all protected areas truly wild. The distinction between wild areas and protected areas focuses attention on the degree to which governments have explicitly set aside wild areas under official protection, e.g., for scientific reserves, ecological reserves, nature reserves, national parks and monuments, wildlife sanctuaries, and protected landscapes and seascapes. A world directory of protected areas using these categories has been maintained by IUCN since the 1960s. Tracing the establishment years of the world's protected areas, Figure 2-14 reveals a very steep rise in their area since the beginning of the century, and especially since about 1970.

Protected areas now exist in about 125 countries, including numerous developing countries (Table 2-9). While calls for nature protection are loudest from people whose stomachs are full, the table suggests that both the appeal and achievement

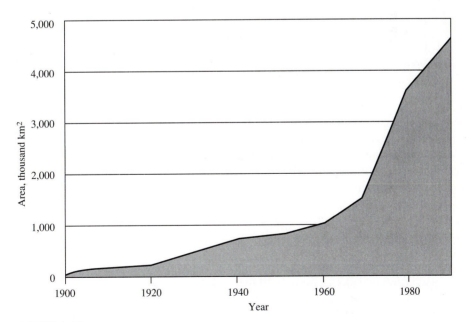

FIGURE 2-14
Cumulative world area under protection status since 1900. *(Source: Reid and Miller (1989, p. 71).)*

TABLE 2-9

Distribution of the world's protected natural areas by countries and territories protecting over one million hectares, late 1980s.

Country/ territory	Protected area (million ha)	Country/ territory	Protected area (million ha)
Greenland	71.0	Iran	3.1
USA	67.5	New Zealand	3.1
Australia	35.7	Kenya	3.1
Canada	22.9	Germany	2.8
USSR	14.5	Zimbabwe	2.8
Indonesia	13.6	Cameroon	2.6
India	12.9	China	2.3
Chile	12.8	Japan	2.2
Brazil	11.9	Senegal	2.2
Tanzania	10.6	Sudan	2.2
Ecuador	10.6	Ivory Coast	2.0
Botswana	9.9	Gabon	1.8
Zaire	8.8	Ethiopia	1.8
Venezuela	7.4	Czechoslovakia	1.8
Pakistan	7.3	Spain	1.7
Namibia	6.6	Poland	1.7
Zambia	6.4	Sweden	1.7
South Africa	5.8	Malaysia	1.6
Peru	5.4	Angola	1.5
Colombia	4.9	United Kingdom	1.5
Bolivia	4.8	Mauritania	1.5
France	4.7	Congo	1.4
Norway	4.7	Uganda	1.3
Mongolia	4.7	Ghana	1.2
Argentina	4.6	Paraguay	1.1
Thailand	4.0	Malawi	1.1
Central African Republic	3.9	Madagascar	1.0

Source: IUCN (1985); WRI and IIED (1988, pp. 294–295).

of nature protection extend more broadly. Despite social, political, and economic turmoil, the developing countries as a whole have demonstrated a remarkably strong commitment to wildlands conservation. Threats to the world's natural areas are unquestionably serious, but even low-income and often densely populated countries have been able to maintain a rich variety and substantial expanse of wildlands.

SYNTHESIS

Systematic knowledge of the world's forest areas and resource conditions is poor. Conceptual frameworks to classify global vegetation are many, but data are few and unreliable for vast regions. Since the 1970s, assessment of forests at the global level has improved, particularly for previously omitted forests in the tropics. However, data on forest area and resource values are still deficient for both natural and manmade forests, and especially for forests in developing countries. Forests are unevenly distributed across countries and in relation to population numbers. A modest but increasing share of world forests is under regular management, mainly in industrialized countries.

Current distributions, conditions, and changes in forest cover require historical understanding for illumination and explanation. Deforestation in the developing countries ("the tropics") is the contemporary extension of forest removal begun centuries ago in ancient China, Japan, the Mediterranean Basin, Europe, and elsewhere to make room for agricultural settlement and other human expansion. European settlement in Africa, the Americas, South and Southeast Asia, and other regions produced additional waves of massive forest clearing. At the same time, some forest clearing was autonomous—not related to colonial economies. While the political and social explanations for deforestation may be different now than a century ago, the form and technology of deforestation have changed very little. Also, the pattern of forest clearing has been universal, beginning with fertile and accessible lands and working towards lands which are increasingly less attractive for clearing and development.

Much policy discussion on forest dynamics in the current era focuses on deforestation amounts and causes. This can lead to sharp disagreements, in part because both the amounts and causes of deforestation are highly variable from one place to another, and because the underlying data base is weak. It is certain that deforestation has been uneven, but that several millions of hectares of forest cover in the developing countries are degraded or converted to non-forest uses each year. The causes for this are many, variable and interrelated. They include continued demand for new lands, problems stemming from distributions of property rights in trees and lands, questions about the adequacy of technical systems to manage tropical forests, and effects of government policies on forest use and stewardship.

The impacts of deforestation on human welfare are highly controversial. This is explained by scientific uncertainty regarding the range and magnitude of impacts, as well as by considerable local variation in the nature and severity of consequences. Various technical and social issues are too complex to be settled with present knowledge, but there can be little doubt that deforestation problems are serious in local contexts.

Importantly, deforestation does not go on indefinitely. Aggregate forest area in important temperate regions—Europe, the USSR, the USA, and Japan—appears to have stabilized following earlier histories of pronounced forest recession. At a world level, forest plantations are gradually replacing natural forests as sources of industrial timber, and this is shifting a considerable share of timber production towards regions previously unimportant in timber growing. These emerging regions include countries in the tropics and subtropics, plus some in temperate zones of the southern hemisphere. The post-1970s enthusiasm for agroforestry, particularly in densely populated low-income countries, aims to raise land productivity by producing trees simultaneously with grazing and cropping. India and China, among others, have been working assiduously to restore tree cover by integrating it into agroforestry production systems for farms and communities. Finally, in the face of deforestation pressures and other threats, both rich and poor countries have set aside thousands of wild areas under protection status. The number and extent of declared wild areas have been increasing dramatically.

In summary, an objective and comprehensive look at trends in global forest cover should confound both Malthusians and Cornucopians. To be observed and explained is a wide mix of positive and negative forces expanding and shrinking the world's forests, sometimes simultaneously or in close proximity of each other. The Malthusian view that the world's forests by now consist of little more than small and isolated fragments is erroneous. It is equally mistaken to believe that tropical deforestation is a small and transient problem that will go away with better planning.

Moreover, while forest cover in the temperate countries is more or less stabilized, there remain questions about lack of adequate forest regeneration in regions of Canada and the western USSR (Honer and Bickerstaff 1985; Barr and Braden 1988). Problems are less those of decreasing forest area than of declining forest condition for particular regions within these two large forested countries. Additionally, while the tropical rainforest is said to be under assault, environmental groups do not hesitate to point out threatened rainforest in Alaska and other zones far from the tropics (Wilderness Society 1986).

Forest plantations are sometimes viewed as compensatory forests to reduce cutting pressures on natural forests for commercial timber. However, the trend towards intensive timber cropping raises environmental debates of its own about long-term sustainability and ecological appropriateness (Chijioke 1980; FAO 1985; Sheldon 1989). Furthermore, since logging for industrial timber is only one of many of deforestation's explanations, the establishment of plantations is only one of many needed adjustments. Lastly, while most evidence is to the contrary, some plantations have been established by removing natural forests to make room for them (Fearnside and Rankin 1980).

Regarding the attention to agroforestry as a development vehicle and mitigator of land scarcity, the model of China is frequently held up for world emulation. China is an excellent example of accomplishment, but accomplishment achieved through a combination of cultural and political circumstances almost unique in the world. Moreover, despite China's major advances in tree planting, the country continues to be deficient in virtually all wood products and forest benefits. Hence even a major success by world standards is far from having solved its tree scarcity problems in a period of only three or four decades. Continued diligence and patience are required.

The number and extent of wild areas around the world should cheer even the gloomiest prophets of doom and extinction. Yet skeptics quickly note that many areas are merely "paper parks," drawn on maps but not managed on the ground. While that perspective has much validity, it is also true that numerous small and large conservation stories provide encouragement for what can be done with limited resources and creative approaches (Green and Barborak 1987; Gradwohl and Greenberg 1988).

Despite China's major advances in tree planting, the country continues to be deficient in virtually all wood products and forest benefits. This rural market for construction materials is located above a deforested valley. Because of forest scarcity, wood is carried to this market over very long distances. *(Photo courtesy of Forest History Society.)*

Is this a black age of forest destruction or a golden age of forest conservation? The question frames a prominent and much needed global debate, but may have no answer in the abstract. Generalizations must be resisted. This reiterates a central theme that there is only one world of forests, but a world of immense diversity and change.

ISSUES FOR DISCUSSION AND INVESTIGATION

1 What are the alternative conceptual frameworks for classifying the world's forests? Why is there no single system?
2 Describe the challenges presented by each of the following in assessing global forest area and uses: (i) ecological gradients of forest cover, (ii) terminology for classifying forests, (iii) economic definitions of forest resources, and (iv) multi-resource forest evaluation.
3 In what ways are aggregate statistics on the picture and trends of global forest cover useful for forest policy and management? In what ways are they not useful?

4 The distribution of the world's forests is highly uneven. Describe the different dimensions and explanations of uneven distribution.

5 What conceptual and practical factors explain the unreliability of data on areas of natural forests? Manmade forests?

6 For which world regions is the historical record of deforestation the most dependable? The least dependable? Why?

7 Summarize current knowledge on the magnitude and geographical context of contemporary deforestation.

8 What is the distinction between deforestation and forest degradation, and what consequence does this have for estimates of forest losses?

9 Why is it difficult to define the causes of deforestation?

10 (i) What are the most prominent differences in deforestation agents when comparing tropical moist forests and semiarid woodlands? (ii) When comparing the main explanations of deforestation across Africa, Latin America, and Southeast Asia?

11 In what ways does the control of disease vectors (e.g., anopheles mosquito and tsetse fly) accelerate or decelerate deforestation (ICIHI 1986)?

12 The solution to tropical deforestation may lie less in forestry than in farming. Explain.

13 Some observers distinguish between shifting agriculture and shifted agriculturalists. What is the difference? What are the implications for deforestation?

14 "It is almost always easier to export an underclass to the frontier than to redivide estates in the heartland" (Durning 1989, p. 39). What does this mean for deforestation dynamics? What will be required to change these policies?

15 Describe how trees both preclude private land tenure and also help establish it. How are these tenure changes related to deforestation?

16 (i) Ownership of forests by national governments does not ensure protection from deforestation. Explain. (ii) How can this be reconciled with doctrines that state ownership keeps forests from being destroyed by private greed?

17 What is the evidence for and against the adequacy of technical methods to manage tropical moist forests?

18 It seems that many government policies are highly unfavorable for the maintenance of forest cover. (i) Identify and describe these policies, and explain why better policies have not yet evolved. (ii) What will be required to put policies on a more positive track with respect to favoring forests?

19 The International Hardwood Products Association, a trade association in the USA which imports tropical woods, released the statement that "tropical forests will be preserved only if they are accorded appropriate economic value" (Baer 1990). The statement was endorsed by important environmental leaders. Explain why forests are conserved by giving them economic value, especially when it might be supposed that only forests without economic value will be spared from cutting.

20 What factors explain forest reversion and stabilization in the USA, Europe, and Japan? To what extent is stabilization permanent, and to what extent are these forests in continued transition?

21 What is the concept of plantations as compensatory forests? What is the concept of emerging plantation regions, and where are they?

22 It is sometimes noted with alarm that annual deforestation greatly exceeds annual reforestation and afforestation. In what contexts is this comparison useful? In what contexts is it meaningless?

23 In some countries forest plantations are necessary to answer the wood supply problem, but may prove insufficient to remedy the deforestation problem. Explain.

24 (i) What are the known and likely impacts of agroforestry on the composition, location, and areal extent of tree cover? (ii) How should tree cover on farms and elsewhere outside of forests be measured for inclusion in a global forest inventory?

25 The world's reservation of protected wild areas is simultaneously impressive and inadequate. Explain.

26 The poet Randall Jarrell once wrote, "People who live in a golden age go around complaining how yellow everything looks." What is the relevance of this comment for today's variety of outlooks on global forest trends?

REFERENCES

Ascher, William and Robert Healy. 1990. *Natural Resource Policymaking in Developing Countries*. Duke University Press, Durham NC, and London, England.

Baer, Wendy. 1990. *Protecting Tropical Forests*. International Hardwood Products Association, Alexandria, VA.

Barr, Brenton M. and Kathleen E. Braden. 1988. *The Disappearing Russian Forest: A Dilemma in Soviet Resource Management*. Rowman and Littlefield, Totowa, NJ.

Boyd, Roy G. and William F. Hyde. 1989. *Forestry Sector Intervention—The Impacts of Public Regulation on Social Welfare*. Iowa State University Press, Ames.

Bruce, John, Louise Fortmann, and James Riddell. 1985. "Trees and tenure: An introduction," pp. vii–xvii in *Trees and Tenure: An Annotated Bibliography for Agroforesters and Others*. University of Wisconsin Land Tenure Center, Madison.

Buschbacher, Robert J. 1990. "Natural forest management in the humid tropics: Ecological, social, and economic considerations," *Ambio* 19(5):253–258.

Camp, Wendell H. 1956. "The forests of the past and present," pp. 35–47 in S. Haden-Guest, J. K. Wright, and E. M. Teclaff (eds.), *A World Geography of Forest Resources*. Ronald Press, New York.

Chijioke, E. 1980. *Impacts on Soils of Fast-Growing Species in Lowland Humid Tropics*. Food and Agriculture Organization of the United Nations, FAO Forestry Paper 21, Rome.

Clawson, Marion. 1979. "Forests in the long sweep of American history," *Science* 204(4398):1168–1174.

Darby, H. C. 1956. "The clearing of the woodland in Europe," pp. 183–216 in William L. Thomas, Jr. (ed.), *Man's Role in Changing the Face of the Earth*. University of Chicago Press, Chicago.

Dearden, Philip. 1989. "Wilderness and our common future," *Natural Resources Journal* 29(3):205–221.

De Montalembert, M. R. and J. Clement. 1983. *Fuelwood Supplies in the Developing Countries*. Food and Agriculture Organization of the United Nations, FAO Forestry Paper 42, Rome.

Duffield, John W. 1982. "Forest regions of North America and the world," pp. 37–66 in Raymond A. Young (ed.), *Introduction to Forest Science*. John Wiley, New York.

Durning, Alan. 1989. "Cradles of life," *World Watch* 2(3):30-40.

ECE/FAO (Economic Commission for Europe; Food and Agriculture Organization of the United Nations). 1986. *European Timber Trends and Prospects to the Year 2000 and Beyond,* Vol. I. United Nations, New York.

Eidsvik, Harold K. 1989. "The status of wilderness: An international overview," *Natural Resources Journal* 29(3):57–82.

Evans, Julian. 1982. *Plantation Forestry in the Tropics*. Clarendon Press, Oxford, England and New York.

FAO (Food and Agriculture Organization). 1963. *World Forest Inventory 1963*. FAO, Rome.

FAO. 1982. *Forestry in China*. FAO Forestry Paper 35, Rome.

FAO. 1985. *The Ecological Effects of Eucalyptus*. FAO Forestry Paper 59, Rome.

FAO. 1988. *An Interim Report on the State of Forest Resources in the Developing Countries*. Report FO:MISC/88/7, Rome.

FAO. 1989. *The Role of Forestry in Combatting Desertification*. FAO Conservation Guide 21, Rome.

Fearnside, Philip M. and Judy M. Rankin. 1980. "Jari and development in the Brazilian Amazon," *Interciencia* 5(3):146–156.

Fernow, Bernhard E. 1911. *A Brief History of Forestry in Europe, the United States, and Other Countries*, 2nd edition. University of Toronto Press, Toronto, Canada.

Fortmann, Louise and John W. Bruce (eds.). 1988. *Whose Trees? Proprietary Dimensions of Forestry*. Westview Press, Boulder, CO.

Gomez-Pompa, A., C. Vasquez-Yanes, and S. Guevara. 1972. "The tropical rain forest: A non-renewable resource," *Science* 177:762–765.

Goodland, R. and H. Irwin. 1975. *Amazon Jungle: Green Hell to Red Desert?* Elsevier Scientific Publishing, Amsterdam, Netherlands.

Goucher, Candice L. 1988. "The impact of German colonial rule on the forests of Togo," pp. 56–69 in J. F. Richards and R. P. Tucker (eds.), *World Deforestation in the Twentieth Century*. Duke University Press, Durham, NC.

Gradwohl, Judith and Russell Greenberg. 1988. *Saving the Tropical Forests*. Earthscan Publications, London, England.

Grainger, Alan. 1984. "Quantifying changes in forest cover in the humid tropics: Overcoming current limitations," *Journal of World Forest Resource Management* 1:3–63.

Grainger, Alan. 1988. "Future supplies of high-grade tropical hardwoods from tropical plantations," *Journal of World Forest Resource Management* 3:15–29.

Green, G. C. and James Barborak. 1987. "Conservation for development: Success stories from Central America," *Commonwealth Forestry Review* 66(1):91–102.

Guppy, Nicholas. 1984. "Tropical deforestation: A global view," *Foreign Affairs* 62(4): 928–965.

Hamilton, Lawrence S. 1987. "What are the impacts of Himalayan deforestation on the Ganges-Brahmaputra lowlands and delta?" *Mountain Research and Development* 7(3): 256–263.

Hardin, Garrett. 1968. "The tragedy of the commons," *Science* 162(3859):1243–1248.

Hecht, Susanna B., R. B. Norgaard, and G. Possio. 1988. "The economics of cattle ranching in eastern Amazonia," *Interciencia* 13(5):233–240.

Holowacz, J. 1985. "Forests of the USSR," *Forestry Chronicle* 61(5):366–373.

Honer, T. G. and A. Bickerstaff. 1985. *Canada's Forest Area and Wood Volume Balance, 1977–1981: An Appraisal of Change Under Present Levels of Management.* Canadian Forestry Service, Victoria, British Columbia.

ICIHI (International Commission on International Humanitarian Issues). 1986. *The Vanishing Forest: The Human Consequences of Deforestation.* ICIHI, Geneva, Switzerland.

IIED and WRI (International Institute for Environment and Development; World Resources Institute). 1987. *World Resources 1987.* Basic Books, New York.

IUCN (International Union for the Conservation of Nature and Natural Resources). *1985. 1985 United Nations List of National Parks and Protected Areas.* IUCN, Gland, Switzerland.

Ives, Jack D. 1987. "The theory of Himalayan environmental degradation: Its validity and application challenged by recent research," *Mountain Research and Development* 7(3):189–199.

Kellison, Robert C. 1988. "The changing quality of the Latin American timber resource," pp. 74–83 in *International Union of Forestry Research Organizations,* Division 5 Conference, São Paulo, Brazil.

Lanly, J. P. 1982. *Tropical Forest Resources.* Food and Agriculture Organization of the United Nations, FAO Forestry Paper 30, Rome.

Lanly, J. P. 1985. "Defining and measuring shifting cultivation," *Unasylva* 37(147):17–21.

Lanly, J. P. and J. Clement. 1979. "Present and future natural forest and plantation areas in the tropics," *Unasylva* 31(123):5–24.

Leonard, Jeffrey H. 1987. *Natural Resources and Economic Development in Central America.* Transaction Books, New Brunswick, NJ.

Lowenthal, David. 1956. "Western Europe," pp. 269–302 in S. Haden-Guest, J. K. Wright, and E. M. Teclaff (eds.), *A World Geography of Forest Resources.* Ronald Press, New York.

Lumpungu, K. 1977. "Land tenure system and the agricultural crisis in Zaire," *African Environment* 2/3:57–71.

Mahar, Dennis J. 1989. *Government Policies and Deforestation in Brazil's Amazon Region.* World Bank, Washington, DC.

Marsh, George Perkins. 1864. *Man and Nature* (David Lowenthal, ed., 1965). Harvard University Press, Cambridge.

McCloskey, J. M. and H. Spalding. 1989. "A reconnaissance-level inventory of the amount of wilderness remaining in the world," *Ambio* 18(4): 221–227.

McGaughey, Stephen E. and Hans M. Gregersen. 1983. *Forest-Based Development in Latin America.* Inter-American Development Bank, Washington, DC.

McNeely, Jeffrey A. 1988. *Economics and Biological Diversity.* International Union for Conservation of Nature and Natural Resources (IUCN), Gland, Switzerland.

Myers, Norman. 1980. *Conversion of Tropical Moist Forests.* U.S. National Academy of Sciences, Washington, DC.

Nair, P. K. R. 1985. "Classification of agroforestry systems," *Agroforestry Systems* 3: 97–128.

Osako, Masako M. 1983. "Forest preservation in Tokugawa Japan," pp. 129–145 in R. P. Tucker and J. F. Richards (eds.), *Global Deforestation in the Nineteenth-Century World Economy.* Duke University Press, Durham, NC.

Palo, Matti and Jyrki Salmi (eds.). 1987. *Deforestation or Development in the Third World?* Finnish Forest Research Institute Bulletin 272, Helsinki, Finland.

Palo, Matti and Gerardo Mery (eds.). 1990. *Deforestation or Development in the Third World?* Vol. III. Finnish Forest Research Institute Bulletin 349, Helsinki, Finland.

Persson, Reidar. 1977. *Scope and Approach to World Forest Resource Appraisals.* Royal College of Forestry, Stockholm, Sweden.

Poore, Duncan, Peter Burgess, John Palmer, Simon Rietbergen, and Timothy Synott. 1989. *No Timber Without Trees: Sustainability in the Tropical Forest.* Earthscan Publications, London, England.

Posey, Darrell. 1985. "Indigenous management of tropical forest systems," *Agroforestry Systems* 3:139–159.

Postel, Sandra and Lori Heise. 1988. *Reforesting the Earth.* Worldwatch Institute Paper 83, Washington, DC.

Reid, Walter V. and Kenton R. Miller. 1989. *Keeping Options Alive: The Scientific Basis for Conserving Biodiversity.* World Resources Institute, Washington, DC.

Repetto, Robert and Malcolm Gillis (eds.). 1988. *Public Policies and the Misuse of Forest Resources.* Cambridge University Press, Cambridge.

Richards, John F. 1986. "World environmental history and economic development," pp. 53–74 in W. C. Clark and R. E. Munn (eds.), *Sustainable Development of the Biosphere.* Cambridge University Press, Cambridge.

Richards, John F. and Richard P. Tucker (eds.). 1988. *World Deforestation in the Twentieth Century.* Duke University Press, Durham, NC.

Rostlund, Erhard. 1956. "The outlook for the world's forests and their chief products," pp. 633–672 in S. Haden-Guest, J. K. Wright, and E. M. Teclaff (eds.), *A World Geography of Forest Resources.* Ronald Press, New York.

Salati, Eneas and P. Vose. 1984. "Amazon Basin: A system in equilibrium," *Science* 225:129–137.

Sanchez, Pedro A., D. Bandy, J. Villachica, and J. Nicholaides. 1982. "Amazon soils management for continuing crop production," *Science* 211:821–827.

Sartorius, Peter and Hans Henle. 1968. *Forestry and Economic Development.* Frederick A. Praeger, New York.

Schmidt, Ralph. 1987. "Tropical rain forest management: A status report," *Unasylva* 39(156):2–17.

Schultes, R. E. 1979. "The Amazonia as a source of new economic plants," *Economic Botany* 33(3):259–266.

Sedjo, Roger A. 1983. *The Comparative Economics of Plantation Forestry: A Global Assessment.* Resources for the Future, Washington, DC.

Sedjo, Roger A. and Marion Clawson. 1984. "Global forests," pp. 128–170 in J. Simon and J. Kahn (eds.), *The Resourceful Earth.* Basil Blackwell, Oxford, England.

Shane, Douglas R. 1986. *Hoofprints in the Forest: Ranching and Destruction of Latin America's Tropical Forests.* Institute for the Study of Human Issues, Philadelphia.

Sheldon, J. C. 1989. "Forestry in balance with conservation—the issues," *Scottish Forestry* 43(1):35–46.

Sommer, Adrian. 1976. "Attempt at an assessment of the world's tropical moist forests," *Unasylva* 28(112/113):5–25.

Spears, John. 1988. *Containing Tropical Deforestation: A Review of Priority Areas for Technological and Policy Research.* World Bank Environment Department Working Paper 10, Washington, DC.

Spurr, Stephen H. and Burton V. Barnes. 1980. *Forest Ecology,* 3rd edition. John Wiley, New York.

Stewart, P. J. 1985. "The dubious case for state control," *Ceres* 18(2):14–19.

Thirgood, J. V. 1989. "Man's impact on the forests of Europe," *Journal of World Forest Resource Management* 4(2):127–167.

Tropical Science Center. 1982. *Costa Rica: Country Environmental Profile.* Trejos Hermanos, San José, Costa Rica.

Tucker, Richard P. and J. F. Richards (eds.). 1983. *Global Deforestation in the Nineteenth-Century World Economy.* Duke University Press, Durham, NC.

Udvardy, M. D. F. 1975. *A Classification of the Biogeographical Provinces of the World.* International Union for the Conservation of Nature and Natural Resources (IUCN) Occasional Paper 18, Gland, Switzerland.

UNESCO (United Nations Educational, Scientific, and Cultural Organization). 1973. *International Classification and Mapping of Vegetation.* UNESCO, Paris, France.

Whittaker, R. H. 1975. *Communities and Ecosystems,* 2nd edition. Macmillan, New York.

Wiersum, Kenneth F. 1982. "Tree gardening and taungya on Java: Examples of agroforestry techniques in the humid tropics," *Agroforestry Systems* 1:53–70.

Williams, Michael. 1988. *Americans and Their Forests: A Historical Geography.* Cambridge University Press, New York.

Wilson, E. O. (ed.). 1988. *Biodiversity.* U.S. National Academy Press, Washington, DC.

Wilderness Society. 1986. *America's Vanishing Rain Forest: A Report on Federal Timber Management in Southeast Alaska.* Wilderness Society, Washington, DC.

World Bank. 1982. *Tribal Peoples and Economic Development: Human Ecological Considerations.* World Bank, Washington, DC.

Worldwatch Institute. 1989. "Reprieve for the rain forest? *World Watch* 2(1):35–36.

WRI and IIED (World Resources Institute and International Institute for Environment and Development). 1988. *World Resources 1988-89.* Basic Books, New York.

Zobel, Bruce J., G. Van Wyk, and P. Stahl. 1987. *Growing Exotic Forests.* John Wiley and Sons, New York.

Zon, Raphael and William N. Sparhawk. 1923. *Forest Resources of the World,* Vols. I and II. McGraw-Hill Book Co., New York.

FORESTS AND DEVELOPMENT: INTRODUCTION AND OVERVIEW

In this and previous centuries, forest depletion and threats of depletion have brought about major adjustments in policies and practices by governments, industries, and individuals. Where such adaptations are inadequate or too late, the consequences are long-run economic burdens and the risk of political and social turmoil. Conversely, where forests have been managed effectively, experiences in several societies show that forests can be an important source of national wealth and amenity values.

THE ROLE OF FORESTS IN DEVELOPMENT

The role of forests in national economic development has been largely neglected. Development economists typically aggregate forests with agriculture, regard forests as something to be removed to make room for true "development," or ignore forest production as a small and unimportant economic activity.

This inattention to forests in development theory is somewhat surprising, given the physical dominance of past and present forests in the land use of so many countries. Moreover, the examples of Sweden, Finland, Canada, and other countries show that forest industries are key components in some national economies. The current environmental revolution dramatically elevates the status of forests in development thinking, but this is very recent. As an indication of newness, the World Bank had no sector paper on forestry until the late 1970s (World Bank 1978).

The recently increased social and political interest in forests demands a more deliberate and systematic treatment of forests in the development process than has been characteristic of the past. Conceptual models of forests in development must fit accepted development theory, and these models require testing and revision in light of shifting development definitions and goals. For example, the ascendancy of "social forestry" to help peasant communities obtain benefits from trees is a dramatic statement that forestry should be explicitly directed to the needs of low-income beneficiaries (Chapter 6). The recent stress on participatory decisionmaking in forestry, both in industrialized and developing countries, likewise signals that forestry must be brought into the development mainstream and its complex tradeoffs.

Forests for Whom and for What?

A few countries in the world may still have no forest laws, policies, programs, or projects. If there are such countries, they are a tiny minority. Everywhere else, it has been decided to steer forest use and practice in socially desirable directions. This requires choices about what mixes of forest goods, services, and values to produce, and for whom these goods, services, and values are intended. In virtually all countries, these central concerns can be summarized in four questions:

• How is material wealth generated from the production aspects of forests?
• How are nonmaterial benefits of forests provided at the same time as material benefits?
• How are the material and nonmaterial benefits distributed between rich and poor, urban and rural, and other components of the population?
• How are future needs from forests weighed against present needs?

Technical and policy options emerge and adjust in relation to this planning framework (Husch 1987). Basic issues include (1) the relative importance of plantation forestry, agroforestry, watershed management, multiple-use areas, protected areas, and other land-use options; (2) the locations, amounts, and justifications for forests in public ownership; (3) differences in policy goals and means appropriate for different classes of forest ownership, e.g., state, private, and communal; (4) the importance and simultaneous limitations of market prices in determining what is produced from forests, and with what level of economic efficiency; and (5) the role of the state in planning, owning, and regulating forest industries and markets.

The whole construct rests on a few central and perennially difficult questions. What is the meaning of development, and what are its goals? Through what social and economic transformations are these goals achieved? What are the links between economic scarcity, development policy, and forest policy? What does it mean to manage forests for sustainable development?

The Meaning of "Development"

The discussion of forests in development is barren without reference to development definitions, goals, and strategies. In its most basic form, development represents the idea of progress, or change in a forward direction. An underlying premise is that no society or individual is fully developed. Rather, all fight for progress from current levels. That humans are able to take charge of their own progress is a bold and even revolutionary break from past centuries of fatalism.

Development in Developing Countries   Since the 1950s, the most widely diffused meaning of development has been framed in economic concepts and language, with development understood as increased production and consumption of material goods and services. Historically, economic development has been achieved by a process, usually driven by industrialization, whereby a country's real per capita income increases over a sustained period of time through continuing increases in per capita productivity. Level of economic development is measured in terms of a ratio of national income per person. Reference to income measures is sometimes supplemented by noneconomic social indicators, e.g., indices of literacy, housing, health conditions, and other quality-of-life measures (Table 3-1).

The vocabulary of economic development presents a number of puzzles. There is no convenient common measure except income per capita for the more than 140 countries which constitute the developing nations. While all are defined by low or intermediate levels of average national income per capita, they are highly diverse in social and political structures, economic bases, histories, cultures, and population sizes.

TABLE 3-1
Quality-of-life indicators, selected countries in the late 1980s.

	SWI	USA	GRE	EGY	IND	ETH
Annual income (GNP/capita, 1000 US$)	27.3	19.8	4.8	0.7	0.3	0.1
Life expectancy at birth (years)	77	75	76	61	58	47
Infant mortality (per 1000 live births)	7	12	13	85	99	154
Population per physician (persons)	696	473	351	786	2,521	77,400
Daily calorie supply (calories/capita)	3,437	3,645	3,688	3,342	2,238	1,749
Illiteracy (% of population aged 15+)	NA *	NA *	8	56	57	38
Annual energy consumption (kg oil equivalent per capita)	4,107	7,265	1,970	588	208	21
Newspaper circulation (per 1000 population)	383	263	120	77	20	1
Population per telephone (persons)	1	1	3	34	189	320
Population per passenger car (persons)	2	2	8	52	543	1,028

SWI = Switzerland; USA = United States of America; GRE = Greece; EGY = Egypt; IND = India; ETH = Ethiopia.
*NA: not available.
Source: World Bank (1989).

Beginning in the 1970s, the meaning of economic development for developing countries became direct reduction of poverty, unemployment, and inequality. This followed observations that the industrial experience of the 1950s and 1960s often met targets of income growth in the aggregate, but failed to provide benefits to other than a small proportion of the world's truly poor people. Countries that were advancing by aggregate measures of income growth were falling behind with respect to living conditions of persons at the bottom of the socioeconomic pyramid. Faith in industrialization as the approach to help countries climb out of poverty yielded to a wider range of ideas. The failure of industry-led growth to "trickle down" spurred demands for "redistribution from growth" (Adelman 1975).

Taking the perspective that development has both material and nonmaterial dimensions and depends on both economic and noneconomic systems, mainstream thinking today proposes that development aim to meet objectives of economic growth, distributional equity, and collective and individual autonomy (Todaro 1985):

• *Economic growth*—This refers to the steady process by which the productive capacity of the economy is increased over time to bring about rising levels of national income.

Development must aim to increase the availability and widen the distribution of food, housing, clothing, and healthcare—as for these children in northeastern Brazil. The younger girl's swollen abdomen is the result of poor nutrition. *(Photo courtesy of FAO)*

• *Distributional equity*—The "basic needs" of the very poorest people must be addressed by increasing the availability and widening the distribution of food, housing, clothing, health care, and other essential elements which lessen the incidence and severity of absolute poverty.

• *Autonomy*—To rise from material deprivation allows individuals and countries to be less dependent on others, fostering greater self-determination and autonomy.

Development in Industrialized Countries   Although poverty in "rich countries" seems an anomaly, a sharp and widening prosperity gap separates the affluent from a socioeconomic underclass in several industrialized societies. The southern USA is a region where forest industries have grown and prospered, but it is also a region where cases of rural poverty pass from one family generation to another (Maharidge 1989). Moreover, evidence suggests widespread material disparity in some countries of Europe (Critchfield 1990). The existence of urban and rural poverty as more than a small and transitory residual is a reminder of problems which were supposed to fade away with high levels of national income. Yet poverty elimination remains a high priority on the development agenda, even if now made more difficult by previous inability to find or apply workable solutions.

A concurrent but separate development impetus with broad implications for forestry leads in the direction of "protecting the environment." *The Greening of America* (Reich 1970) portrayed the symptoms and values behind a counterculture's rejection of contemporary urban-industrial life. This has since expanded into a "green view" of development among segments of virtually all Western societies, as well as among educated elites in the developing countries. This is because unprecedented material progress in the industrialized countries has taken a heavy toll in depersonalization and alienation (Wachtel 1983). Pointed questions focus on conflicts between material accumulation and other dimensions of human progress, and on the ways in which industrialized countries are developed in some respects while underdeveloped in others.

Accompanying the frequent skepticism about urban-industrial growth as a model of development is heightened attention to the nonmaterial measures of the "good life." This refers to indicators of social and psychic well-being such as health, self-esteem, autonomy, justice, work satisfaction, recognition, and democratic participation. Other goals are to increase self-direction; to strengthen mutually beneficial interdependence with other persons, communities, and societies; and to enrich the aesthetic quality of life (UNESCO 1988).

Debates about the balance of forest uses and the distribution of their benefits must be understood within this larger context of remaking the world according to new images. A whole set of social movements dedicated to peace, feminism, spiritual growth, solidarity with oppressed peoples, human rights, consumer cooperatives, alternative technologies, and ecological harmony have been underway since the 1960s. Ideas and values once confined mainly to a radical counterculture have caught on more widely, and this wider diffusion now has far-reaching consequences in issues of "forests for whom and for what" (Figure 3-1).

FIGURE 3-1
Connections between selected "green values" and forestry issues.

"Green values"	Forestry issues or impacts
Responsible consumerism	–Biodegradable products (e.g., paper vs. plastic) –Demand for wood and furniture from sustainable sources –Recycled paper and containers; unbleached paper
Concern for psychic and physical health	–Forests as sanctuaries from pressures of everyday life –Popularity of hiking, camping, and other forest recreation and sports –Wholesomeness of nature study –"Health of the planet" as preoccupation
Personal growth and self-realization	–Forests as "sacred temples" for spiritual growth –Wilderness as learning and self-study –Adventure travel as personal exploration
Commitment to community	–Battle of "little people" against big companies and government agencies –Mobilization of "ecology watchdogs" –Environmental advocacy as lifestyle

Forest Endowment and Forest-Based Wealth

An important historical idea is that the wealth of nations is a consequence of ownership of natural resources or access to the natural resources of other countries. The European imperialist powers of previous centuries laid great stress on possessing natural resources and conquering new territories to obtain them. The British navy, for example, was constantly in search of new timber sources to maintain its sea power (Albion 1926). In this century, scholarly inquiries point out that adverse climate, poor soils, and lack of minerals and forests explain the "backward condition" of materially poor countries and regions (Huntington 1924; Markham 1942).

Yet the case for natural resources determinism is increasingly difficult to argue and defend. If scarcity of natural resources causes economic deprivation, then the world's poorest countries should include Japan, Taiwan, Singapore, Hong Kong, Korea, Israel, Denmark, and Switzerland. Conversely, one should observe exceptional material prosperity in Zaire, Amazonia, Papua New Guinea, Siberia, Alaska, and other regions well-endowed with minerals, forests, water, and fish and game. That the opposite is true presents serious challenges to arguments about the role of resource endowments in material wealth.

That endowments of forests and other natural resources do not correspond well with material wealth rests on several explanations. Land-based wealth has been joined in these last two centuries by wealth built on manufacturing and services, and these are increasingly traded internationally. Raw materials and finished goods are financed and transported in worldwide networks, so that possession of raw materials is no guarantee that the wealth they generate stays at home.

A large forest endowment does not ensure forest-based wealth. On the contrary, many of the world's heavily forested regions are materially impoverished. *(Photo courtesy of FAO.)*

A society's economic resources are not its natural resources, but its organizational and technological skills (Rosenberg and Birdzell 1985). On this point it is also instructive to consider the dozen or so countries with the world's highest ratios of forest stocks to human population (Table 3-2). All of these are forest-rich countries. Yet only Canada, Finland, Sweden, and Australia have built up substantial forest industries, with the other countries not much advanced beyond a stage of casual exploitation. This helps illuminate the conceptual distinction between forest inventory (i.e., physical stocks) and economic supply (i.e., affordable raw materials). In terms of using social organization and technical knowledge to extract wealth from forests, the comparison of Finland and Sweden with the other countries is indeed striking. The difference between utilizing boreal versus tropical moist forests is critical, but it would be difficult to maintain that this is the principal reason for forest-based wealth in the Nordic countries and lack of it in many others.

Forests and the Stages of Economic Development

The history of forest uses and values in most forested regions reveals a pattern of developmental stages. Forest removal is followed by incipient conservation, and finally by forest management. The timing and progress of these stages vary substantially across countries and historical eras. The stages are determined by

TABLE 3-2
Countries with highest ratios of forest area
to human population

	Ha/capita
French Guiana	114
Suriname	42
Guyana	22
Papua New Guinea	12
Bolivia	12
Canada	11
Belize	10
New Caledonia	5
Finland	4
Sweden	3
Australia	3

Source: FAO (1988, Table1a)

demographic and economic conditions, by social and political forces, and by biogeographical features of the forest itself.

At first, the forests are the home of indigenous tribes and the bane of settlers. Little if any of the forest is private property, and the state's claim to forests is an unenforceable piece of paper. With or without assistance from the state, settlers claim forested lands for their farms and pastures. Forests are cleared in the path of population diffusion and agricultural extensification. Timber is extracted as an abundant and seemingly limitless resource, with little or no regard for future regrowth. Indigenous peoples are assimilated, displaced, or die.

In the second stage the state reacts to forest loss, often because of forecasts of timber famine, environmental disruption, and associated political stirrings for forest protection. Laws and policies are formulated to conserve remaining forest resources. Measures include prohibitions against certain types of forest use, regulation of timber cutting, and attempts to protect forests against fire, cattle, poachers, and squatters. On lands meriting special attention as forest reserves, the state retains certain segments of public domain or later reclaims private property.

The third stage is genuine forest management. As the land frontier closes, emphasis turns from extensive to intensive land use. Initiatives are taken to reestablish forests through varying combinations of natural regeneration and manmade planting. Silviculture for timber production is economically justified. Management for continuity becomes a societal goal, and forested areas are organized for sustained yield. Imports of forest products become important for economies which cannot efficiently supply domestic consumption from domestic forest resources. National wealth is sufficient to increase emphasis on forests for recreation and amenities.

The latest chapters in the stages towards forest management are still being written. The USA provides an example of trends in one industrialized country. Over the last half century, forest management in the USA has evolved away from intuition towards more formal planning and science as the framework for management. The role of the public in policy decisions has increased enormously. Special interest groups have become far more numerous and powerful. Fears of timber famines have faded into the background, while concerns for preservation of ecosystem health and biological diversity assume increasing importance. Public influence over private land use is far more constraining than in past decades. Through increased production per unit area and various changes in the mix of forest products and services, the USA's forests supply three times the human population as at the turn of this century (Healy and Shands 1989).

Looking ahead to the year 2000, the ECE/FAO Timber Committee for Europe observes increasing demand everywhere in Europe and North America for recreational use of forests. Traditional demands on forests for soil protection and water conservation are increasing in certain regions (e.g., the Mediterranean Basin). Urban tree planting for environmental amenities is becoming a specialized practice, and concern for landscape management is on the rise (ECE/FAO 1986).

The stages of economic development are not linear, repeating, or of determined length. Moreover, historical stages in the presently industrialized countries are only partly relevant for today's developing countries. Figure 3-2 shows material advance moving from left to right, but with a very important flow of power and influence moving from right to left. This refers to the political, financial, technological, and intellectual influences exerted by industrial societies on the rest of the world.

The developing countries, benefiting from technologies and experiences in the now industrialized countries, may be able to omit certain steps in the sequence of industrial wood processing. Also, the developing countries are being asked, and sometimes pressured through political and financial means, to implement forest conservation much earlier relative to their present stage of industrial progress than was characteristic of Europe or North America in past eras. A further observation concerns reversals or temporary upsets in long-term trends, as when rapid rises in petroleum prices induce increased fuelwood consumption in industrialized countries (Prins 1979). Thus while historical evolutionary patterns are not quickly transformed, neither are past sequences adequate guides for the future.

FACTORS BEARING ON DEVELOPMENT PROSPECTS

Forests present a number of unique production features. These give forestry its identity, and define the special problems of making forests serve development. Beyond these shared characteristics are variations across countries in forest endowment, income level, and other differentiating factors. Development prospects are given by the shared production features on the one hand, and by the differentiating contextual factors on the other.

Distinctive Features of Forest Production

The subject matter of forestry is technical, economic, social, and political. These several dimensions come together when considering forestry's unique production

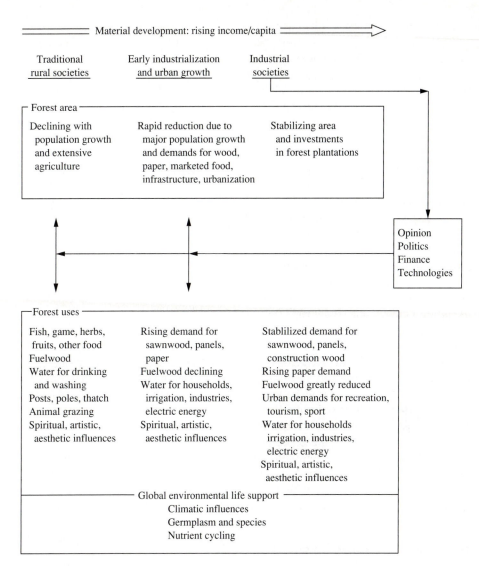

FIGURE 3-2
Dynamics of forest area and use with progressing stages of material development.

features. The discussion of forestry in development makes sense only in relation to this individuality of forestry as distinguished from agriculture and other sectors.

Long Production Periods   Production periods in forest management are vastly longer than the usual period in agriculture and industry. This makes planning difficult because of substantial risk and uncertainty. It makes investment in timber management difficult because of capital illiquidity over many years. It makes political interest difficult because results materialize only long after terms of office expire. The world now has three times the population, and one hundred times the industrial activity, of just a century ago. Yet a century is the relevant time frame for conservative forest practice in many cold climates. An error can take centuries to correct, if it can be remedied at all. The classic problem is then how to manage the interface between fast socioeconomic change and slow biological change.

Calendar time has to be converted into social and economic time, or the weighting of early consumption needs against the willingness and ability to defer benefits into the future. In principle, public landowners are able to wait longer than private landowners, and wealthy landowners longer than impoverished ones. Hence an 80-year timber rotation on public forests in Switzerland may be more feasible, economically and socially, than a 5-year rotation of fuelwood by a peasant farmer in Haiti. Yet both of these periods may be long from the standpoint of those who intend to receive benefits.

The long production period creates intergenerational tradeoffs. A forest can be depleted or converted to alternative land uses rapidly for the benefit of present generations, but restoration and replacement take decades and entire human generations. Complex economic, political, and primarily ethical considerations arise in weighting this generation's claim on forests against claims allowed for persons yet unborn. Seemingly technical issues of forest regulation are in reality ethical and political issues when probed more deeply.

Complex Production Relations   An unavoidable complication is that multiple forest outputs are produced simultaneously. Cutting old-growth timber on the USA's Olympic Peninsula reduces populations of the spotted owl. Altering grazing patterns in the semiarid Sahelian regions of Africa affects regeneration of woody vegetation for fuel and construction materials. Joint production everywhere complicates decisions on what and how to produce.

The complexity of forest growth means that the economist's "production function" is highly variable from one place to another. Yields of radiata pine (*P. radiata*) in Chile may be a poor guide to yields of the same plantation species in Ecuador. Swedish silviculture is introduced into Canada, but not without adjustment problems (Soyez 1988). The ecological variability of forests obligates forest practices to be adapted to local conditions. It implies that technologies in forestry are not as easily transferred from country to country as technologies in many other sectors.

External Benefits and Costs   Externalities in forest management are costs and benefits accruing to persons other than forest owners. A frequently cited negative externality is deforestation of upland watersheds causing property damage, loss of irrigation water, siltation of reservoirs, and other problems downstream (Gregersen et al. 1987). Positive externalities occur when recreational experiences are enjoyed by persons allowed free access on private forest holdings, as in western Europe (Stephenson 1989). These are only two among dozens of impacts, both positive and negative.

Technologies in forestry have to be adapted for local conditions. These tropical pines in Costa Rica exhibit highly uneven growth, suggesting that the seed source is not appropriate for the planting site. *(Photo courtesy of World Bank.)*

The implication is that activities in forests spill over to improve or diminish human welfare beyond the welfare of forest owners alone. This complicates public forest management enormously for it means taking into account gainers and losers off-site, theoretically around the world (e.g., the issue of global climate). Social conflict is produced to the extent that external costs are ignored or cannot be controlled.

Renewability and Nonrenewability   Traditional doctrines in forest management regard forests as renewable. This proposition is valid in the abstract, but critical aspects fail under closer scrutiny. Renewability applies to some attributes of forests, but not to all.

Some germplasm resources, and some forest ecosystems, are exhaustible and irreplaceable. The management concept of "endangered species" is a direct reflection of this. In the aesthetic domain, second-growth forests are not equivalent to virgin forests when considering attributes of wildness. In timber production, industrial qualities and potentials of old-growth logs are different from those of second-growth and plantation logs. Thus nonrenewability and irreversibility are indeed important constraints in forest management. This adds significance to the intergenerational tradeoffs described previously.

Unpriced Values   As indicated earlier, many essential forest goods, services, and values have no market prices. This refers to almost all environmental services and influences, almost all contributions to education and science, most contributions to phychophysiological well-being, and most contributions of forests as a source of land and human habitat for indigenous peoples. Even among directly consumable and tangible products, only a minority pass through markets.

That the forest's contributions are largely unpriced poses two great efficiency problems. The first is to bias land use away from forests in general, e.g., relative to agriculture and other competing uses. The second is to bias production away from unpriced outputs in particular, e.g., wildlife and watershed protection in relation to timber. A restatement of the first problem is that forest owners are not fully compensated by the world for all that they contribute to it. The second problem calls attention to the conflict between commodity versus non-commodity uses of forests, and to the perpetual dilemma that user tradeoffs never can be compared in strictly monetary terms.

Variations in Contexts Across Countries

On a global basis, the development contexts for forestry are hugely different across countries, and often across subregions within them. These contexts are critical for sectoral planning and policy formulation.

Country Size and Population   A country's physical size and population level explain much about existing and potential patterns of forestry in development. Large physical size often presents a diversity of forest types, while large populations imply correspondingly large domestic markets for forest products. Hence the USA, USSR, and Brazil stand in contrast with small countries like Cyprus, Dominica, and the Solomon Islands in terms of forest base and wood-processing enterprises that can be supported by domestic demand. Many small countries are highly dependent on linkages with the international economy for imports and exports of goods, services, and investment capital. Also, size is a critical determinant of number and diversity of forestry schools, conservation organizations, industry trade associations, and other institutional dimensions of the sector.

Forest Endowment and National Income   Forest endowment and national income combine to define alternative development typologies for forestry. By typologies is meant the prominent characteristics of different forestry situations which define policy directions and priorities. Besides country size, important elements in development typologies for forestry include degree of forest abundance, population densities and distributions, level of industrialization, and numerous other variables (World Bank 1978).

FIGURE 3-3
Forest abundance and national income, selected countries.

Income per capita	Forest area per capita		
	High	**Moderate**	**Low**
High	Canada	USA	Netherlands
	USSR	France	England
	Sweden	Austria	Switzerland
	Finland	Australia	Japan
Moderate	Brazil	Yugoslavia	Poland
	Colombia	Bulgaria	Ireland
	Venezuela	Panama	Israel
	Malaysia	Costa Rica	Turkey
Low	Republic of Congo	Indonesia	China
	Zaire	Laos	India
	Gabon	Myanmar	Afghanistan
	Angola	Ivory Coast	Pakistan
	Cameroon	Ghana	Bangladesh
	Guyana	Guinea	Ethiopia
	Suriname	Liberia	Haiti

Figure 3-3 is a two-dimensional classification which considers just national income and forest area, using selected countries for illustration:

• *High income and abundant forest*—The upper-left corner shows major producers of forest products, all of which are net exporters.

• *High income and scarce forest*—Countries in the upper-right corner have little forest area per capita, but are sufficiently wealthy to import forest products from elsewhere.

• *Low income and abundant forest*—The lower-left corner includes countries with abundant forests, but relatively little industrial wood processing due to other constraints.

• *Low income and scarce forest*—The lower-right corner identifies a few of the countries with chronic unmet needs in protective reforestation, timber supply, fuelwood management, and virtually all other forest goods and services.

These typologies rarely portray the variety of situations for individual countries. There is much unevenness within individual countries in both forest distribution and income distribution. Many large countries—Canada, Australia, Brazil, China, and others—exhibit examples of many typologies simultaneously. Also, forest endowment and level of national income are only two elements in the context of forestry policy and development. Additional differentiating factors are contrasts between humid and arid zones, availability of land and other inputs for afforestation and reforestation, and other biogeographical variables.

Forestry History and Traditions   The depth of forestry experience and traditions ranges from hundreds of years in central Europe to a few decades in some of the developing countries. The forestry of the nineteenth century in the Nordic countries, the USA, Britain, Australia, and even India and Japan bore a pronounced influence from Germany. On the other hand, some of the forestry institutions in today's developing countries descend from colonial models implanted by Britain, France, Spain, Portugal, Belgium, the Netherlands, and the USA. Varying administrative and legal structures for forestry—as well as educational and social institutions in the forestry sector—have sprouted from these different historical roots.

Up until the 1960s and 1970s, most forestry matters in Latin America were handled by agronomists. There were few foresters. Even now, some of the world's smallest developing countries have only one or two professional foresters—normally educated in other countries—who are handicapped by virtually no forestry data, budgets, or management models to guide their work. This is in contrast to strong forestry legal foundations, administrative systems, university programs, and research institutes in places such as Europe, North America, Australia, and New Zealand.

Culture and Natural Resources   A study of forests in development is incomplete without reexamining the classic gulf on ideas about "man and nature." The separation of Western sciences from all others has produced contrasting ideas of time, causality, and the place of man in nature. In turn, this has produced differences in moral obligations and legal understandings. Among the key implications for forests and forestry are differences in culture affecting whether land can be owned, dispute settlement in the case of conflicting claims of rights to trees and land, and moral obligations regarding balance with nature (Northrop 1956; Spoehr 1956).

To simplify, nontechnological peoples have myths and legends which tell them they are descended as a part of nature, and that their cosmological system operates under irreversible natural laws. To simplify again, Western societies—through scientific power to predict and control—have conceptually separated themselves from nature, and are looking for ways to manipulate it to human advantage. Goodness for someone inside nature is complete immersion in it, and absolute harmony with it. Goodness for someone outside is taking control and establishing mastery. The notion that forests offer "natural resources" as something separate from the entirety of nature may be a purely Western concept, without counterpart in non-Western cultures. It follows that objectives to "use" forest resources to improve human welfare often run counter to the understanding of local interests (Moody 1988).

Economic Organization   Economic organization in forestry reflects economic wealth and political ideologies. Major structural differences in forestry are observed between industrialized and nonindustrialized economies, socialist and capitalist production systems, and regions of large forest enterprises versus small ones.

Sources of investment capital and operating budgets range broadly. They include almost exclusive reliance on allocations from central governments in the usual case of socialism, dependence on external aid in many low-income countries, and extensive private financing in industrialized market economies.

The availability and cost of labor and capital determine the range of technologies in forestry and the forest industries. In Europe and North America, the separation of forest work from agricultural work occurred quickly and dramatically after the Second World War. This compares with today's developing economies, where much forest work is still casual and seasonal, and still drawn from agricultural sectors.

One extreme is severe scarcity of forest labor in forested zones of the Nordic countries, the USSR, and parts of Canada. This compares with abundant and low-cost labor in most of Asia and Africa, and in many regions of Latin America. Hence in the late 1980s, a day's services for a forest worker cost the equivalent of US$140 in Sweden, but US$2 in the Philippines. Both as cause and effect of this wage gap, productivity of forest labor in northern Europe exceeds that in most developing countries by huge margins.

Scarcity of labor in the Nordic countries explains forest mechanization, which in turn raises productivity and wages per worker. *(Photo courtesy of Jonas Palm.)*

Political Power and Interest Groups   To an extent seldom fully recognized, the possibilities and limitations of forestry in development are explained by the distribution of political power and the organizational structure of forestry interests (Chandrasekharan 1983). This refers especially to structures of producers and sellers of forest products, conservation groups, associations of forest landowners, and labor unions and cooperatives. Among these interest groups are found the ruling elites. These elites include leaders of political parties, large industrialists, large forest landowners, trade union leaders, leading bankers and financiers, military leaders, and others. The contest for power among these elites directly or indirectly determines which policies and strategies for forestry are possible.

The urban bias in development (Lipton 1977) can be a severe problem for forestry. Forestry is predominantly rural in its social, cultural, and economic setting. Yet not all organizations affecting forestry are rural in composition or interests. Frequently, wood manufacturers' associations and environmental interest groups have offices in the urban metropolis, but agendas outside of it. In many respects, both represent urban interests more than rural ones.

The strength of social and political organization among private forest owners can be a key ingredient in forestry for economic growth. Forest owners' associations in the Nordic countries are among the world's most respected models of forest cooperatives. There farm and other nonindustrial forest owners collectively own and manage logging and wood-processing facilities, negotiate timber selling prices with industrial wood buyers, and contract for professional silviculture and reforestation. The success of forestry cooperatives in the Nordic region is explained by the importance of forestry in national economies, political acceptability of strong government intervention in forestry, and long experience in forest methods and farm forestry.

In Japan and the Republic of Korea, village forestry associations bring together tiny and fragmented forest ownerships within a larger social and economic framework (Gregersen 1982). Ancient traditions of community cooperation are combined with strong government support and thorough organizational planning (Morita 1988).

The examples of forest owners cooperatives in the Nordic countries, Japan, and Korea contrast with experiences in the USA and Latin America (McGaughey and Gregersen 1988). Characteristic problems are unsound planning, inadequate financial resources, internal management quarrels, little or no government help, small membership base, lack of technical know-how, and vulnerabilities to corruption. In these situations, the inability of forest owners to collectively organize themselves for political and economic advantages rules out various possibilities in forest management.

In summary, it is not a certain form of economic organization which alone explains economic and social performance in forestry. Progress also depends on the ways in which different forestry interests organize themselves to cooperate and to contend with competing interests.

FORESTS AND SUSTAINABLE DEVELOPMENT

The preceding discussion indicated why it can be inappropriate to generalize about the development role of forestry in a highly diverse world. Nevertheless, a few common themes orient forestry in a broadly similar framework. One dominating theme is that of forests in "sustainable development."

Sustainability is used in various contexts, and the term has different meanings across social, economic, and ecological disciplines. The classical forestry doctrine of forest management for sustained yield fits a biophysical definition of sustainability. That is, total wood removals must not exceed annual forest growth over the long run (Lönnstedt 1984).

Yet this meaning is too narrow for the larger concept of sustainability which has taken root since the 1980s. This larger concept envisions an entire world which combines global economic and social progress with respect for natural systems and environmental quality.

The challenge for forestry is to work towards this complex goal with institutions, policies, and technologies already available or to be created in the immediate future. The concept of sustainability in forestry implies that the total welfare effects of forest management should never decrease (Hagglund 1990), and that environmental protection and economic development should be integrated as a single management problem. The premise is that economic development cannot be effective on a declining resource base, and that environmental protection is not possible without economic growth to satisfy basic material needs.

These generalizations are readily accepted. More problematic are policies and strategies to work towards sustainability in light of real-world complexities. An immediate complication is that sustained timber yield does not ensure stable communities. Moreover, countries follow alternative pathways to managing for sustainability, including a pathway of forest depletion.

Sustained Yield and Sustainable Development

The issues of forestry in sustainable development have European foundations going back several centuries. Beginning in the 1500s, the German states imposed strict ordinances for the management of forests for local production following previous centuries of deforestation and destructive forest practices. Charcoal burning was regulated, bricks substituted for wood shingles in roofs, and hedges and ditches supplanted wooden fences. Some cities regulated the amount of wood allowed per person, and Saxony ordered that all houses be built of stone. Foresters designated what was to be cut even for fuelwood, and no cutting was allowed in private forests unless authorized by foresters (Fernow 1911).

During the seventeenth and eighteenth centuries, wood prices in the German states rose so rapidly that sales to outsiders were prohibited. Because commerce in forest products was restricted, each political unit had to be self-sufficienct in forest products and fuelwood. Only local production could satisfy local needs. Local forests had to be managed for the indefinite future, and management for "sustained yield" became deeply embedded in forestry thinking. Interestingly, the arguments for conservation to protect the environmental values of forests came only later in the nineteenth century.

The governments of almost all countries now endorse in principle the concept of sustained yield of forests. The objective is to "facilitate the continuous and optimal provision of all tangible and intangible effects of the forest for the benefit of present and future generations" (Wiebecke and Peters 1984, p. 178). The policy problem is to turn this possibly universal objective into guidelines which can be implemented.

Many industrialized countries which otherwise adhere to political and economic liberalism justify considerable inroads into private ownership to attempt to sustain forests. Switzerland, the Nordic countries, and Japan regulate private timber felling and mandate compulsory reforestation on private lands. Additionally, private owners are offered subsidies, tax credits, guaranteed prices, etc., for implementation of management practices specified by public authorities. An erosion of some private ownership rights is exchanged for a public welfare function which emphasizes forest continuity (Sartorius and Henle 1968).

Other approaches towards sustainability include aggregation of small forest holdings into larger management units through cooperatives and other institutional means, as noted earlier for the Nordic countries, Japan, and Korea. Still another strategy is nationalization of all forest holdings, as in socialist countries. A dominant approach in the USA and Canada is to control the flow of timber from public owners to private industry buyers. In summary, the mix of approaches to sustain production varies from country to country in response to distinctive cultural, historical, and ownership differences. The unifying factor is that virtually all industrialized countries have been making efforts towards these goals for some time, with varying amounts of success and failure.

The question arises whether sustained timber yield brings to local communities the sustainability implied in the term. Continuity and even flow of timber supply— if that can be achieved through forest management—is no guarantee that forest industries remain viable. The USA's policy of nondeclining even flow of government timber is nowhere more evident than in the region of the Pacific Northwest, where forest industries suffered a wrenching crash in the early 1980s. Plant closures and widespread unemployment were immediate consequences (Keegan and Polzin 1987). The example illustrates that a collapse in market demand destabilizes forest industries just as surely, and usually more quickly, than diminution of timber supply. Moreover, demand-side policies are well beyond the conventional influence of most forestry agencies.

Even when timber is renewed and supplied on a sustainable basis, mechanization can greatly reduce employment. During the highly expansive periods of industrial growth in the 1950s and 1960s, employment in the forest industries of Canada, the USA, France, Britain, and the USSR fell or grew by only a few percentage points (ILO 1975). Workers in Swedish forestry and forest industries fell from over 300 thousand in 1960 to 240 thousand in 1980, even though annual timber harvest increased substantially over the same period (Lönnstedt 1984). In

Even when timber is renewed and supplied on a sustainable basis, mechanization can greatly reduce employment. In Finland, the forestry labor force fell from 90 thousand persons in 1970 to less than half that number only 20 years later. *(Photo courtesy of Erkki Oksanen and Finnish Forest Research Institute.)*

Japan, the number of forest workers fell from 220 thousand in 1962 to 130 thousand by 1983 (Okuchi 1988). Australia expected substantial increases in forestry and forest industries employment from the 1970s to the end of this century, only to find actual employment falling rather than rising (Dargavel 1982).

In the final analysis, relationships among economic stability, local communities, and sustained timber yield are vague and poorly defined (Machlis and Force 1988). Conceptual foundations are weak (Waggener 1977). Beyond aspects of timber production for forest industries, issues of forest sustainability show huge gaps between expectations and realities (Baskerville 1990). Sustainability often reduces to simple rules of thumb (e.g., extinction of plants and animals must be avoided), given that "sustainable development" is often more a matter of ethical responsibility for the future than of appeal to economic principles (Hagglund 1990).

The new initiatives on sustainable development and conservation, with reference to forests in the developing countries, must begin with these lessons being learned and not learned in the industrialized countries. While a few economists have pointed out the inadequacies of sustained yield policies (Lemaster and Beuter 1989), their arguments have had little real effect. Perhaps in future decades, policies will more deliberately aim at stabilizing economic and social indicators rather than timber flows. A major complication is the jointly produced flow of non-timber outputs, whose optimal management may require different scheduling. These problems suggest the huge amount of future work to answer the sustainability question in ways which are both theoretically defensible and operationally useful. This matter will continue to provoke much disagreement in all countries where it is seriously studied.

Forestry in Alternative Paths to Development

Profiles of countries which have many decades of experience in forestry—mainly today's industrialized countries—show a variety of pathways along which forestry has evolved in the course of national development. Sweden exemplifies forest-rich development, or the deliberate favoring of forests and forestry as a major provider of national income. The USA presents a second type of model, depleting a large proportion of its precolonial forest endowment as a form of land-based capital to fuel economic takeoff into agriculture and other forms of growth. A third model is given by Japan, which depleted a large share of its forest endowment, turning to imported logs to supply Japanese wood-processing industries during Japanese economic growth. Yet another model is New Zealand, which over the course of several decades created assets in the form of forest plantations for future exports. These patterns for Sweden, the USA, Japan, and New Zealand are highly instructive for the differences they reveal about forests in relation to sustainable development.

Sweden and Forest-rich Development   Sweden was a poor agrarian country at the turn of the last century, and 90 percent of its population was rural. Poverty was a primary factor in the emigration to North America of more than one-third of Sweden's population. Today Sweden is a prosperous country of eight million people, enjoying one of the world's highest standards of living.

During its economic transformation, Sweden deliberately invested in its forests. This refers to significant allocations of national income for silviculture, forest plantations, and transportation infrastructure in forested regions. The country also invested heavily in forestry education and vocational training, technologies for timber harvesting and processing, and workers' skills and safety. Sweden has spent considerable sums for detailed forest data systems, and for extension services and cooperatives to serve farmers and other nonindustrial landowners who own 50 percent of Sweden's forests.

Over many decades, Sweden's forest growth has increased even as total wood consumption also has expanded (Figure 3-4). With less than one percent of the world's forest area, Sweden commands roughly ten percent of global forest products exports. Exports of forest products constitue about one-half of Sweden's net export earnings. This share is smaller than in the early part of the century, even though the absolute value of forest products exports has been growing steadily.

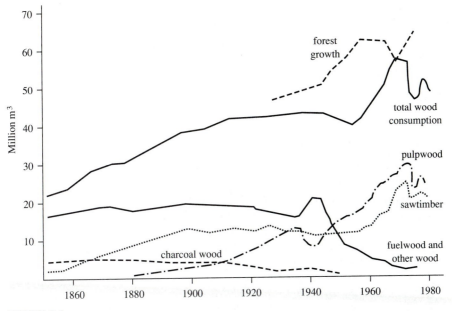

FIGURE 3-4
Trends in wood consumption and forest growth in Sweden. *(Source: Lonnstedt (1984, p. 708).*
Used with permission of National Research Council Canada.)

Many factors explain Sweden as a case of forest-rich economic development. These include (Richards 1987; Hagglund 1990):

• Low population density on the land due to last century's emigration, this century's urbanization, and rising agricultural productivity throughout
• Proximity to the wood-hungry markets of Central Europe and Britain
• A long coastline, well-protected harbors, many navigable rivers and inland waterways, a good railroad network, increasing road density in forested areas, and other transportation advantages

These positive features of population and geography combine with a favorable social setting for forestry. A forest law—first implemented in 1903 and periodically modified through the decades—prescribes that forests must be regenerated, and lays down other conditions of forest management. The success of the forest law, and of a system of 250 forest districts which implement forest policy under the jurisdiction of forestry boards, is due in very large measure to "Swedish consensus." This consensus is difficult to define and evaluate, but builds on democratic ideologies and national solidarity. The consensus also rests on an early and widespread belief in Sweden that forests and forestry are good for the long-run benefit of the country, an article of faith whose political and economic importance cannot possibly be measured.

Swedish forest policy is decided by the country's parliament in consultation with government agencies, large forest products companies, farm and other

Spruce pulpwood awaits processing at a modern facility in Sweden. To maintain its exports of forest products in a global economy, Sweden's production costs have to be competitive internationally. *(Photo courtesy of Jonas Palm.)*

nonindustrial forest owners, trade unions, and environmentalists. Political solutions in Swedish forestry are achieved not because everyone agrees on the issues, but rather because different viewpoints are accommodated in a national dialogue and in the inevitable compromises this requires. Moreover, the forest law and other elements of social control over forests have been exercised flexibly to suit variations across local situations. These somewhat intangible qualities of Swedish political and social life go far in explaining why forest-rich development has been possible.

Transformation of Forest Capital in the USA   When the USA was a younger agrarian country, a large part of its endowed wealth was in the form of forests over fertile lands. Since the time of European settlement, approximately 100 million hectares of this forest capital have been converted into other forms of capital for the advancement of agriculture, mining, the construction industry, and additional economic activities. The most rapid clearing occurred between 1800 and 1920, mainly east of the Mississippi River (Williams 1988).

The USA's deforestation was not a deliberate strategy to produce national wealth, but was an inevitable consequence of making room for agricultural expansion. Stocks of timber were converted into liquid capital, yielding arable land beneath them as an even greater source of national wealth. Previously unproductive forest assets produced an injection of housing materials, railroad ties, mine

In the USA, forests were cleared to yield arable land beneath them as an even greater source of national wealth. Pictured is a farm in North Carolina in 1901, with stumps and girdled trees attesting to previous forest cover. *(Photo courtesy of Forest History Society.)*

timbers, and other products for industry and household consumption. The newly converted lands under agriculture provided an increased flow of food products for both subsistence and market sales, helping propel the country's industrial urbanization. Forest conversion financed much of the USA's early economic development (Sedjo 1991).

In a physical sense, the USA's forest depletion during the nineteenth century was wasteful. Catastrophic forest fires often burned unchecked, unregulated grazing of cattle and sheep damaged pastured woodlands, and various species of fish and wildlife were pushed to critically low population levels or driven to extinction.

Were these losses justified in the building of a new nation trying to gain economically from what was then an untamed wilderness? From an economic perspective, the argument has been made that last century's forest clearing in regions such as the upper midwestern states was not destructive (Libecap and Johnson 1975). Forests were abundant in other regions of the country, and practices of "careless" logging and burning in the pine forests of Michigan, Wisconsin, and Minnesota were consistent with the economy and social climate of the times. Views such as this will always remain controversial, particularly when explored with criteria other than economic rationality.

Important in the case of the USA, the historical experience of forest depletion was reversed, bringing the USA's forest estate into a very healthy current condition (Fedkiw 1989). Principal reasons for this include effective control of forest fires; widespread substitution of alternative energy sources for fuelwood; rising real prices of timber, which spurred forest management and use of wood substitutes; the resilience of cutover forests, which allowed them to regenerate once adverse pressures were removed; and appropriate subsidies and tax incentives to encourage afforestation and reforestation on private lands.

Japan's Imported Forests   Like Sweden, Japan is very heavily forested. Unlike Sweden, Japan's forests furnish only relatively small quantities of industrial timber despite Japan's sizable population. Although it is a forest-rich country, Japan has not pursued forest-rich economic development. Especially in recent decades, economic growth has been propelled very rapidly by high-technology industries, not by resource-based sectors like agriculture and forestry. The national wealth created by these industries allows the country to import logs and processed forest products from around the Pacific Basin (Chapter 5).

Japan has a very long tradition of "wood culture," due in part to the historical scarcity of iron and steel, cement, fossil fuels, and other wood substitutes in the mountainous archipelago. The early stages of Japanese industrialization after the 1890s led to impressive increases in timber consumption of about 10 percent per year for pulp and paper plants, coal mines, power transmission poles, railroad construction, packaging, and other industrial uses. Industrial growth brought with it rapid urbanization, and wood was the least expensive building material for massive numbers of small and low-cost houses in Japanese cities. In Japan the use of firewood and charcoal for household heating and cooking continued very late, and was still 30 percent of the gross value of forestry output around 1950.

However, Japanese economic expansion ultimately overwhelmed the country's ability—and lessened its need—to be self-supporting in forestry. From 1885 to 1985, Japan's population tripled, and its real income per capita increased by a factor of 18. Somewhat surprisingly, Japan was able to meet its rapidly growing wood consumption from its domestic forests during most of this period. Only after 1960 did Japan turn increasingly to imports (Figure 3-5).

Beginning in the late 1800s, Japanese forestry was responsive to increasing timber demand. The early stages of Japanese economic expansion were accompanied by an expanding supply of sugi (*Cryptomeria japonica*), hinoki (*Chamaecyparis obtusa*), and other timber species under conditions of rapidly rising timber prices, low-wage rural labor, and pronounced shortages of land. Highly favorable for tree planting were tenure changes allowing private forest ownership, and leases to private individuals to grow trees on degraded state lands. Not to be overlooked is that traditional Japanese farmers had the moral sense of "bequesting beautiful forests to their descendants" (Kumazaki 1988).

Since 1960, fundamental changes have occurred in Japanese forest products consumption. Mine timbers, railroad ties, and utility poles have been replaced

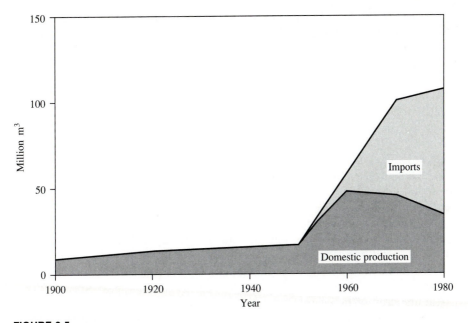

FIGURE 3-5
Production and imports of industrial wood in Japan. *(Source: Adapted from Kumazaki (1988, p. 8).)*

by iron and concrete substitutes. Wooden boxes and crates have been replaced by metal and corrugated boxes. In construction, the ratio of wood to all building materials has fallen dramatically. Household fuelwood use by now has become minimal. The forestry sector was 6.5 percent of Japanese national product in 1890, 2.4 percent in 1960, but less than 0.2 percent in 1985 (Kumazaki 1988).

Clearly, the Japanese economic miracle had profound consequences for forestry. Former surpluses of rural labor were assimilated in urban-industrial sectors, producing wage escalation throughout the Japanese economy. From 1961 to 1985, the price of standing sugi timber did not even double, while the average wage for forestry workers rose by a factor of 14 (Kumazaki 1988). This illustrates why traditional forest practices, which developed under conditions of cheap labor and high-priced timber, no longer are economically attractive. More rational is to import logs and processed forest products from other countries, managing Japan's extensive forest cover for watershed protection and amenity benefits, as increasingly favored by Japanese public opinion.

It could be argued that timber growing in Japan is a victim of the country's economic prosperity. Because prices for domestic timber currently are low by historical standards, Japan's forest growth now exceeds its harvests by a ratio of three to one. Many private forest owners are reluctant to cut their timber and face the high costs of compulsory reforestation. Because these problems reflect Japan's transition from poverty to wealth, they are problems many other countries would envy.

New Zealand's New Forests   New Zealand presents yet another variation of forests in national development, one in which the principal source of forest capital comprises timber plantations of an exotic (non-native) species, radiata pine. In 1913, New Zealand's Royal Commission on Forestry concluded that the country would face a severe timber shortage by 1950 unless actions were taken to replace the depleted natural forests. A report to New Zealand's parliament rejected forest products imports, recommending instead a strategy of afforestation, and creating the nucleus of what was later to become the New Zealand Forest Service. Not only the government, but also a number of private capitalists were attracted to afforestation by low land prices, prospects of future timber scarcity, and several years of technical and organizational experience in afforestation pioneered by the government. In the private sector, funds from small investors were pooled in special financial companies to raise afforestation capital (Le Heron 1988).

New Zealand's first flurry of afforestation during the 1920s and 1930s was of unprecedented scale at the time (Roche 1990). By 1935, young plantations of 300 thousand hectares were almost equally divided in ownership between the New Zealand Forest Service and a single private company, New Zealand Forest Products.

The first crop of radiata plantations matured in the 1940s and 1950s, bringing new challenges for both the government and private companies. New Zealand had no prior experience with large-scale wood processing, even though the government's industrialization proposal called for integrated production of sawnwood,

In New Zealand, the principal source of forest capital comprises timber plantations of *Pinus radiata*. *(Photo courtesy of New Zealand Forestry Corporation.)*

pulp, and newsprint. Furthermore, market acceptance of radiata forest products was untried, and doubts existed about the reliability of plantation wood supply. In order to attract investors to process radiata timber from its Kaingaroa Forest, the New Zealand Forest Service set very low timber prices and guaranteed a log supply for 25 years (renewable for two more 25-year periods). The government also provided for a mill site, electricity, modern port, railroad between mill and port, rental housing, immigration of skilled workers, and rights to transfer net profits of foreign investors to home countries. Capital requirements were large, and a business venture finally went forward on shareholding divided among the New Zealand government, two private companies, the Commonwealth Development Fund Corporation, and the New Zealand public (Le Heron 1988).

From these experimental beginnings emerged a forestry sector which is assuming increasing importance in New Zealand's economy. Several aspects of this growth are noteworthy:

• Investments in afforestation and subsequent reafforestation generated a demand for the best available plantation science and technology: tree breeding, fertilization, thinning and pruning, and mechanization. These practices are intended to reduce the risks of biological failure, shorten production periods, reduce costs, and improve the volume and quality of timber harvest.

• New Zealand's exotic forests developed from historical concern to avoid domestic timber scarcity, but then shifted in orientation. The first period of intensive

From the 1990s onward, New Zealand's forest products increasingly will be exported to countries of the Pacific Basin and elsewhere. *(Photo courtesy of New Zealand Forestry Corporation.)*

planting (1925–1936) was aimed at avoiding domestic scarcity. The second planting phase (since 1960) has been export-oriented in its justification. From the 1990s onward, the country's forest products increasingly will be exported to Australia, Japan, China, and elsewhere.
• Forest products industries in New Zealand are inseparable from the integrated global economy. Companies from Britain, Australia, and Japan provided technical assistance and equity capital when New Zealand's forest products industries were still in their infancy. The cycling of multinational capital continued when, only a few decades later, two of New Zealand's largest forest products corporations purchased holdings of forest-based companies in North America, Brazil, and Chile.

Through the decades, relations between the New Zealand Forest Service and private forest industries have been redefined many times. The state has provided substantial grants, incentives, and subsidies to private companies to help them export, and to offset the costs of afforestation. On the other hand, the New Zealand Forest Service has disagreed sharply with private companies on prices at which the government's plantation timber should be sold. In the late 1980s, the New Zealand Forest Service was dissolved to make room for a state Forestry Corporation and the transfer of almost half of the state's plantation forests to private ownership. These progressions in New Zealand illustrate that forestry is not immune from dramatic changes in politics and economics (Kirkland 1988).

SYNTHESIS

This overview of the role of forests in development identifies fundamental challenges in making forests serve development goals. Development is multidimensional, producing an occasional clash of views on where progress should lead and how it should be measured. Thus development economics concerns itself with material progress, or strategies to attack the absolute poverty of the world's masses of poor persons. The principal yardsticks for measuring progress in the climb out of poverty are growth of national income and the way it is distributed. This economic view of development is not the only perspective. Hence a number of development theorists look towards progress in human cooperation, altruism, pursuit of ecological harmony, respect for diversity, benevolence, compassion, and other values. In this broadened view, no particular model or level of economic development ensures progress in the other dimensions. Indeed, "green values" of development often are at odds with the traditional orientation of forestry for commodity production.

These varying outlooks on the meaning and goals of development have critical consequences for forestry. On the one hand, this gives forests their special importance in satisfying a broad range of human needs. On the other, the multidimensional character of both forests and development is precisely why the "for whom and for what" issues are especially difficult. Forests are wanted by the poor and by the rich, and for material and nonmaterial satisfactions. Fulfillment of each of these claims on forests contributes to "development" at some level.

Because forestry models tend to be specific to biogeographical and sociopolitical circumstances, they are not easily transferred from one country to another. Forestry in the presently industrialized countries went through a sequence of developmental stages from forest clearing to forest conservation, and finally to forest management. This previous historical sequence may not be entirely descriptive of forestry in today's developing countries, in large part because of pressures and influences exerted from industrialized countries in this now highly interdependent world.

Variations in cross-country patterns of forestry development are explained by country size and population, forest endowment and national income, the origins of forestry history and traditions, the different views of nature in technological vs. nontechnological cultures, the structure and effectiveness of economic organization as it affects forestry, and the political power and influence of groups with special interests in forestry. Yet around the world, the possibilities of forestry are constrained by shared distinctive features: long periods required to grow trees, complex production relations among the multiple products and services of forests, the presence of benefits and costs from forests accruing to other than forest owners, complex issues of forest renewability and nonrenewability, and the presence of significant unpriced values.

The "sustainable development" thesis is advanced by stressing that forests are part of a nation's capital to be carefully invested and husbanded. This capital can be intensively managed to produce national income directly. It can be transformed to alternative forms of capital to fuel takeoff of the economy as a whole. It can be built up from a degraded condition for protection purposes and as a contingency reserve. It can be created through manmade plantations to generate exports.

Different countries represent each of these models reasonably well and with reasonable degrees of success. Yet in reality most countries coordinate management of multiple forms of forest capital simultaneously. A realistic perspective recognizes the advantages of forest conversion in some areas, forest preservation in others, and forest creation in still others. In sum, the role of forests in development is a highly dynamic one which aims for ever greater production of forest goods, services, and values through efficient management of several types of forest capital.

The profiles presented here for a small set of industrialized countries lead to questions about the relevance of these profiles for today's developing countries. In particular, the link between forest depletion and the takeoff thesis of economic development is controversial for developing countries which still have abundant forests. What would constitute a pathway of justifiable forest transformation for countries such as Brazil, Zaire, and Indonesia? Is it possible to use the lessons of forest conversion in North America in the nineteenth century, or of Europe in earlier centuries, as a guide for the developing countries of the current era?

As widely interpreted, the problem of forest transformation in many of today's developing countries is that it does not generate the capital required for takeoff. Only a small share of forest capital is actually transformed into other productive investments, while the rest is wasted. Unlike forest depletion in Europe, which occurred over centuries, contemporary forest transformation in some of the developing countries is compressed into decades. This increases the difficulty of achieving efficient capital conversion. Consequently, as a country finally reaches a stage where it has both the technological and organizational capability to achieve a high degree of forest utilization, it may discover that its forests already have dwindled (Leonard 1985). The country finds itself on a "treadmill" (Burns 1986) of using up potential resources before they become true resources for economic growth.

For deforestation to work as a strategy for economic takeoff, a number of favorable factors must come together. The USA's takeoff into sustainable growth was aided by sufficient national wealth and political will to ultimately take control of deforestation problems. Other factors were competent organizational structures between different levels of governments (e.g., for fire protection), and the good fortune of benevolent soil and climate for forest renewal. It is obvious that many of today's developing countries do not share these conditions.

As illustrated by Sweden, sustainability of forest-rich development results not only from the protection and management of forest stocks, but also from conducive social and political factors. This helps ensure gradual rather than convulsive policy shifts for forestry and natural resources. A disturbingly large number of countries suffer the effects of civil wars, ethnic conflicts, violent political overthrows, and gross economic mismanagement. Forest-rich development is a long-term and highly conservative undertaking having little chance for takeoff and eventual sustainability in the middle of economic and political chaos.

New Zealand built a substantial base of plantation assets during this century using an exotic species. This required available lands, the diligent application of forest science and technology, and the ability to make progress despite frequent differences between state and private interests. With the possible exception of Chile, Brazil, and a few countries in southern Africa, New Zealand's circumstances are uncommon in the developing world.

The forestry pathway followed by Japan likewise is not easily imitated by today's developing countries. Japan harnessed farm labor during slack agricultural seasons to create what later amounted to millions of hectares of intensively managed forests. Low-priced labor and degraded lands were transformed into valuable forest capital. This was possible because of Japan's market-oriented economy, which signalled that profits could be made in timber growing. Supporting factors were key reforms in Japan's forest tenure policies to enable private forest ownership, and overall cohesion within Japanese society.

Examples can be found of developing countries which have circumstances resembling Japan's at the end of the last century: rural labor surpluses, shortage of usable land, and depleted natural forests. Less in evidence are the other elements which made farm-based forestry in Japan successful: historical traditions of "wood culture," strong market signals for timber growing, suitable land and tree tenure, and national sociopolitical unity.

In the final analysis, a country must identify policy and technical options for forestry, and then defend and pursue chosen options in the face of competing claims and interests. At the most basic level, these options cannot be implemented unless the following conditions are met:

- Tenure claims on trees, land, and other forest resources are secure.
- The society is able to maintain law and order in forested regions. Where relevant, this includes strategies which respond to illegal logging, shifting agriculture, and other forest encroachments.
- Authorities in executive and legislative posts, forestry agencies, the military, the judiciary, and elsewhere in the public service do not have conflicts of interest with sound forest policies. Furthermore, these authorities cannot be corrupted by persons whose economic or political fortunes are at odds with such policies.
- Basic infrastructure is adequate for forestry planning and management. This refers not only to transportation networks and other physical infrastructures, but also to maps, resource inventories, and other decision-making information.
- Forest management rests on a sound scientific and technical basis with respect to methods of forest regeneration, protection, and control of growth and yield.
- Policies in forestry are predictable, even as governments change. This allows producers and consumers of forest goods and services to go forward with decisions which are precluded where forestry policies have a history of instability.
- The society is able to identify and weigh competing social and economic interests in forests, both now and in the future. This demands that a citizenry and its decisionmakers understand the multiple contributions of forests, and relate these to national goals through a political process which is widely understood and accepted.
- Prices, taxes, and regulations in forestry make sense within the social, economic, and political context of the society. Policies are able to balance forestry's production and protection aspects, and blend incentives and disincentives which steer forestry behavior in directions favorable to national interests.

Conspicuously missing from the forestry scenes of many developing countries are secure tenure, dependable law enforcement, incorruptible governments, basic infrastructure, open and competitive markets, and policy predictability. Even the industrialized countries struggle with the difficult balancing of production and protection, incentives and regulations, and competing interests. Ultimately, the successes and limitations of forestry in development are explained by a country's ability or inability to resolve these issues.

In summary, forests contribute to economic and social advancement in particular places at particular times. Yet there are no recipes for achieving this result. Abundance of forests is a poor indicator of economic and social potential. Management for sustained yield is no guarantee of sustainable economic development. Finally, the pathways of economic growth in relation to forests split off in many directions.

ISSUES FOR DISCUSSION AND INVESTIGATION

1 Issues in forests for development seem more numerous and complicated now than three or four decades ago. Discuss this assertion in relation to the following possible explanations: (i) increased global population, particularly in the developing countries; (ii) widening income disparities between the world's rich and poor; (iii) improved popular and political recognition of how forests serve human needs; (iv) rising environmental concerns and the spread of "green values"; and (v) other factors considered important.

2 (i) Development has material and nonmaterial dimensions. Explain. (ii) With respect to making forestry serve development goals, this presents both opportunities and problems. Why?

3 According to most international statistics, the USA is a "developed" country while India is a "developing" one. What factors support the comparison as valid? What factors make the comparison false? How are the "for whom" and "for what" questions about forests in development the same and different in the two countries?

4 It is commonly asserted that development policies should strive to promote economic growth, distributional equity, and collective and individual autonomy. Discuss how these objectives may complement or conflict with each other in the following instances: (i) implementation of reforestation programs, and (ii) establishment of pulp and paper industries.

5 The outspoken economist John K. Galbraith finds that the relation of natural resources to economic prosperity "is so erratic as to be flatly worthless" (Galbraith 1979, p. 16). Indeed, the possession of abundant forests is no assurance that they produce wealth for a country. (i) Illustrate with specific examples. (ii) If ownership of natural resources is not the key to national wealth, then what alternative explanations are important?

6 Historically, the areas and uses of forests have been transformed through successive stages of economic growth and development. (i) What are those stages, and what transformations do they exert on forests? (ii) To what extent do these stages and transformations continue? To what extent are these stages and transformations no longer relevant because of changed circumstances?

7 Forestry has unique production features which distinguish it from other sectors when considering how forests contribute to development. Describe the significance for national development of each of the following features in forestry: (i) long production periods, (ii) complex production relations, (iii) presence of external benefits and costs, (iv) issues of renewability and nonrenewability, and (v) presence of unpriced values.

8 Possibilities and constraints bearing on forestry in development are explained by critical variations across countries in several dimensions. Describe how cross-country differences in the following dimensions affect the prospects and limitations of forestry in development: (i) geographical size and population, (ii) forest endowment and national income, (iii) forestry history and traditions, (iv) presence of technological versus nontechnological cultures, (v) economic structure of forestry, and (vi) distribution of political power and presence of special interest groups.

9 What is the "urban bias" in development (Lipton 1977)? How does it affect forestry?

10 Where and why did attention to sustained yield in forestry begin? Is sustained yield of forests a good guide to managing forests for "sustainable development"? Explain and defend.

11 Briefly compare and contrast the pathways of forestry in the national development of Sweden, the USA, Japan, and New Zealand.

12 What countries besides Sweden have successfully pursued forest-rich development? What countries besides Japan have been "importing forests"?

13 In what ways is Brazil's current forest depletion a pathway to economic development, similar to the economic expansion accompanying the USA's forest depletion last century? In what respects are there major differences between Brazil of today and the USA of yesterday with respect to forest depletion and national development?

14 Investigate how Chile's model of forest development based on exotic plantations does and does not parallel experience in New Zealand.

15 Policies to make forests serve national development have little chance of success unless a number of preconditions are met. What are they?

REFERENCES

Adelman, Irma. 1975. "Development economics: A reassessment of goals," *American Economic Review* 65(2): 302–309.

Albion, Robert G. 1926. *Forests and Sea Power: The Timber Problem of the Royal Navy, 1652–1862.* Harvard University Press, Cambridge.

Baskerville, Gordon. 1990. "Canadian sustained yield management: Expectations and realities," *The Forestry Chronicle* 66(1):25–28.

Burns, David. 1986. *Runway and Treadmill Deforestation: Reflections on the Economics of Forest Development in the Tropics.* International Union for Conservation of Nature and Natural Resources (IUCN), Perfect Images Ltd., Southend, England.

Chandrasekharan, C. 1983. "Rural organizations in forestry," *Unasylva* 35(142):2-11.

Critchfield, Richard. 1990. *An American Looks at Britain.* Doubleday, New York.

Dargavel, John. 1982. "Employment and production: The declining forestry sector reexamined," *Australian Forestry* 45:255-261.

ECE/FAO (Economic Commission for Europe; Food and Agriculture Organization). 1986. *European Timber Trends and Prospects to the Year 2000 and Beyond*, Vol. I. United Nations, New York.

FAO (Food and Agriculture Organization). 1988. *An Interim Report on the State of Forest Resources in the Developing Countries.* FAO Report FO:MISC/88/7, Rome.

Fedkiw, John. 1989. *The Evolving Use and Management of the Nation's Forests, Grasslands, Croplands, and Related Resources.* USDA (United States Department of Agriculture) Forest Service General Technical Report RM-175, Fort Collins, CO.

Fernow, Bernhard E. 1911. *A Brief History of Forestry in Europe, the United States, and Other Countries*, 2nd edition. University of Toronto Press, Toronto, Canada.

Galbraith, John K. 1979. *The Nature of Mass Poverty*. Penguin Books, Harmondsworth, England.

Gregersen, Hans M. 1982. *Village Forestry Development in the Republic of Korea*. Food and Agriculture Organization of the United Nations, Rome.

Gregersen, H., K. Brooks, J. Dixon, and L. Hamilton. 1987. *Guidelines for Economic Appraisal of Watershed Management Projects*. Food and Agriculture Organization of the United Nations, FAO Conservation Guide 16, Rome.

Hagglund, Bjorn. 1990. "Sustained-yield forest management: The view from Sweden," *The Forestry Chronicle* 66(1):29–31.

Healy, Robert G. and William E. Shands. 1989. "A conversation with Marion Clawson," *Journal of Forestry* 87(5):18–24.

Huntington, Ellsworth. 1924. *Civilization and Climate*. Yale University Press, New Haven.

Husch, Bertram. 1987. *Guidelines for Forest Policy Formation*. Food and Agriculture Organization of the United Nations, FAO Forestry Paper 81, Rome.

ILO (International Labor Organization). 1975. *The Woodworking Industries and the Creation of Employment*. Second Tripartite Technical Meeting for the Woodworking Industries, Report II, Geneva, Switzerland.

Keegan, Charles E. and Paul E. Polzin. 1987. "Trends in the wood and paper products industry: Their impact on the Pacific Northwest economy," *Journal of Forestry* 85(11):31–36.

Kirkland, A. 1988. "The rise and fall of multiple-use forest management in NZ," *New Zealand Forestry* 33(1):35–37.

Kumazaki, Minoru. 1988. "Japanese economic development and forestry," pp. 1-15 in R. Handa (ed.), *Forest Policy in Japan*. Nippon Ringyo Chosakai, Tokyo, Japan.

LeHeron, R. 1988 "The internationalization of New Zealand's forestry companies and the social appraisal of New Zealand's exotic forest resource," *Environment and Planning A* 20:489–515.

Lemaster, Dennis C. and John H. Beuter. 1989. *Community Stability in Forest-Based Economies*. Timber Press, Portland, OR.

Leonard, H. Jeffrey. 1985. *Divesting Nature's Capital: The Political Economy of Environmental Abuse in the Third World*. Holmes and Meier, New York.

Libecap, Gary A. and Ronald N. Johnson. 1975. "Property rights, nineteenth century federal timber policy, and the conservation movement," *Journal of Economic History* 39(1):129–142.

Lipton, M. 1977. *Why Poor People Stay Poor: Urban Bias in World Development*. Harvard University Press, Cambridge.

Lönnstedt, Lars. 1984. "Stability of forestry and stability of regions: Contradictory goals? The Swedish case," *Canadian Journal of Forest Research* 14:707–711.

Machlis, Gary E. and Jo Ellen Force. 1988. "Community stability and timber-dependent communities," *Rural Sociology* 53:220–234.

Maharidge, Dale. 1989. *And Their Children After Them*. Pantheon Books, New York.

Markham, S. F. 1942. *Climate and the Energy of Nations*. Oxford University Press, London, England.

McGaughey, Stephen E. and Hans M. Gregersen. 1988. *Investment Policies and Financing Mechanisms for Sustainable Forestry Development*. Inter-American Development Bank, Washington, DC.

Moody, Roger (ed.). 1988. *The Indigenous Voices: Visions and Realities*. Zed Books, London, England.

Morita, Manabu. 1988. "Forest cooperative promotion policy," pp. 266–280 in R. Handa (ed.), *Forest Policy in Japan*. Nippon Ringyo Chosakai, Tokyo, Japan.

Northrop, F. S. C. 1956. "Man's relation to the Earth in its bearing on his aesthetic, ethical, and legal values," pp. 1052–1067 in W. L. Thomas, Jr. (ed.), *Man's Role in Changing the Face of the Earth*. University of Chicago Press, Chicago.

Okuchi, Sho. 1988. "Development of forestry production and forestry labor," pp. 309–320 in R. Handa (ed.), *Forest Policy in Japan*. Nippon Ringyo Chosakai, Tokyo, Japan.

Prins, Kit. 1979. "Energy derived from wood in Europe, the USSR, and North America," *Unasylva* 31(123):26-31.

Reich, Charles A. 1970. *The Greening of America*. Random House, New York.

Richards, E. G. (ed.). 1987. *Forestry and Forest Industries: Past and Future*. Martinus Nijhoff Publishers, Dordrecht, Netherlands.

Roche, Michael. 1990. *History of New Zealand Forestry*. New Zealand Forestry Corporation and G.P. Publications, Wellington, New Zealand.

Rosenberg, Nathan and L. E. Birdzell, Jr. 1985. *How the West Grew Rich: The Economic Transformation of the Industrial World*. Basic Books, New York.

Sartorius, Peter and Hans Henle. 1968. *Forestry and Economic Development*. Frederick A. Praeger, New York.

Sedjo, Roger A. 1991. "Forest resources: Resilient and serviceable," pp. 87–132 in K. D. Frederick and R. A. Sedjo (eds.), *America's Renewable Resources: Historical Trends and Current Challenges*. Resources for the Future, Washington, DC.

Soyez, D. 1988. "Scandinavian silviculture in Canada: Entry and performance barriers," *Canadian Geographer* 32:133–140.

Spoehr, Alexander. 1956. "Cultural differences in the interpretation of natural resources," pp. 93–102 in W. L. Thomas, Jr. (ed.), *Man's Role in Changing the Face of the Earth*. University of Chicago Press, Chicago.

Stephenson, Tom. 1989. *Forbidden Land: The Struggle for Access to Mountain and Moorland*. Manchester University Press, Manchester, England.

Todaro, Michael P. 1985. *Economic Development in the Third World*, 3rd edition. Longman, New York.

UNESCO (United Nations Educational, Scientific, and Cultural Organization). 1988. *Goals of Development*. UNESCO, Paris, France.

Wachtel, Paul L. 1983. *The Poverty of Affluence: A Psychological Portrait of the American Way of Life*. Free Press, New York.

Waggener, Thomas R. 1977. "Community stability as a forest management objective," *Journal of Forestry* 75(11):710–714.

Wiebecke, Claus and W. Peters. 1984. "Aspects of sustained yield history: Forest sustention as the principle of forestry—ideas and reality," pp. 176–201 in Harold K. Steen (ed.), *History of Sustained-Yield Forestry*. Forest History Society, Santa Cruz, CA.

Williams, Michael. 1988. *Americans and Their Forests: A Historical Geography*. Cambridge University Press, New York.

World Bank. 1978. *Forestry Sector Policy Paper*. World Bank, Washington, DC.

World Bank. 1989. *Social Indicators of Development 1989*. Johns Hopkins University Press, Baltimore and London, England.

FORESTS AND DEVELOPMENT: FOREST INDUSTRIES

For centuries, processed wood has been one of the most versatile and ubiquitous industrial materials. The least-processed wood products are posts, poles, squared construction timbers, railroad ties, and the like. The next degree of processing is for sawnwood, one of the largest and most widespread of wood-processing industries. Sawnwood is both an intermediate and end product, with uses in construction (i.e., lumber), furniture, cabinetry, wooden crates, and a variety of other applications. Competing with sawnwood in many uses and markets are veneer and plywood, particleboard, fiberboard, and other wood-based panels.

These solidwood industries are joined by those which use wood in the form of fiber, i.e., wood pulp. Normally it is the fiber-based industries which require the greatest degree of processing, and therefore also the largest investments. This refers to the production of newsprint, printing and writing papers, wrapping and packaging papers, household and sanitary papers, and numerous specialty papers and paperboards.

Besides wood, other industrial raw materials from forests are used in a wide range of sectors. Those finding greatest industrial application include latexes and gums, oils and resins, waxes, tannin, skins and furs, rattan and bamboo, medicinal extracts, and numerous food products for commercial preparation and sale. Especially for forests in the developing countries, these "minor" forest products can be significant in total sectoral output. However, the current chapter concentrates on those forest industries which use industrial wood.

WORLD PRODUCTION AND CONSUMPTION OF WOOD AND PAPER PRODUCTS

The mixes of feasible wood-processing industries vary widely across countries and regions according to quantity and quality of timber trees, level of economic development, and technological capability. Likewise, consumption mixes of wood-based products vary with population size and national income, together with a whole series of other demand determinants.

Consumption Patterns and Trends

As shown in Figure 4-1, production and consumption of wood-based forest products are concentrated in the world's industrialized regions. Over three-fourths of the world's sawnwood is produced by North America, Europe, the USSR, and other industrialized regions. These regions also account for over three-fourths of the world's sawnwood consumption (i.e., production plus imports minus exports). The industrialized countries hold even larger shares—varying between 80–90 percent—of world production and consumption of wood-based panels, paper, and paperboard.

Conversely, most of the countries of the developing world have not built up wood-processing facilities commensurate with their population sizes. Thus India

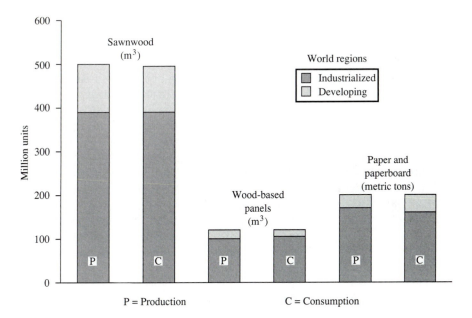

FIGURE 4-1
Production and consumption of wood-based forest products, industrialized and developing countries. *(Source: FAO (1989).)*

All of Africa produces only two percent of the world's sawnwood. The blade of a band saw is sharpened at a forestry training and demonstration center in the Congo. *(Photo courtesy of FAO.)*

and China combine for almost forty percent of global population, but only six percent of global production of industrial wood. The whole of Africa produces only two percent of the world's sawnwood, two percent of its wood-based panels, and one percent of its paper and paperboard. Yet Africa possesses 13 percent of world population and 20 percent of the world's closed forests. This helps reiterate a central point from the previous chapter: the wealth of the forest is not its possession, but rather the infrastructure, markets, technologies, and social and economic policies to use it.

Disparities in consumption can be pronounced. Consumption of paper and paperboard, in particular, closely reflects income differences across countries (Figure 4-2). The USA leads the world in per capita consumption of paper and paperboard, at over 300 kg per person per year. This compares with typical annual consumption of 3–10 kg per person in Africa, the developing countries of Asia, and the poorest regions of Latin America and the Caribbean Basin. Consequently, less than one-fifth of the world's population consumes 75 percent of the world's paper and paperboard.

Since the end of the Second World War, aggregate world demand for sawnwood, wood-based panels, and paper and paperboard has been increasing. However, growth patterns and trends are highly variable among different products, time periods, and levels of economic development:

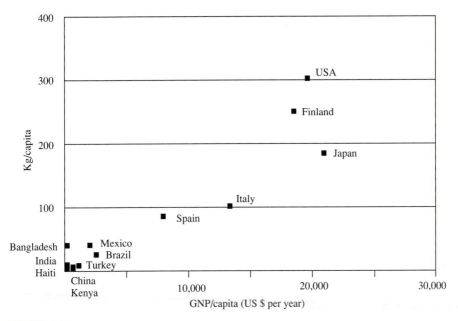

FIGURE 4-2
Per capita consumption of paper and paperboard in relation to per capita income, selected countries. *(Sources: FAO (1989); World Bank (1989).)*

• *Sawnwood*—Global consumption of sawnwood has been expanding, but at decreasing rates. Vigorous sawnwood demand in the aggregate of developing countries contrasts with slowing of demand in the industrialized countries (Figure 4-3). Housing construction in the industrialized countries has stabilized in response to demographic and economic factors, following a lengthy postwar construction boom that began in the 1950s and tapered off in the 1970s. Hence the USA's peak year of housing starts was in the year 1972. The slowing of residential construction since the mid-1970s reduced the demand for sawnwood. Additionally, sawnwood markets have been eroded by substitution of plywood, particleboard, aluminum, and other alternative materials. This differs from the developing countries, where substitutes for sawnwood typically are not as abundant nor as competitive in cost. Sawnwood consumption remains strong in the developing countries because of rapid population growth, large unmet needs for construction, and scarcity of cheap substitutes.

• *Wood-based panels*—Plywood demand grew rapidly through the 1950s and 1960s as construction activity expanded in the industrialized countries, and as plywood substituted for sawnwood. However, plywood use slowed in response to the decline of postwar construction, and as new substitutes replaced plywood. Among these new substitutes are particleboard, fiberboard, waferboard, oriented strand board, and other panels reconstituted from wood particles. Recent slow growth in consumption of wood-based panels in the industrialized countries

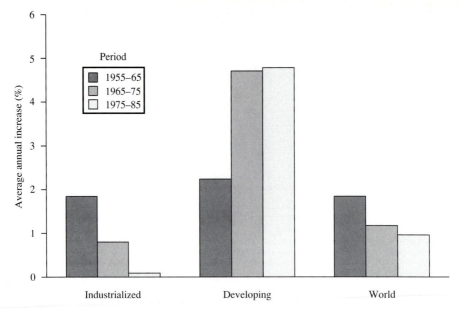

FIGURE 4-3
Growth rates in sawnwood consumption, industrialized and developing countries. *(Source: Ewing and Chalk (1988, p. 7).)*

Housing starts in the USA peaked in the early 1970s, after which residential demand for sawnwood began to diminish. *(Photo courtesy of Forest History Society.)*

Especially in the industrialized countries, plywood use grew rapidly as a substitute for sawnwood in many applications. Later, panels of reconstituted wood (e.g., particleboard, oriented strand board, etc.) substituted for plywood. *(Photo courtesy of Forest History Society.)*

contrasts with substantial growth in the developing countries, where demand is far from saturated (Figure 4-4).

• *Paper and paperboard*—World demand for paper tracks general economic growth since the end of the Second World War. Changes in newsprint consumption in the industrialized countries are determined largely by advertising expenditures allocated to newspapers. This share remains relatively constant at about 28 percent in the USA, and about 50 percent in Europe (Ewing and Chalk 1988). Regarding printing and writing papers, the diffusion of high-speed copying machines and computer printers has increased the demand for office paper in both industrialized and developing countries. To date, forecasts of the "paperless office" are baseless. Consumption of wrapping and packaging papers has been slowing in the industrialized countries because of substitutes (e.g., plastics), streamlining of handling and transportation methods, and other factors. Reverse trends are observed in the developing countries, where the general demand for packaging is growing wherever economies are growing, and where paper and paperboard are viable substitutes for wooden boxes, cloth sacks, and other forms of packaging.

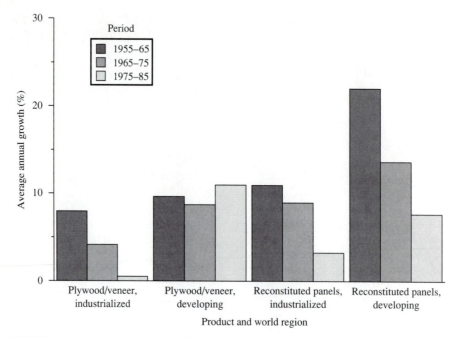

FIGURE 4-4
Growth rates in consumption of wood-based panels, industrialized and developing countries.
(Source: Ewing and Chalk (1988, p. 9).)

The world's production and consumption of industrial roundwood—comprising sawlogs, veneer logs, pulpwood, chips, and wood residues—derive from the summed production of these various wood and paper products. As shown by Figure 4-5, production of industrial roundwood increased rapidly during the 1950s and 1960s, but slowed during the 1970s and 1980s. At a world level, industrial roundwood expanded by 3.5 percent per year in the 1950s, 2.2 percent in the 1960s, 1.1 percent in the 1970s, and by less than 1.0 percent in the 1980s (Sedjo and Lyon 1990). This slowing is explained by overall moderation of world economic growth, and by the leveling of demand in the industrialized countries for sawnwood, panels, and wrapping and packaging papers. Still other explanations rest with various forms of technological change which affect the supply of or demand for roundwood input (Richards 1987).

Role of Technological Change

Moderating the world's industrial roundwood consumption—particularly in the industrialized countries—are various technological innovations. Technological change helps offset wood scarcities, keeping prices from rising as rapidly as they would in the absence of these innovations. Data on the price of industrial roundwood in Europe and various other parts of the world since the mid-1960s re-

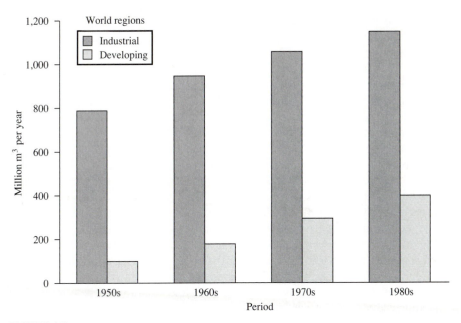

FIGURE 4-5
Production of industrial roundwood, industrialized and developing countries. *(Source: FAO, Yearbook of Forest Products (various volumes).)*

veal considerable price volatility, but no persistent upward pressure on real prices. That the real price of industrial roundwood has not risen very much in the major consuming centers—despite substantial postwar population growth and rising real incomes—implies that technological change has been particularly powerful (Sedjo and Lyon 1990).

Historically, a number of substitutes have emerged to displace wood and paper. A century ago, about 50 percent of all wood utilized in the USA was for fuel. By 1970, this proportion had fallen to about five percent because of substitution by fossil fuels. Examples of wood-substituting products in recent decades include aluminum window frames, metal doors, plastic grocery sacks, plastic milk containers, and petroleum-based synthetic fibers. In each case the rate of product substitution has been governed by new technical processes, changing cost relationships, and changing consumer standards of product acceptability.

New techniques for treating wood against fire and decay offer prospects of expanding wood use in construction, possibly displacing non-wood products. Moreover, rising petroleum prices could once again augment demand for fuelwood and cellulosic fibers (i.e., rayon and acetate). However, these are the exceptions. The broader trends show that forest industries are struggling to retain traditional markets, and that main substitution trends are from wood to non-wood products.

Within the forest industries, much technological change is wood-saving. This results when an increased proportion of the biomass from a given timber harvest can be used for production, or when technologies require less wood input per unit of product output. The newsprint industry presents an example of dramatic wood-saving technological change. In the 1970s, newsprint producers achieved a 10 percent increase in printable area per ton of newsprint by reducing basis weight (i.e., weight per unit area of paper). Moreover, while thermomechanical pulp (TMP) was virtually unknown in commercial applications in 1980, today it is the dominant technology in new pulping capacity for newsprint. Pulp yields from TMP are considerably higher than yields from the processes they replaced, and the effect is to conserve wood inputs. Still another technological development is chemi-thermomechanical pulp (CTMP), which raises pulp yields still higher.

Additionally, the paper industry's pulpwood consumption is reduced by wastepaper recycling. Since 1960, wastepaper recycling in Japan and Western Europe has risen gradually but persistently to current levels of 50 and 45 percent, respectively. This reflects both responsiveness to economic forces, and a philosophy that recycling is socially responsible (Gottsching 1988).

Several wood-saving technologies have found increasing rationale in the solid-wood industries. In plywood production, techniques have been developed to increase the amount of veneer that can be peeled from a log. Product quality in sawmilling is improved through computerized log scanning to determine how to maximize the value of sawnwood recovery. Wood-saving techniques in construction include increased use of wood trusses, which are lumber pieces joined together to form framing members in roofs, floors, and walls.

Some technologies do not reduce the volume of wood consumed, but make new use of what had been low-quality and non-merchantable wood. Supply is increased by allowing a previously inferior forest resource, not viewed as part of the industrial timber base, to substitute for a higher-quality resource. Hence between 1950 and 1986, the USA's use of short-fiber (i.e., non-coniferous) pulpwood increased from 14 to 38 percent of total fiber input. This was facilitated by development and diffusion of new types of pulping and pulp-drying technologies. Moreover, the development of waferboard and oriented strand board makes it possible for the USA and Canada to use "low-quality" aspen for a product that competes directly with plywood in many applications. Short-fiber pulp and oriented strand board are examples of technologies which relieve constraints on the economic supply of wood, and thus moderate wood prices.

Another factor moderating wood prices is cost-reducing innovation in timber harvesting and transport. Beginning in the early part of this century, the use of trucks to replace railroads halved the cost of timber hauling in the USA, and thus vastly increased the amount of timber that could be supplied to market. In recent decades, the southern USA presents an example of productivity gains in logging more than sufficient to offset sharp increases in the prices of logging equipment.

Finally, technology raises industrial wood output through the yield effects and cost savings of intensified forest management, particularly in forest plantations. Worldwide evidence of substantially increased activity in forest plantations since about 1960 reflects a judgment about the adequacy of future timber supplies from naturally regenerated forests, as well as considerable progress in improving plantation technologies. Tree-breeding programs lead to faster tree growth, higher

TABLE 4-1
Costs to grow plantation wood, various plantation types and regions.

Type and region	Rotation age (years)	Carrying costs on one cubic meter of plantation wood at 10 percent rate of interest		
		Yield at rotation (m³)	Cost of establishment (US$/ha)	Future cost of wood (US$/m³)
Spruce/fir (boreal forest)	80	560	300	1,097.36
Douglas-fir (western North America)	45	810	450	40.49
Loblolly pine (southern USA)	25	350	370	11.45
Caribbean pine (tropics and subtropics)	15	240	500	8.35
Paraserianthes (i.e., Albizia; Southeast Asia)	8	280	350	2.68
Eucalyptus (tropics and subtropics)	8	480	350	1.56

Source: Adapted from Johnson (1976).

harvestable volumes, and better log quality. When such plantations are given intensive management, the result is to greatly expand economic supply.

Table 4-1 shows cost comparisons when rotation ages can be shortened and growth rates increased, as for fast-growing tropical and subtropical plantation species compared with temperate species. The effects of plantation technology on the world's markets can be grasped by noting that eucalyptus now accounts for 13 percent of world exports of bleached kraft pulp, up from only 4-5 percent a decade earlier. Major producers of eucalyptus pulp are Spain, Portugal, and Brazil. None of these countries was a supplier until recently, and in none is eucalyptus an indigenous species.

Future Potentials and Constraints

A once common view in forestry was that increasing scarcity of timber would drive up timber prices, causing timber famines where shortages were particularly severe. Yet evidence suggests that consumption and price of industrial roundwood have moderated since 1950, especially in the industrialized countries. While it is unlikely that there will be a global shortage of industrial wood, an important question concerns wood availability in different world regions. In this respect it is critical to distinguish between increasing availability in the industrialized countries, and shortages in many of the developing countries.

Industrialized Countries   Modest growth in the demand for industrial wood in the industrialized countries is explained by the maturing of their economies. Populations are growing very slowly or even declining in western Europe, eastern Europe, the USSR, Canada, Japan, and other parts of the industrialized world. In many of these countries, housing is approaching levels consistent with long-term requirements for replacement and repair, but not expansion. At the same time and just as importantly, wood-saving technology allows the demand for wood raw materials to grow less rapidly than demand for final wood products. Hence most forecasts of world demand for industrial roundwood to the year 2000 and beyond show low projected growth rates (Table 4-2).

Most parts of the industrialized world have the potential to increase timber harvests in future years. Critical issues are whether prices will be attractive, and how environmental pressures will affect patterns and rates of timber cutting. Yet in light of increased forest growing stock and assumed continuation of technological progress, major producing regions are in a position to supply substantially increased volumes of industrial roundwood (ECE/FAO 1986; Ewing and Chalk 1988):

• *North America*—Together, the USA and Canada produce over one-third of the world's industrial roundwood. Studies by the USA's Forest Service indicate that forest growth consistently exceeds timber removals in all regions of the USA except the Pacific Northwest. Major silvicultural opportunities exist to increase forest productivity in all regions. Canada's total forest area is massive, and Canada's tim-

TABLE 4-2
Forecasts of demand for industrial roundwood to the year 2000 and beyond.

Organization/ Study	Year made	Projected to year	Forecast volume (billion m^3)	Implicit growth rate (percent per year)
World Bank	1978	2000	2.8	4.2
		2025	5.9	3.4
Stanford Research Institute	1979	2000	1.9	1.6
FAO, Industry Working Party	1979	2000	1.8	1.2
Food and Agriculture	1982 (high)	2000	2.6	3.7
Organization	(low)	2000	2.3	2.9
IIASA	1987	2000	1.8	1.2
		2030	2.6	1.2
Resources for the Future	1988 (base case)	2000	1.7	0.8
		2035	2.0	0.6

Source: Sedjo and Lyon (1990, p. 177) and sources therein cited.

ber removals increased rapidly after 1960. Future production of industrial wood in Canada depends on the pace of opening up new areas, intensifying forest management, expanding reforestation, and increasing the use of forest residues.

• *Europe*—During the last 40 years, almost all European countries invested significantly in forestry. This has expanded forested area by 15 percent, and produced even larger increases in forest growing stock and forest growth. For Europe as a whole, forest growth is well above timber removals. European experts foresee continued increases in growing stock, forest growth, and timber removals.

• *USSR*—Over half of the Soviet Union's vast forests are biologically suitable for timber production, but a much smaller area of forests is economically served by transportation networks. In relation to its forested area, the USSR's production of industrial timber is modest. The volume of timber cut is well below that permitted. Harvesting intensity is low, and considerable scope exists to take a wider range of timber species, dimensions, and qualities. An expanded timber cut—in combination with more intensified forest management—could theoretically double or triple forest growth. This depends on resolving political and economic issues.

• *Japan*—Japan's major reforestation investments throughout the country imply that Japan has the option to harvest increasing amounts of its own timber, should that prove desirable or necessary in Japanese policy. Many of Japan's plantations are reaching cutting age, and Japanese timber harvests after the mid-1990s have the potential to rise significantly.

• *Australia, New Zealand, South Africa*—Each of these countries has significant investment in plantations which supply industrial wood for export as well as for domestic consumption.

In summary, it appears that modest growth in market demand for industrial wood over the next few decades can be adequately accommodated by forthcoming economic supplies. Numerous surprises could intervene to upset markets and disrupt production. In particular, political pressures to stop or modify timber cutting, responding to concerns of environmentalists, merit careful attention. Yet even when allowing for increasing areas of natural forest excluded from logging, no serious scarcity of wood is likely to occur in any major part of the industrialized world.

Developing Countries   During 1975–1990, the aggregate of developing countries increased their sawnwood consumption by over 60 percent. Consumption of paper and paperboard more than doubled, as did consumption of wood-based panels. This represents an approximate doubling of roundwood input in just 15 years. The next 15 years could witness another doubling of demand in view of population increase and the essential role of construction materials, paper, and other wood-based products in economic growth.

Will the combination of domestic timber production plus wood and paper imports meet rising demand at reasonable prices? This is a complex issue. Substantial

From 1975–1990, the developing countries increased their consumption of sawnwood by over 60 percent. This small sawmill in Nicaragua is typical of many in the region. *(Photo courtesy of FAO.)*

increases in plantation harvests are expected from Brazil, Chile, Zimbabwe, and several other tropical and subtropical producers. Yet many countries have only small or insignificant plantation forests, and are rapidly depleting their natural forests through deforestation.

For example, traditional African log suppliers in Ghana and Nigeria have reached production limits because of past overcutting. Thailand and East Malaysia (i.e., Sabah and Sarawak) may be facing a similar constraint. The Ivory Coast, Philippines, and Costa Rica illustrate countries in which industrial roundwood production has been steadily declining (Figure 4-6). This is not explained by shrinking demand, but rather by forest depletion. Countries in this predicament must contemplate decreased consumption or increased wood imports. Hindering imports is that several of these countries are saddled with large international debts.

On the other hand, several developing countries still have large areas of natural forests which theoretically can be opened for timber cutting. In Africa, these

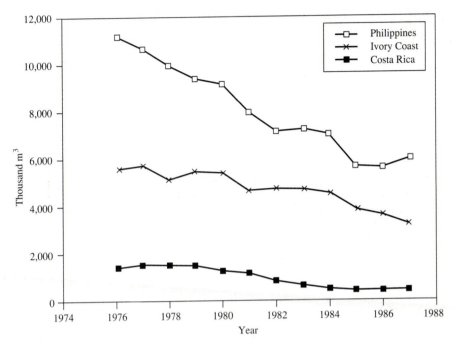

FIGURE 4-6
Declining production of industrial roundwood in the Philippines, Ivory Coast, and Costa Rica. *(Source: FAO (1989).)*

countries include Gabon, Zaire, Equatorial Guinea, the Republic of Congo, Benin, and the Central African Republic. Amazonia and the Guianas contain huge stocks of standing timber in Latin America. According to the government of Indonesia, that country's natural forests with management potential exceed 57 million hectares (Indonesia Ministry of Forestry 1990).

These remaining natural forests of Africa, Latin America, and Asia are future sources of industrial timber under the right conditions of infrastructure expansion, market demand, technical progress to utilize the mixed species, and underlying social and political stability. Even more critical is the political climate for and against logging in light of competing interests for the forests, especially the interests of environmentalists and indigenous peoples. Concern to protect tropical forests is almost certain to preclude timber cutting over increasingly larger areas.

In summary, the outlook for the production and consumption of industrial wood in the developing countries is clouded by many uncertainties. Demand for wood and paper products is growing rapidly. Yet serious questions remain about adequacy and specific sources of timber supply for many countries. The world as a whole is not running out of industrial wood, but developing countries which do not have much production forest will continue to experience low consumption of wood and paper well into the future.

FOREST INDUSTRIES IN REGIONAL GROWTH: ALTERNATIVE VIEWS

One notable exception to the past neglect of forests in economic development was the work by FAO in forest industries for developing countries. A seminal and now classic paper by Jack Westoby (1962) defined the role of forest industries in attacking economic backwardness. That analysis described the importance of forests in a national economy, stressed linkages with other sectors, and discussed the potential for evolution from simple to more progressive products and technologies.

The theory of incremental growth—as Westoby interpreted it for forestry—maintains that a region which begins with a strong base of one or more natural resources exports those resources. This eventually creates sufficient wealth in the region for the establishment of infrastructure and primary processing. In turn, infrastructure and primary processing provide employment for population increase. As earnings accumulate from the primary resource industries, investments are made in secondary economic activities. Each developmental stage leads to more employment and higher population density. At a sufficient size, the economy becomes more diverse and increasingly stronger.

Growth theory has a competing opposite in dependency theory. Dependency theory argues that the resource-producing region remains a perennial hinterland controlled by external wealth and power emanating from one or more metropolitan poles. The hinterland can be a developing country dependent on industrialized countries, or a poor rural region dependent on a national metropolitan center. Instead of gaining self-sufficiency and wealth from its natural resources, the hinterland remains perpetually dependent on outsiders for capital and management. Profits are not reinvested in the hinterland, but rather are remitted to the metropolis. Because secondary industry is not developed in the hinterland, there is no basis for population increase. The regional economy remains undiversified, often relying on just one or two commodity exports (i.e., staples) for its entire economic existence. This makes the hinterland's economy vulnerable to immediate booms and busts with fluctuations in metropolitan demand.

Growth Theory

The intuitive arguments for forest industries are compelling. Management of forests for timber presents an opportunity to use otherwise low-value, erodible lands to produce raw materials for industrial growth. Rural economies are diversified from their dependence on crops and livestock. Employment in logging and wood-processing is scheduled to complement work in agriculture. Forest industries play their part in holding rural residents from migrating to crowded cities. They produce or save foreign exchange, assisting national progress towards economic self-sufficiency. Managed forests provide a wide range of non-timber benefits for persons at all socioeconomic levels.

These are the idealized attributes of forest industries against which actual performance must be compared. The question is then the extent to which the forest industries contribute to the economic well-being of people living in and near the forested regions. Criteria to be considered include the volume and quality of local employment provided, the level of wages and salaries paid, and the stability of forest industries in supporting local communities over a substantial period of time.

The forest industries connect with the rest of the national economy through backward and forward linkages. These linkages measure the degree of an industry's mutual integration with the rest of the economy. Backward linkages sum the purchases of an enterprise to satisfy its demands for logs, manufactured goods, labor, and all other inputs. Forward linkages show the extent to which an enterprise's sales generate further economic transactions for transport, additional processing, and other value-added. Specifically, Westoby (1962) argued as follows:

• *Favorable nature and properties of the raw material*—In development policy, priority should be given to industries which process local raw materials. Wood is one of the few raw materials that nearly all inhabited regions of the world have available and can regenerate from existing forests, or could possess by establishing plantations.

• *Forests and poor regions*—Forests frequently are located in the least developed rural areas, where the subjective need to improve living standards is the greatest. Even regions possessing little natural forest of commercial value can transform the situation fairly rapidly through manmade planting, opening new perspectives for employment and income.

• *Essential goods and sectoral priorities*—Forest products should rank subjectively high in development priorities. These priorities are value judgments, but it can be argued that many forest products are "essential" and satisfy basic needs. This includes wood and fiber for housing, furniture, newspapers, and books. Suitable housing and furniture, and the expansion of learning through books and newspapers, are indicators of material well-being and social standards.

• *Demand expansion and import-saving effect*—The majority of developing countries experience deficits in net trade of forest products, aggravating their balance of payments situation. They export low-value forest products (e.g., logs and sawnwood), and import high-value products (e.g., panels, pulp, paper, and paperboard). Yet demand is projected to increase for goods with high income elasticity, especially paper and wood-based panels. Hence a move towards domestic production of presently imported forest products can lead to import savings.

• *Capturing value-added from exported logs*—Developing countries which export logs have the opportunity to capture income and provide employment by investing in domestic processing. Processing capacity increases not only to satisfy growing internal demand, but also to substitute exports of processed wood for exports of logs. Because logs are bulky and costly to transport, the export of processed wood in place of unprocessed wood results in cost savings due to freight reductions.

• *Flexible combination of inputs and outputs in forestry*—Forest management can be adapted to take account of changing conditions. With shifts in technologies and demands, standing timber can be allocated to any of multiple end products (e.g., fuel, sawlogs, or fiber). The timing of harvesting is flexible within fairly

Forest products should rank high in development priorities. Here Ethiopian children share a few tattered books at a rural school. *(Photo courtesy of World Bank.)*

broad limits, permitting adjustment to demand fluctuations. Moreover, timber can be produced intensively on a small amount of land, or extensively over large areas. Different species and species groups often substitute for each other. Hardwoods substitute for softwoods in products such as sawnwood, wood-based panels, and certain kinds of wood pulp. These various options offer a multitude of strategies to supply timber for domestic industry or export.

• *Absorption of underemployed and unemployed rural labor*—Activities in tree planting, silviculture, and certain kinds of logging are labor-intensive, or at least amenable to a range of technology alternatives. Many tasks in silviculture can be mechanized only with great difficulty, even in high-wage industrialized countries. Some forestry activities can be scheduled to coincide with slack agricultural seasons, thus absorbing cyclically idle farm labor. Important working routines, skills, and know-how in agriculture are often readily transferred to forestry and wood processing.

• *Flexible scale and technology in logging and processing*—Enterprises in logging and wood processing vary greatly in scale and labor intensity. In logging, manual labor assisted by draft animals or relatively inexpensive logging devices often competes favorably in costs with more capital-intensive alternatives in regions where rural labor is still inexpensive. In processing, the physical properties of wood render it relatively easy to work mechanically, enabling a wide variety of products to be made with relatively simple machinery. Small production scale can be economical in the processing of basic products (e.g., sawnwood, veneer,

Elephants are used for logging in the Mai Sa region of Thailand. Manual labor assisted by draft animals often competes favorably in costs with mechanized alternatives where rural labor is still inexpensive. *(Photo courtesy of FAO.)*

mechanical pulp). This is due to the difficulty of transporting the raw material on the one hand, and the ease with which wood can be worked on the other.

• *Enterprise growth by degrees*—A small wood-processing enterprise can expand incrementally as conditions permit. Certain types of processing integration are technologically possible and economically feasible even at small scales of operation. Mechanization can substitute for manual methods as the process of industrialization proceeds, particularly in materials handling. This possibility of gradual growth, step by step, is advantageous under the conditions of most developing regions.

• *Dynamic growth through linkages*—Forest industries are thought to be a propulsive sector, given that expansion of forest industries has strong forward linkages with other sectors. High interindustry interdependence induces demand and provides supplies for other sectors, making forest industries a good starting point for industrial growth.

Cases Illustrating Growth Theory

Growth theory applied to forest industries is perhaps nowhere better illustrated than in the Nordic countries, particularly Sweden and Finland, and in the southern

USA. Forest industries in the Nordic countries are heavily oriented towards exports, while those in the southern USA produce primarily for the huge USA market. Significant is the prominent role of private forest ownership, by corporations and particularly by farmers and other nonindustrial owners, in each case. Sweden was discussed as an example of forest-rich development in Chapter 3. From the beginning of its modern era of industrial development, Sweden generated income from its mining and metal industries in addition to its forest sector. In comparison, Finland has relied more exclusively on forestry until industrial diversification after the Second World War.

Finland   Finland's forest area per capita is the highest in Europe. Forestry and forest industries are critical in the export-led economic growth of the country. Since 1860, the contribution of the forestry sector in annual Finnish exports has ranged from 37–90 percent, dominating export flows throughout the period. Exports began with logs and sawnwood, and through the decades diversified and expanded to include increasing shares of high-valued products in pulp and paper. The country's long-term economic growth compares favorably with economic growth in other industrialized countries. Thus for the century covered by the period 1870–1976,

Finland's exports of forest products include increasing shares of high-valued pulp and paper. *(Photo courtesy of Erkki Oksanen and Finnish Forest Research Institute.)*

per capita income growth in Finland and Sweden was second only to Japan (Palo 1988).

The continuous growth and development of Finland's forest industries can be attributed to several factors. Initial advantages included nearness to the wood-importing countries of western Europe, abundant and cheap water transport, extensive peasant ownership of the forested land (i.e., egalitarian society), and an abundance of Finnish entrepreneurs experienced in sea commerce of forest products. Up until the 1960s, linkages between agriculture and forestry were strong, so that economic effort could be seasonally rotated between farming and forest work.

Finland's growing export income from forest products generated strong reinvestment, including reinvestment in the manufacture of machinery and other capital goods. Mill machinery was built first for the Finnish industries, and then for export. Especially since the 1950s, Finland has been exporting not only forest products but also paper machines, engineering consulting services, and logging equipment. Integration between forest industries and the rest of the Finnish economy has been increasing, and Finland's forest industries are linked with the country's high-growth industries (Haltia and Simula 1988).

Not least important is Finland's heavy investment in the people and institutions of forest management. This refers to research, education, professional societies, and extension. Much of this system was put into place in the early decades of this century, including an important forestry law for private forests, comprehensive forest inventories, and public grants and credits for forest improvements.

Southern USA   The southern USA is among the world's leading producers of wood and paper products. The forest base is large and diverse, and 90 percent of it is owned privately. The 12 southern states produce more than one-third of the USA's softwood sawnwood, two-fifths of its hardwood sawnwood, about half of its plywood, and two-thirds of its pulp. Timber harvests rank among the top agricultural crops in all parts of the region. In relationship to total manufacturing, forest industries in the early 1980s employed one of every nine workers, paid $1 of every $10 in wages and salaries, and produced $1 of every $11 in value-added. This was sufficient to exceed employment and income in each of the region's other major industries (USDA Forest Service 1988).

Forest industries in the southern states expanded rapidly after the Second World War. This occurred for a number of reasons. First is forest regeneration and improved timber stocking in response to fire protection, reforestation, and other forest management programs begun decades earlier. Second is the USA's construction boom during the 1950s and 1960s, coinciding with key advances in the production of laminated beams, southern pine plywood, log debarking, and other important technologies. New pulping technologies developed since the 1930s explain a steady shift from low-paying and unstable employment in the sawnwood industry to higher wages and more continuous employment in the pulp and paper industries.

Pulping technologies developed since the 1930s have generated high wages and stable employment in the pulp and paper industries of the southern USA. *(Photo courtesy of Forest History Society.)*

Besides being large and dynamic, the region's forest industries are well integrated with the surrounding economy through backward and forward linkages. In the southern USA, forest industries purchase a high proportion of their timber and labor locally, and sell much of their output for further manufacturing and distribution within the region. In this way, each dollar of income generated by forest industries is "multiplied" to produce substantial regional benefits. Hence economic multipliers compare favorably with those in other sectors (Figure 4-7).

Dependency Theory

By the mid-1970s, Westoby registered serious disappointment in the forest industries model, rejecting much of his original formulation (Westoby 1978). At the 1978 World Forestry Congress, Westoby unequivocally stated that conventional forest industries had contributed little or nothing to socioeconomic development in the developing countries. While 100–150 million hectares of tropical forest had been logged in the previous two decades, most log production had been exported. Weak government forest services were in large part responsible for unregulated forest cutting, although typically because of circumstances beyond their control.

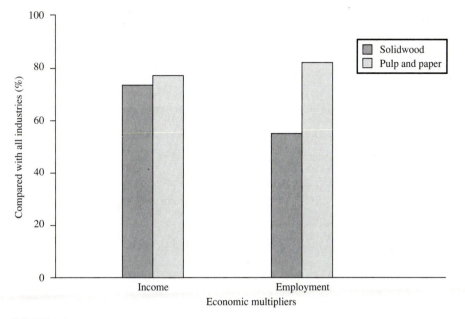

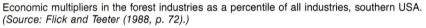

FIGURE 4-7
Economic multipliers in the forest industries as a percentile of all industries, southern USA.
(Source: Flick and Teeter (1988, p. 72).)

Of the meager revenue flow generated by forest concessions, very little had been reinvested in forest management, regeneration, or research. The modest development of forest industries which had taken place was externally oriented. This produced few multiplier effects for local people, but generated a steady stream of cheap raw materials for importers outside of the tropics. Dependency theory, rather than growth theory, appeared to provide a better explanation of the actual role of forests in development.

According to dependency theory, a forested region which produces timber for processing elsewhere increases its income from timber extraction, but usually not as rapidly as income accumulates in wood manufacturing and sales. This typically produces unequal economic development in favor of the manufacturing pole (Riihinen 1981). In other words, resources are drawn from the forested region to contribute to the incomes of those who control processing and product sales. Unless processing and sales are controlled by those who reside in the forested region, the process represents a net transfer of economic surplus from the forested hinterland to an external metropolis. The transferred surplus may be particularly large where exporters and manufacturers obtain timber at subsidized prices, as in diverse countries around the world. Framed in dependency theory, capitalist powers in the metropolis manipulate production and commerce to their advantage and at the expense of politically weaker and economically backward forested regions (Figure 4-8).

FIGURE 4-8
Dependency theory applied to economic underdevelopment of forested regions. *(Sources: Leslie (1980); Marchak (1983).)*

Hinterland and metropolis:
- Forested regions are part of economically poor "hinterland."
- Capital, management, and markets are dominated by wealthy "metropolis."
- Dominant economic class in metropolis controls terms of investment, production, and commerce in forest indutries.
- Metropolis places managers in hinterland, but they are transients whose values and priorities are allied with metropolis.

Net economic exchange:
- Value-added from wood processing flows from poor hinterland to rich metropolis (i.e., "trickle up").
- Accumulation and growth occur in metropolis more than in hinterland, leading to unequal economic progress.
- Forested hinterland is forever dependent on metropolis for new investment and consumer goods.
- No imperative for metropolis to invest in hinterland except to keep log supplies flowing.

Vulnerability of forested hinterland:
- Form and rate of technological advance are governed by profitability to dominant economic class in metropolis.
- Modern corporate methods displace local indigenous methods.
- Specialization in timber growing and processing produces accentuated economic swings in hinterland when wood products demand fluctuates in metropolis.

Cases Illustrating Dependency Theory

Dependency perspectives have been used to describe forest industries in Canada, Australia, and Brazil. These cases are briefly summarized.

British Columbia, Canada   Canada is the world's largest exporter of pulp, newsprint, and coniferous sawnwood. Instability in global economic conditions, particularly conditions in the USA, has a pronounced negative effect on Canada's forest industries, and hence on an estimated three hundred dependent communities across the country (Ketcheson 1986). Also, much of the employment and income in Canada's forest industries is captured by Ontario, while less-industrialized but more heavily forested regions like British Columbia derive relatively fewer jobs and value-added in manufacturing (Jacques and Fraser 1989).

Dependency began early. In the 1860s and 1870s, the valley of the Ottawa River was a vast "sea of pine." At that time, nearly half of Canada's adult male population was engaged in logging and sawmilling. These industries provided immense exports, mainly to supply the large markets of Britain and the USA. Yet the mid-1800s were times of periodic catastrophic market collapse because of production gluts and rapid forest depletion. Moreover, Canada's forest industries were highly dependent on the USA for sawmill technology, investment capital, and export markets. Downturns in either British or USA markets led to immediate and sharp economic recessions (Gillis and Roach 1986).

Canada's historical dependency on external markets continues into the present era, especially in the heavily forested province of British Columbia. Between the late 1970s and early 1980s, British Columbia's forest industries went from a period of expanded timber cut and high world prices for exports into a depression so serious that more than one-third of the sector's labor force was unemployed, many permanently. Large corporate operations were affected more severely than small independent ones. This undercut a long-standing assumption in western Canada that integrated and corporate forest industries provide financial stability to withstand adverse times (Drushka 1985).

Importantly, many enterprises in British Columbia's forest industries are managed from outside the forested regions. Foreign owners, together with owners from eastern Canada, control many of British Columbia's largest companies with timber rights and manufacturing capacity. This has led one Canadian sociologist to assert that decisions on industry expansion, contraction, and other issues critical to British Columbia's welfare are made in Toronto, Montreal, New York, San Francisco, and Tokyo (Marchak 1983).

In the dependency interpretation, only few skilled and semiskilled workers are needed in the forest industries. Jobs for workers with advanced education are very limited. Young local residents who manage to achieve advanced education leave the hinterland in search of opportunities in the metropolis. Hence the forested region loses the few members of its population who might otherwise find alternatives to resource dependency.

Historically, work in Canadian logging and sawmilling camps was strenuous, prone to frequent and severe accidents, and highly seasonal (Bradwin 1972). Some camps later become towns, frequently remote single-industry towns of precarious stability because of youth out-migration, and the ultimate uncertainty of the sole economic base (Lucas 1971). Surveys in Canada show that these towns bring with them a high proportion of unmarried men, lack of good employment opportunities for women, and vulnerabilities to economic recession when layoffs occur simultaneously. "Boom and bust" economic cycles in the forest industries create high transience rates for workers, such that instability is the outstanding feature of the labor force (Marchak 1983).

Tasmania, Australia   Australia's island state of Tasmania has lower income and higher unemployment than the national average. Three pulp and paper companies derive their fiber from Tasmanian forests, with beginnings traced to British and Australian capital invested in the 1920s and 1930s. These three companies provide a significant share of Tasmania's manufacturing employment, wages, taxes, and local purchasing.

Because of their economic and political power in one of Australia's least-developed regions, the companies have been able to obtain generous subsidies and assistance from the Australian and Tasmanian governments. Through the decades, the companies have been granted cheap electricity, roads, preferential tariffs, forest concessions at only nominal royalty rates, help in battling

Single-industry towns and camps have a precarious existence because of youth out-migration and the ultimate uncertainty of the sole economic base. *(Photo courtesy of Forest History Society.)*

environmental pressures, and state assistance to regenerate cutover forested lands. To demonstrate seriousness and reinforce their hold on political power, the companies have on occasion closed mills and dismissed workers to leverage even more government assistance.

In this variation of dependency theory, profits for shareholders in Tasmania's pulp and paper companies are paid from subsidies borne by Australian taxpayers as a whole. Furthermore, since most shareholders are not Tasmanian, the process transfers wealth from the state, reducing the possibility for reinvestment in other sectors of Tasmania (Dargavel 1984).

Mahogany Exports, Brazil Brazil heavily subsidized export of mahogany sawnwood during the early 1980s. Through this policy, a metropolitan merchant class was able to take control of mahogany production and export, squeezing out small local sawmills or making them dependent on large trading companies for supplies of logs and operating capital. Mahogany exporters earned large profits from the subsidies, while the small sawmills were paid less than their production costs. Side effects included illegal invasion of forest reserves, and ensuing intimidation of the indigenous tribes who lived there. Sawnwood needed for local construction often was not available because milling capacity was concentrated on exports. The episode is interpreted as just one in a series of self-impoverishing extractive cycles in Brazil's economic history (Browder 1987).

Interpreting the Conflicting Paradigms

These competing ideas on successes and failures of forest industries merit closer scrutiny by mustering appropriate criteria, valid empirical data, and plausible interpretations. Was Westoby's original model of forest industries flawed in concept? Is the concept sound, but the implementation lacking? Or has the rejection of forest industries been exaggerated, with successful industrialization ignored in the rush to push new development agendas? Each of these perspectives has merit, and none is correct alone.

The perception that forest industries are to be questioned as a development vehicle goes beyond the bounds of ordinary forest policy and management. It is deeply rooted in widespread public opinion, which since the 1970s has lost confidence in industrial development because of environmental concerns and distrust of business motives. Forest industries are particularly embattled because they cut trees. A skeptical view is doubly reinforced by the rapid infusion into decisionmaking circles of persons without traditional forestry educations, especially many who by formal education or personal inclination see themselves as environmentalists.

Hence a leading problem of forest industries is an ideological one, or a conflict in paradigms. This refers to mutually inconsistent beliefs, values, criteria, and methods for interpreting the real world. Competing paradigms are especially prevalent when political, analytical, and data issues are many and complex (Kuhn 1970). Jack Westoby may not have been entirely wrong about the dynamic role of forest industries in economic growth, but neither was he entirely right.

At least three interpretations arise when confronting the claims of competing paradigms. The first is that experience with forest industries across regions indeed has been variable, and that observers who argue successes and failures are describing true variations stemming from different historical, geographical, market, and political contexts. Especially important are the patterns of forest ownership, industry ownership, and their interaction. The breadth and depth of a region's non-forest economic activities determine linkage possibilities, and the extent of diversification in sources of regional income.

A second interpretation is that individuals ideologically immersed in a particular paradigm are unable to be objective, whether these individuals are chief executive officers of forest products companies or leaders of conservation organizations. Because of basic disagreements over perceptions and values, those immersed in opposing paradigms frequently are unable to understand each other. They speak different "languages," and only translation can open possibilities for persuasion or conversion. Translation requires developing, formalizing, and presenting competing views in a unified and comprehensive framework understandable to both sides of the debate (Kuhn 1970). This has not happened widely for forest industries.

A third factor in the battle of paradigms is that conventional approaches to understanding regional economic impact often fail to take sufficient account of political factors. In central India, a World Bank project to establish pine plantations in a region of natural forests was stopped by social protests which reverberated to top political levels (Anderson and Huber 1988). In the early 1980s, the USA's Weyerhaeuser Company exited a large forest industries venture in Indonesia for reasons which might also be described as political (Bethel et al. 1982). These political factors so paramount in the coming and going of forest industries were not even mentioned in Westoby's original paper.

Political and social factors also confound the dependency school. The implications of dependency theory lead to arguments for deliberate hinterland isolation, a view which can be faulted as myopic and unrealistic. Secondly, dependency models frequently forget or ignore the history of social resistance in limiting hinterland exploitation. For example, workers in logging and milling in the northwestern USA and western Canada have a long history of social unrest and militancy in collective movements to improve social and economic conditions (Jensen 1945; Bergren 1967).

Moreover, the assumption that an external metropolis dominates capital and management leaves unexplained the emergence of local independent producers, a characteristic of forest industries in many regions. Foreign ownership in Finland's

Thousands of small sawmills were owned and managed by local entrepreneurs during southern Brazil's agricultural expansion. Conspicuously absent were foreign owners and large-scale operations. *(Photo by Jan Laarman.)*

forest industries was small since the beginning, disappearing entirely by 1918 (Palo 1988). Southern Brazil presents an equally interesting case. Literally thousands of small sawmills were owned and managed by local entrepreneurs during southern Brazil's principal agricultural expansion, mainly from the 1950s through the 1970s. Conspicuously absent were foreign owners and large-scale operations.

The contest over paradigms cannot avoid difficult questions. If forest industries do not promote the economic growth and development of forested regions, then what non-forest alternatives would be superior? Are some regions poor because they are forested, or are they forested because they lack certain desirable characteristics of location and infrastructure? If forest industries serve as a leading sector for a period of years and later fade into lesser importance, does this mean that they did not make a major contribution to development? Gregersen (1973) raised these issues in reply to Kromm's (1972) contention that forestry is a space-using residual land use, and hence unable to contribute much to regional development in the USA's northern Michigan. This exchange of perspectives needs to be wider than for Michigan alone, for it penetrates to fundamental concerns.

It is unrealistic to believe that the competing paradigms for forest industries can be resolved, but much could be done to explore and compare them more rigorously than in the past. This depends on the availability of conceptual tools, data, and explicit professional interest. Since the 1970s, these ingredients have found their most articulate expression in the search for "appropriate" enterprises and technologies.

APPROPRIATE ENTERPRISES AND TECHNOLOGIES

The many unanswered questions about development impacts of forest industries lead quite naturally to attempting to define and ultimately promote industries and technologies which are "appropriate." An appropriate industry or technology is a production system suitable for the particular economic, social, institutional, and physical environment in which it operates. Hence appropriateness is defined only in a particular context.

Thus the conditions of labor costs and skills which make the manufacture of handmade paper and bullock carts appropriate in some regions of South Asia (Chetty 1985) may be precisely why these industries are inappropriate in Europe and North America. Conversely, large pulp and paper plants of the kind found in industrialized countries seldom can be imitated in developing countries, even if governments there show great psychological attraction to them (King 1977).

On the other hand, a number of criteria defining appropriateness are nearly universal. From a national viewpoint these include the desire to limit industrial pollution, protect and regenerate forests, and protect workers from accidents. Differences across countries are more a matter of degree than kind, explained by varying capacities to afford and implement the stated goals (FAO 1986).

Experience in Forestry and Forest Industries

The range of development tradeoffs in forest industries can be appreciated by comparing the roles and constraints of small private enterprises, large private enterprises, and state corporations. Each category presents degrees of appropriateness and inappropriateness for forest industries in regional development. This three-way classification does not exhaust the possibilities, nor is each category easily defined.

Small Enterprises   The proposition that "small is beautiful" (Schumacher 1973) has won enthusiasts to small scale as an indicator of appropriateness, especially in the context of developing countries. The contention is that large-scale forms of economic organization provide few employment opportunities and other benefits for the poorer elements of society. In comparison, small enterprises are argued to be more labor-intensive, simple to operate and maintain, and meet "quality of life" attributes such as increased local self-sufficiency and minimal disruption of village and rural life. Yet these issues cannot be settled by assertion, since numerous exceptions and contradictions undermine attempts to generalize. The reality is that small enterprises provide many advantages for regional growth and development, while simultaneously suffering many disadvantages.

An extensive survey by FAO in six developing countries found that forest-based activities represent one of the most common types of small enterprise (FAO 1987). One-person operations in households are very common, including many operations run by women entrepreneurs. Only a small proportion of enterprises employ 10 or more workers. A typical employment level is 2–4 persons, many of them family members (Table 4-3). Despite their very small size, aggregate employment can be large. Hence Table 4-4 shows that employment in the forest sector of the Philippines is concentrated in cottage industries, not in the "modern" subsector of higher capital investment.

Typical small enterprises are those producing firewood and charcoal, furniture, woodwork, agricultural implements, wagons, carts, and boats. Small forest-based enterprises in a broadened definition also include those which use canes, reeds, vines, and grasses to make mats, baskets, and similar products. A third activity is handicrafts of wood and non-wood materials.

The appropriateness of small enterprises is highly subjective and variable by context, but may be summarized in a few generalizations (Arnold et al. 1987). First and perhaps most importantly, they provide nonagricultural rural employment in regions where alternative off-farm employment may be difficult to find. In this way, earnings from small enterprises help smooth out seasonal income cycles. Much of the output from small enterprises is consumed by poor segments of society not reached by modern industries. Many small enterprises are able to get along without sophisticated management, and they harness and develop local entrepreneurial talent. Very often, they use sources of capital and raw materials which might otherwise remain unproductive. Yet the technical efficiency of small enterprises is difficult to resolve, and competing analyses show marked disagreement on this issue.

TABLE 4-3

Summary characteristics of small forest-based enterprises in six developing countries.

	Jamaica	Honduras	Zambia	Egypt	Sierra Leone	Bangladesh
Proportion of all small forest-based enterprises (percent)						
Rural location	88	100	96	80	99	97
Production at home	52	72	81	76	NA	NA
One-person operations	58	59	69	69	NA	36
Women's ownership	32	10	12	65	NA	3
Main enterprise:						
Sawmilling	1	3	6	0	0	1
Carpentry, furniture	23	71	14	24	67	27
Wood carving, bamboo, cane	13	0	12	0	6	12
Baskets, mats, hats	63	11	60	70	24	32
Others	0	15	8	6	3	28
Mean values per enterprise						
No. workers	2.2	2.2	1.7	1.9	1.8	3.8
Investment (thousand US$)	3.0	1.1	NA	NA	0.4	0.3
Production value (thousand US$ per year)	5.0	2.5	NA	1.5	1.4	2.4

Source: Fisseha (1987).

TABLE 4-4

Employment in modern and traditional subsectors, forest industries in the Philippines.

	Establishments (number)	Employment (persons)	Labor/capital (persons per million US$ fixed assets)
"Modern" subsector			
Logging	137	39,235	93
Sawmills	450	17,278	343
Wood panels:			
Veneer	24	4,300	107
Plywood	29	9,000	64
Blockboard	13	480	343
Particleboard	2	200	29
Fiberboard	1	352	129
Pulp and paper	19	6,713	43
"Traditional" subsector (cottage industries)			
Handicrafts	5,720	129,000	43,040
Minor forest products	3,160	85,360	90,960
Furniture	5,600	45,430	9,740

Source: Laarman et al. (1981, p. 11).

Small forest-based enterprises include those which use canes, reeds, vines, and grasses to make mats, baskets, and similar products. *(Photo courtesy of World Bank.)*

Besides the inconclusive debate on technical efficiency, problems of smallness include poor working conditions and low wages for hired labor. Another concern is lack of access to long-term credit for enterprise growth, and to sufficient working capital to meet peak periods of demand. Competition among small enterprises in a single product line may be intense, limiting ability to accumulate capital from earnings. Markets are constrained by the low purchasing power of rural and village customers, the principal buyers of many products. Additionally, handicrafts may be subject to seasonal fluctuations if a main demand is the tourist industry. Small woodworking shops which use power tools experience overcapacity unless machinery is fully utilized. Finally, small enterprises typically lack personal contacts and political power to influence policies affecting their welfare, including policies on access to forest raw materials.

The relation between small enterprise and access to raw materials can pose serious dilemmas, as illustrated by sawnwood production in Ecuador. Only a small proportion of the country's sawnwood is produced in sawmills. The rest originates in labor-intensive chainsaw operations in the forest. Trees are felled to the ground, and the chainsaw operator cuts logs lengthwise to make boards carried out of the forest on mules or by manual carrying. Chainsaw operations account for a full 75 percent of primary sawnwood production and 89 percent of industry employment. Yet chainsaw operations are opposed by the main forest industries as a competitor for timber. They are opposed by the government and environmental groups as difficult to monitor and control, and as a likely source of forest destruction. Chainsaws could be officially prohibited from sawnwood production to reduce deforestation pressures, but this would cost Ecuador the loss of several thousand jobs (Prestemon and Laarman 1989). This conflict between employment promotion and other social goals is typical of the tradeoffs in technology policy for small enterprises.

Large Enterprises The broad outline of benefit-cost impacts attributable to large enterprises, particularly enterprises of transnational companies, is well known. These impacts have been explored to a limited extent in the forest industries. However, the information to systematically evaluate the appropriateness of large enterprises is often anecdotal, incomplete, and contradictory. Additionally, realities are clouded by differences in perception and interpretation. This makes it difficult to compare and reconcile the "good" done by Olinkraft and Westvaco in Brazil (Blake and Driscoll 1977) with the "harm" attributed to Japan and New Guinea Timbers in Papua New Guinea (Lamb 1990).

In forest industries as elsewhere, the large enterprise is often the victim of polarized opinion on whether industry itself is inherently good or bad. The controversies infuse disputed claims between growth theorists and dependency theorists, and between developers and preservationists. Disagreements over the suitability of an enterprise can be particularly volatile when it represents direct foreign investment by a parent company from another country. Private foreign investment is viewed by some as having neocolonial connotations, enormous political power, and corrupting influences. Yet without a factual basis for analysis, the rhetoric can be simpleminded. The challenge is to produce objective accounts of large enterprises in the development context of forestry to fairly represent aspects of both appropriateness and inappropriateness.

To be remembered is that most transnational investment in the world's forest industries is among industrialized countries. The USA and Canada are home to the majority of the world's largest forest products transnationals, with the others headquartered mainly in Europe and Japan. When studied in the early 1980s, two-thirds of the foreign subsidiaries of the USA's forest products companies were located in Europe, Canada, and other industrialized regions. Many subsidiaries, both in industrialized and developing countries, are engaged in product sales rather than manufacturing (Bilek and Ellefson 1987). Moreover, manufacturing often depends on purchased raw materials rather than timber supplied from forestlands owned by the subsidiaries (Bethel et al. 1982). Therefore, connections to forest management are few and indirect.

In reference to the developing countries, profiles of transnational investment in forest industries vary considerably by region (Contreras 1987). Hence European companies—most of them small by international standards—dominate logging and milling in West Africa. This compares with the dipterocarp region of Indonesia, Malaysia, and the Philippines, where foreign presence has declined rapidly since the late 1970s. Unlike Africa or Southeast Asia, foreign investment in the forest industries of Latin America is mainly in pulp and paper companies. While some Brazilian companies are now large exporters, most foreign investment in Latin America's pulp and paper industries has been to satisfy internal markets by

European companies, most small by international standards, dominate logging and milling in West Africa. *(Photo courtesy of FAO.)*

substituting domestic production for imports. These contrasts across world regions help explain why the links between forestry, foreign investment, and development impact are difficult to summarize.

The debate over large enterprise, particularly large transnational enterprise, is usually one of conflicting goals. Directly or indirectly, goals of the parent company emphasize profits and company diversification and expansion. In comparison, national social policy in the host country typically stresses generation of tax revenues and employment, net gains in foreign exchange, and steering of investment towards neglected sectors and regions. This dichotomy of goals makes "appropriateness" a contentious issue, and harmonization of goals through negotiation and compromise the primary task of policy (Gregersen and Contreras 1975). Some basic dilemmas of large transnational enterprise have no real answers (Frank 1980, pp. 29–36):

• If the company repatriates profits, it is depriving the developing region of newly created wealth. On the other hand, reinvestment locally increases the company's hold on the regional economy.

• If the company pays the standard local wage, it is accused of exploiting cheap labor. If it pays more, it is accused of rendering local firms noncompetitive.

• If the company favors the latest and best production methods, it is said to be importing a technology too advanced for the skills and employment needs of the local area. Yet if it uses simpler technologies, the company is blamed for holding back regional progress.

The large enterprise normally argues its appropriateness in terms of improved technologies and management, generous wages and allowances, leadership in safety and pollution control, ability to produce for export markets, and contributions to local infrastructure (e.g., roads, schools, recreation facilities, etc.). Thus Paper Industries Corporation of the Philippines is a world pioneer in the integrated processing of tropical timbers, and has provided technical assistance to thousands of individual tree farmers (Picornell 1986). In Chile, the Cholguan companies built up a sizable group of enterprises from radiata pine plantations they established over several decades on soils too poor for agriculture (Cortes 1986). In Brazil, the company Aracruz Florestal exports eucalyptus pulp earning hundreds of millions of dollars in foreign exchange from a region which is otherwise economically poor and sparsely populated (Jaakko Pöyry Oy 1986). Factors claimed in the appropriateness of Cholguan and Aracruz are outlined in Figure 4-9.

Yet each potential benefit has, as its counterpart, a potential cost. Among them are heavy demands on scarce inputs (e.g., loan capital, skilled labor), technologies which do not employ many local people in relation to the amount of capital invested, dominance of outsiders in management decisions, and outflow of profits and managerial income from the local area. Costs of a largely noneconomic character may include threats to autonomy, as when a country's natural resources are in foreign hands, or when the power of large business is used to corrupt government officials.

FIGURE 4-9
Factors in appropriateness of two large forest-based enterprises in South America. *(Sources: Cortes (1986); Jaakko Pöyry Oy (1986).)*

Aracruz Florestal, Brazil:
- Located in sparsely populated, poor region
- Brazilians have 65 percent of ownership
- Brazilians made 60 percent of equipment
- Production scale sufficiently large to keep costs competitive
- Annual export earnings highly significant for sector and region
- Self-sufficient in most pulping chemicals
- Pollution control far more stringent than reqired by law
- Among world leaders in technologies for plantation forestry

Cholguan Companies, Chile:
- Established several thousand hectares of pine plantations on poor sandy soils
- Company is main source of stable work in its region
- Strong net positive contribution to foreign exchange earnings
- Strong net positive contribution to government revenues
- Substantial rise in level of wages and salaries through time
- Company able to do much of its own plant design and engineering
- Forestry research in genetic improvement, fertilization, disease management
- Company contributions to schools, recreation centers, workers' housing, literacy programs, electricity network, health and dental services

In recent times, impacts of large-scale enterprise in forestry and forest industries are perhaps nowhere more controversial than in the case of Brazil's Jari Florestal (the "Jari project"). In the late 1960s, the North American billionaire Daniel K. Ludwig purchased over one million hectares of land along the Jari River in the lower Amazon Basin. On this land he started various enterprises in rice production, cattle raising, mining, sawmilling, and pulp production. From the late 1960s through the late 1970s, approximately 100 thousand hectares of native forests were cleared and burned to make room for pulpwood plantations of gmelina (*Gmelina arborea*), pine (*P. caribaea*), and eucalyptus (*E. deglupta*). In many plantations, growth performance turned out far lower than expectations, partly because early methods of clearing used bulldozers which removed topsoil and led to compaction. Also, Jari's plantations provoked criticisms that nutrient removal in the harvested biomass would make continued tree growing unsustainable unless costly fertilization were applied (Fearnside and Rankin 1980; 1982).

Having invested enormous sums reportedly exceeding one billion dollars in land development and installation of a pulp mill towed from Japan on barges, Ludwig sold the Jari project at a huge financial loss to a Brazilian consortium in the early 1980s. Many mistakes in technology were made when Jari began. Yet

At Brazil's Jari Florestal, thousands of hectares of natural forest were removed to make room for pulpwood plantations. This is a plantation of 2-year old *Gmelina arborea*. *(Photo courtesy of C.B. Davey.)*

visitors to the project were impressed with the imagination, innovativeness, and flexibility with which problems were addressed and, in many cases, solved (Kelly and London 1983; Hornick et al. 1984).

The Jari project epitomizes the kind of undertaking for which financial, environmental, political, and psychological criteria must enter the debate on appropriateness. Was Jari a colossal failure as the news media claimed, or was the sale forced by Ludwig's extreme secrecy and the political and bureaucratic problems this caused in Brazil? Was Ludwig a mad eccentric, or an exceptional visionary of what massive enterprise can do to transform a poor and sparsely populated region? Is the Jari project another hurried and failed Amazon "experiment" on a mammoth scale, or could the developing world use another 50 entrepreneurs with the energy and zeal of Daniel Ludwig? The symbolic value of the Jari project cannot be overstated, and questions on its appropriateness are bound to be asked long into the future.

State Corporations   Public enterprises, particularly state corporations, are a significant component of forest industries in many countries. Although most characteristic of socialist systems, the state corporation also is important elsewhere. A substantial share of logging in India and other regions of South Asia is by government companies. Mexico's newsprint enterprises are entirely in government hands, as is virtually all pulp and paper production in Bangladesh. Presently or in the recent past, state-owned companies comprise the largest sawmilling enterprises in small economies like Gambia and Guyana. These are isolated examples, since a systematic inventory of the world's forest industries does not exist.

The rationale for state corporations mixes economic arguments with political ideology. Private markets may not be able to raise the funding required for large and capital-intensive projects like pulp and paper plants, meaning that it is left to the government to form a state enterprise. Moreover, it is sometimes claimed that state corporations are better positioned than private capitalists to close the gap between social and market costs of production. This is because the state corporation has more reason to regard the profit motive as just one among many management objectives.

Regarding ideology, state corporations have been used to avoid the unwanted dominance of foreign capital, thus extending state power in place of transnational power. Historically, socialist thought emphasizes the ownership and management of a country's basic large-scale production units. More generally, public ownership and control of key sectors and enterprises is a political means to mitigate the concentration of private wealth (Lal 1980).

Typical problems which arise in state ownership of enterprises are economic dislocations caused by monopoly power and other insulation from market signals. On the one hand, a state corporation may not have to be financially profitable if other national objectives are being promoted. On the other, a state corporation cannot be allowed to bankrupt a country through waste and ineffective management.

Efficiency issues are illustrated in Blandon's (1983) account of logging industries in the USSR. At the time of analysis, state logging companies emphasized physical targets (i.e., production measured in cubic meters) rather than monetary values. This led to questionable timber harvesting practices. So as not to be penalized for falling short of production goals, logging managers tended to conceal true production capacity. Economic models to compare costs of alternative logging systems were flawed by theoretical problems in accounting for cost of capital. The fact that administrative "price lists" for timber changed only infrequently made logging unprofitable, discouraged the harvesting of small-sized timber, led to shipping of logs over unnecessarily long distances, and perpetuated the expansion of extensive logging. Together, these many problems with the planning and price system conspired to produce disappointing logging productivity.

The pulp and paper industries of Bangladesh furnish another example of difficulties which can arise with state-owned enterprises (Douglas 1983). A large state conglomerate owns and manages the handful of companies which produce pulp, newsprint, and other paper. A study in the early 1980s showed heavy dependence on foreign imports, scarcity and high costs of both wood and non-wood raw materials, limited domestic demand for the final products, and export sales at prices below production costs. Despite emphasis on forest industrialization for export, import value exceeded export value by wide margins even after many years of operation. Foreign exchange losses were enormous, and the pulp and paper companies were high on the list of top money losers in the Bangladesh economy. Inappropriateness was ascribed to mistaken government perceptions that large and capital-intensive forest industries could be successful in Bangladesh, and inability or unwillingness to retreat from this position once investments were committed.

Strategies to Promote Appropriateness

As indicated by the preceding accounts, small private enterprises, large private enterprises, and state corporations offer certain theoretical advantages accompanied by troublesome real-world problems. Analysis of these issues in the forest industries has been extremely restricted. The many criteria of appropriateness often are competing and contradictory. The cross-country view is weak, and observations are clouded by ideological and emotional biases. The discussion of what works and what does not is hampered by gaping holes in information. Genuine progress requires broader strategies. Two such strategies are reform of economic policies, and encouragement of an expanded array of technologies.

Economic Policies   The wide range of achievements in forest industries among countries not too different in production technologies and forest endowments suggests that economic policies are critical in explaining some of the differences. These policies influence the scale and location of enterprises; the relative sizes and compositions of "traditional" and "modern" subsectors; the prices of timber, wood products, and their substitutes; and barriers to entry by new enterprises.

As for almost all types of industries, economic policies pertinent to forest industries tend to fall into two main classes. First are national and sectoral policies affecting the prices at which enterprises buy and sell goods and services. Taxes, subsidies, and price controls are among the conventional instruments. Second are indirect controls such as licensing of firms, public ownership of forests and processing plants, regulation of timber cutting and reforestation, regulation of imports and exports, and other stipulations regarding the conditions under which individual industries and enterprises are sanctioned to operate (Cody et al. 1980).

These policy options are numerous, complex, and have consequences often poorly understood in the forestry sector. Problems begin with timber pricing. Publicly-owned timber has been underpriced in a substantial number of countries, both developing and industrialized. This is a main impediment to rational forest use, and a leading explanation for the existence of socially inefficient forest industries.

Obstacles in the way of revised timber pricing include pressures by vested business interests to postpone reforms, political commitments to provide timber to dependent industries, lack of forest valuation frameworks and data to apply them, and overall administrative weaknesses (Repetto and Gillis 1988). Thus impediments are simultaneously political, conceptual, and operational. Still, reform of timber pricing is a necessary if not sufficient condition for the rationalization of forest industries in terms of their composition, location, and environmental impacts. Here is a worldwide challenge in both temperate and tropical regions, and in both socialist and market economies.

Revision of timber pricing is just one among many potential economic shifts. Others include (1) transferring wood-processing plants, logging companies, and other commercial undertakings from government to private management; (2) phasing out government marketing boards which administer prices and quotas for forest products, including products which are imported and exported; (3) allowing market forces rather than government regulations to determine the numbers and types of enterprises in the forest industries; (4) encouraging creative use of incentives and payment-by-results in industrial afforestation and reforestation; and (5) insuring that subsidies, taxes, and credits do not distort sectoral investments in peculiar and undesirable ways. Each of these is an argument, directly or indirectly, for allowing market approaches to govern the direction of forest industries development.

In this respect, China engaged in remarkable policy measures during the 1980s to allow the level and structure of timber prices to more closely reflect market demand, and to lay the groundwork for market allocation of timber and wood products (Jinchang et al. 1988). More widely, the social and political turbulence sweeping many of the world's socialist and formerly socialist countries raises important questions about how economic reforms will affect the future structure and performance of their forest industries.

Technology Development and Transfer   In the continuing debate on appropriate technology, some development specialists have called for "intermediate technologies" to better suit the conditions of developing countries. Intermediate technologies represent a middle position in the tradeoff between labor absorption and labor productivity. From the social viewpoint in labor-abundant settings, the aim is to keep capital costs low and employment high without unduly sacrificing productivity. Additionally, new technologies should improve working conditions, enhance safety, contribute to local self-sufficiency, and minimize negative environmental effects.

Do such technologies exist, or are they a romantic but mythical abstraction? If they do not now exist, could they be generated in the future by redirecting science, research, and social policy towards these ends? In forest industries these questions have been insufficiently considered, and answers are correspondingly few and inconclusive.

In the late 1970s, FAO began a program to produce a portfolio of small-scale forest industries for developing countries. Objectives were to adapt modern plant design to labor-intensive, small-scale operations without seriously reducing product quality or financial viability. In this way appropriate technology would be "created" (Leslie and Kyrklund 1980).

The outcome of this inherently difficult proposition can be debated. FAO claimed success in intermediate technologies for wood-based panels, e.g., fiberboard and particleboard. Pulp and paper proved more difficult, with conclusions

The aim of technology policy in labor-abundant settings is to keep capital costs low and employment high without sacrificing productivity. The introduction of chainsaws to replace manual felling reduces employment. How can labor-intensive methods be improved so that jobs are not lost to mechanization? *(Photo courtesy of FAO.)*

qualified to say that there are no standard designs which can be applied everywhere (Leslie and Kyrklund 1980). Also, technology blueprints are but a first and tentative step to be followed by revised engineering specifications, testing of pilot plants, manufacture of modified equipment, and actual diffusion of the new technologies through commercial sales. Because this sequence is long, expensive, and risky, the degree of success or failure cannot be evaluated in the short term.

In the Philippines, the International Labor Office funded a project to determine the range and viability of intermediate technologies in logging, silviculture, and reforestation methods. Activities ranged across both government and private sectors, and included technologies of potential use to large industrial enterprises. The intermediate methods depended on improved hand tools, reorganized working techniques, and other approaches using only modest financial inputs (Ahmed and Laarman 1978).

On an experimental basis, these methods compared very well in cost, working conditions, and environmental impacts with the existing alternatives. However, many obstacles must be overcome for these methods to be accepted on a commercial scale. Main challenges include psychological preferences ("prestige value") associated with equipment-intensive technologies. Substantial investments are required to train and supervise workers, many of whom are employed only temporarily. Also, local workshops sometimes have difficulty making and supplying reliable hand tools and related implements. Manual and intermediate technologies in logging are limited by timber size and terrain conditions. Finally, labor surplus can be a seasonal phenomenon, and resident labor is particularly limited in some forested regions. In light of these constraints, prospects for widespread adoption of intermediate technologies should not be exaggerated.

The governments of a few industrialized countries with extensive experience in technology development show strong interest in transferring manual and semi-mechanized methods to developing countries. For example, Sweden's Forest Operations Institute produced a manual of systems, methods, and equipment judged to have possible applications in developing countries. These same technologies had reached peak use in Sweden during the 1950s and 1960s (Skogsarbeten 1983). Finland's handbooks on appropriate technologies are based on the same concept, i.e., that labor-using but technically efficient methods once widespread in Finland might have current application in the developing countries (Kantola and Virtanen 1986; Kantola and Harstela 1988). The premise that countries like Sweden and Finland have older technologies now appropriate in the developing countries should not be accepted uncritically until much more is known about successes and failures in the transfer process.

SYNTHESIS

Production and consumption of wood-based forest products are concentrated in the industrialized economies. The industrialized economies consume over three-fourths of the world's sawnwood, and even higher proportions of its wood-based panels, paper, and paperboard.

Growth in the consumption of wood-based forest products is uneven across different countries and products, and through different time periods. Demand in the industrialized countries for sawnwood, wood-based panels, and wrapping and packaging papers has been slowing due to demographic, economic, and technological factors. This compares with most of the developing countries, where population increase and scarcity of substitutes explain high rates of demand increase for most industrial wood products.

Especially in the industrialized countries, the substitution of non-wood products moderates the consumption of industrial roundwood. Moreover, wood-saving technologies reduce wood inputs in production of newsprint, sawnwood, plywood, and other product lines. Advances in timber harvesting and transportation contain or reduce costs of timber extraction. Development of reconstituted wood-based panels, and of technologies to use short-fiber pulp, expand use of what once had been inferior timber supplies. Intensified forest management through plantation forestry makes it possible to grow industrial wood of desirable qualities in desirable locations. Together, these technological changes help explain why previous forecasts of "timber famines" have not materialized, and why they are unlikely to occur in the future.

In the developing countries, prospects for expanded production and consumption of forest products are less optimistic. Substantial increases in plantation harvests are expected from several tropical and subtropical producers. Yet countries like the Philippines, Ivory Coast, and Costa Rica have only insignificant plantation forests, even as their natural forests have become seriously depleted through deforestation. Amazonia, Indonesia, and several countries of Africa have large expanses of natural forests to be opened for timber production, but will almost certainly face increasing political and social pressures to limit timber cutting. Thus serious questions remain about overall adequacy and specific sources of timber supply in many countries.

The role of forest industries in economic growth is interpreted from the contrasting perspectives of growth theory and dependency theory. Growth theory maintains that forest industries provide a very wide range of products, including those produced and consumed by persons living at a subsistence level. The industries which process wood as a raw material vary greatly in the way they combine logs, labor, and capital investment. This wide range of technologies permits small and technologically simple forest industries to be feasible even where technical skills and capital are scarce. Forest products flow into many sectors of the economy, stimulating economic growth and development well beyond the forested region and sector. The demand for forest products increases as economic growth takes place, thus assuring a continuing place for forests and forest industries in national priorities. Industrialization evolves towards more sophisticated wood processing as regional development advances and consolidates. At a sufficient size, the economy becomes more diverse and increasingly stronger. For example, forest industries in Finland and the southern USA generate impressive economic growth along lines consistent with this framework.

Dependency theory argues that a forested region is a hinterland dominated by an outside metropolis. Contrary to the arguments of diffusion (i.e., "trickle down") in growth theory, the hinterland remains perpetually dependent on outside investors and suppliers. This is not due to purposeful exploitation as an end in itself. Rather, the hinterland remains economically backward as a consequence of greater income accumulation in wood manufacturing and sales than in extraction of timber. Variations on dependency themes have been used to describe forest industries across contexts ranging from regions of Canada and Australia to some of the developing countries.

The competing claims of growth theory and dependency theory cannot be resolved in the abstract. Some individuals are unable to take a detached viewpoint on these issues, meaning that ideologies get in the way of objective appraisals. Also, economic development of forested regions rests on complex variables in resource ownership and geography, market structures, and distribution of political and economic power. These complexities cast doubt on any single doctrine proposing to explain economic contributions of forest industries.

Questions about the development impacts of forest industries lead to defining and promoting "appropriate" enterprises and industries. Complex tradeoffs exist among the many criteria of appropriateness, such as when comparing attributes of small private enterprises, large private enterprises, and state corporations. Various countries have the opportunity to move towards greater appropriateness of forest industries by reforming timber pricing and other economic policies. Some development specialists argue for "creating" appropriate technologies through increased investments to design and promote production technologies especially suitable for the developing countries. Additionally, Sweden and Finland are among the industrialized countries attempting to transfer manual and semi-mechanized methods to developing countries. Most of these efforts date from the 1980s, and it is too early to assess their effectiveness.

ISSUES FOR DISCUSSION AND INVESTIGATION

1 How and why are patterns of wood and paper consumption different in the industrialized countries than in the developing countries?

2 In the forest industries, technological change helps mitigate wood scarcities by reducing wood demand and by expanding timber supplies. (i) What evidence supports this? (ii) How does technological change enter the prognosis on future adequacy or inadequacy of world timber supply? (iii) In what ways does this prognosis not apply uniformly around the world?

3 Compelling intuitive arguments can be made for forest industries in the attack on economic underdevelopment (Westoby 1962). What are they?

4 What are the forward and backward linkages from forest industries? How are they important in the economic growth of a country or subregion?

5 Outline the economic and political dimensions of dependency theory as it pertains to forest industries in some regions.

6 Hayter (1985) observes the presence of considerable foreign ownership in Canada's forest industries. In Hayter's view, this has accelerated investments, provided good access to international markets, and stimulated inflows of managerial and financial inputs. Yet foreign ownership also explains a number of dependency problems. What are they?

7 Jack Westoby was not entirely wrong about the dynamic role of forest industries in economic growth. Yet in light of post-1962 observations, neither was he entirely right. Explain.

8 In interpreting the economic contributions of forest industries, growth theory and dependency theory stand as competing paradigms. (i) What factors account for this contest of perspectives? (ii) Can both paradigms be true simultaneously? Why or why not?

9 The evaluation of appropriateness in forest industries is a complex and multidimensional study in who pays, who benefits, and by how much (Simula 1986, p. 54). (i) Explain. (ii) Do the criteria of appropriateness vary across countries, or are they universal? Explain and defend.

10 Why is the appropriateness of a forest-based enterprise or industry normally framed in terms of tradeoffs?

11 A technological and economic dualism characterizes the forest industries of many countries, separating large and capital-intensive enterprises from those which are smaller and not as "modern" in the use of production methods. How does dualism enter debates on appropriate enterprises and industries?

12 Each of small private enterprises, large private enterprises, and state corporations offers certain theoretical advantages accompanied by troublesome real-world problems. Describe in the context of the world's forest industries.

13 Skeptics maintain that large-scale, capital-intensive forest industries are inappropriate in the context of most developing countries. However, this viewpoint is not universally accepted. (i) Provide arguments for and against "modern" forest industries in the economic growth of developing countries. (ii) From the standpoint of engineering and financial feasibility, what is the evidence that methods of large-scale production can be modified to make them economic on a smaller scale?

REFERENCES

Ahmed, Iftikhar and Jan G. Laarman. 1978. "Technologies for basic needs: The case of Philippine forestry," *International Labor Review* 117(4):491-499.

Anderson, R. S. and W. Huber. 1988. *The Hour of the Fox: Tropical Forests, the World Bank, and the Indigenous People in Central India*. University of Washington Press, Seattle.

Arnold, J. E. M., M. E. Chipeta, and Y. Fisseha. 1987. "The importance of small forest-based processing enterprises in developing countries," *Unasylva* 39(157/158):9–16.

Bergren, Myrtle. 1967. *Tough Timber: The Loggers of British Columbia*, 2nd edition. Progress Books, Toronto, Canada.

Bethel, James S., David G. Briggs, Stanley P. Gessel, Robert G. Lee, and Gerard F. Schreuder. 1982. *The Role of U.S. Multinational Corporations in Commercial Forestry*

Operations of the Tropics. College of Forest Resources, University of Washington, Seattle.

Bilek, Edward M. and Paul V. Ellefson. 1987. *Organizational Arrangements Used by U.S. Wood-Based Companies Involved in Direct Foreign Investment*. University of Minnesota Agricultural Station Bulletin 576—1987, Minneapolis.

Blake, David H. and Robert E. Driscoll. 1977. *The Social and Economic Impacts of Transnational Corporations: Case Studies of the U.S. Paper Industry in Brazil*. Fund for Multinational Education, New York.

Blandon, Peter. 1983. *Soviet Forest Industries*. Westview Press, Boulder, CO.

Bradwin, Edmund W. 1972. *The Bunkhouse Man: A Study of Work and Pay in the Camps of Canada, 1903–1914*. University of Toronto Press, Toronto, Canada.

Browder, John O. 1987. "Brazil's export promotion policy (1980–1984): Impacts on the Amazon's industrial wood sector," *The Journal of Developing Areas* 21:285–304.

Chetty, N.V. Ramachandra. 1985. "Social forestry and forest-based small-scale rural industries," *Indian Forester* 111:678–692.

Cody, John, Helen Hughes, and David Wall (eds.). 1980. *Policies for Industrial Progress in Developing Countries*. Oxford University Press, New York.

Contreras, Arnoldo. 1987. "Transnational corporations in the forest-based sector of developing countries," *Unasylva* 39(157/158):38–52.

Cortes, Hernan. 1986. "Development impact of an integrated forestry industry in Chile," pp. 287–310 in *Appropriate Forest Industries*. Food and Agriculture Organization, FAO Forestry Paper 68, Rome.

Dargavel, John. 1984. "Pulp and paper monopolies in Tasmania," pp. 69–89 in Michael Taylor (ed.), *The Geography of Australian Corporate Power*, Croom Helm Australia, Sydney, Australia.

Douglas, James J. 1983. *A Re-Appraisal of Forestry Development in Developing Countries*. Martinus Nijhoff/Dr. W. Junk Publishers, The Hague, Netherlands.

Drushka, Ken. 1985. *Stumped: The Forest Industry in Transition*. Douglas and McIntyre, Vancouver, Canada.

ECE/FAO (Economic Commission for Europe; Food and Agriculture Organization of the United Nations). 1986. *European Timber Trends and Prospects to the Year 2000 and Beyond*, Vol. I. United Nations, New York.

Ewing, Andrew J. and Raymond Chalk. 1988. *The Forest Industries Sector: An Operational Strategy for Developing Countries*. World Bank Technical Paper 83, Industry and Energy Series, Washington, DC.

FAO (Food and Agriculture Organization of the United Nations). 1986. *Appropriate Forest Industries*. FAO Forestry Paper 68, Rome.

FAO (Food and Agriculture Organization of the United Nations). 1987. *Small-Scale Forest-Based Processing Enterprises*. FAO Forestry Paper 79, Rome.

FAO (Food and Agriculture Organization of the United Nations). 1989. *Yearbook of Forest Products, 1976–1987*. Rome.

Fearnside, Philip M. and Judy M. Rankin 1980. "Jari and development in the Brazilian Amazon," *Interciencia* 5(3):146–156.

Fearnside, Philip M. and Judy M. Rankin 1982. "The new Jari: Risks and prospects of a major Amazonian development," *Interciencia* 7(6):329–339.

Fisseha, Yacob. 1987. "Basic features of rural small-scale forest-based processing enterprises in developing countries," pp. 31–60 in *Small-Scale Forest-Based Processing Enterprises*. Food and Agriculture Organization of the United Nations, FAO Forestry Paper 79, Rome.

Flick, Warren A. and Lawrence D. Teeter. 1988. "Multiplier effects of the southern forest industries," *Forest Products Journal* 38(11/12):69–74.

Frank, Isaiah. 1980. *Foreign Enterprise in Developing Countries*. Johns Hopkins University Press, Baltimore, MD.

Gillis, R. Peter and Thomas R. Roach. 1986. *Lost Initiatives: Canada's Forest Industries, Forest Policy, and Forest Conservation*. Greenwood Press, New York.

Gottsching, Lothar. 1988. "Issues and opportunities in wastepaper recycling," pp. 212–227 in Gerard F. Schreuder (ed.), *Global Issues and Outlook in Pulp and Paper*. University of Washington Press, Seattle.

Gregersen, Hans M. 1973. "The role of forestry in regional economic development: An alternative view," *Journal of Forestry* 71(2):98–99.

Gregersen, Hans M. and Arnoldo H. Contreras. 1975. *U.S. Investment in the Forest-Based Sector in Latin America*. Johns Hopkins University Press, Baltimore, MD.

Haltia, Olli and Markku Simula. 1988. "Linkages of forestry and forest industry in the Finnish economy," *Silva Fennica* 22(4):257–272.

Hayter, Roger. 1985. "The evolution and structure of the Canadian forest product sector: An assessment of the role of foreign ownership and control," *Fennia* 163:439–450.

Hornick, John R., John I. Zerbe, and Jacob L. Whitmore. 1984. "Jari's successes," *Journal of Forestry* 82(11):663–667.

Indonesia Ministry of Forestry. 1990. *Indonesia National Forestry Action Plan, Country Brief*. Government of Indonesia and Food and Agriculture Organization of the United Nations, Jakarta.

Jaakko Pöyry Oy. 1986. "A case history of the Aracruz pulp mill project in Brazil," pp. 341–357 in *Appropriate Forest Industries*. Food and Agriculture Organization of the United Nations, FAO Forestry Paper 68, Rome.

Jacques, Romain and G. Alex Fraser. 1989. "The forest sector's contribution to the Canadian economy," *The Forestry Chronicle* 65:93–96.

Jensen, Vernon H. 1945. *Lumber and Labor*. Farrar and Rinehart, New York.

Jinchang, Li, Kong Fanwen, He Naihui, and Lester Ross. 1988. "Price and policy: The keys to revamping China's forestry resources," pp. 205–245 in Robert Repetto and Malcolm Gillis (eds.), *Public Policies and the Misuse of Forest Resources*. Cambridge University Press, Cambridge.

Johnson, Norman E. 1976. "How susceptible are tropical tree plantations to insect depredations?" pp. 406–414 in *Proceedings of Sixteenth World Congress*, Division 2. International Union of Forest Research Organizations (IUFRO).

Kantola, Mikko and Klaus Virtanen. 1986. *Handbook on Appropriate Technology for Forestry Operations in Developing Countries*, Part I. National Board of Vocational Education, Government of Finland, Helsinki.

Kantola, Mikko and Pertti Harstela. 1988. *Handbook on Appropriate Technology for Forestry Operations in Developing Countries*, Part II. National Board of Vocational Education, Government of Finland, Helsinki.

Kelly, Brian and Mark London. 1983. *Amazon*. Harcourt Brace Jovanovich, New York.

Ketcheson, D. E. 1986. "An overview of Canadian forest and wood products trade," pp. 248–258 in Gerard F. Schreuder (ed.), *World Trade in Forest Products 2*. University of Washington Press, Seattle.

King, K. S. F. 1977. "The political economy of pulp and paper," *Unasylva* 29(117):2–8.

Kromm, David E. 1972. "Limitations on the role of forestry in regional economic development," *Journal of Forestry* 70(10):630–633.

Kuhn, Thomas S. 1970. *The Structure of Scientific Revolutions*, 2nd edition. University of Chicago Press, Chicago.

Laarman, Jan, Klaus Virtanen, and Mike Jurvelius. 1981. *Choice of Technology in Forestry: A Philippine Case Study*. New Day Publishers, Quezon City, Philippines.

Lal, Deepak. 1980. "Public enterprises," pp. 211–234 in John Cody, Helen Hughes, and David Wall (eds.), *Policies for Industrial Progress in Developing Countries*. Oxford University Press, New York.

Lamb, D. 1990. *Exploiting the Tropical Rain Forest: An Account of Pulpwood Logging in Papua New Guinea*. Man and the Biosphere Series, Vol. 3, UNESCO, Paris, France.

Leslie, A. J. 1980. "Logging concessions: How to stop losing money," *Unasylva* 32(129):2–7.

Leslie, A. J. and Borje Kyrklund. 1980. "Small-scale mills for developing countries," *Unasylva* 32(128):13–15.

Lucas, Rex A. 1971. *Minetown, Milltown, Railtown: Life in Canadian Communities of Single Industry*. University of Toronto Press, Toronto, Canada.

Marchak, M. Patricia. 1983. *Green Gold: The Forest Industry in British Columbia*. University of British Columbia Press, Vancouver, Canada.

Palo, Matti. 1988. "Forest-based development theory revisited with a case study of Finland and prospects for developing countries," pp. 13–157 in Matti Palo and Jyrki Salmi (eds.), *Deforestation or Development in the Third World?* (Vol. II). Finnish Forest Research Institute Bulletin 309, Helsinki, Finland.

Picornell, P. M. 1986. "Technology and people at Paper Industries Corporation of the Philippines," pp. 169–179 in *Appropriate Forest Industries*. Food and Agriculture Organization of the United Nations, FAO Forestry Paper 68, Rome.

Prestemon, Jeffrey P. and Jan G. Laarman. 1989. "Should sawnwood be produced with chainsaws? Observations in Ecuador," *Journal of World Forest Resource Management* 4:111–126.

Repetto, Robert and Malcolm Gillis (eds.). 1988. *Public Policies and Misuse of Forest Resources*. Cambridge University Press, Cambridge.

Richards, E. G. (ed.). 1987. *Forestry and Forest Industries: Past and Future*. Martinus Nijhoff Publishers, Dordrecht, Netherlands.

Riihinen, Paivo. 1981. "Forestry and the timber economy in economic development," *Silva Fennica* 15(2):199–207.

Schumacher, E. F. 1973. *Small Is Beautiful: Economics As If People Mattered*. Harper and Row, New York.

Sedjo, Roger A. and Kenneth S. Lyon. 1990. *The Long-Term Adequacy of World Timber Supply*. Resources for the Future, Washington, DC.

Simula, M. 1986. "What is appropriate?" pp. 43–50 in *Appropriate Forest Industries*. Food and Agriculture Organization of the United Nations, FAO Forestry Paper 68, Rome.

Skogsarbeten (Forest Operations Institute of Sweden). 1983. *Swedish Forestry Techniques with Possible Applications in the Third World*. Tryckeri AB, Primo, Oskarshamn, Sweden.

USDA (United States Department of Agriculture) Forest Service. 1988. *The South's Fourth Forest*. Forest Products Report 24, USDA Forest Service, Washington, DC.

Westoby, Jack C. 1962. "Forest industries in the attack on economic underdevelopment," *Unasylva* 16(4):168–201.

Westoby, Jack C. 1978. "Forest industries for socioeconomic development," *Commonwealth Forestry Review* 58(2):107–116.

World Bank. 1989. *Social Indicators of Development 1989*. The Johns Hopkins University Press, Baltimore and London, England.

CHAPTER 5

INTERNATIONAL TRADE OF FOREST PRODUCTS

Timber harvests from some regions of the globe provide industrial roundwood and processed wood products to other regions. Regions poorly endowed with accessible and usable timber often look abroad for provision of logs, sawnwood, wood-based panels, wood chips, pulp, paper, and paperboard. Conversely, regions well endowed in utilizable timber and industrial capacity often supply both domestic and foreign markets. Thus forest products flow from regions where production exceeds domestic consumption ("surplus regions") to where production falls short of domestic consumption ("deficit regions"). These trade flows are governed by market factors, but subject to a wide range of trade restrictions.

At more than US$80 billion annually and growing, trade in forest products represents about three percent of world trade. In the forest industries, international trade has been expanding slightly more rapidly than overall production.

WORLD PATTERNS IN FOREST PRODUCTS TRADE

Although there are hundreds of international trade flows in forest products, most trade flows are towards three high-population regions (Figure 5-1). The first of these is trade within or towards Europe, dominated by exports from the Nordic countries and the USSR to the densely populated countries of western, central, and eastern Europe. The second major trade flow is within North America, mainly a net flow from Canada to the USA. The third is exports from around the Pacific Basin to Japan, China, Taiwan, the Republic of Korea, and other importing countries in East Asia. In addition to international flows of wood products, a number of countries record substantial trade in non-wood products.

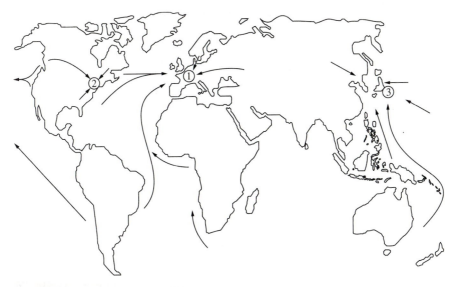

FIGURE 5-1
Major flows of forest products in international trade.

Wood and Paper Products

As shown in Table 5-1, the USA is the world's largest importer of forest products, mainly from Canada. Japan, the second largest importer, draws its imports from numerous suppliers, particularly from various parts of the Pacific Basin. Similarly, the UK imports from a host of suppliers worldwide. Germany relies to a greater extent on European supply sources, but also imports forest products from around the world.

The world's major exporting regions are North America, the Nordic countries, the USSR, and Southeast Asia. The position of top exporter goes to Canada (Table 5-2). Canada's ability to produce large quantities of forest products vastly exceeds

TABLE 5-1
Largest importers of forest products, 1987

	Imports, US$ billion
USA	13.0
Japan	9.9
Germany	8.1
UK	8.1
France	5.0
Italy	3.3
China	3.3

Source: FAO, Yearbook of Forest Products, 1976–1987

TABLE 5-2
Largest exporters of forest products, 1987

	Exports, US$ billion
Canada	15.1
USA	8.2
Sweden	7.3
Germany	4.5
Finland	4.2
USSR	3.0
Malaysia	2.6
Indonesia	2.5

Source: FAO, Yearbook of Forest Products, 1976–1987

the country's domestic consumption, thereby making Canada a region of "wood surplus." Canada is followed by the USA as the world's second leading exporter of forest products. Sweden, Germany, Finland, and the USSR are other major exporters in the temperate zones. Malaysia and Indonesia are the world's largest exporters of tropical hardwoods.

Note that the USA and Germany are leading importers as well as leading exporters. This has multiple explanations. First, countries commonly import different products than they export. Thus the USA imports tropical hardwood plywood from Indonesia, and exports coniferous logs to Japan and China. Germany purchases coniferous sawnwood from the Nordic countries and the USSR, and sells paper and paperboard to France and the Netherlands.

Secondly, countries often export a product from one region while simultaneously importing the same product elsewhere because of location and transportation costs. Transportation routes and costs explain why the USA exports Douglas-fir sawnwood from its Pacific Northwest to Japan and Mexico, but also imports Douglas-fir sawnwood from Canada for consumption in Chicago and Boston.

Table 5-3 shows that the world has only two major regions of net exports in forest products, North America and the USSR. All other regions are modest to large net importers. This pattern is broadly similar to that observed since the 1950s and 1960s. Despite substantial growth in forest products trade, the structure of trade flows remains remarkably stable.

The USA is a large exporter of forest products. Plywood made in the USA is loaded onto a German vessel for shipment to Australia. (Photo courtesy of Forest History Society.)

TABLE 5-3
Trade balances in forest products by world regions, 1987

	Exports	Imports	Net
	US$ billion		
Canada and USA	23.3	14.3	+9.0
USSR	3.0	0.7	+2.3
Oceania	0.9	1.1	−0.2
Latin America and Carribean	1.8	2.1	−0.3
Africa	1.1	2.1	−1.0
Asia (excluding Japan)	7.3	8.9	−1.6
Europe	34.9	41.1	−6.2
Japan	0.9	9.9	−9.0

Source: FAO, Yearbook of Forest Products, 1976–1987

Europe and the USSR   The Nordic countries of Europe—particularly Sweden and Finland—are major exporters of forest products. Most Nordic production goes to other European countries, much of it in the form of pulp and paper. Significant producers of forest products within western and central Europe are Germany, France, Austria, and Switzerland. Much of this production is traded within the region. However, Europe as a whole is a net importer of forest products. Many countries outside the region sell forest products to Europe, among which the most important are Canada and the USA.

The USSR, with its vast forests stretching from Europe across northern Asia, is a major producer and significant exporter of forest products. The USSR has been the dominant supplier of wood products and pulp and paper to eastern Europe (Volkov 1988). The country also exports large volumes of coniferous sawnwood to western Europe, together with coniferous logs to Japan. The USSR's export pattern reflects both its forest endowment and the nature of economic and political ties within what had been the socialist countries of Europe.

In the economic and political framework which emerged after the Second World War, eastern Europe has been a modest producer of forest products, relying instead on imports from the USSR. For this reason, exports of forest products from market economies to eastern Europe have been modest. The major restructuring of economies in both the USSR and eastern Europe is certain to affect former trade patterns, but the dimensions of change are not yet clear.

North America   Within North America are large interregional flows of forest products, some of which are international flows between Canada and the USA. Additionally, both Europe and East Asia are major offshore markets for North America (Stairs and Salinger 1988).

Forest products of western Canada and the USA's Pacific Northwest flow east and south to all regions of the continent. Similarly, eastern North America is a large producer and exporter of forest products. Eastern Canada, the Great Lakes region, and the southern USA are each distinctive regarding mixes of forest products exported interregionally and internationally.

Canada's largest foreign market for forest products is its neighboring country to the south. Regarding the USA's consumption of coniferous sawnwood, Canadian imports rose from 12 percent of the USA's consumption in 1960 to over 30 percent by the 1980s. Moreover, the USA purchases nearly one-half of Canada's pulp exports, and 80 percent of Canada's newsprint exports.

The Pacific Basin   The East Asian countries of Japan, Korea, Taiwan, and China are among the world's large wood-consuming markets. These are "wood deficit" countries, meeting demands for wood and paper through substantial imports (Schreuder 1986).

Just after the Second World War, Japan was a growing market for logs as the country actively engaged in reconstruction. Tropical hardwood logs were imported from Southeast Asia to be processed into plywood and sawnwood. Japan also imported rough sawnwood from the eastern regions of the USSR. As the Japanese economy grew, so did Japanese demand for wood imports. In the early 1960s, log flows to Japan from the USA's Pacific Northwest became significant. Despite opposition from various interests, the USA's log exports to Japan continue to be substantial, with log exports in recent years consistently exceeding US$1 billion (Cox 1988). Although Japan's forests are increasingly capable of providing addi-

An increasing diversity of exports to East Asia includes logs from New Zealand. *(Photo courtesy of New Zealand Forestry Corporation.)*

tional industrial production, environmental considerations and the high costs of extraction explain why imports continue to be Japan's preferred supply source (Nectoux and Kuroda 1989).

By the late 1960s, the rapidly expanding economies of Taiwan and Republic of Korea also became important wood importers. In the early 1980s, China added its demand to that of the others for imports of mainly unprocessed wood. Hence especially since the 1970s and 1980s, large volumes of wood chips and logs—and some sawnwood and plywood—have been moving from the western forests of North America to East Asia. Simultaneously, an increasing diversity of exports to East Asia includes logs from New Zealand, wood chips from Australia, pulp from Chile and Brazil, and plywood from Indonesia. Trade of forest products in the Pacific Basin now resembles a huge wheel, with forest products of various types originating along the rim and flowing along the spokes to East Asia, the importing center.

Other Trade Flows   Some trade flows in forest products are modest on a world scale, but are significant sources of income for individual countries (Ewing and Chalk 1988; Palo 1988). Myanmar (i.e., Burma) and Thailand are the world's principal exporters of teak (*Tectona grandis*), and teak exports constitute more than one-fourth of Myanmar's export earnings. In recent years, Paraguay's exports include substantial flows of sawnwood and veneer to Brazil. Exports of wood pulp from Swaziland, a small country in southern Africa, account for almost half of Swaziland's merchandise exports. Yet the high ranking of forest products among all exports is sometimes explained mainly by undiversified economic structure (e.g., Myanmar and Swaziland), or by temporary export surpluses because of forest clearing (e.g, Paraguay).

As a group, the share of the developing countries in the world's trade of forest products is still small. Between 1970 and the late 1980s, this share rose only modestly to 16 percent of imports and 14 percent of exports (Table 5-4). The developing countries increased their shares of world exports in sawnwood and

TABLE 5-4
Shares of the developing countries in the trade of forest products, 1970 and 1987

	Shares held by the developing countries			
	Imports		Exports	
	1970	1987	1970	1987
		(percent by value)		
Industrial roundwood	10	20	44	34
Sawnwood	10	13	13	18
Wood-based panels	8	17	29	43
Wood pulp	8	13	2	6
Paper and paperboard	19	17	2	4
Total:	13	16	13	14

Source: FAO, Yearbook of Forest Products, various volumes.

especially wood-based panels, but these solidwood products are a smaller part of world trade than pulp and paper. For the developing countries in aggregate, trade surpluses in logs, sawnwood, and wood-based panels are more than offset by trade deficits in pulp, paper, and paperboard.

Moreover, trade deficits appear to be growing. Figure 5-2 shows a higher ratio of imports to exports since 1980 compared with preceding years. Important exceptions are Indonesia, Brazil, and Chile, each of which substantially increased net exports (Figure 5-3). Indonesia phased out log exports in the early 1980s, shifting instead to massive investment in plywood production and exports. Export expansion in Brazil and Chile is explained by large production increases from plantation-grown timber.

Non-Wood Products

Particularly in some developing countries, non-wood products comprise a substantial share of forest-based exports and imports. For centuries, the tapping of gum arabic from *Acacia senegal* has been a traditional source of export earnings in Africa's Sahel. India's non-wood forest products provide over half of that country's exports from forestry (Gupta and Guleria 1982). The forestry statistics of Thailand show an active trade in bamboo canes, fresh bamboo shoots, wood tar, various kinds of bark, charcoal, roots, medicinal plants and spices, gums and

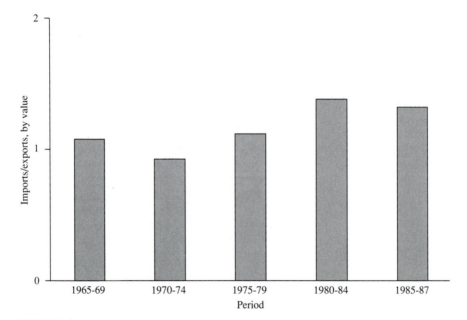

FIGURE 5-2
Ratio of imports to exports of forest products in the developing countries. *(Source: FAO, Yearbook of Forest Products, various volumes.)*

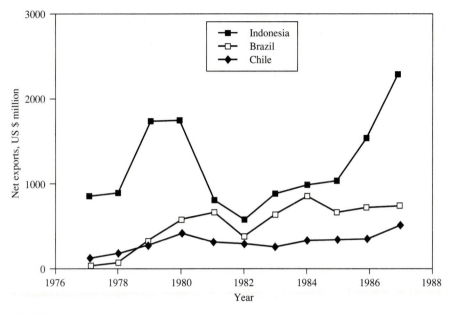

FIGURE 5-3
Net exports of forest products from Indonesia, Brazil, and Chile. *(Source: FAO, Yearbook of Forest Products, 1976-1987.)*

oils, orchids, live animals, reptile skins, birds' feathers, edible birds' nests, lac, and honey (DeBeer and McDermott 1989). Because of underreporting, the traded volumes and values of non-wood forest products typically are larger than shown by official statistics.

In Southeast Asia, rattan is by far the leading non-wood forest product entering international trade. Rattans are climbing palms, of which 20–25 of approximately 600 species are used for furniture, weaving, baskets, mats, and handicrafts. In 1987, Indonesia exported about US$150 million of raw and semi-processed rattan, and an additional US$60 million in processed products. This compares with less than US$15 million only ten years earlier (Priasukmana 1988). World markets for rattan products have grown rapidly since the 1970s, with annual exports of finished rattan products approaching US$3 billion by the late 1980s.

In the past, the main rattan producers—Indonesia, Malaysia, the Philippines, and Thailand—exported raw and semi-processed rattan canes to Taiwan, Hong Kong, and Singapore for manufacture into finished products. Increasingly, the producer countries are attempting to limit exports of raw canes in order to encourage the manufacture of rattan domestically. Moreover, depletion pressures on wild sources of rattan obligate Thailand and the Philippines, once major exporters of rattan canes, to turn to imports in order to support their furniture industries (DeBeer and McDermott 1989).

DETERMINANTS OF TRADE FLOWS

What determines the direction of trade among countries? The broad patterns of international trade, including trade of forest products, reflect differences in production efficiencies from country to country (Kallio et al. 1987). The West African countries of Gabon and Cameroon produce and export logs to the world. Finland and Sweden produce and export paper. In light of current industrial efficiencies, this division provides more forest products for everyone than if Gabon and Cameroon exported paper, and Finland and Sweden exported logs. More generally, countries export goods and services which they produce at low cost, trading them for imports of goods and services they produce less efficiently. In the pure theory of trade, this provides gains for all trading partners.

A Theory of Trade

The Heckscher-Ohlin theory, named after the two Swedish economists who developed the theory in the 1920s, explains why a country has a comparative advantage in producing some goods and services but not others. Their theory maintains that a country's trading pattern reflects its resource base, broadly defined. In this view a country has a comparative advantage in the production of goods and services requiring major inputs of those resources with which the country is well-endowed. The endowment of productive resources includes labor, capital, and natural resources—and important subcategories within each of these broad divisions. Taking the Heckscher-Ohlin view, a country with substantial stocks of timber is likely to have a comparative advantage in the production of industrial roundwood, and thus be a roundwood exporter. Conversely, countries with limited timber are likely to be at a comparative disadvantage in roundwood production, and thus be roundwood importers.

Countries with large populations in relation to other resources are expected to have a comparative advantage in producing labor-intensive goods, e.g., handmade furniture. Other countries may have a comparative advantage in the production of roundwood by virtue of their forest endowments, but may lack the labor, skills, and capital to allow them a comparative advantage in wood processing. Many of the industrialized countries are well-endowed with management talent and investment capital, implying that their comparative advantage lies with aspects of forestry and forest industries requiring those inputs.

Various realities modify the basic Heckscher-Ohlin model. For example, the USA is well endowed with timber and is the world's largest producer of forest products. Yet the USA remains a huge importer of forest products. The USA's large domestic market consumes more forest products than the USA produces domestically. This illustrates why the simple view of comparative advantage must be modified to recognize production levels in relation to domestic demand. A country is an exporter only if it generates a surplus above its own consumption.

Forest Resources and Comparative Advantage

From a Heckscher-Ohlin perspective, a number of different types of forest resources provide comparative advantage in production and trade of forest products. Many export flows originate with old-growth timber, characterized by high commodity values per tree in relation to costs of logging, processing, and transportation. Other regions are favored by rapid and abundant natural regeneration of forest cover, so that their comparative advantage lies in the extent and productivity of second-growth forests. Still a third type of comparative advantage lies with regions able to practice intensified management of forest plantations.

Historically, access to appropriate sources of timber offered countries comparative advantage in shipbuilding, and therefore also in exploration, trade, and warfare. The existence of quality old-growth forests stimulated trade as far back as the cedars of Lebanon, providing exports to Egypt several thousand years ago. To this day, most exports of roundwood and forest products from western North America, the USSR, West Africa, Indonesia, and many other regions derive from

Most exports of roundwood and forest products from western North America derive from old-growth forests. *(Photo courtesy of Forest History Society.)*

old-growth forests. The possession of old-growth forests alone, however, is not sufficient. They must be of desired species and qualities, accessible at reasonable cost, well-located with respect to markets, and not set aside as protection forests excluded from logging.

In other regions, comparative advantage lies with successful forest regeneration. Hence in eastern and southeastern North America, forest products derive mainly from timber harvested in second-growth forests. Many of these forests are found on lands that were once under grazing and cropping but were later abandoned because of low agricultural productivity. As noted previously, a similar land-use shift has been occurring in various regions of Europe, especially regions which currently are net exporters of forest products.

The third variation of comparative advantage in forest resources occurs where conditions are right for highly productive forest plantations. Plantations allow for immediate regeneration, control of species and location, introduction of improved genetic stock, and consequent high growth rates. Necessary but not sufficient conditions for plantations are favorable soils, precipitation, and climate. These ecological factors must be complemented by low-cost access and transportation, minimal competition from alternative land uses, and continuity of plantation management from establishment through maturity. Just as importantly, plantations increasingly are required to meet social tests of environmental acceptability and harmonization within the landscape.

Brazil is one of the "emerging regions" in world timber supply. These 5-year old eucalypts at Aracruz Florestal exhibit very fast biological growth and high productivity per hectare. *(Photo courtesy of William Dvorak.)*

Regions which to date have exhibited comparative advantage in plantation forestry include the southern USA, New Zealand, central Chile, southern and central Brazil, regions of southern Africa, and regions of Spain and Portugal. As noted previously, many of these are "emerging regions" which never before were important in world timber supply, but which promise to compete very successfully because of fast biological growth and high productivity per hectare (Sedjo 1983; Stier 1990).

Comparative Advantage in Wood Processing

A region's strengths in growing and harvesting timber, rattan canes, and other raw materials do not necessarily imply comparative advantage in industrial processing. Comparative advantage in processing depends on efficient use of additional capital, labor, technology, energy, entrepreneurial talent, and other inputs. Secondary and tertiary uses of sawnwood and rattan for furniture—and pulp for paper and paperboard—require efficiencies in still other facets of processing and marketing.

This is demonstrated in Table 5-5, which ranks countries according to observed comparative advantage in different groupings of forest products. Malaysia, the Ivory Coast, Gabon, Papua New Guinea, and the Republic of Congo rank high for comparative advantage in trade of roundwood. The ranking changes radically for manufactured products like paper, where comparative advantage belongs to Finland, Sweden, Canada, Norway, and Austria.

In general, the availability of low-cost forest resources tends to confer a comparative advantage in the early stages of processing. This is reflected in the large-scale production and export of sawnwood and pulp from regions which indeed produce most of the world's industrial roundwood. Major examples are interregional and international exports of sawnwood and pulp from western Canada, the Nordic countries, the USSR, the southern USA, and the plantation regions of the tropics and subtropics.

Yet ready availability of low-cost wood does not guarantee a pronounced advantage in the international market. Table 5-6 shows only a small cost differential between Chile and Sweden in exporting kraft pulp to western Europe, even though wood costs are US$61 in Chile and US$189 in Sweden.

Physical location close to the forest or the market is not always necessary to obtain a comparative advantage, even in primary processing. A country may be so effective in processing that it can import the raw material, process it domestically, and export at a profit. An example is the Republic of Korea, which during the 1960s and 1970s imported tropical hardwood logs from the Philippines, Malaysia, and Indonesia. These logs were processed into plywood and exported extensively to buyers such as Japan and the USA.

The basis of Korea's comparative advantage in producing tropical hardwood plywood was not its forest endowment, since the country has no domestic tropical timber. Rather, it was an efficient labor force and favorable transport rates for ocean shipping with respect to both log suppliers and plywood markets. This made international transportation costs low, despite long distances.

TABLE 5-5

Index of observed comparative advantage in trade of forest products, by product groups

	Index of net trade per 1,000 US$ of GDP, Early 1980s				
	Comparative advantage (Highest 5 countries)			**Comparative disadvantage (Lowest 5 countries)**	
Roundwood:	Malaysia	42.3		Republic of Korea	−7.7
	Ivory Coast	34.1		China	−3.9
	Gabon	33.2		Japan	−3.5
	Papua New Guinea	29.4		Singapore	−3.0
	Republic of Congo	10.5		Finland	−2.4
Sawnwood:	Malaysia	17.3		Egypt	−9.0
	Swaziland	16.1		Trinidad and Tobago	−8.1
	Finland	13.6		Tunisia	−6.7
	Sweden	11.9		Cuba	−5.7
	Ivory Coast	11.5		Algeria	−4.6
Wood-based panels:	Republic of Congo	14.2		Hong Kong	−2.8
	Gabon	9.7		Trinidad and Tobago	−2.7
	Singapore	5.9		Kuwait	−2.4
	Finland	5.8		Eqypt	−2.1
	Indonesia	5.8		Saudi Arabia	−2.1
Wood pulp:	Swaziland	99.9		Republic of Korea	−2.5
	Finland	12.2		Netherlands	−1.9
	Sweden	11.6		Italy	−1.8
	Portugal	10.2		Ecuador	−1.8
	Chile	8.3		Germany	−1.8
Paper and paperboard:	Finland	51.6		Hong Kong	−9.5
	Sweden	22.8		Ireland	−8.9
	Canada	12.0		Singapore	−8.8
	Norway	6.1		Ecuador	−7.9
	Austria	5.3		Malaysia	−6.2

Source: Bonnefoi and Buongiorno (1990).

TABLE 5-6

Costs of producing and exporting bleached kraft pulp to western Europe, comparison of Chile and Sweden

	Chile	Sweden
	(US$ per delivered ton) *	
Cost element		
Roundwood (logs)	61	189
Energy	26	10
Chemicals and other materials	78	54
Labor and overhead	39	54
Capital Charges †	109	49
Transport	55	25
Total:	368	381

* Data for 1985 compared at 1985 exchange rates.
† Capital charges include interest and depreciation. Chile's figures are higher because the capacity is relatively newer.
Source: Ewing and Chalk (1988, p. 36)

Japan is another exception to the need for primary processing to be located near the forest raw material. The Japanese wood-processing industries, which initially developed around Japanese timber, today depend to a large degree upon imported logs and wood chips. Japan takes over 40 percent of world imports of hardwood logs, over 50 percent of world imports of coniferous logs, and over 75 percent of world imports of wood chips.

The processing of imported wood in Japan reflects, in part, the unique requirements of Japanese wood consumption. For example, Japanese plywood standards require 3' by 6' panels rather than the 4' by 8' standards of North America. Also, Japanese construction techniques pose special requirements in terms of sizes and visual characteristics of exposed wood surfaces. It may be argued that Japan's unique wood requirements negate some of the comparative advantage otherwise attributed to the world's major exporters of processed wood. An alternative argument is that these major producers have failed to manufacture products which meet Japanese specifications—even if technically and financially feasible—because of reluctance to commit to the Japanese market on a regular and continuing basis.

Exchange Rates

The international trade of goods and services requires the exchange of currencies. For the Japanese to buy logs from the USA requires that the Japanese convert their yen to dollars (i.e., buy dollars) to pay for the logs. To the Japanese log buyers, two prices are important. They are the price of logs, which is quoted in dollars, and the price of dollars in exchange for yen. For example, if the price of 145 yen is US$1, and the price of the USA's logs is $100 per cubic meter, then 1 m^3 of logs costs the Japanese

$$\$100 \times 145 \text{ yen/dollar} = 14,500 \text{ yen}$$

A rise in the price of either the logs or the dollar increases the price that the Japanese pay for logs. At a price of 200 yen for US$1, then 1 m^3 of logs costs the Japanese

$$\$100 \times 200 \text{ yen/dollar} = 20,000 \text{ yen}$$

Finally, if the exchange rate remains at 145 yen per dollar, but the dollar price of logs rises to $137.93, the price to the Japanese is still 20,000 yen because 1 m^3 of logs costs the Japanese

$$\$137.93 \times 145 \text{ yen/dollar} = 20,000 \text{ yen}$$

Similar computations must be carried out for any trade across countries with different currencies. Exchange rates usually are determined by factors that affect the supply and demand of currencies, country by country. These factors include monetary and fiscal policies, which increase or decrease a country's aggregate production and consumption of goods and services. Currencies exchanged in international financial markets are called "hard currencies," and can be bought and sold in major banks. Because of their importance in world trade of forest products, the upward and downward movements of the Japanese yen, the Canadian dollar, and the USA dollar have significant implications for the volumes and directions of forest products trade in the Pacific Basin and elsewhere.

In some cases, exchange rates are controlled by governments rather than by market forces. Governments impose exchange controls to ration the availability of foreign exchange, and thereby influence trading decisions. Countries with "soft currencies" find that their currencies are not traded everywhere, and often are worthless outside of the country. Socialist economies typically use an exchange control system, as do some of the capitalist developing countries. To import requires a government allocation of adequate foreign currencies to undertake the transaction. A variant of this system is found in some countries that have multiple exchange rates, in which different rates apply for different sectors or for different products.

An example is the Cooperative Republic of Guyana, which exports greenheart (*Ocotea rodiaei*) and other forest products to the UK, USA, and other markets. Guyana's exporters of forest products are allowed to retain 15–50 percent of their hard currency earnings, with the retained portion determined in negotiations between the government and individual producers. Retained hard currencies are usable only for approved business purposes, and the time required for approval often causes costly delays. This has made it difficult for the sawmills and other producers to cover large export orders, and to import the machinery and spare parts they need for continued production and exports. Other Guyanese industries retain 50 percent of their hard currencies across the board, and experience fewer complications.

TRADE RESTRICTIONS

Although comparative advantage explains general patterns in the international trade of forest products, these patterns are distorted by trade barriers (Bourke 1988; Wiseman 1990). Trade barriers take the form of tariffs, quotas, and other controls limiting the type or volume of forest products that would be traded in a free market. Trade restrictions are imposed for various reasons, especially by the desire to protect producers of forest products in the domestic economy from foreign competition.

Since the end of the Second World War, international tariff negotiations have attempted to reduce trade restrictions across a wide range of products and services, including forest products. Tariffs have decreased as a result of these negotiations. However, decreasing tariffs have been replaced by a growing number of nontariff barriers, which maintain protection in different forms.

Tariffs

A tariff is a tax imposed upon an imported good, increasing its price. An exporter's product enters the importing country at a higher price than without the tariff. In this way the tariff restricts market competitiveness, and sometimes excludes imports entirely. Because of the tariff, domestic producers capture some of the market otherwise held by foreign suppliers. To the extent that domestic producers are less efficient than their international competitors, the tariff means that product buyers face higher prices. Hence the overall effect of a typical tariff is to protect producers but injure consumers in the country imposing the tariff.

Table 5-7 illustrates tariff rates for three major traders of forest products. Tariffs on raw materials generally are low, with tariffs rising as the level of processing increases. Importing countries rarely apply tariffs or other restrictions on round-wood. Moreover, tariffs usually are absent or modest on sawnwood, pulp, and other products representing the first stages of processing. Tariff rates normally begin to rise for products like plywood and various categories of paper and paperboard. This phenomenon of graduated tariffs is called tariff escalation, and is a deliberate policy to encourage the import of products which add income and employment to the domestic economy through further processing. As a corollary, tariff escalation is a deliberate policy to discourage the import of finished products which would displace domestic production, causing opposite effects for income and employment.

While tariffs of under 20 percent may seem low, they can have a pronounced impact on market competition. This is because the nominal amount of a tariff sometimes greatly understates effective protection. For example, Japan's tariffs are zero on imports of coniferous logs, but 15 percent on imports of coniferous plywood. Suppose that Japan faces import prices of US$100 per cubic meter for logs, and US$200 per cubic meter (roundwood equivalent) for plywood made from similar logs. The nominal tariff of 15 percent adds US$30 to the price of imported plywood, giving Japanese plywood producers effective protection of 30 percent. This is because Japanese costs of plywood production could rise by US$30 (above the log price of US$100) before Japan finds it cheaper to import plywood rather than logs. Actual estimates from Japan, the USA, and western

TABLE 5-7
Tariffs on selected forest products in three principal importing regions

	Japan	USA	European Community
Coniferous roundwood	Free	Free	Free
Coniferous sawnwood	6.0	Free	3.8–4.9
Particleboard	12.0	4.0	5.0
Fiberboard	6.5	3.0	6.5
Coniferous plywood	15.0	20.0	10.0

Sources: Bourke (1988); tariff schedules, respective regions.

Europe indicate that effective protection is almost always higher than nominal tariffs (Bourke 1988).

Nontariff Barriers

In addition to tariffs, a host of trade restrictions are grouped together in the category of nontariff barriers. Among them are quotas setting limits on the total amount of a product which can be imported or exported. Other nontariff barriers include quality standards for imports, government licensing to control numbers and composition of importers and exporters, government policies to purchase from certain suppliers and no others, discriminatory treatment of foreign shipping companies, subsidies to domestic producers, and special fees and taxes (other than tariffs) applying to imports and exports. These nontariff barriers are extensive in the international trade of forest products, although many of them are subtle and difficult to detect.

Export Restrictions   One of the most important trade restrictions in forest products is a limit on the export of raw materials. The usual rationale is to maintain low prices and sufficient volumes of the raw material to favor domestic processing industries. A related restriction is imposed through government control of the types and grades of raw materials that may be harvested. Control of harvests is tantamount to a control of domestic production, and thus indirectly a control of exports.

Although it continues to be one of the world's largest log exporters, the USA maintains partial restrictions on the export of coniferous logs from the western states. Canada bans the export of logs from government lands, but this policy can be modified during periods of domestic "surplus."

Among the developing countries, commitment to restrict log exports has spread and intensified over the last 10–15 years, but with important variations across regions. The Philippines tried to limit log exports during the 1970s, but achieved only limited success at first due to the high profitability of log smuggling. Indonesia phased out log exports during 1980–1985 to foster the establishment of its domestic plywood industry. Thus Indonesia's log exports were about 20 million cubic meters annually during the late 1970s, declining to less than one million cubic meters presently. Peninsular Malaysia prohibits log exports, even as East Malaysia (Sabah and Sarawak) allows them. Although Chile is an exception, most of Latin America restricts log exports. This compares with Africa, where restrictions on log exports are the exception rather than the rule.

Product Standards   Differing standards for wood products from one country to another may constitute trade barriers. This issue arises within North America in the trade of plywood between the USA and Canada. Knot size is smaller in Canada's spruce plywood than in the USA's southern pine plywood. Canadian housing standards limit the size of knots in plywood acceptable for construction on the grounds that plywood with large knots lacks sufficient strength. The impo-

For many years the Philippines tried to limit log exports, eventually managing to retain most logs for processing. *(Photo courtesy of World Bank)*

sition of a small-knot standard by the Canadians would effectively preclude the use of much of the USA's plywood in the Canadian market. This example raises the difficult question of the extent to which standards are used as a policy device to obtain trade protection, versus the extent to which standards are truly essential for product performance.

Another facet of the standards question relates to product delivery. An interesting case is found in the Japanese newsprint industry. North American newsprint exporters have found it difficult to convince Japanese newspaper firms to use the imported product. This is despite the fact that North American newsprint is of comparable quality and is less expensive than Japanese newsprint. However, Japanese resistance to imports is explained less by quality and price than by inventories and delivery services. North American newspaper companies maintain several months of newsprint in their inventories. Responsibility for the next day's newsprint resides within the newspaper companies. In contrast, Japanese newspaper companies typically keep only a day or two of newsprint inventory, relying on "just in time" delivery of newsprint from their suppliers. The responsibility to provide newsprint on a daily basis rests with these suppliers. That is, Japanese newspaper companies are buying not only newsprint, but also inventory services and punctual delivery. This explains much about why North American newsprint exporters have been unable to sell much newsprint in Japan.

In the late 1980s, Australia's Building Workers Industrial Union and Timber Workers Union banned the use of imported tropical woods from building sites in Sydney and Melbourne. The unions maintained that the strength of imported hardwood plywood is below levels considered safe by Australian authorities. The

Australian government opposed the ban on grounds that it violates international conventions of fair trade, asking for clarification of the issues through an independent study (USDA Foreign Agricultural Service 1990).

Other Nontariff Barriers   The preceding illustrations suggest that it can be difficult to separate product standards and market features from nontariff barriers which impede international trade. Negotiations over nontariff barriers often take on contentious tones because of these differences in interpretation. Other examples of real or alleged nontariff barriers include the following:

• Citing the possibility that oak wilt would spread to Europe, the European Community requires that imported oak logs and sawnwood be debarked and fumigated. The USA's oak exporters regarded these measures as unnecessary. During the 1980s, Europe restricted oak imports from North America until an agreement could be reached on fumigation policy and procedures. The European Community later expanded its phytosanitary standards on imported wood to cover several other temperate species.

• Japanese agricultural standards require that imported sawnwood be inspected in Japan rather than prior to shipment. This necessitates costly unbundling and re-sorting.

• Taiwan and the Republic of Korea prohibit foreign shipping companies from conducting their own unloading, warehousing, trucking, and marketing.

• Honduras, Guyana, and Gabon are among the countries which have used marketing boards as exclusive exporters of forest products. Bureaucratic inefficiencies and lack of export competition can present serious bottlenecks. Similarly, wood imports in Venezuela require a permit from the Ministry of Agriculture.

Finally, trade inertia results when political, cultural, and historical alignments modify purely market forces (Kornai 1987). Traders are free to find the most profitable transactions possible, but in practice confine themselves to known and proven channels of information and commerce. This is because trade typically evolves from contacts and agreements established only over long periods of time. The search for new trading partners may entail more cost and effort than expected benefits.

The importance of political and historical ties is illustrated in the origins of forest products imported by countries and territories of the Caribbean Basin. Thus Puerto Rico imports a large share of its forest products from the USA, while Cuba imports from the USSR. Guadeloupe and Martinique purchase forest products from France, while the country of Trinidad and Tobago imports heavily from Commonwealth partners like Canada and Guyana. None of these markets is closed to competition, but the patterns suggest that much more than market price explains trade flows.

Complexities of Trade Restrictions

The economic and political consequences of trade restrictions are highly complex, and special interests compete for attention and favor. This is illustrated by reviewing the debates on Canada's sawnwood exports to the USA, the USA's log exports to East Asia, and proposals to boycott imports of tropical hardwoods.

Canadian Sawnwood Exports to the USA   Canada has been a major exporter of coniferous sawnwood to the USA for many decades. By the early 1980s, over one-third of the coniferous sawnwood consumed by the USA consisted of imports from Canada. The USA's sawnwood industry, alarmed by the imports and seeking to reduce competition, argued that Canada was selling government timber using administrative prices rather than market prices. The USA's producers charged that this gave an indirect subsidy to Canadian sawmills, and therefore violated international principles of fair trade. Based upon the evidence presented to it, the USA's International Trade Commission ruled against Canada, supporting the claim that Canada's administered prices constituted "unfair" subsidies (Percy and Yoder 1988).

When Canada refused to change its system of timber sales and pricing, the USA imposed an import tax of 15 percent to offset the alleged subsidy. After further negotiations, the Canadians proposed a sawnwood export tax to be levied in Canada if the USA would drop its import tax. Canada's self-imposed tax had the beneficial effect from the Canadian viewpoint of allowing the tax revenues to be retained within Canada. The arrangement was acceptable to sawnwood producers in the USA, since the tax barrier afforded them sufficient price protection. Ultimately, most Canadian provinces modified their methods of timber pricing to approximate market pricing, and the export tax was removed.

The example illustrates the complicated politics of trade disputes. They began with allegations of export subsidy, the subsequent imposition of an import tax, and the substitution of an export tax for the import tax. Finally, the pricing system was modified to eliminate the alleged subsidy.

Log Exports from the USA   The USA accounts for over one-fourth of world exports of coniferous sawlogs and veneer logs. The major offshore markets for these logs are in East Asia, primarily Japan but also China and the Republic of Korea. In the early 1960s, the USA's log exports to Japan began as an expedient means to salvage large volumes of timber blown down by a violent storm in the Pacific Northwest. As log exports increased rapidly thereafter, domestic wood processors had to compete with Asian buyers for adequate supplies of logs. Moreover, sawmills, plywood plants, and other processors found it politically useful to argue that the export of logs was an export of employment.

More recently, the issue of log exports has assumed environmental dimensions. Environmentalists contend that a reduction in log exports helps decrease timber cutting in the Pacific Northwest's old-growth forests. This makes it easier to save the habitat of the spotted owl, and to achieve other environmental benefits because of old-growth protection.

In response to these and other political pressures, a law was passed in 1990 that permanently prohibits the export of coniferous logs from lands of the federal government west of the 100th meridian. This followed a series of temporary restrictions dating from 1969. The 1990 law also limits the volume of logs which can be exported from lands of state governments, e.g., the state of Washington cannot export more than 25 percent of its harvest.

The United States Forest Service estimates that the new law will reduce log exports by about 15–20 percent. Criticisms of the restrictions are of two types, economic and environmental. Decreased log exports from the Pacific Northwest lead to short-term and perhaps permanent employment losses in logging, shipping, and other facets of international commerce within the region. A second concern is that Asian log buyers will adjust to diminished exports by increasing their log purchases from other sources, including tropical sources. In this scenario, environmental gains for the USA are purchased at the price of environmental disturbances in other countries. Herein lies a dilemma, since no one wants to be accused of exporting deforestation.

Boycott of Tropical Hardwoods   Beginning in the late 1980s, environmentalists in Europe, North America, and elsewhere have proposed either consumer boycotts or official government restrictions on imports of tropical woods. Their thesis is that tropical deforestation can be slowed by reducing the international demand for tropical wood products. The argument continues that reduction of international demand removes an important cause of forest cutting in tropical regions. This view has been challenged on several grounds (Vincent 1990):

• Only a modest proportion of wood removed from tropical forests is exported. For the aggregate of developing countries, some 60 percent of industrial round-wood is converted into products consumed domestically. Secondly, four of every five cubic meters of roundwood are consumed for fuel and other nonindustrial purposes. Thus even though a large industrialized country like the USA is a major importer of tropical hardwoods, the USA's imports account for only a very small share (about two percent) of total wood removals in the tropics.

• A boycott of imported tropical woods can do little to address shifting agriculture, inadequate forest policies, and other fundamental problems explaining deforestation. Logging is but one of several interrelated deforestation agents which vary in importance from one local region to another.

• Most tropical forests are located in developing countries struggling with debt and other serious economic constraints. Boycotting their products adds to their economic difficulties. This continues and possibly accelerates pressures for forest cutting.

• Unless otherwise protected, tropical forests must have commercial value to compete with alternative land uses if they are to remain as forests. Because a boycott depresses prices of marketable forest products, forests might experience even greater pressures for conversion to non-forest uses.

• Restrictions against tropical woods run counter to the general philosophy that industrialized countries should help developing countries by buying their products.

Because of these limitations, several alternatives to boycotts have been suggested. One is that a "stamp of approval" be assigned to products from tropical forests which are managed in sustainable ways. Although this idea originated with environmentalists in the importing countries, it is strongly supported by certain exporters, importers, and distributors as a marketing aid. Properly administered, the labeling approach allows consumers to purchase products which are certified as coming from sustainable sources. While labeling of tropical imports as sustainable faces difficult challenges of definition and verification, it puts a positive emphasis on incentives for forest management (Vincent 1990).

Trade Restrictions and Economic Welfare

Views on the role of international trade in economic development divide into two main schools of thought. The first emphasizes the advantages of free trade following the principles of comparative advantage. The second finds it reasonable to apply trade restrictions as a means to initiate industrialization and diversify economies, particularly in developing countries. Both groups agree that trade barriers significantly affect the quantity, direction, and composition of goods and services which enter international trade.

Economists adhering to the classical doctrine of benefits from free trade take the view that unrestricted international trade promotes economic development, and therefore that trade barriers hurt the development process. Economic efficiency at both national and global levels is promoted when countries open themselves to international competition, so that countries specialize along production lines which use their comparative advantages. This expands markets, lowering costs and prices for all countries.

An outward-looking strategy in the production and trade of forest products is characteristic of many world regions which have done well in using forest industries for economic growth. Examples drawn upon in this book include Sweden, Finland, and New Zealand. To this can be added Brazil and Chile among the developing countries, together with other emerging regions producing plantation-grown products for world consumption. It was noted that Korea became an important producer and exporter of tropical hardwood, even without a domestic supply of logs. By virtue of their export-led strategies, these producers have been obligated to seek efficiency by world standards. Their development policies for forestry and forest industries require open markets in the rest of the world.

Advocates of open markets point out that policies which interfere with free trade lead to costly inefficiencies. Hence during the first years of Indonesia's restrictions on log exports, a doubling of export revenues from plywood and sawnwood was insufficient to balance huge losses from the drop in log exports (Figure 5-4). Indonesia's plywood exports have grown enormously since the early 1980s, although partly because of continued subsidies and protection. While governments almost always believe that protection for their "infant industries" can be removed as these industries mature, often such industries demand and are granted perpetual protection. This shifts burdens onto other economic sectors, since too many national resources are committed to propping up high-cost producers.

Some governments apply selective export quotas or differential export taxes to influence the composition of their forest industries. This, too, can distort efficiency. For instance, Indonesia imposed a very high export tax on sawnwood in 1990, more than doubling the export price of Indonesian sawnwood. According

Indonesia phased out log exports in the early 1980s. Before the imposition of the export restriction, this front-end loader moved export logs on the beach at the Holtekang forestry area, West Irian. *(Photo courtesy of FAO.)*

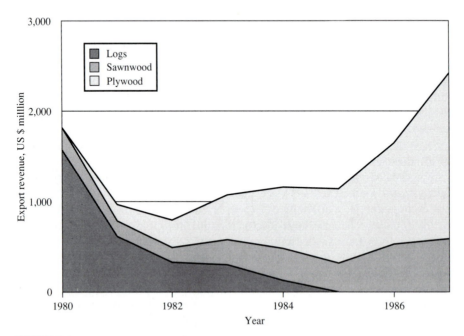

FIGURE 5-4
Changes in Indonesia's export of logs, sawnwood, and plywood since 1980. *(Source: FAO, Yearbook of Forest Products, 1976-1987.)*

to preliminary estimates, the export tax will generate US$100 million per year for the government. Yet the most important effect of the tax is to divert roundwood from sawmills to plywood plants. Plywood plants face less competition for logs as sawmills are forced to close or sharply curtail production. Thus the export tax has winners and losers, with obvious losers including owners and workers of Indonesia's 2,700 sawmills.

In summary, the classical doctrine of free trade maintains that restricting imports and exports has negative or ambiguous consequences for a country's economic health. Most often, arguments to raise trade barriers originate with special interests competing for political favor. Indonesia's export tax on sawnwood illustrates that protection of one type of industry can adversely affect another. As suggested by efforts of the USA's sawnwood producers to hold back competing imports from Canada, trade protection for a country's producers is likely to increase prices paid by that country's consumers. Moreover, the export-led strategies of Finland, Sweden, New Zealand, Chile, and other regions indicate that economic growth from forest industries requires cost competitiveness in relation to other producers.

However, a competing school of thought maintains that free trade may be best for the world in a theoretical sense, but not for some countries or regions individually. These dissenters generally acknowledge the desirability of international production efficiency, but add social and political criteria to the purely economic framework. The dissenting perspective emphasizes equitable income distribution and national self-sufficiency as development priorities. In this view, developing regions legitimately apply trade barriers to attempt to diversify their production, become more self-reliant, and eventually reduce dependency on outside markets. This final objective reflects an assumption that the structure of world trade is not neutral, but distributes gains in favor of the rich at the expense of the poor. This is the alleged problem of an unfavorable "international economic order," loudly vocalized by the developing countries since the 1970s.

In the asymmetrical world seen by these dissenters, the developing countries specialize in the production of primary commodities for export to the industrialized countries. In exchange, they import manufactured products for which prices have been rising rapidly. This is a deterioration in their terms of trade, or a decrease in the weighted prices of exports relative to imports. Thus a developing country might have to export ever larger quantities of logs and rough sawnwood to earn the foreign exchange required to purchase a given amount of manufactured paper from year to year. By remaining a perpetual exporter of raw wood, the developing country cannot reap the benefits of increased employment, skills diffusion, and manufacturing value-added presently enjoyed by the industrialized countries.

A second focus of the dissenters revolves around the question of who owns the investment capital and management skills rewarded through trade. For instance, to what extent do nationals in West Africa gain by the export of logs and veneer to western Europe, given that a large share of this enterprise is in the hands of Europeans? The principal benefits of the trade may accrue to nonnationals who repatriate substantial shares of their earnings back to Europe (Nectoux and Dudley 1987). The trade appears as if income is received by Africans, but this is not entirely true. In short, patterns of income distribution from international trade can be deceptive, particularly in a world of great international mobility of capital and earnings (Todaro 1985).

In conclusion, the desirability of international trade as a growth strategy depends on its linkages with the rest of the economy, and on the level and distribution of the incomes it generates. Different analysts strongly disagree about the actual terms of trade between industrialized and developing countries, given high variability through time and across different commodities and regions (Blake and Walters 1987). Likewise, the important matter of who captures the income from trade requires an understanding of ownership patterns as well as trading patterns. The complexities of international trade rest on economic and political considerations which defy simplistic interpretations according to any single theory or world view.

CHANGING INSTITUTIONS AFFECTING INTERNATIONAL TRADE

Because of international disputes and potential disputes arising over international trade, governments have cooperated to set up a number of institutions to facilitate trade and establish the "rules of the game." These institutions include the General Agreement on Tariffs and Trade, the Canadian-USA Free Trade Agreement, and the common market within the European Community. An institution intended to facilitate the trade of tropical hardwoods is the International Tropical Timber Organization.

The General Agreement on Tariffs and Trade

The General Agreement on Tariffs and Trade (GATT) was part of the machinery devised to restore health to the international economy after the Second World War. During the worldwide economic depression of the 1930s, countries applied tariffs and other trade restrictions to protect their domestic industries and employment. During that period, the application of tariffs by one country would lead a trading partner to retaliate by applying its own tariffs. The result was a dramatic reduction in overall trade, contributing to the severity and duration of the depression.

The GATT was formed to keep those problems from occurring again. A set of rules governs the trade policies of GATT's members, and GATT provides a forum in which international trade disputes can be mediated. An important objective of GATT is to eliminate the selective application of trade restrictions, and to block retaliatory tariff increases (Caves et al. 1990).

Importantly, GATT has organized a series of multilateral trade negotiations to promote trade liberalization, primarily through tariff reductions. As a result of these negotiations, average tariffs in industrialized countries on industrial products declined from over 40 percent in 1947 to about five percent by the late 1980s (Kelly et al. 1988). The "Tokyo Round" of these negotiations concluded in 1979. For the major industrialized countries, tariffs on primary wood products declined from an average of 2.4 percent before the Tokyo Round to 1.7 percent after it. Corresponding figures for secondary wood products were 7.8 and 5.7 percent, respectively (UNIDO 1983).

The Tokyo Round also attempted to address nontariff barriers, although with little success. These issues have carried through to the most recent negotiations which began in 1986, known as the Uruguay Round. The problems of identifying and evaluating nontariff barriers are formidable, making it difficult to assess whether they are increasing or decreasing. For international trade of forest products, a recent partial inventory shows that nontariff barriers are numerous (Bourke 1988, p. 70–73):

• Export controls on volumes and prices of forest products have been used in many countries since the 1970s, and commitment to them has increased greatly in recent years.

• Import quotas and other quantitative import controls are most common in the European Community and in some developing countries. This has limited imports, despite growth in consumption of forest products in these markets.

• The USA and the European Community have made increasing use of official complaints to argue against export subsidies, "dumping" (i.e., exporting at prices below prices in the exporter's domestic market), and other pricing tactics considered unfair under GATT.

• Product standards, import licensing, inspection procedures, and technical and sanitary regulations have become increasingly important sources of disagreement among traders of forest products.

• Export subsidies are defined by GATT as unfair competition, but countries have found subtle and sometimes "invisible" means to subsidize exports, including exports of forest products. These include low-interest loans and tax benefits for exporters, together with government financing of export promotion.

Hence while tariffs on forest products are generally modest and declining, it is the nontariff barriers which may be more constraining to freer trade. In many cases, no single nontariff barrier is a major problem. Rather, it is the combination of many nontariff barriers together which add complexity and costs to the international movement of forest products.

The Canadian-USA Free Trade Agreement

Signed in 1988, the Free Trade Agreement (FTA) is a collection of policies, procedures, and formal guidelines to facilitate mutual trade and investment between Canada and the USA. The FTA is intended to reduce trade barriers, speed dispute resolution, and overcome past practices which interfered with cross-country business relations. The agreement calls for the elimination of all tariffs between the two countries by the year 1999, including tariffs on forest products.

The trade flow of forest products between Canada and the USA is the world's largest. In the late 1980s, the trade balance showed Canada exporting US\$9 billion of forest products to the USA, and the USA exporting US\$0.8 billion

TABLE 5-8

Canada's leading exports of forest products to the USA, 1987

	Canadian exports to the USA	
	As a percent of USA's imports	As a percent of Canada's exports
Coniferous sawnwood	100	83
Wood pulp	85	45
Paper and paperboard	55	68

Source: FAO, Yearbook of Forest Products, 1976–1987

to Canada. Three product groups constituted over 98 percent of Canada's forest products exports to the USA: paper and paperboard, coniferous sawnwood, and wood pulp (Table 5-8). The effect of the FTA is to reduce tariffs on most kinds of paper and paperboard, even though pulp and coniferous sawnwood already move freely (Table 5-9).

TABLE 5-9

Tariffs on forest products traded between Canada and the USA, rates as of January 1989

	Canada	USA
	(percent)	
Solidwood products		
Coniferous sawnwood	Free	Free
Shakes and shingles	Free	20
Wood chips	Free	Free
Wood veneers	Free	Free
Coniferous plywood	15	20
Particleboard	5	4
Waferboard/OSB	4	4
Doors	11.3	7.5
Windows	9.2–12.5	5.1
Manufactured houses	5.1	9.2
Pulp and paper products		
Wood pulp	Free	Free
Newsprint	Free	Free
Uncoated groundwood	Free	Free
Sack kraft (unbleached)	Free	Free
Kraft linerboard	6.5	Free
Kraft papers (bleached)	9.2	2.4
Coated groundwood	2.5	2.5
Writing papers	6.5	2.4
Sanitary tissue	10.2	5.3
Paper sacks	9.2	5.3

Source: Tariff schedules, respective countries.

One analysis predicts that tariff removal will increase the USA's exports of forest products to Canada by US$15 million annually, and Canada's exports to the USA by US$13–23 million annually (Schott and Smith 1988). In relation to the very large volume of current trade, these impacts are small. Likely to be more significant are aspects of the FTA related to investment rules and regulations as they affect location and production decisions about forest industries on both sides of the international border.

The European Community 1992

Initially established in the 1950s, the European Community has expanded to become a twelve-nation group to promote the economic integration of European countries. Members now include the majority of western Europe's largest economies: France, Germany, Italy, Belgium, Luxembourg, the Netherlands, Denmark, Ireland, the UK, Greece, Portugal, and Spain. For many years, members of the European Community have been moving progressively towards liberalized trade among themselves. These measures include the elimination of tariffs among member countries, the establishment of a common tariff schedule for imports from nonmember countries, and the free movement of investment and labor among members. By the end of 1992, individual countries will have made progress on domestic policy reforms in agriculture and other sectors to bring about substantial harmonization of economic policies within the Community.

Not surprisingly, nonmember countries fear that they face increased difficulties exporting to the Community. Harmonization of construction regulations and other policies within the Community not only increases opportunities for trade among members, but also creates the potential for barriers to be erected against imports from nonmembers. Among exporters of forest products, this is an important concern for Sweden, Finland, Canada, the USA, the USSR, Austria, and other nonmember countries.

That outsiders might encounter difficulties trading with the European Community was highlighted in the case of kraft paper and paperboard during the 1980s. In 1983, the European Community accused the USA of "dumping" kraft linerboard in the Community's market. This was the Community's stated reason for imposing an import tax. This import tax was then extended in 1987 to also include kraft imports from Austria, Canada, Finland, Sweden, and the USSR. The European Community justified this action as serving the long-term interests of its consumers. Yet the Community's consumers lost economic benefits because of higher prices, while the Community's kraft producers gained them, through the imposition of the tax (Wiseman 1990).

The International Tropical Timber Organization

During the 1970s, many countries urged the formation of a commodity agreement to manage issues in the international trade of tropical hardwoods. Discussions towards this end began in 1977 under the auspices of the United Nations Conference on Trade and Development (UNCTAD). This eventually led in 1983 to the adoption of the International Timber Trade Agreement (ITTA). The ITTA entered into force in 1985, after a sufficient number of countries ratified it. The administrative body to implement the terms of the agreement is the International Tropical Timber Organization (ITTO). Many years were required to work out details regarding location of the ITTO's headquarters (Yokohama, Japan), size and composition of its secretariat, decision powers of its council, and other issues relating to ITTO's purpose and governance.

Unlike organizations which manage many of the world's other commodity agreements, the ITTO does not attempt to influence commodity prices. Rather, main objectives are to improve market data on tropical hardwoods, upgrade the efficiency of forest industries in the producing countries, and strengthen management practices in tropical forestry. The ITTO provides a forum in which industrial and environmental perspectives can be presented and debated. This refers to perspectives on managing tropical forests and combatting deforestation. Moreover, the ITTO is a forum for the exchange of views between exporting and importing countries on perceived trade barriers and other issues affecting market policies.

The ITTO's council is composed of both producing (exporting) and consuming (importing) countries, with equal voting strength. The votes of consuming countries are allocated in proportion to the volumes of tropical timber they use, which gives Japan one-third of all votes held by the consuming countries. Votes of producing countries are weighted partly by their export volumes, and partly

One of the objectives of ITTO is to upgrade the efficiency of forest industries in the producing countries. *(Photo courtesy of World Bank.)*

by the areas of their tropical forests. Hence Brazil casts the largest number of votes among the producing countries, even if Brazil is not a particularly large exporter of tropical woods.

The ITTO faces many divisive problems. From the beginning, support for the ITTA and formation of the ITTO were hampered by controversies over whether the new arrangements would interfere with free trade. This was symptomatic of wider disagreements about the terms of commodity trading between the industrialized and developing countries. Moreover, skeptics question the ability of the ITTO to bring about needed reforms in the forest policies of the producing countries, and to marshall resources to control tropical deforestation. Clearly, the ITTO cannot hope to address the many daunting issues of the tropical timber trade on its own. Its most appropriate role is as catalyst in seeking a wider search for cooperation.

SYNTHESIS

The world's most important international trade flows in forest products are towards Europe, East Asia, and between Canada and the USA. Forest products flow from "surplus regions" to "deficit regions," as determined by domestic production of forest products in relation to domestic demand. Countries commonly export a certain mix of forest products, while importing a different mix. Moreover, it is not unusual for a given country to both export and import a similar product for reasons of transportation networks.

The share of the developing countries in the world's trade of forest products is small. In aggregate, the developing countries show trade surpluses in logs, sawnwood, and wood-based panels. However, this is more than offset by deficits in the trade of pulp, paper, and paperboard. Trade flows of teak and some of the non-wood forest products (e.g., rattan) are modest on a world scale, but are significant for some individual countries.

Comparative advantage in the production and export of forest products depends on the characteristics of the forest resource, and on the quantity and productivity of the inputs required to process it. Most of the world's exports of roundwood and processed forest products originate from old-growth forests of desirable species and qualities. These must be forests that are accessible to markets, and that are not excluded from logging because of environmental constraints or other reasons. Other exporting regions have a comparative advantage because of the abundance and productivity of their second-growth forests. Still a third type of comparative advantage rests on possession of highly productive plantations, including plantations in regions never before important in world timber supply.

Yet physical location close to low-cost timber is not sufficient to confer a comparative advantage in wood processing. The examples of Korea and Japan illustrate that it can be profitable to import raw wood and process it domestically, despite being located long distances from the sources of raw material. More broadly, comparative advantage in wood processing rests on utilization efficiencies, labor productivities, transportation costs, and other processing inputs. Additionally, patterns of trade depend very much on currency exchange rates between countries.

Restrictions on international trade of forest products include both tariff and nontariff barriers. Countries typically apply an escalated tariff structure to encourage imports of unprocessed wood, but discourage imports of more highly manufactured products. Compared with other traded goods, tariffs on forest products are not particularly high. Yet effective protection can be greater than suggested by the nominal amount of the tariff.

In the trade of forest products, nontariff barriers are numerous. They include trade disruptions because of alleged subsidies to exporters, as in the case of the USA's import of coniferous sawnwood from Canada. In an increasing number and variety of countries, governments restrict exports of logs and other raw wood on the grounds that this helps domestic producers and reduces forest cutting. In the industrialized countries, some environmentalists have argued for boycotts or other strategies to discourage the import of tropical hardwoods.

Other nontariff barriers are subtle and difficult to detect. Among them are disagreements over product standards, inspection procedures, and technical and sanitary regulations. Some developing countries export forest products only through marketing boards, and import forest products only with government authorization. Historical, political, and cultural connections explain why trading patterns are not determined by market forces alone.

Views on the role of international trade in economic development are divided into two schools of thought. Advocates of free trade explain how all trading partners benefit when countries follow the principles of free trade along lines of comparative advantage. The Nordic countries, New Zealand, Chile, and Brazil illustrate that a liberalized trading regime for forest products provides healthy export earnings, while simultaneously distributing substantial quantities of forest products to the world's consumers. A dissenting perspective finds it reasonable to use trade restrictions as a means to increase the self-reliance of developing countries, particularly those which want the employment and skills which come with early industrialization. Dissenters further argue that the earnings produced from trade do not necessarily stay at home, but rather depend very much on who owns and manages the exporting enterprises. In a world of highly diverse trading partners, no single theoretical framework is sufficient to encompass all of the arguments for and against free trade.

Various multilateral and bilateral institutions manage the problems of international trade, including the trade of forest products. The General Agreement on Tariffs and Trade has helped reduce tariffs to well below what they were at the end of the Second World War. The GATT has been less successful in reducing nontariff barriers. By the end of this century, the Free Trade Agreement signed by Canada and the USA will eliminate all tariffs on forest products flowing between the two countries. The consolidation and strengthening of the European Community promises to increase internal trade among its members, but raises questions among nonmembers with respect to possible new impediments in exporting to the Community. The International Tropical Timber Organization arose in the 1980s to facilitate dialogue between countries which export and import tropical hardwoods, offering a forum to discuss and debate the many complex problems of that trade.

ISSUES FOR DISCUSSION AND INVESTIGATION

1 Describe the principal international flows of forest products, and explain what accounts for the direction of trade.

2 Current patterns of forest products trade are not too different from broad patterns observed 30–40 years ago. (i) What could explain this? (ii) What departures from past patterns can be expected in the future?

3 The possession of abundant forests is a necessary but not sufficient condition for a country to have comparative advantage in exporting forest products. True or false? Explain and defend.

4 That some countries live with low wood and paper consumption in a world of potential timber surplus is more a matter of income distribution than forest distribution. Explain this statement within the context of international trade of forest products.

5 The prices at which countries buy and sell each other's currencies determine the quantities and directions of trade in forest products. Suppose that the Canadian dollar is falling and the Swedish crown is rising in relation to the major currencies of western Europe. How will this affect Europe's imports of pulp and paper from Canada compared with Sweden?

6 What is an escalated tariff structure, and how is it manifested in the international trade of forest products?

7 (i) In what ways can standards for the strength, size, appearance, or sanitary condition of wood products become a trade barrier? (ii) Can these barriers be removed? How?

8 The USA is one of the world's largest importers and exporters of forest products. Unlike most of the rest of the world, the USA uses English rather than metric units of measurement. Is this a barrier in the trade of forest products? Explain, and cite examples.

9 Many countries have tightened restrictions on the export of unprocessed or lightly processed wood, especially logs. (i) In what ways can this lead to economic inefficiencies? (ii) Who are the winners and losers from these restrictions? (iii) Are the arguments for and against restricting log exports the same in North America as in Southeast Asia? Explain and defend.

10 Tariffs have fallen dramatically since the end of the Second World War, and world trade has expanded enormously. This is applauded by advocates of open economies and liberalized trade, who show the global benefits of extensive international commerce. Another viewpoint is far less positive about the gains to trade, especially from the perspective of developing countries. (i) Describe how these two schools of thought might clash on important issues in the international trade of forest products. (ii) Can both schools be right at the same time? Why or why not?

11 An alternative to boycotting the import of tropical hardwoods is to allow consumers to buy tropical hardwoods produced from "sustainable sources." What challenges does this raise for identifying such sources, and for administering a certification system?

12 The International Tropical Timber Organization is a relatively new body to facilitate international trade of tropical hardwoods. What problems does it face, and what will be required to make this an effective organization?

REFERENCES

Blake, David H. and Robert S. Walters. 1987. *The Politics of Global Economic Relations*, 3rd edition. Prentice-Hall, Englewood Cliffs, NJ.

Bonnefoi, Benoit and Joseph Buongiorno. 1990. "Comparative advantage of countries in forest products trade," *Forest Ecology and Management* 36(1):1–17.

Bourke, Ian J. 1988. *Trade in Forest Products: A Study of the Barriers Faced by the Developing Countries*. FAO Forestry Paper 83, Food and Agriculture Organization, Rome.

Caves, Richard E., Jeffrey A. Frankel, and Ronald W. Jones. 1990. *World Trade and Payments: An Introduction*, 5th edition. Scott, Foresman, Little, Brown Higher Education, Glenview, IL.

Cox, Thomas R. 1988. "The North American-Japanese timber trade: A survey of its social, economic, and environmental impact," pp. 164–188 in J. F. Richards and R. P. Tucker (eds.), *World Deforestation in the Twentieth Century*. Duke University Press, Durham, NC.

DeBeer, Jenne H. and Melanie J. McDermott. 1989. *The Economic Value of Non-Timber Forest Products in Southeast Asia*. Netherlands Committee for IUCN, Amsterdam, Netherlands.

Ewing, Andrew J. and Raymond Chalk. 1988. *The Forest Industries Sector: An Operational Strategy for Developing Countries*. World Bank Technical Paper No. 83, Industry and Energy Series, Washington, DC.

FAO (Food and Agriculture Organization of the United Nations). 1989. *Yearbook of Forest Products, 1976–1987*. Rome, Italy.

Gupta, T. A. and A. Guleria. 1982. *Non-Wood Forest Products from India*. IBH Publishing Co., New Delhi, India.

Kallio, Markku, Dennis P. Dykstra, and Clark S. Binkley (eds.). 1987. *The Global Forest Sector: An Analytical Perspective*. John Wiley and Sons, New York.

Kelly, Margaret, Naheed Kirmani, Miranda Xafa, Clemens Boonekamp, and Peter Winglee. 1988. *Issues and Developments in International Trade Policy*. International Monetary Fund Occasional Paper No. 63, Washington, DC.

Kornai, G. 1987. "Historical analysis of international trade in forest products," pp. 432–456 in M. Kallio, D. P. Dykstra, and C. S. Binkley (eds.), *The Global Forest Sector: An Analytical Perspective*. John Wiley and Sons, New York.

Nectoux, Francois and Nigel Dudley. 1987. *A Hardwood Story: An Investigation into the European Influence on Tropical Forest Loss*. Friends of the Earth Trust and Earth Resources Research, Ltd., Gwynne Printers, UK.

Nectoux, Francois and Yoichi Kuroda. 1989. *Timber from the South Seas: An Analysis of Japan's Tropical Timber Trade and Its Environmental Impact*. WWF International, Gland, Switzerland.

Palo, Matti. 1988. "Export prospects for the forest industries in developing countries," *UNITAS, Finnish Economic Quarterly Review* 60(4):76–83.

Percy, Michael B. and Christian Yoder. 1987. *The Softwood Lumber Disputes and Canada-U.S. Trade in Natural Resources*. Institute for Research and Public Policy, Halifax, Nova Scotia, Canada.

Priasukmana, Soetarso. 1988. "Indonesia as a supplier of rattan products in the international market," pp. 217–222 in J. A. Johnson and W. R. Smith (eds.), *Forest Products Trade: Market Trends and Technical Developments*. University of Washington Press, Seattle.

Schott, Jeffrey J. and Murray G. Smith (eds.). 1988. *The Canada-United States Free Trade Agreement: The Global Impact,* Institute for International Economics, Washington, DC.

Schreuder, Gerard F. (ed.). 1986. *World Trade in Forest Products 2*. University of Washington Press, Seattle.

Sedjo, Roger A. 1983. *The Comparative Economics of Plantation Forests: A Global Assessment*. Resources for the Future, Washington, DC.

Stairs, Gerald R. and Marion C. Salinger (eds.). 1988. *Canada/U.S. Forest Products: Analysis of North American and World Trade Opportunities*. Duke University, Center for International Studies, Durham, NC.

Stier, J. C. 1990. "The world eucapulp industry and its impacts on the northern U.S. pulp and paper industry," *Northern Journal of Applied Forestry* 7(4):158–163

Todaro, Michael P. 1985. *Economic Development in the Third World,* 3rd edition. Longman, New York and London, England.

UNIDO (United Nations Industrial Development Organization). 1983. *Tariff and Non-Tariff Measures in the World Trade of Wood and Wood Products*. Sectoral Working Paper Series No. 6, UNIDO/IS 396, Vienna, Austria.

USDA (United States Department of Agriculture) Foreign Agricultural Service. 1990. *Wood Products: International Trade and Foreign Markets*. Circular Series WP 4-89, Washington, DC.

Vincent, Jeffrey R. 1990. "Don't boycott tropical timber," *Journal of Forestry* 88(4):56.

Volkov, V. O. 1988. "USSR: Trends and prospects in the forest products trade," pp. 183–196 in Andras Nagy (ed.), *International Trade in Forest Products*, A B Academic Publishers, Bicester, UK.

Wiseman, A. Clark. 1990. *Recent International Developments Impacting United States Forest Products Trade*. RFF Discussion Paper ENR90-06, Resources for the Future, Washington, DC.

CHAPTER 6

FARM AND COMMUNITY FORESTRY

Through the last two decades, the world's forestry profession and the international agencies have shown rapidly escalating interest in tree growing by farmers and local communities, especially in the developing countries. "Social forestry," as it is frequently known, is equated with tree growing "by the people, for the people." Social forestry commonly makes use of agroforestry technologies, or the integration of trees with various forms of agricultural crops and livestock. For some purposes, only blurred lines separate social forestry, agroforestry, and farm and community forestry. Each of these labels directly or indirectly refers to growing and using trees to provide food, fuel, medicines, livestock fodder, building materials, and cash incomes. Farm and community forestry typically emphasizes a self-help aspect—people's participation—as a social objective ranking in importance with the production objectives.

CONTEXT AND RATIONALE

A great stirring in support of farm and community forestry occurred in the late 1970s. In 1978, the Eighth World Forestry Congress in Indonesia addressed the theme "Forests for People." This focused attention on policies and projects for improved integration of tree growing with other forms of land use, and on strategies to shift benefits of tree growing towards people struggling with poverty. The International Council for Research in Agroforestry (ICRAF) was established in 1977, with a mission to advance and diffuse knowledge about how to increase the productivity of different systems of raising trees, crops, and animals on the same piece of land. At about the same time, the World Bank announced its policy to

Farm and community forestry takes the benefits and services of trees to the doorstep of persons who use them. This is a small farm south of Maracaibo, Venezuela. *(Photo courtesy of FAO.)*

commit vastly increased funding to fuelwood production, small-scale tree farms, and other projects aimed to benefit the rural poor (World Bank 1978).

A focus on farm and community forestry represents a sharp conceptual break from the context of traditional forestry. The object of organization and management is not so much large masses of woody vegetation called forests, but rather smaller groups of trees in home gardens and agricultural fallows, along fences and roads, and in other settings not meeting the conventional definition of forests. It is sometimes said that farm and community forestry aims to take the benefits and services of trees to the doorsteps of persons who could use them.

Yet tree growing by farmers and peasant communities faces major obstacles. It is misleading to believe that every indigenous community or peasant family should want to grow trees, is able to do so, and reaps rewards from this practice. Much remains to be learned about constraints of tree and land tenure, suitability of biological technologies, determinants of social and economic feasibility, effectiveness of extension methods, and other factors which together explain success or failure in farm and community forestry.

Ancient Art, New Science

A number of contemporary societies consist mainly of forest farmers. On the bank of the Amazon River, the 2,000 villagers of Tamshiyacu engage in a large number of production activities combining tree products with products from other plants and animals. The production mix includes cultivated fruits, wild forest fruits and nuts, root crops, charcoal, palm hearts, medicinal plants, and animal skins and meat. Cleared plots in the forest are planted with a variety of annual and semi-perennial crops, later followed by perennial tree crops. These cyclic production methods provide the Tamshiyaquinos with a reasonably steady income (Padoch et al. 1985).

A very different biogeographical context is that of livestock herders from the Pokot and Turkana tribes in arid and semiarid East Africa. In the dry season, trees along rivers and streams are a valuable source of leaves and twigs to feed livestock, as well as fruit and pods to feed people. The only woody species cut back are the less useful bush species—used for fencing and livestock corrals—in order to promote better ground cover of perennial grasses. Wood is used for fuel, and several woody species are used for medicines. Building materials are selectively cut from certain trees. The Pokot and Turkana attach great value to trees, and individual herders possess well-defined user rights in particular sections of riverine forest (Barrow 1988).

Of course, the practice of tending trees and other woody plants in association with agriculture and grazing is an old one. In the temperate world, Britain has a thousand years of experience with hedges and hedgerow trees (Rackham 1989). Until the Middle Ages, it was common practice in Europe to clearcut degraded forests, burn the slash, and cultivate food crops and tree crops in conjunction with each other. Similar practices of shifting cultivation continued in Finland until the beginning of this century, and in parts of Germany into the 1920s (King 1987).

Much earlier, the ancient Greeks and Romans grew coppices of oak, chestnut, and willow for forage, firewood, and vineyard stakes. Writings from more than two thousand years ago describe methods of tree sowing and planting, grafting and layering, and pruning and pollarding (Meiggs 1982). Practices to help trees during drought were known, and it was observed that goats were undesirable in woodlands. Dead owls were a precaution against hail. The remedy for ants—which were considered harmful—was to put out a donkey's heart, or ashes with vinegar (Fernow 1911).

While these latter practices are unimaginable today, the science of farm and community forestry nevertheless is young and immature. Tree growing in association with agriculture is said to be an ancient art, but a new science. The new science is called upon to integrate the best available knowledge about agroforestry technologies with accumulating field experience regarding how these technologies fit particular social and ecological settings.

To what extent can Western science enhance traditional methods of tree growing and use? How should Western science build on centuries of indigenous ecological knowledge and folk science? These are highly challenging issues.

Trees for Basic Needs

Tree growing is a dominant feature in the way of life of some indigenous societies and peasant households, but has a peripheral or even negligible role in others. These differences are explained by local biogeographical contexts, patterns of agricultural land use, patterns of tree and land tenure, cultural traditions, and economic incentives and pressures. The purposes of tree growing vary across this wide spectrum. Yet they can be summarized in terms of producing food, fuelwood, construction materials, cash income, and savings and security (Figure 6-1).

Food   When considering the role of forests in meeting basic needs, a logical beginning is food supply (FAO 1989a). The interfaces between trees and food are multiple and complex, and not well articulated in forestry theory. Forests are cleared to provide new lands for cultivation and grazing, trees furnish food sources directly, and trees stabilize adjacent or downstream agriculture through soil and water protection and microclimate effects. Nitrogen-fixing trees and shrubs

FIGURE 6-1
Rationale for tree growing and management in farm and community forestry. *(Sources: FAO (1978, p. 6); Chambers and Leach (1987).)*

Contribution	Benefits
Food, fodder, grazing	Protects croplands against wind and water erosion. Increases productivity of marginal croplands. Provides direct food consumption for humans and livestock.
Firewood and charcoal	Reduces costs compared with non-wood alternatives. Substitutes for agricultural residues. Reduces household labor. Lessens pressure for depletion of woody vegetation in sparsely wooded areas. Contributes to nutrition through availability of cooked food.
Poles, posts, and other building materials	Maintains housing standards. Provides rural infrastructure at low cash costs.
Saleable products	Raises incomes of farmers and communities. Diversifies local economies. Furnishes inputs to industries and handicrafts.
Saving and security	Meets contingencies requiring needs for cash. Provides countercyclical food and incomes (e.g., during dry seasons in agriculture). Compares favorably with other assets managed by the rural poor.

provide low-cost fertilizer. Tree shade, fodder, and litter can raise livestock productivity, and hence the supply of meat and milk. These contributions are not fully compatible, as when too much tree clearing precludes the other contributions.

Where tree cover is scarce, the links between forests and food production are most readily observed as agricultural losses after more trees are removed, or agricultural gains after trees are restored. These losses and gains are difficult to quantify, and often are valid only for localized areas or controlled tests on experimental farms. Despite these qualifications, there can be little doubt that tree cover is linked with crop and livestock production (Table 6-1).

Besides their role in affecting the yields of crops and livestock, trees contribute to food production directly (Hoskins 1990). This refers to tubers, fruits, leaves, oils, gums, fish, game, honey, mushrooms, insects, and numerous other edible products. These foods supplement existing food sources and incomes, and often make up for seasonal shortages. Some of these foods are smoked, dried, or fermented, making it possible to store them over extended periods. Numerous fruits and leaves are excellent sources of vitamins, minerals, and protein. Certain leaves and seeds add flavor and seasoning—as in sauces and soups—to otherwise bland diets. Tree fruits and nuts are common snack foods, especially for children (FAO 1989b).

TABLE 6-1
Selected examples of food production in relation to tree cover

Region	Action/context	Impact
Denmark (Jutland)	Over 100 thousand hectares planted on dunes, heath, and degraded lands (19th century).	Reduced crop losses by over 40%.
Greece	Deforestation effects from thousands of years ago.	Responsible for annual crop losses of US$25 million (in 1960s).
USSR (Armavir wind corridor)	Shelterbelts planted in 1930s.	Crop yields up 100–400%
China (arid regions)	Extensive networks of shelterbelts planted beginning in 1950s.	Farm productivity increased 50–100%. Sizable deserts reclaimed.
Senegal (coastal region)	Dune stabilization, windbreaks, and on-farm tree planting to protect farms and gardens.	Modest investment (US$1.7 million) protects crops valued in millions of dollars.
Niger (Majjia Valley)	Over 1,000 hectares protected by windbreaks planted 1975–1980.	Millet yields increased 23%
Nepal (Phewa Tal watershed)	Trees and grasses planted on eroded slopes and gullies. Livestock off.	Increased fodder quadrupled family income in 3 years.

Sources: Sartorius and Henle (1968, pp. 77–98): WRI et al. (1985, Part II, "Case Studies").

Tree fruits and nuts are comon
snack foods, especially for children.
*(Photo courtesy of Yosef Hadar and
World Bank.)*

Fuelwood   In most developing countries, a substantial proportion of rural households use fuelwood (firewood plus charcoal) for all or part of their cooking and heating needs (Arnold and Jongma 1979). Although urban residents have access to fuelwood substitutes such as kerosene and electricity, these substitutes are not always affordable. This means that firewood and charcoal continue to be major energy sources in many cities. Also consuming considerable quantities of firewood and charcoal are tobacco curing, brick making, ore smelting, bakeries, restaurants, and other industrial and commercial establishments.

In the many local regions of the world where fuelwood is scarce, the shortages are as much a consequence as a cause of deforestation. The clearing of forests and woodlands for agriculture reduces available wooded area. At that point, continued extraction of fuelwood may exceed the capacity of the remaining wooded area to regenerate itself. Importantly, much firewood and charcoal is not from forest sources, but rather derives from farm trees and other vegetation dotted all over the landscape. Particularly in sparsely vegetated arid zones and mountain uplands, fuelwood gathering in combination with heavy grazing has been known to deplete woody vegetation over broad areas. Furthermore, these pressures change the composition of the vegetation towards increasingly inferior species and qualities (Eckholm et al. 1984).

Fuelwood scarcities are believed to entail high social and environmental costs. In rural zones the collection of fuelwood from increasingly distant or marginal sources requires more and more labor time, usually of women and children. The rising price of firewood and charcoal in cities and towns may take significant proportions of meager cash incomes. Hence the purchase of a cubic meter of firewood in the Tibetan city of Lhasa costs an entire average annual income in that region (Richardson 1990).

Substitution of agricultural wastes for fuelwood has become extreme in some cases. Because many of these wastes would otherwise be used as mulches and fertilizer, this substitution is associated with reductions in crop productivity (Bajaracharya 1983). Additionally, although the matter is not well researched, fuelwood scarcity is postulated to adversely affect health and nutrition. This is because meals are undercooked, or not cooked at all (Agarwal 1986; Brouwer et al. 1989).

However, collective knowledge of these issues is highly inadequate. Fuelwood demand is variable from region to region and household to household for reasons which are not completely understood. Also, fuelwood users may adjust to scarcities in ways which are more numerous and less burdensome than ordinarily assumed (DeWees 1989).

In light of the complex dynamics of adjustment, the forestry solution to grow more trees is often only a partial solution if indeed a solution at all. Where fuelwood is scarce, development strategies generally aim both to decrease demand and augment supply. The appropriate lines of action vary with the circumstances, but are likely to include fuelwood conservation, expanded forest protection and tree planting, and diversification of energy sources (Figure 6-2).

FIGURE 6-2
Strategies to manage fuelwood scarcities. *(Source: DeWees (1989).)*

Decrease demand

Conserve fuelwood
• improve woodstoves and charcoal kilns
• improve industrial boilers and combustion processes
• encourage easy-to-cook foods (households)
• promote communal cooking (households)

Diversify energy sources
• promote rural electrification, hydropower, wind power, solar cooking boxes, and other energy alternatives
• subsidize locally available commercial fuels (e.g., kerosene)

Increase supply

Protect and manage existing forests and woodlands
• rest depleted areas
• control fire and grazing
• turn over control to local groups for management

Expand tree planting
• emphasize agroforestry approaches and multipurpose trees
• encourage fuelwood plantations where appropriate
• address obtention of "free" wood from open-access areas

This father and son make charcoal stoves in Kenya. In some countries, governments and aid agencies attempt to promote low-cost stoves as a strategy to reduce fuelwood consumption. *(Photo courtesy of World Bank.)*

Construction Materials   Trees, shrubs, bamboos, and palms provide an enormous variety of materials used in construction. Among the most visible of these are posts and poles to build houses, bridges, and fences. Branches and leaves are common thatching materials for roofs and walls. Other construction applications include furniture, boats, agricultural implements, ladders, scaffolding, carts and wagons, coffins, fish traps, and storage containers.

The bamboos and palms are particularly popular as construction materials, even if conventionally neglected in forestry. In Asia, bamboo has been called "the poor man's timber." Villagers in Asian countries from China to India use a variety of methods to regenerate and cultivate several species of bamboos. Likewise, rattans have been an ancient and invaluable source of construction material.

Cash Income   Where markets permit, numerous forest and tree products are sold for cash rather than consumed directly. These cash sales sometimes generate badly needed supplementary incomes, especially during slack months in

In Asia, bamboo is "the poor man's timber." This Chinese carpenter teaches apprentices how to make pine furniture in the shade of a bamboo stand. *(Photo courtesy of FAO.)*

agricultural cycles. In other cases, sales of tree products are a year-round activity and a primary source of income. Activity patterns vary greatly across contexts:

• The babassu palm (*Orbignya* sp.) provides food, fiber, edible oil, and cash to over 450 thousand households in an economically poor region of Brazil. The processing of babassu kernels for oil occurs during the slack period in agriculture, providing one-fourth of household income during this "hungry period" (May et al. 1985).

• For the Tagbanua people of the Philippines, the sale of rattan and resin provides daily earnings considerably higher than in agricultural wage labor (Conelly 1985).

• In Ecuador, coffee and cacao farmers generate modest amounts of occasional income by selling culled shade trees to wood buyers from furniture factories (Mussack and Laarman 1989).

• In China, a proliferation of "sideline enterprises" includes the growing or gathering of ginseng, marten fur, cinnamon, bamboo, pine seeds, mushrooms, honey, and a variety of products from wild and farmed deer (Richardson 1990).

• Almost everywhere in the developing countries, wood and other forest materials are used for the production and sale of arts and handicrafts.

Tree farming can be a primary source of income in response to emerging markets. The match industry of India is based largely on smallholder tree growing.

Private plots of *Casuarina equisetifolia* are major sources of firewood and poles for the Indian cities of Madras and Bangalore (Foley and Barnard 1984).

Production of pulpwood as a cash crop is the main source of livelihood for several thousand rural families living within wood transportation distance of Paper Industries Corporation of the Philippines (PICOP). Most farms devote 1–2 hectares to food crops and domestic animals, and another 8–9 hectares to growing trees of *Paraserianthes falcataria* under a contract system with PICOP (Hyman 1983b).

Savings and Security   Trees can be a means of holding assets and meeting urgent or large needs for income. Importantly, the food and cash which can be derived from trees lessen impacts of agricultural failures and other rural emergencies. Hence trees are sometimes regarded as a form of rural insurance, deliberately retained or planted to provide an asset for savings and security. In many respects, trees offer advantages over other types of assets (Figure 6-3).

FIGURE 6-3
Characteristics of trees compared with other assets of the poor.
(Source: Adapted from Chambers and Leach (1987, p. 13).)

Desirable characteristics	Type of Asset					
	Trees	**Jewels**	**Land**	**Bank deposits**	**Cattle**	**Sheep/ goats**
Low starting costs	+	−	−	0	−	0
Low maintenance costs	+/−	+	−	++	−	−
Low vulnerability to disease, accidents, damage, droughts	+/−	++	+	++	−	−
Low vulnerability to theft	+/−	−	+	++	−	−
Assured property rights and cashability	+/−	++	+	++	+	++
Generates value by reproducing, growing	+	0	+/0	+/−	+	+
Stores well	+	++	+	++	−	−
Easy to pledge, mortgage, or use as security for loans	0	++	+	++	+	0
Easy to transport	−	++	− −	++	+	+
Divisible into small units for sale	+	+/−	+/−	++	−	0
Regenerates after disposal	+/0	−	−	−	−	−

++: strongly positive; +: positive; 0: usually neutral; +/−: sometimes positive, sometimes negative; −: negative; − −: strongly negative

Various studies show that trees and tree products are sold or traded to pay for dowries, weddings, funerals, and other social and ceremonial functions. Thus in countries like Turkey and India, it is traditional to plant trees upon the birth of a female child in anticipation of her future wedding (Foley and Barnard 1984).

Moreover, trees help meet expenses stemming from educational fees, medicines, childbirth, physical incapacity, business failures, livestock deaths, gambling debts, and other contingencies. In different contexts, trees are cut and their products sold, or trees serve as tangible assets against which to borrow money (Chambers and Leach 1987).

In ordinary circumstances, the presence of trees and tree crops reduces ecological and economic risks by diversifying agricultural and grazing systems. Especially critical are trees whose leaves flush or whose fruits mature during seasons when crop and livestock production is low. In times of dire emergency, trees and shrubs have been known to provide food products and cash to help victims survive famines, floods, wars, and other disasters. For the rural poor, the consumption and sale of tree products may be one of the few survival options in the face of these catastrophes.

Patterns of Tree Management and Cultivation

Observed methods of managing tree cover—whether on farms or on communal lands—reflect continuing adaptations to changes in ecological, cultural, social, demographic, and economic forces. At one extreme, approaches to tree management comprise the highly sophisticated manipulation of trees, crops, and livestock in close association with each other. These are the world's most elaborate agroforestry systems, found principally in regions of high population density and small landholdings. Elsewhere, tree management is more passive, relying mainly on natural regeneration and attempted control of depletion pressures to retain at least the most valued trees in the rural landscape. Between these two ends of the spectrum lies a variety of management strategies, many of which are described in the rapidly growing literature on agroforestry.

Agroforestry systems can be classified in a number of ways (Nair 1985; Vergara 1985). However, most classifications recognize three basic variations: (1) agro-silviculture, or the integration of trees and annual crops; (2) silvo-pastoralism, or the integration of trees with livestock on grazing lands, and (3) agro-silvo-pastoralism, or the integration of trees, crops, and livestock in a single system of management. Each of these systems produces two or more outputs, and each has at least one production cycle which extends beyond a year. Most critically, each system is intended to provide positive ecological or economic interaction between the woody perennials and the other elements of the production mix (Lundgren and Raintree 1983).

A few examples of tree management illustrate a wide range of practices and purposes (Winterbottom and Hazelwood 1987; MacDicken and Vergara 1990):

• *Enhanced shifting cultivation*—Traditional shifting cultivation is characterized by sequential stages of crops and trees through time. Most forest trees are

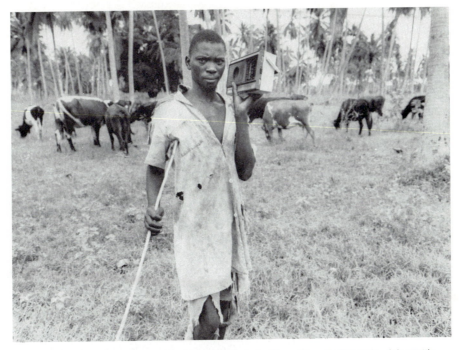

Silvo-pastoral systems integrate trees with livestock. In this pasture in Tanzania, dairy cattle graze under a tree cover which is mainly palms. *(Photo courtesy of FAO.)*

removed from a patch of land in order to plant crops. After a few years, crop productivity diminishes because of weed competition and declining levels of nutrients and soil organic matter. With declining productivity, the farmer moves to clear a new plot of forest, allowing the previously cultivated plot to lie fallow. The forest or woodland vegetation reestablishes itself in the fallow through natural regeneration, and through trees and shrubs deliberately introduced or helped along by the farmer. Through this enhancement process, the farmer is able to return to the forest fallows for fruits and nuts, construction poles, and other useful products.

• *Taungya*—Last century in Burma, the British colonial administration favored a method of teak establishment called "taungya," roughly translated as "hill cultivation." This system has since spread to numerous other countries, particularly in the humid tropics. Shifting cultivators are given rights to clear forest land in order to plant temporary food crops, but are required to plant and tend seedlings of timber plantation species interplanted among these food crops. As the tree canopy closes and shades out the food crops, the farmers are moved to another area, where the cycle is repeated. Substantial areas of timber plantations have been established through taungya methods in Southeast Asia and West Africa.

• *Dispersed farm trees*—In most of the developing world, trees are deliberately planted or allowed to grow from natural regeneration in and near farm fields and pastures. These trees are protected to provide food products, construction materials, fuelwood, shade, livestock fodder, medicines, and beneficial impacts for crops. The Chinese intercrop *Paulownia* with annual crops like wheat and vegetables on an estimated two million hectares. *Cordia alliodora* is a valuable timber species which is cultivated in and around pastures in several countries of Latin America. The nitrogen-fixing *Acacia albida* increases yields of millet and sorghum in the relatively infertile soils of the Sahel. *Prosopis cineraria* plays a similar role in India's arid northwestern region. Both *Acacia albida* and *Prosopis cineraria* are multipurpose species which also produce fuelwood, livestock feed, and wood for farm tools.

• *Shelterbelts, windbreaks, hedges, and living fences*—Shelterbelts and windbreaks are strips of trees and shrubs to protect crops, livestock, orchards, and homesites from wind, sun, or snow. Hedges and living fences provide many of the same functions, while also demarcating field boundaries and controlling livestock movements. Moreover, it is common to observe trees planted along roads, railroads, and waterways. Each of these variations of "linear forestry" often features multipurpose or mixed species. The objective is to increase productivity of adjacent crops and livestock while simultaneously furnishing by-products. Management methods often emphasize coppicing, pollarding, or pruning. This permits a continuous flow of fuelwood, livestock fodder, and other products over many years.

• *Canopy trees for plantation crops*—Shade trees form the canopy over plantations of coffee, cacao, and other estate crops. Shade trees include *Cordia alliodora* and *Erythrina* in Latin America, and *Paraserianthes falcataria* and *Gliricidia sepium* in Southeast Asia. Many shade trees, when overmature, can be harvested for wood. However, their most important functions are to favorably influence microclimate and soil conditions for the plantation crops.

• *Shade and fodder trees for livestock*—In the context of raising livestock, trees and shrubs have their greatest utility in providing shade and fodder. Fodder from woody species is especially vital when grass and crops have ceased production during a growing season, and during episodic droughts (Okafor 1980). Dependence on trees for fodder is perhaps nowhere greater than in South Asia. Roughly 80 percent of the fodder to feed Nepal's domestic livestock derives from trees (Singh et al. 1984). In India, the number of species of trees and shrubs used for livestock fodder is counted in the hundreds (Singh 1982).

• *Alley cropping*—This refers to a practice in which farm crops are grown in "alleys" between rows of nitrogen-fixing trees or shrubs. The trees and shrubs are pruned frequently, and leaves and twigs from the prunings are used as a mulch to add organic matter and nitrogen to the cultivated crop. This mulch substitutes for chemical fertilizers, providing what sometimes can be a low-cost approach to growing food crops simultaneously with fuelwood, fodder, and other by-products.

• *Home gardens*—Home gardens refer to multistoried associations of multipurpose woody perennials integrated with annual and semi-perennial crops. Sometimes these gardens include chickens, ducks, rabbits, and other domestic animals. Home gardens are among the most intensive and complex of agroforestry systems, providing a wide range of different products and ecological services on small plots near homesteads.

Roughly 80 percent of the fodder to feed Nepal's domestic livestock derives from trees. A Gurung woman feeds tree leaves to her buffalo, which eats 40 kilograms of fodder each day. *(Photo courtesy of FAO.)*

Community Forestry, Farm Forestry

Since the 1970s, the Western world has learned a few vital lessons about social and economic factors as they pertain to tree management on farms and in communities of the developing world. These lessons frequently return to the question posed previously: farm and community trees for whom and for what?

This focus is paramount because incentives and obstacles in tree management are generally distinct for relatively well-off farmers compared with smallholder farmers, tenant farmers, tribal and nomadic groups, and other socioeconomic groups. Each grouping may have subgroups within it, so that a useful profile of human motivations and constraints in tree growing becomes very complex. In fact, the basic concept of "community" in community forestry may rest on false premises if many disparate groups and interests are considered simultaneously. The benefits and costs of growing trees are divided according to the interrelated variables of social class, political power, land tenure, wealth, kinship, age, and gender. Consequently, a principal challenge is to make the technical aspects of tree management feasible and beneficial for one or more target groups within what is often a highly stratified socioeconomic structure.

Not many years ago, many foresters and development specialists assumed that massive tree planting could be organized over large areas of communal lands.

Yet recent experience in numerous developing countries shows that community management of trees frequently fails for one or more of several reasons (Gregersen et al. 1989, pp. 133–134):

• The diversity of interests in a "community" implies that often it is unable to pull together cooperative efforts today for delayed and uncertain benefits projected several years into the future.

• For community forestry to be effective, a collective entity of persons must agree on how and why trees are being husbanded. Secondly, this collective entity must work together on more or less a perpetual basis to protect trees from grazing, fires, premature cutting, and other depletion pressures. Unified action is not possible when different individuals and subgroups have varying and even conflicting interests.

• Often the user rights to the products and services of trees on communal lands are uncertain and change through time as societies themselves change. Rights might be different for natural vegetation versus planted trees. Moreover, the weaker elements of a community may fear that the politically and economically stronger elements will appropriate most of the benefits in one way or another, no matter what formal agreements might exist.

For community forestry to be effective, a collective entity of persons must agree on how and why trees are being managed. Members of a village in the Uppalo Gherku region of Nepal meet with a forest extension agent to discuss tree planting. *(Photo courtesy of FAO.)*

• Only sometimes are communities organized as joint producers and managers of other programs and resources. The management of a community forest, or a community woodlot, frequently requires the development of a special "grass roots" organization to take charge of details. For a variety of reasons, the building of grass roots organizations for tree management can be difficult and time-consuming to achieve.

Some of the early disappointments with community forestry shifted increasing interest towards farm forestry. In farm forestry, the social units targeted for attention are individual farmers and households. Unlike community forestry, decisions and actions in farm forestry rest with individual landowners and families. Individual ownership simplifies decisionmaking, clarifies rights, and ensures that those who work and invest in tree growing are those who reap the benefits. From the perspective of providing international development assistance, programs in farm forestry tend to be simpler to design and implement than community-based alternatives. Moreover, success with a particular tree-management practice on a few farms may induce other farmers to accept similar practices. This allows innovations to spread at relatively low cost, as with *Leucaena leucocephala* in regions of Southeast Asia and the Western Pacific.

However, farm forestry also has its share of problems. The example of the Gujarat Social Forestry Project (GSFP) in India illustrates several of them. The GSFP began in 1969, expanding greatly after 1980 due to an infusion of funding from the World Bank. Activities in GSFP were (1) distribution of tree seedlings for farm forestry; (2) strip plantings of trees along roadsides, canal banks, and railroad lines; (3) village woodlots of about four hectares each; (4) reforestation and afforestation of degraded lands; and (5) construction and diffusion of improved stoves and crematoria to reduce fuel consumption. As measured by demand for seedlings to plant, GSFP has been highly successful. In the planting season of 1983 alone, nearly 200 million seedlings were distributed. By the late 1980s, approximately 250 thousand hectares had been planted, of which about 40 percent were on farms. However, critics advanced the following arguments (Longhurst 1987):

• A major use of seedlings in GSFP has been eucalyptus for block planting by Gujarat's relatively larger farmers—including farmers with irrigation facilities—to supply the urban market for construction poles. This has provided few products and little income for the region's landless and truly poor.

• Gujarat's farm forestry has contributed little to agricultural production and food supply. About 30 thousand hectares were converted from cultivation of food crops to cultivation of trees.

• The amount of genuine agroforestry combining tree crops and food crops is minimal. This is because of the inherent qualities of eucalyptus compared with multipurpose trees, lack of coordination between the Forest Department and the Agriculture Department, and other institutional constraints.

• One analysis for the Gujarat village of Dhanori indicates that Dhanori's establishment of a small woodlot directed benefits to even the most disadvantaged villagers (Verma 1988). Yet it requires far more time and resources for the Forest Department to help a village plan and set up a small woodlot than for it to distribute seedlings to larger farmers who are literate, progressive, and not suspicious of outsiders. To meet production and distribution targets, project personnel favored these larger farmers.

• Because of their role in household management, the interests of women in the state of Gujarat would have been served by greater emphasis on fuelwood. As it turned out, the preferred fuelwood species made up less than 10 percent of the seedlings distributed through GSFP in its early years.

This example of Gujarat illustrates the social tradeoffs inherent in farm forestry. Trees were established on good agricultural soils rather than on wastelands and other marginal sites. The production objective of getting trees in the ground was well served by working with larger farmers, but the distribution objective of reaching the state's poorest people was not fully attained.

More broadly, emphasis on individual rights to trees through farm forestry is most difficult to make work for shifting cultivators on public lands, indigenous groups for which individual ownership is an alien concept, and landless families who work as laborers or tenants on the farms of others. Yet these groups rank high on most lists of subjective "need" in programs of rural development. This frequent

In India's state of Gujarat, eucalyptus trees have been planted on good agricultural soils rather than on wastelands and other marginal sites. *(Photo courtesy of World Bank.)*

conflict between production goals and distribution goals is a familiar story in rural development, and not at all unique to farm and community forestry. Moreover, the Gujarat case is but a microcosm of what is happening in farm and community forestry more widely (Romm 1989).

In some contexts, social units intermediate in size between the individual household and the "community" (i.e., entire village) appear to be functional alternatives for tree management. In several developing countries, school children are charged with the care of tree nurseries. These children provide seedlings for their families and sell them to farmers. Just as importantly, children may learn about environmental conservation in the process. Church groups and women's groups also comprise appropriate social units in some cases. In Kenya, women's church groups of about fifteen members per group have proved enthusiastic tree raisers and planters (Shepherd 1985).

In summary, the search for approaches which aim for progress in both production and equity demands the constant and diligent study of different cases linking tenure, social organization, and technical achievement. Very clear is that neither farm forestry alone nor community forestry alone provides a complete framework.

PROGRAMS AND PROJECTS: MAKING THEM WORK

Deliberate interventions to initiate or expand farm and community forestry take the form of programs and projects. Since the 1970s, dozens of programs and projects have been evaluated for lessons learned. Most evaluations indicate that program and project success requires workable solutions across four broad areas: planning and design, social incentives and constraints, technologies, and institutions and extension.

Planning and Design

The role of planning and design in farm and community forestry is to debate the social, economic, and environmental objectives of programs and projects, and to compare the advantages and disadvantages of alternative means to achieve them. Objectives extend beyond physical targets such as numbers of seedlings distributed, or hectares of forest and woodlands protected. True objectives consider a more sophisticated framework of food consumption, labor time, disposable income, and other welfare measures.

Planning and design are not simple exercises. The multiple objectives of a particular program or project usually reveal subtle tradeoffs or even basic incompatibilities. Few programs and projects are without negative effects, and few are acceptable to everyone concerned, particularly when a "community" is seen to comprise diverse socioeconomic groups. For these reasons, planning and design generally entail a series of compromises and subjective judgments. Five characteristics of good planning and design are identified in Figure 6-4, and are briefly summarized in the following paragraphs.

FIGURE 6-4
Desirable characteristics of plans and designs for farm and community forestry.

- Builds upon existing knowledge, priorities, and practices
- Aims at target beneficiaries, not at amorphous and undifferentiated "communities"
- Anticipates and accommodates uncertainties
- Is realistic regarding time to achieve results
- Gives explicit and early attention to how efforts will be managed by beneficiaries

First, plans and designs demand a thorough understanding of how trees and shrubs are managed according to current knowledge, priorities, and motivations (Rocheleau 1987). This informs the planner about the nature of problems and opportunities, sheds light on where and why they exist, and suggests interventions and resources which might help improve social and economic welfare. The baseline information on perceived needs, wants, and conditions usually derives from one or more surveys and assessments. Such analyses range in scope from a few interviews with farmers and villagers to elaborate sampling schemes covering hundreds of informants. Survey scale and complexity are determined by the purposes of data collection, and the time and budget available (Raintree 1989).

An entire science has grown up around methods to learn about local communities in a development context, but this science is inexact. It commonly relies on opinions and perceptions—in parallel with observed behavior—for its conclusions. This process is vulnerable to a variety of errors in communication, interpretation, and judgment. For example, governments and development agencies strongly advocated tree planting for fuelwood 10–15 years ago, even though it has since been concluded that fuelwood production alone rarely interests farmers and communities. Time and resources were wasted as various fuelwood projects collapsed for lack of local support. Likewise, nitrogen-fixing tree species have proven less popular in African agroforestry than initially assumed by program designers (Kerkhof 1990). Either social assessments have been faulty or, just as seriously, project planners have ignored the assessments actually provided for them.

A second main point is that programs and projects aim to improve the welfare and fit within the constraints of specific target beneficiaries (Noronha and Spears 1985). In Central America, large farmers and ranchers are interested in tree planting to the extent that this provides them with marketable products. This compares with small farmers, who are motivated more by desires for self-sufficiency in wood, positive effects of trees on crops and livestock, and emotional or aesthetic factors (Tschinkel 1987).

This example for Central American landowners emphasizes the rationale for accurate diagnosis of attitudes, objectives, and resources by different socioeconomic segments. With good reason, small and landless farmers are more averse to taking risks—including adoption of agroforestry innovations—than are landowners who are larger and more diversified. Similarly, most experience shows that ability to wait for tangible returns from tree management is positively related to scale and diversity of economic activities. Hence it makes little sense to speak of harmonizing project objectives with community interests if the community is differentiated. More accurate is to attempt to provide benefits to particular socioeconomic elements within a larger population.

Thirdly, practical experience indicates that planning and design must accommodate considerable uncertainty. Projects in farm and community forestry often have the character of social experiments, meaning that outcomes and impacts are difficult to predict. In India's state of Uttar Pradesh, demand for tree seedlings during the early years of a social forestry program was 30 times greater than anticipated (FAO 1985). Even though Gujarat's farm forestry was criticized for straying from its socioeconomic mission, the program was continuously redesigned and refocused (Blair and Olpadwala 1988). In Haiti, the Agroforestry Outreach Project found it necessary to shift from a central seedling nursery to several decentralized

To the extent that tree-growing demonstrations succeed on the lands of progressive farmers in Central America, it takes at least another two years before interest spreads more widely. A farmer in Honduras examines teak (*Tectona grandis*) planted on a hillside. *(Photo courtesy of FAO.)*

nurseries (Murray 1986). Each of these cases illustrates that good planning and design allow for almost inevitable adjustments to circumstances not foreseen at the outset.

The fourth guideline stems from the preceding one. Because many interventions in farm and community forestry are in fact experimental, adequate time is required for them to succeed in an evolutionary way. Farm forestry in Gujarat had an experimental period of 10 years before it was ready to move ahead on a significant scale (Blair and Olpadwala 1988). To the extent that tree-growing demonstrations succeed on the lands of progressive farmers in Central America, it takes at least another two years before interest spreads more widely (Tschinkel 1987). Yet a number of governments and funding agencies expect visible results at early stages. Programs under pressure to move fast often risk major difficulties at later stages if basic steps in social and technical learning are skimped or omitted.

Finally and usually most importantly, tree management on farms and communal lands is a "people's forestry" in which decisions and actions should be in the hands of persons living locally. As passionately expressed in numerous conferences and articles, the professional is motivator rather than manager or policeman. To the extent that it becomes increasingly spontaneous and self-supporting, a people's forestry is not forever dependent on external funding and management. The ideal of autonomy is aptly articulated in the title of a conservation project in Guatemala, "We Did This Ourselves" (Nations et al. 1987).

At the start of a project, an external funding agency or private voluntary organization typically shares project management with an indigenous tribe, peasant community, or farmers' group. Eventually, the beneficiaries are expected to take complete control. This progression from joint to sole management faces numerous hurdles, and projects easily disintegrate if local people feel they do not truly "own" them. Approaches to organizing and sustaining local management usually work through extension agents, who are expected to build local management capability by means of education, demonstration, and technical guidance. This is a long-term prospect which cannot be hurried.

Social Incentives and Constraints

Accomplishments in farm and community forestry depend on removing social constraints and increasing social incentives. Prominent in this discussion are attitudes about tree growing, issues of tenure and ownership, and gender roles.

Attitudes Towards Tree Growing and Protection   Customs, myths, and attitudes define the human meaning of forests and trees (Burch 1988a). Successful efforts in farm and community forestry build upon positive attitudes, and attempt to overcome or at least work around negative ones. Various surveys in cultural anthropology and economic botany reveal the following:

• Even in regions with pronounced scarcities of forests and trees, tree planting may be low among priorities compared with immediate and often desperate needs for water and food, healthcare, and employment.

• Some indigenous peoples feel that tree growing is the work of nature and gods, and that human intervention is neither necessary nor appropriate.

• From the perspective of individual peasants or tribal groups, tree or woodland depletion may appear totally beyond their control, or irrelevant in the time scale of their lives.

• Various beliefs about the effects of trees, such as the belief that eucalyptus dries the soil and kills adjacent plants, are based on a folk science that is sometimes accurate and sometimes faulty.

Antipathy to forests and trees may be explained as a result of inherited traditions, or because of strictly practical and contemporary reasons. Farmers cut down trees to reduce populations of crop-eating birds, to eliminate hiding places for thieves and other threatening persons, and to get rid of snakes and ghosts. In African countries, people have been taught that tsetse flies can be controlled by cutting down the trees which harbor them. Providing persuasive arguments why this should not be done—and why trees should be protected—can be very difficult (Foley and Barnard 1984).

On the other hand, the reverence for certain forests and trees can work positively for their protection and establishment. In India, an avenue of research explores how sacred trees and shrubs might be produced in nurseries for planting and care on farms and communal lands. Similarly, various components of the tree and shrub cover in West Africa are protected because of their spiritual significance in local cultures. In general, the Western scientific view of tree management gives inadequate attention to spiritual dimensions of trees and shrubs in strategies for their propagation and husbandry.

Ownership and Tenure In the heavily populated regions of the developing world, land tenure arrangements are progressively tightening with increasing competition for land. This threatens various traditional social arrangements for collectively managing communal lands, and various customary rights of villagers and farmers to use tree products and services on the lands of others (Raintree 1987). Long-term activities like tree establishment and protection simply do not occur without secure rights to the future goods and services that will be produced (Fortmann 1988). Moreover, traditional usufruct rights of villagers and farmers to collect fuelwood, fodder, and food products on state lands are far from permanent in a context of rapid changes in land ownership and uses (Singh 1986).

Simultaneously, many traditional types of common lands and tribal tenure carry over successfully into the current era. In fact, a number of governments seem increasingly willing to transfer certain forests, woodlands, and other nonagricultural lands to local communities for administration and management. In central Nepal, the Hattisunde Forest has been protected over several years by four villages without resort to fences or posted guards (Winrock International 1988). In 1990, the government of Niger turned over management responsibilities for several Sahelian woodlands to the villages near them, based on positive testing of this approach with an experimental forestry cooperative at Guesselbodi forest (Heermans 1986). The Dhanori village woodlot in India was galvanized when the Gujarat government agreed to give 100 percent of the woodlot's future products and services to the village, rather than the 50/50 split proposed originally (Verma 1988).

Also in India, the Forest Department of West Bengal has encouraged villages to take charge of restrictions on grazing and cutting in degraded forests of sal (*Shorea rubusta*). Efforts began with a single pilot project in the early 1970s. By 1990, forest protection committees had been formed in nearly 1,300 villages. In return for their protection services, the Forest Department gives the villages 25 percent of the revenues from the sale of fuelwood and timber. Additionally, the villages are allowed to gather leaves, silk cocoons, medicinal herbs, fodder grasses, oil seeds, and other forest products from the regenerating forests. Village management of grazing and wood cutting appears to be a low-cost approach to regenerating extensive forested areas (Malhotra and Poffenberger 1989).

The management of common property, such as through village forestry, seems most successful where individuals are relatively undifferentiated in social rank and economic status. Trust and cooperation tend to reflect conditions of only small differences in ethnic, political, and educational rank. Also, management of common property often works best in remote regions where the power of central government is relatively weak, and where local political governance still flourishes. Management of common property is most vulnerable to collapse where central government displaces former local authority, where human populations are increasing rapidly, where land scarcity is severe, and where markets and new technologies drive up land values (Shepherd 1985).

In the Western world, there is much romantic and practical sentiment that indigenous peoples and peasant communities should maintain harmonious social and ecological relationships with the land (e.g., Posey and Balee 1989; UNESCO 1989). Does this depend on defending common property from forces that will harm it? Through what policies and programs should the rural poor empower themselves to protect their communal lands from outside intervention? Is it inevitable that village and tribal management of natural resources will break down because of far-reaching social change ("modernization") now affecting many of these communities? These questions frame ongoing debates about rural tenure in general, with major implications for strategies in farm and community forestry.

Gender Roles   In numerous traditional cultures, women are separated from men in terms of economic sphere and decisionmaking authority. It is not unusual for women to have to work longer and harder than men, but for less wealth, prestige, and leisure. Some African women claim that their social and economic status is no more than as "tenants on their husbands' lands" (Shepherd 1985, p. 10).

Yet it is the women who often are the local experts in key matters of farm and community forestry (Fortmann 1986). Because they generally hold primary responsibility for family food and health, women customarily know more than men about local fuelwood supplies, medicinal plants, and food products from trees and shrubs. In the West African country of Sierra Leone, interviews with villagers found that women named 31 products gathered or made from adjacent woodlands, while men identified eight (Hoskins 1984).

In numerous traditional societies, women work longer and harder than men, but for less wealth, prestige, and leisure. These young Ethiopian women work in erosion control and afforestation. *(Photo courtesy of FAO.)*

Because they generally hold primary responsibility for family food and health, women customarily know more than men about local fuelwood supplies, medicinal plants, and food products from trees and shrubs. *(Photo courtesy of World Bank.)*

223

Additionally, women have taken the lead in significant environmental initiatives such as the Chipko Movement in India and the Greenbelt Movement in Kenya. Chipko ("embrace the trees") refers to the nonviolent protest in which female activists were among those who demonstrated effectively against timber cutting practices which conflicted with village interests (Shiva and Bandyopadhyay 1986; Weber 1989). The Greenbelt Movement and other Kenyan projects in tree planting have been inspired mainly by women, with women also providing most of the labor.

In thousands of villages around the world, women do not speak out when men are present, and in other ways are expected to follow conventional norms of social stratification by gender. Thus while it is frequently urged that women be given adequate representation in the planning and implementation of farm and community forestry, this can be a hollow recommendation unless accompanied by specific strategies. The recruitment of women as professionals and technicians in farm and community forestry is one such strategy, and other strategies depend on local circumstances.

Technologies

Some observers believe that technical problems in farm and community forestry are minor compared with the complexity of social issues. This is open to debate. In many cases, trees and shrubs are managed on sites which are small, dispersed, and unproductive for all but the hardiest of plants and animals. Critical factors related to soils and climate may be variable and unknown. To the extent that practices are in the hands of many different persons rather than a few technical specialists, there may be a minimal degree of control over methods of establishing and caring for trees. Written technical instructions can be useless in regions where a majority of persons are illiterate, and where individuals are not accustomed to receiving formal technical guidance.

The price of technical failure can be high. This price is measured not only in time and money, but also in lost confidence. Project sponsors and organizers accept a heavy responsibility each time they persuade farmers and villagers to invest land and labor in tree management. Losses because of droughts, insects, pathogens, livestock browsing, and other technical problems may seriously hurt targeted "beneficiaries" in a way that discourages them from further interest and participation. Unfortunately, such losses have been all too frequent. Examples include drought and termite damage to seedlings of eucalyptus and *Acacia albida* in some of the Sahelian projects, and widespread defoliation of *Leucaena* plantings in the Philippines because of a psyllid insect (*Heteropsylla cubana*). In view of these and other experiences, technical choices in farm and community forestry increasingly favor diversity, versatility, and adaptability in strategies to help manage risk.

Agroforestry Systems   The explosion of interest in farm and community forestry since the 1970s has produced several research initiatives to improve the productivity and usefulness of agroforestry technologies. In Central America, the Center for Tropical Agricultural Research and Training (CATIE) manages a program to compare the performance of different multipurpose tree species across a range of the region's climates and site qualities. Similar objectives guide the Forestry/Fuelwood Research and Development (F/FRED) Project in several countries of Asia. In Nigeria, the International Institute for Tropical Agriculture (IITA) has been experimenting with different ways of intercropping maize with nitrogen-fixing woody species. The International Council for Research in Agroforestry (ICRAF) was established specifically to guide and coordinate agroforestry research.

In view of the huge diversity of existing and potential agroforestry technologies, the choice of research priorities should adhere to a systematic approach. Over the course of several years, a team at ICRAF evolved a formal methodology to help assess agroforestry research issues and priorities. ICRAF's "Diagnostic and Design Methodology for Agroforestry" comprises four stages. The pre-diagnostic stage surveys existing agronomic and tree-growing practices in a local area. The second phase, the diagnostic stage, identifies possible agroforestry solutions in relation to findings on perceived problems and opportunities. The technology design stage focuses on selection, design, and evaluation criteria for the testing of specific agroforestry techniques. Finally, the planning stage specifies the details of an agroforestry research project, including an implementation plan to carry it out (Lundgren and Raintree 1983).

In principle, this process of diagnosis and design is iterative, and research is constantly reviewed and evaluated on the basis of results from field trials. This helps develop agroforestry improvements in the shortest possible time, and with minimum expenditure of resources.

Yet in practice, agroforestry research is vulnerable to a certain amount of criticism. The agroforestry literature contains hundreds of papers describing individual practices combining crops, livestock, and woody perennials. A major emphasis is inventories and classifications of different systems. Less in evidence are policy evaluations and cost-benefit analyses which draw this information together to provide a sense of what is being learned, and where research is leading. Moreover, only some of the past research reflects a truly interdisciplinary effort which integrates perspectives of anthropologists, agronomists, soil scientists, foresters, and other specialists.

Many of these concerns arise when considering research on multipurpose tree species, such as those often preferred by farmers and villagers. Three challenges are to determine for whose benefit the research is intended, to take advantage of previous knowledge on the subject, and to generate findings which have immediate applications for beneficiaries (Figure 6-5). The agroforestry research of the future must move rapidly from description to experiment, and from experiment to feasible practice (Huxley 1990).

Species Selection   In programs and projects where trees are grown from seed or seedlings, a fundamental question is the choice of species. Technical criteria for selection include ecological suitability, growth and yield, water requirements, seed availability, and resistance to pests, fires, and droughts. Above all, the species

FIGURE 6-5
Challenges in research on multipurpose trees for agroforestry.
(Source: MacDicken (1989).)

Identifying Clients and Their Problems
Clear identification of end users (beneficiaries) and their perceived priority of problems
• Issue: some research fails to begin with a clear sense of which issues to address, and why
Using Existing Knowledge
Incorporation of findings from past studies in current research design and field practices
• Issue: attention to historic work and parallel work in other countries can make research more efficient and relevant
Generating Useful Results
Development of guidelines and practices which are within the user's capacity to implement
• Issue: researchers are expected to think beyond academic findings to how results can be used in the field

must satisfy the objectives of why trees are being planted in the first place—whether for cash crops, shelterbelts, live fences, fuelwood, fodder, fruit, shade, ornamental purposes, or other ends.

In a people's forestry, the people choose the species, and foresters and extension agents advise on technical methods of production. In reality, foresters and extension agents have their own perspectives regarding what could and should be grown, and these views often conflict with views of target beneficiaries. Sorting out these differences requires ample care and deliberation, since many years of subsequent work rest on initial species selection. A review of experience in Africa suggests that projects which are able to accommodate a dialogue on species fare more successfully than projects which retain fixed ideas (Kerkhof 1990).

In farm and community forestry, the choice of species can be a difficult matter. This is because trees are expected to survive a range of planting sites and ecological conditions. In particular, many programs seek trees and shrubs which are able to grow on "wastelands" and marginal sites subject to harsh climates, fires, grazing pressures, and other adverse circumstances.

During the 1970s and 1980s, numerous reports highlighted trees and shrubs deserving further study for use in farm and community forestry. For example, the FAO Panel of Experts on Forest Gene Resources identified 35 candidate species in this category (Burley 1980). The USA's National Academy of Sciences published two volumes on promising fuelwood species for the tropics (NAS 1980, 1983a). It also published a series on *Leucaena, Casuarina, Acacia mangium,* and *Calliandra* as deserving increased attention in the fight against deforestation.

Such worldwide summaries of what is known and not known about individual genera and species provide useful starting points. Yet they do not identify "miracle trees," as some persons apparently hoped. Rather, the leading perspective today is that choices on what to plant should be variable and specific in relation to purposes of tree growing, local familiarity with species, and available information on biological performance. A project in the Atlantic coastal plain of Costa Rica screened dozens of exotic and native trees as potential candidate species to be planted on farms and in degraded pastures, concluding that initial survival and growth favor native species like *Vochysia hondurensis, V. ferruginea, Stryphnodendron excelsum*, and *Hyeronima oblonga* (Butterfield 1990). These species appear on few world lists, illustrating that appropriate species for Costa Rica's Atlantic coastal plain are not identified except in the regional context.

Where doubts exist about seed availability or expected biological performance, many projects rely on species already known in the project area. This minimizes risks of failure, even if performance may be less than with species which are promising but untried. Prudent strategies typically begin with familiar species while simultaneously testing the survival, yield, and local acceptance of several alternatives. However, a frequent dilemma finds that the commercial pines and eucalypts familiar to foresters are not familiar to local farmers, and the native species familiar to farmers are not well known by foresters.

Particularly where growing conditions are adverse and introduced species are at their ecological limits, much current opinion argues for managing and regenerating the natural woody vegetation. Choice of species becomes growing what can be regenerated on the site through soil mulching, water conservation, weeding, and improvement cuttings.

This is perhaps nowhere clearer than in the Sahelian zone of Africa, where eucalyptus and neem (*Azadirachta indica*) were established at very high costs by bulldozing "useless brush." Foresters in the World Bank estimated that costs

A frequent dilemma in farm and community forestry finds that the commercial pines and eucalypts familiar to foresters are not familiar to local farmers. Are these pines a good choice for farm forestry in Costa Rica? *(Photo courtesy of World Bank.)*

to grow irrigated eucalyptus in Niger exceeded US$5,000 per hectare, while *E. camaldulensis* in Senegal cost over US$800 per hectare. Yet wood yields of the planted species are no greater, and are often poorer, than yields of the mixed native shrubs and small trees. Moreover, these bushland species furnish a variety of by-products, and management practices do not expose and compact the soil as often happens when introduced trees are planted in blocks (Heermans 1986).

The perspective that trees and shrubs are not so much to be planted as regenerated naturally is by no means unique to the African Sahel. This strategic direction conforms with broader sustainability themes now on many lips, receiving particularly strong endorsements from environmentalists.

Risk Reduction   Many proposed projects in tree planting and stewardship demand inputs of land and labor which subsistence-level people are unable or unwilling to commit. With some exceptions, the decision environment is highly conservative because persons living in poverty take few risks with their meager resources. To the extent that changes are possible, they tend to be small and gradual, evolving only after demonstrated successes and other assurances that efforts will not fail. Tree projects face the additional constraint that results often require many years to materialize. These realities focus attention on policies and strategies to reduce biological and economic risks.

The decision environment in farm and community forestry is highly conservative because persons living in poverty take few risks with their meager resources. *(Photo courtesy of FAO.)*

The principles of risk reduction include diversification of project activities and technical approaches, use of pilot tests to precede larger efforts, and clear differentiation between experiments and demonstrations. Risk-reducing subsidies include low-cost loans to help farmers or communities cover initial costs of tree establishment, payments of cash or food as a supplement or bonus for participating in tree planting, and distribution of seeds and seedlings at low or zero cost to recipients. The provision of technical assistance through extension services is yet another form of risk reduction. Additionally, risk is managed through broad strategies identified previously: clarification of tenure, choice of appropriate units of social organization, attention to gender roles, and initial use of familiar and versatile agroforestry systems and tree species.

A particularly important aspect of risk reduction is to ensure early payoffs so that beneficiaries quickly see tangible results. Sometimes this takes the form of encouraging the collection of grass and leaves for fodder—and branches for fuel—from rows or plots of trees which are not yet mature for poles and construction timbers. Moreover, some species grow exceptionally rapidly. An example on the Indonesian island of Java is *Calliandra*, a shrub taller than a village house in nine months, and harvestable for fuelwood in just one year. Resprouting enables the stump to send up new stems rising above the houses again within only six months (NAS 1983b). Fast growth is characteristic of numerous other trees and shrubs growing in the humid tropics, so that time scales familiar in temperate regions can be quite irrelevant.

In some projects, cash payments have been used to induce farmers and villagers to plant and take care of trees. These subsidies are paid upon planting, after measured tree survival, or upon some combination of initial establishment and subsequent survival. However, much successful tree planting takes place with low material incentives, or no incentives at all. This is because generous subsidies tend to attract persons more interested in the cash payments than in tree growing. Typically, these individuals abandon tree growing soon after the subsidies end. To be effective, cash subsidies should be sparing, restricted to socioeconomic groups who need them, and confined to just the early stages of a project. Subsidies work best when tied to results (e.g., number of hectares planted and trees surviving) rather than number of days worked (Tschinkel 1987).

As with other crops, credit at satisfactory terms may help reduce financial problems in growing tree crops. Yet for the most part, credit is more easily obtained by relatively well-off landowners than by smallholders and the landless. Lenders generally are reluctant to extend loans to persons who lack title to the land, or who have insufficient collateral. Even farmers who have land titles may be unwilling to risk losing their property by using their land as loan collateral. In some cases, cultural attitudes discourage the borrowing of money, as in an unsuccessful fuelwood project in the Ilocos region of the Philippines (Hyman 1983a). Shifting cultivators and other landless persons face great difficulties obtaining loans, and are wary of formal agreements which tie them to governments and legal systems. In summary, credit may be less important in reducing risk for smallholders than marketing assistance, price guarantees, and technical assistance (Arnold 1983).

As with other crops, credit at satisfactory terms may help reduce financial problems in growing tree crops. However, lack of credit is only one among several constraints, particularly for small holders. *(Photo courtesy of World Bank.)*

A large number of projects in farm and community forestry rely heavily on the distribution of subsidized tree seed or seedlings as a primary activity. The intent is to offer a means of getting local people to initiate or expand tree planting at little cash cost to themselves. Also, project organizers have the opportunity to learn which kinds of seed and seedlings are in local demand, providing still another strategy to lessen project risk.

The provision of seed and seedlings raises challenging policy questions on what prices (if any) to charge different categories of persons and groups, what limits to apply on quantities of seed or seedlings per client, and what choices to make on nursery locations and seedling distribution systems. A major issue in many projects is that availability of subsidized seed and seedlings discourages the start-up of nurseries by farmers and businesses, since they are unable to compete with the low-cost supply. Hence continued subsidization beyond an introductory phase can be counterproductive (FAO 1985).

Institutions and Extension

Success in farm and community forestry relies on effective coordination between the targeted communities and the responsible government agencies. Frequently, development banks and other funding organizations play important financial and

Numerous projects in farm and community forestry rely heavily on the distribution of subdidized tree seed or seedlings. *(Photo courtesy of FAO.)*

policy roles. Moreover, various programs and projects are implemented through intermediaries, particularly nongovernmental organizations (NGOs) like religious groups and other charitable agencies. A supportive institutional environment is one which promotes good working relationships across this spectrum.

Government organizations for farm and community forestry are highly variable. Usually, the scope of the activity is sufficiently different from management of government forests as to require new administrative units. Secondly, many forestry agencies realize that they cannot win the trust of a farm and community constituency as long as they continue to present an image of being rural police whose primary function is to enforce forest laws. For both of these reasons, several of India's state forest departments have created separate divisions of social forestry. Senegal has assigned foresters without uniforms and guns to work with special offices for rural development. Before it launched its highly successful village forestry program, the Republic of Korea shifted responsibility for forestry to the Ministry of Home Affairs in order to give priority to village tree planting at the level of local governments (Eckholm 1979).

A "people's forestry" attracts a variety of NGOs interested in the broad connections between tree management, socioeconomic development, and environmental protection. At the local level, these NGOs include various kinds of cooperatives for tree planting and forest products marketing. At the international level, many

NGOs are conduits for directing foreign funds into local projects. Thus the Agro-forestry Outreach Project in Haiti was implemented through CARE and the Pan American Development Foundation (PADF), with funding from the USA and Switzerland. In turn, CARE and PADF worked through more than 170 Haitian NGOs to carry out local extension, supplying over 27 million tree seedlings to 110 thousand farmers (Winterbottom and Hazelwood 1987).

Several NGOs are successful in farm and community forestry because of their grass-roots orientation, genuine commitment to the poor, and the trust this wins among project participants. Some NGOs are able and willing to implement small and dispersed activities not feasible for either governments or development assistance agencies. On the other hand, governments sometimes view NGOs as overturning their policies, competing for external funding, and in other ways opposing government programs. Also, many NGOs lack technical expertise unless given considerable outside assistance. None of these virtues or deficiencies is universally applicable, given that NGO experiences in farm and community forestry are highly variable from case to case.

Farm and community forestry typically rests on public information, project promotion, and technical assistance provided through extension programs (Kenny Jordan 1988). Extension agents both gather information (e.g., on existing patterns of tree management) and transmit information (e.g., publicity for a government campaign on fire prevention and reforestation). Extension agents in farm and community forestry have the difficult assignment of assessing how the products and services of trees are perceived and used, how the cultural setting shapes land-use practices, how different individuals and social units might respond to changes in government policies, and how local people perceive relationships between the new social forestry and traditional state and corporate forestry.

The educational role of extension workers is to communicate at the level of farmers, villagers, and tribal groups on matters pertaining to the management of tree cover (Pelinck et al. 1984). Ideally, this builds upon local knowledge and works within local constraints. It is by now very well accepted that "technical packages" rarely work unless designed and tested through a participatory strategy. This implies that extension workers and their clients engage in a perpetual exchange of opinions, ideas, and evaluations of field experiments (FAO 1985).

PROFESSIONAL DEVELOPMENT

Farm and community forestry now attracts widespread interest as both a conceptual framework and policy priority. This raises difficult issues for forestry organizations and professionals, many of which are striving to remake themselves for a truly social forestry managed by professionals called social foresters. This calls for a modified "social contract" and new professional skills.

The Social Contract

Especially in many of the developing countries, the social contract between foresters and their clients is changing dramatically. The traditional forester works on state or company lands, where ownership issues and management objectives are conceptually straightforward. The social forester usually struggles with greater ambiguity. Importantly, the social forester frequently chooses an advocacy role, representing the needs and rights of the socially disadvantaged before higher authority. This breaks with the historical role of foresters as protecting state interests from poor people who squat and poach on forest lands. As farm and community forestry moves ahead in the 1990s, the rewriting of the social contract contends with the following issues (Shepherd 1985, pp. 18–19):

- *Putting people first*—The aim of farm and community forestry is to satisfy the pressing needs which drive villagers and shifting agriculturalists to overcut forests and woodlands.
- *Gaining trust*—In areas where forestry officials have repeatedly fined villagers and taken them to court for violating forest laws, forging a new relationship of trust is difficult but essential for both sides.
- *Defining benefits*—Benefits are not fuzzy and distant objectives at a national level. Rather, they are tangible gains in a local setting for specifically targeted peasants, villagers, or tribal groups.
- *Clarifying distribution*—Farm and community forestry has its greatest potential to succeed where distributional issues regarding ownership, costs, and benefits are thoroughly discussed and clarified.

Professional Skills

The questions of greatest concern in farm and community forestry, and those about which the least is known, fall outside the range of conventional forestry knowledge (Zulberti 1987). This is why anthropologists, sociologists, political scientists, economists, and management specialists must be systematically drawn into farm and community forestry, meeting the foresters half way (Romm 1982).

Meanwhile, the making of social foresters and agroforesters is gradually evolving into a specialized field of study. On the one hand, the social forester is expected to master various social sciences which help him or her with social analysis and organization. On the other, the agroforester knows the components and operation of complex ecological systems. To explore the juncture of these social and natural sciences is to identify many new areas of curriculum and field training important in farm and community forestry.

Figure 6-6 shows a framework of needed parallel development in technical skills and social skills. Among the key skills are abilities to (1) listen, inform, persuade, and in other ways communicate with peasants, villagers, and tribal groups; (2) interpret social and anthropological theories of rural life in terms of management guidelines for trees, shrubs, woodlands, and forests; (3) link social processes with ecological processes, explaining each in terms of the other; and (4) create and influence the direction of social organizations which help the rural poor to manage trees and forests (Burch 1988b).

Among the key skills in farm and community forestry is the ability to communicate with peasants, villagers, and tribal groups. *(Photo courtesy of World Bank.)*

FIGURE 6-6
Parallel technical and social skills for development of professionals in farm and community forestry. *(Source: Adapted from Burch (1988b, p. 102).)*

Technical skills	Social skills
Diagnosis: how to increase growth, reduce biological risk	**Diagnosis:** how to connect trees/shrubs to reduction of poverty/dependence
Planning/prescription: harvest schedules, management areas, forest protection	**Planning/prescription:** benefit-cost frameworks, social impact assessments
Flora/fauna inventory: species, growth rates, age distribution, volumes, etc.	**Social inventory:** demographic structure, ethnic composition, fertility/mortality
Site preparation: boundaries, marking, roads and trails	**Project preparation:** social units, training systems, work assignments
Market analysis: end uses, delivered costs, competing products	**Market analysis:** household consumption, time budgets
Monitoring and evaluation: seedling survival, tree growth, hectares protected	**Monitoring and evaluation:** employment distribution, social change and adaptation, negative and positive social indicators

SYNTHESIS

For thousands of years, villagers and farmers have been husbanding trees and shrubs for household needs and to provide cash incomes. However, it is mainly since the 1970s that governments and international agencies have been committing personnel and budgets to strengthen a "people's forestry" in the developing countries. The hopes for farm and community forestry are framed within the broad context of combatting food shortages, energy scarcities, environmental degradation, and the continuing scourge of material poverty. A leading perspective argues for a self-help strategy. That is, governments and development banks cannot do for the management of tree cover what millions of individual persons can do with the right mixes of knowledge, resources, motivations, and social arrangements.

The benefits of managing tree cover on farms and near villages can be classified in a number of ways. One is increased food production, either directly or through influences on crop and livestock yields. A second is the provision of fuelwood as an energy source less costly than most energy alternatives. A wide variety of construction materials derives not only from trees and shrubs, but also from bamboos and palms. Under some circumstances, tree farming for monetary income is a viable economic opportunity, as is the collection and sale of non-wood forest products. Passive retention or deliberate cultivation of trees can represent savings and security, helping to meet special contingencies and compensating for reduced income during hardship periods.

Trees and shrubs are passively protected or actively managed only insofar as they furnish net benefits to someone. At the same time, trees and shrubs occupy land area, and require attention and labor to manage. Thus the protection and management of trees is not without cost. Each farmer and each community is in many ways unique in its perceptions of the benefits and costs of husbanding trees. It is these differences which explain wide variations in the purposes and practices of tree management. Some of the best-known agroforestry practices include enhanced shifting cultivation, taungya intercropping, dispersed and linear patterns of farm trees, canopy trees for plantation crops, shade and fodder trees, alley cropping, and home gardens.

Beginning in the late 1970s, the renewed interest in ancient practices stimulated considerable enthusiasm for farm and community forestry in development policy. Tangible accomplishments like the establishment of ICRAF, and the funding of farm and community forestry by the World Bank, created high expectations. However, only some of the early programs and projects in farm and community forestry materialized according to plan. Others were redirected or abandoned because initial perceptions and assumptions later proved faulty. Accumulating experience in farm and community forestry leads to the following current perspectives:

• Intervention in farm and community forestry begins with understanding the ecological, social, and economic processes which govern tree management practices at a local level.
• The scope for intervention is shaped by cultural attitudes about tree management, the economic and political circumstances of land and labor availability, the

range of possible technologies for managing tree cover, and the place of trees in overall household priorities. These constraints are not immutable, and a primary objective of intervention is to relax them.

 • Successful interventions in farm and community forestry are those which pay particular attention to distributional impacts. Almost universally, key concerns are divisions of benefits and costs across gradients of land ownership, social class, and gender.

Neither "community" nor "farm" forestry alone provides an exclusive focus for activities. Appropriateness of social organization is a matter of building upon existing social units on the one hand, and of working towards particular social objectives on the other. Moreover, farm and community forestry is not solely tree planting, nor is it solely community management of adjacent forests and woodlands. It is not confined to a single product like fuelwood, and it is more than a search for miracle trees.

Prospects in farm and community forestry depend on continued efforts to revise the social contract between foresters and rural communities. By this is meant targeting the poor and socially disadvantaged as participants and beneficiaries of tree husbandry. Special emphasis is placed on the ability of social foresters to blend technical and social skills for the particular aims and constraints they face in these challenging tasks.

ISSUES FOR DISCUSSION AND INVESTIGATION

1 A basic issue in farm and community forestry is "how to change land use so that people get what they need on a sustainable basis from a relatively fixed or even shrinking land base" (Gregersen 1988). What are the other basic issues, and why are they issues?

2 Describe the degree of overlap and separation within the following pairs: (i) social forestry and agroforestry; (ii) farm forestry and community forestry; and (iii) social forestry and community forestry.

3 Tree management on farms and near villages is an ancient art, but a new science. Explain. What justifies the term "science" in this context?

4 In India, "social forestry is a program for the development of society as well as land resources" (Chand and Singh 1983, p. 317). Explain.

5 What defines community in community forestry?

6 Relationships between trees and food production are both complementary and competitive. Explain and illustrate.

7 How does the intensification of agroforestry systems help curb tropical deforestation? What assumptions are necessary for this to be an effective strategy?

8 Fuelwood dynamics remain grossly understudied in relation to fuelwood's prominent place in global wood consumption. (i) What factors explain this, and what (if anything) should be done about it? (ii) Explain why fuelwood scarcity is simultaneously an energy problem, a food problem, and an environmental problem. (iii) Why is it so difficult to grow fuelwood (Noronha 1981)?

9 (i) Describe trees as an "insurance policy" for subsistence-level people. (ii) In what ways are trees superior and inferior to other assets which may play a similar role?

10 That a village such as Dhanori in India managed a successful woodlot on four hectares of village commons is in many ways an exceptional accomplishment (Verma 1988). Explain.

11 In a people's forestry, the professional is expected to have implicit confidence in the ability of local people to make good choices about forests and trees in overall land use. Discuss this proposition as (i) naive and dangerous; and (ii) sound and irrefutable.

12 Tree species favored by foresters and extension workers for a certain program or project frequently are not the ones considered most desirable by the people who live there. Why not? Through what policies and procedures should these differences be resolved?

13 Investigate the suitability of *Eucalyptus* in farm forestry and community forestry.

14 Each of the many agroforestry systems carries with it numerous social implications. What are the social implications of taungya methods, and under what social circumstances is taungya not viable?

15 In some regions, local communities have enjoyed tree tenure without land tenure. (i) In what contexts is this possible? (ii) Where and why are tenure arrangements changing, and what are the implications for tree management?

16 (i) What general considerations should enter the design of an incentives package to encourage people to manage tree cover in their locality? (ii) How will these incentives be different for large farmers compared with small farmers? For individual farmers compared with villagers on common lands? For tree planting compared with management of nearby woodlands?

17 Tree farming for cash incomes has been successful in certain regions of the Philippines and India. Why does tree farming not exist in virtually every developing country experiencing wood scarcities?

18 Describe the role of women as overlooked experts in farm and community forestry.

19 Innovations in farm and community forestry depend on reducing risks of failure. Identify alternative strategies of risk management.

20 It is often said that progress in farm and community forestry requires a new "social contract" between the forestry profession and its clientele. Explain. Who writes this contract, and through what means?

21 Summarize leading challenges in agroforestry research, and explain why they are challenges.

22 Summarize leading challenges in forestry extension with farmers and communities, and explain why they are challenges.

23 Who or what are social foresters, and how are they educated and trained?

24 A large share of the intellectual leadership, literature, and applied work in farm and community forestry originates in Asia. Explain why, and evaluate whether Asia's prominence will continue.

25 Within the forestry and agriculture professions, the conceptual framework for farm and community forestry has advanced considerably since the 1970s. What are likely to be the next stages in conceptual development? Explain and defend.

REFERENCES

Agarwal, B. 1986. *Cold Hearths and Barren Slopes: The Woodfuel Crisis in the Third World.* Zed Books, London, England.

Arnold, J. E. M. 1983. "Economic considerations in agroforestry projects," *Agroforestry Systems* 1(4):299–311.

Arnold, J. E. M. and Jules Jongma. 1979. "Fuelwood and charcoal in developing countries," *Unasylva* 29(118):2–9.

Bajaracharya, Deepak. 1983. "Fuel, food, or forest? Dilemmas in a Nepali village," *World Development* 11(12):1057–1074.

Barrow, Edmund. 1988. *Trees and Pastoralists: The Case of the Pokot and Turkana.* Social Forestry Network Paper 6b, Overseas Development Institute, London, England.

Blair, Harry W. and Porus D. Olpadwala. 1988. *Forestry in Development Planning: Lessons from the Rural Experience.* Westview Press, Boulder, CO.

Brouwer, I. D., L. M. Nederveen, A. P. den Hartog, and A. H. C. Vlasveld. 1989. "Nutritional impacts of an increasing fuelwood shortage in rural households in developing countries," *Progress in Food and Nutrition Science* 13:349–361.

Burch, William R., Jr. 1988a. "Gods of the forest," *Farm Forestry News* 2(3):1–3.

Burch, William R., Jr. 1988b. "The uses of social science in the training of professional social foresters," *Journal of World Forest Management* 3(2):73–109.

Burley, J. 1980. "Choice of tree species and possibility of genetic improvement for smallholder and community forestry," *Commonwealth Forestry Review* 59(3):311–326.

Butterfield, R. 1990. "Native species for reforestation and land restoration: A case study from Costa Rica," *Proceedings of the XIX IUFRO World Congress*, Division 1, Vol. 2:3–14. Montreal, Canada.

Chambers, Robert and Melissa Leach. 1987. *Trees to Meet Contingencies: Savings and Security for the Rural Poor.* Institute of Development Studies Discussion Paper 228. University of Sussex, Brighton, England.

Chand, Kanwar Prakash and Ranveer Singh. 1983. "People's participation and social forestry: A case study of Himachal Pradesh," *Indian Journal of Agricultural Economics* 38:317–322.

Conelly, W.T. 1985. "Copal and rattan collecting in the Philippines," *Economic Botany* 39(1):39–46.

DeWees, Peter A. 1989. "The woodfuel crisis reconsidered: Observations on the dynamics of abundance and scarcity," World Development 17(8):1159–1172.

Eckholm, Erik. 1979. "Community forestry: The South Korean experience," *Development Digest* 17(4):11–20.

Eckholm, Erik, Gerald Foley, Geoffrey Barnard, and Lloyd Timberlake. 1984. *Fuelwood: The Energy Crisis that Won't Go Away.* International Institute for Environment and Development with Earthscan, London, England, and Washington, DC.

FAO (Food and Agriculture Organization of the United Nations). 1978. *Forestry for Local Community Development.* FAO Forestry Paper 7, Rome.

FAO. 1985. *Tree Growing by Rural People.* FAO Forestry Paper 64, Rome.

FAO. 1989a. *Forestry and Food Security.* FAO Forestry Paper 90, Rome.

FAO. 1989b. *Forestry and Nutrition: A Reference Manual.* FAO Forestry Department (Policy and Planning Service) and Economic and Social Policy Department (Food Policy and Nutrition Division), Rome.

Fernow, Bernhard E. 1911. *A Brief History of Forestry in Europe, the United States, and Other Countries,* 2nd edition. University of Toronto Press, Toronto, Canada.

Foley, Gerald and Geoffrey Barnard. 1984. *Farm and Community Forestry.* International Institute for Environment and Development, Energy Information Program Technical Report 3. Earthscan, London, England.

Fortmann, Louise P. 1986. "Overlooked experts in subsistence forestry," *Journal of Forestry* 84(7):39–42.

Fortmann, L. 1988. "The tree tenure factor in agroforestry, with particular reference to Africa," pp. 16–33 in L. Fortmann and J.W. Bruce (eds.), *Whose Trees? Proprietary Dimensions of Forestry.* Westview Press, Boulder, CO.

Gregersen, Hans M. 1988. "People, trees, and rural development: The role of social forestry," *Journal of Forestry* 86(10):22–30.

Gregersen, Hans, Sydney Draper, and Dieter Elz. 1989. *People and Trees: The Role of Social Forestry in Sustainable Development.* Economic Development Institute (EDI) of the World Bank, Washington, DC.

Heermans, John G. 1986. "The Guesselbodi experiment: Bushland management in Niger," *Rural Africana* 23/24:67–77.

Hoskins, Marilyn. 1984. "Observations on indigenous and modern agroforestry activities in West Africa," pp. 46–50 in J.K. Jackson (ed.), *Social, Economic, and Institutional Aspects of Agroforestry.* United Nations University, Tokyo, Japan.

Hoskins, M. 1990. "The contribution of forestry to food security," *Unasylva* 41(160):3–13.

Huxley, Peter A. 1990. "Experimental agroforestry," pp. 332–353 in K.G. MacDicken and N.T. Vergara (eds.), *Agroforestry: Classification and Management.* John Wiley and Sons, New York.

Hyman, Eric L. 1983a. "Loan financing of smallholder treefarming in the provinces of Ilocos Norte and Ilocus Sur, the Philippines," *Agroforestry Systems* 1(3):225–243.

Hyman, Eric L. 1983b. "Smallholder tree farming in the Philippines," *Unasylva* 35(139):25–31.

Kenny Jordan, C. B. 1988. "Forestry program fights rural poverty," *Journal of Forestry* 86(5):37–41.

Kerkhof, Paul. 1990. *Agroforestry in Africa: A Survey of Project Experience.* PANOS Institute, London, England.

King, K. S. F. 1987. "The history of agroforestry," pp. 1–11 in H.A. Steppler and P.K. R. Nair (eds.), *Agroforestry: A Decade of Development.* International Council for Research in Agroforestry (ICRAF), Nairobi, Kenya.

Longhurst, Richard. 1987. *Household Food Security, Tree Planting, and the Poor: The Case of Gujarat.* Social Forestry Network Paper 5d, Overseas Development Institute, London, England.

Lundgren, B. O. and J. B. Raintree. 1983. *Sustained Agroforestry.* International Council for Research in Agroforestry (ICRAF), Reprint No. 3, Nairobi, Kenya.

MacDicken, Kenneth G. 1989. "Challenges for multipurpose tree research," *Farm Forestry News* 3(2):1.

MacDicken, Kenneth G. and N. T. Vergara (eds.). 1990. *Agroforestry: Classification and Management.* Wiley, New York.

Malhotra, K. C. and Mark Poffenberger (eds). 1989. *Forest Regeneration Through Community Protection: The West Bengal Experience*. West Bengal Forest Department, Indian Institute for Bio-Social Research and Development, Ramakrishna Mission, and Ford Foundation. Calcutta, India.

May, Peter H., A. B. Anderson, J. M. F. Frazão, and M. J. Balick. 1985. "Babassu palm in the agroforestry systems in Brazil's mid-north region," *Agroforestry Systems* 3(3):275–295.

Meiggs, Russell. 1982. *Trees and Timber in the Ancient Mediterranean World*. Clarendon Press, Oxford, England.

Murray, Gerald F. 1986. "Seeing the forest while planting the trees: An anthropological approach to agroforestry in rural Haiti," pp. 193–226 in D. W. Brinkerhoff and J. C. Garcia Zamor (eds.), *Politics, Projects, and People: Institutional Development in Haiti*. Praeger, New York.

Mussack, Michael F. and Jan G. Laarman. 1989. "Farmers' production of timber trees in the cacao-coffee region of coastal Ecuador," *Agroforestry Systems* 9:155–170.

Nair, P. K. R. 1985. "Classification of agroforestry systems," *Agroforestry Systems* 3: 97–128.

NAS (National Academy of Sciences, USA). 1980. *Firewood Crops: Shrub and Tree Species for Energy Production*. National Academy of Sciences, Washington, DC.

NAS. 1983a. *Firewood Crops: Shrub and Tree Species for Energy Production*, Vol. 2. National Academy of Sciences, Washington, DC.

NAS. 1983b. *Calliandra: A Versatile Small Tree for the Humid Tropics*. National Academy of Sciences, Washington, DC.

Nations, James D., B. B. Burwell, and G. R. Burniske. 1987. *We Did This Ourselves: A Case Study of the INAFOR/CARE/Peace Corps Soil Conservation and Forest Management Program*, Republic of Guatemala. U.S. Peace Corps, Washington, DC.

Noronha, Raymond. 1981. "Why is it so difficult to grow fuelwood?" *Unasylva* 33(131):4–12.

Noronha, Raymond and John S. Spears. 1985. "Sociological variables in forestry project design," pp. 227–266 in Michael M. Cernea (ed.), *Putting People First: Sociological Variables in Rural Development*. Oxford University Press, New York.

Okafor, J. C. 1980. "Trees for food and fodder in the savanna areas of Nigeria," *International Tree Crops Journal* 1:131–141.

Padoch, C., J. Chota Inuma, W. De Jong, and J. Unruh. 1985. "Amazonian agroforestry: A market-oriented system in Peru," *Agroforestry Systems* 3(1):47–58.

Pelinck, E., P. K. Manandhar, and R. H. Gecolea. 1984. "Forestry extension: Community development in Nepal," *Unasylva* 36(143):2–13.

Posey, D. A. and W. Balee (eds.). 1989. "Resource Management in Amazonia: Indigenous and Folk Strategies." *Advances in Economic Botany*, Vol. 7. New York Botanical Garden, Bronx, New York.

Rackham, Oliver. 1989. *Hedges and Hedgerow Trees in Britain: A Thousand Years of Agroforestry*. Social Forestry Network Paper 8c, Overseas Development Institute, London, England.

Raintree, J.B. (ed.). 1987. *Land, Trees, and Tenure: Proceedings of an International Workshop on Tenure Issues in Agroforestry*, Nairobi, May 27–31, 1985. International Council for Research in Agroforestry (ICRAF), Nairobi, Kenya.

Raintree, J. B. 1989. "The diagnosis and design methodology," pp. 11–17 in P. A. Huxley and S. B. Westley (eds.), *Multipurpose Trees: Selection and Testing for Agroforestry*. International Council for Research in Agroforestry (ICRAF), Nairobi, Kenya.

Richardson, S. D. 1990. *Forests and Forestry in China: Changing Patterns in Resource Development*. Island Press, Washington, DC.

Rocheleau, D. E. 1987. "The user perspective and the agroforestry research and action agenda," pp. 59–87 in H.L. Gholz (ed.), *Agroforestry: Realities, Possibilities, and Potentials*. Martinus Nijhoff, Dordrecht, Netherlands.

Romm, Jeff. 1982. "A research agenda for social forestry," *International Tree Crops Journal* 2:25–59.

Romm, Jeff. 1989. "Forestry for development: Some lessons from Asia," *Journal of World Forest Resource Management* 4:37–46.

Sartorius, Peter and Hans Henle. 1968. *Forestry and Economic Development*. Frederick A. Praeger Publishers, New York.

Shepherd, Gill. 1985. *Social Forestry in 1985: Lessons Learnt and Topics to be Addressed*. Social Forestry Network Paper 1a, Overseas Development Institute, London, England.

Shiva, Vandama and J. Bandyopadhyay. 1986. "The evolution, structure, and impact of the Chipko movement," *Mountain Research and Development* 6(2):133–142.

Singh, Chatrapati. 1986. *Common Property and Common Poverty: India's Forests, Forest Dwellers, and the Law*. Oxford University Press, Delhi, India.

Singh, J. S., U. Pandey, and A. K. Tiwari. 1984. "Man and forests: A central Himalayan case study," *Ambio* 13:80–87.

Singh, R.V. 1982. *Fodder Trees of India*. Oxford and IBH, New Delhi, India.

Tschinkel, H. 1987. "Tree planting by small farmers in upland watersheds: Experience in Central America," *International Tree Crops Journal* 4:249–268.

UNESCO (United Nations Educational, Scientific, and Cultural Organization). 1989. *Traditional Ecological Knowledge: A Survey of Phytopractices in Tropical Regions*. UNESCO, Paris, France.

Vergara, Napoleon T. 1985. "Agroforestry systems: A primer," *Unasylva* 37(147):22–28.

Verma, D. P. S. 1988. "Some dimensions of benefits from community forestry: A case study regarding the flow of benefits from the Dhanori village woodlot," *Indian Forester* 114(3):109–127.

Weber, T. 1989. *Hugging the Trees: The Story of the Chipko Movement*. Penguin Books, New York.

Winrock International. 1988. "Locally managed forest excels in Nepal," *Farm Forestry News* 2(3):4.

Winterbottom, Robert and Peter T. Hazelwood. 1987. "Agroforestry and sustainable development: Making the connection," *Ambio* 16:100–110.

World Bank. 1978. *Forestry Sector Policy Paper*. World Bank, Washington, DC.

WRI (World Resources Institute), World Bank, and United Nations Development Program (UNDP). 1985. *Tropical Forests: A Call for Action* (Parts I and II). WRI, Washington, DC.

Zulberti, Ester (ed.). 1987. *Professional Education in Agroforestry: Proceedings of an International Workshop*. International Council for Research in Agroforestry (ICRAF), Nairobi, Kenya.

FORESTS AND GLOBAL ENVIRONMENT

Environmentalism refers to a social revolution which perceives that wild nature is scarce and must be protected. Although Plato worried about the consequences of deforestation in the hills of Attica thousands of years ago, it is only since the Industrial Revolution that the roots of an environmental movement can be discerned. Yet the true revolution in politics, legislation, economic priorities, and other actions on the environment occurred only after the Second World War, and in particular since the early 1960s. Thus in virtually every country, owners of forestlands are under increasing public pressure to manage forests for their environmental services and ecological functions.

ENVIRONMENTALISM IN SOCIAL CONTEXT

The origins of environmentalism have grown from separate desires to control nature, understand nature, and preserve nature. From these separate origins there very recently emerged an environmental movement claiming millions of adherents, most of whom are relatively affluent and well educated. Environmentalism is the reason for entire new bureaucracies and political parties, large research projects on how the earth's biosphere operates, and complex layers of legislation intended to conserve and protect natural resources. Especially when viewed at the international level, the environmental movement manifests a profound desire to defend the perceived organic wholeness of nature and natural systems in a world otherwise badly fragmented by ethnic, religious, economic, and political differences.

Characteristics and Themes

The character and aims of environmentalism lack clear and consistent definitions. Environmentalism in the late twentieth century can be any one or all of the following: a state of mind, a way of life, an attitude about priorities, or a political philosophy (McCormick 1989). While there is no universally accepted definition of environmentalism or the environmental movement, a few leading themes describe their complexities.

Caring for Mother Earth   Views on man's relationship with the natural world have shifted dramatically through historical periods. The forested wilderness has been a hostile place of loneliness, menacing beasts, and other immediate dangers. The ancient Asians appreciated the aesthetic qualities of wilderness, but mainly in the context of nature worship (Callicott and Ames 1989). Early Western societies respected nature and its elements in their beliefs, but wild landscapes and wilderness held little attraction. Nature became less threatening with the advance of agricultural and industrial technology (White 1967). Good nature was tamed nature, and mastery over the environment was considered absolutely essential for human progress.

It was only in the eighteenth and nineteenth centuries that the negative impacts of the human subjugation of nature became a concern among educated elites in Europe and North America. Several writings on natural history gradually shifted opinion to the view that the material progress of civilization was exerting too high a price on nature. In Britain, a widely read book by the amateur field naturalist Gilbert White (*The Natural History of Selbourne*, 1789) expressed the Arcadian view of desiring that man lead a simple life in order to restore himself to peaceful coexistence with nature. The English poet Wordsworth wrote of the "violated rights" of nature, while the USA's Thoreau reflected on nature as the interdependence of life at Waldon Pond. In 1864, George Perkins Marsh described in *Man and Nature* how deforestation and other abuses of nature were making the Earth unfit for human habitation, drawing on examples from the Mediterranean Basin and elsewhere. Charles Darwin's pioneering work on species evolution strengthened scientific views that man was indeed a part of nature.

By the late 1800s, Victorian Britain had some 100 thousand members in its several hundred natural history societies. Their emphasis was mainly nature study and contemplation. However, protectionist campaigns first begun in the 1860s led to legislative acts protecting birds and other wildlife, and then to preservation of open lands for recreation and amenity values (McCormick 1989). The late 1800s also witnessed establishment of the world's first national parks (in the USA, Australia, Canada, and New Zealand), early discussions on controlling European slaughter of African wildlife, and a philosophical split of the USA's environmental movement into preservationists and conservationists.

From these roots among mainly aristocratic elites and middle-class progressives grew a wider following through the course of the present century. This following ultimately became the ecology movement during and after the 1960s. Its arrival has been heralded as the "silent revolution" (Inglehart 1977) and the "new environmental paradigm" (Milbrath 1984). Its world view seeks, among other goals, a long-run sustainable relationship with nature (Figure 7-1). Its driving forces are the education and affluence of the Western middle classes, especially where material needs are ensured but wild nature is scarce (Ophuls 1977). Its "green values" are inspired by a doctrine that man is expected to be a caring and competent custodian of Mother Earth, whose life-support functions depend on proper stewardship of natural resources in a balanced biosphere. According to the recent Gaia hypothesis, this biosphere forms a single and vast self-regulating organism of interrelated living components (Lovelock 1979).

In forestry, many of these ideas converge in the "land ethic." As articulated by the USA's Aldo Leopold, this is the proposition that man is member and citizen of the land community rather than its conqueror (Leopold 1949). Leopold's land ethic followed by several decades other ethical-aesthetic philosophies on land and nature propounded in central Europe and Soviet Russia. Out of these and other origins has emerged a powerful environmental movement of substantial global size and influence (McCormick 1989, p. viii):

• Founded in 1865, the world's first nongovernmental organization (NGO) with aims to protect the environment was the Commons, Footpaths, and Open Spaces Preservation Society in Britain. By the late 1980s, the global number of NGOs with environmental objectives was over 15 thousand.

• The first international agreement on environmental matters was signed in 1886. This number expanded to more than 250 international agreements by the late 1980s, of which three-fourths were drawn up after 1960.

FIGURE 7-1

Values and attitudes of environmentalists in the USA, Britain, and Germany in the early 1980s. *(Source: Adapted from Milbrath (1984, pp. 21–41).)*

High valuation of nature implies:
• Appreciation of nature for its own sake
• Environmental protection favored over economic growth

Avoidance of risk implies:
• Development and use of "soft" technologies
• Government responsibility to protect nature and humans

Limits to growth imply:
• Conservation policies to combat resource shortages
• Control of human population numbers

Needed are societies:
• With compassion towards other species, peoples, and generations
• With openness and participation in public affairs
• Using foresight and planning for the public good
• Favoring cooperation over competition
• Leading simple lifestyles (post-materialism)

- In 1972, the United Nations Conference on the Human Environment met in Stockholm, Sweden, to formulate what became the United Nations Environmental Program (UNEP). By 1980, nearly all of the world's major international organizations had promulgated policy positions on the environment.
- The world's first Green political party began in New Zealand in 1972. By 1988, active Green parties existed in 14 countries, offering an alternative to the conventional right-left spectrum of traditional politics. While not strong in any country, the rise of the Greens challenges the older and larger political parties to respond to the needs and demands of the new environmental constituencies.

Accommodating Diverse Ideologies A notable feature of the world's so-called environmental "movement" is its fragmentation. Environmentalism is not at all a single social effort, but more correctly a loose and sometimes incompatible collection of groups and coalitions varying enormously in objectives, philosophies, strategies, and underlying ideologies. Environmental organizations like the World Wildlife Fund are large and growing (Figure 7-2). Others are tiny grass-roots groups, working locally without budgets or paid personnel. Different environmental groups pursue varying blends of educational, scientific, social, and political aims. Objectives range from protecting wildlife to stopping nuclear power plants, and from preserving rainforests in the tropics to preserving rainforests in western North America.

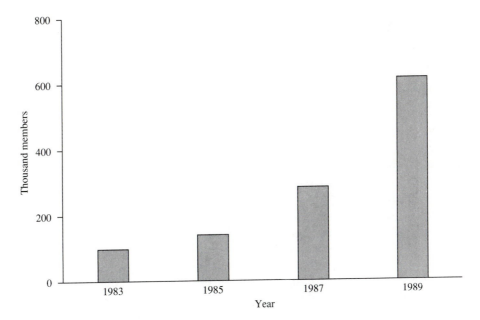

FIGURE 7-2
Membership growth in the World Wildlife Fund, USA affiliate (WWF-US), 1983-1989. *(Source: World Wildlife Fund (1989, p. 58).)*

Guiding philosophies vary from adamant opposition to economic growth ("deep ecology") to purposeful accommodation between economic growth and nature conservation. The first group sees the second as too permissive and compromising to foster a deep environmental consciousness. The second sees the first as too radical and threatening to be taken seriously. The "deep ecology" faction pursues a biocentric perspective to the limit, arguing that human and nonhuman species are inherently equal in nature. Its philosophical counterpart prides itself on being less extreme.

Not suprisingly, strategies and tactics range broadly. The Chipko protest against logging in India follows the Ghandian tradition of nonviolent resistance (Guha 1990). This compares with Earth First!, a group which has advocated deliberate confrontation and occasional "eco-terrorism," such as actions taken to deter logging in California (Russell 1988).

Motivating arguments range from spiritual convictions that nature is holy (the nature worshippers) to pragmatic reasoning that waste is evil (the utilitarians). This ideological split separates the preservationists from the conservationists, as played out at the beginning of this century in the USA by John Muir and Gifford Pinchot. Expressing a simple but crucial difference persisting today, Muir's ultimate commitment was to wilderness and preservation, while Pinchot's was to civilization and forestry (Nash 1973).

John Muir and his philosophical allies worked to set aside wildlands for exclusion of all but recreational and educational purposes. For Muir, California's Sierra Nevada mountains were a sacred place of "high temples" for "worship with Nature." Muir distinguished himself by the passion of his nature mysticism, and by the zeal of his nature evangelism. One of Muir's biographers argues that nature preservation was Muir's religious protest against modernity (Fox 1981).

Gifford Pinchot led the way for the utilitarians, for whom forest conservation meant that humans had the capability and moral responsibility to manage forests for their many different uses. Such uses included, and sometimes emphasized, commodity production for commercial objectives. Pinchot contended that forests can and should be exploited wisely and sustainably, applying management approaches borrowed from the German model of rational forest science. The Pinchot ideology stressed development (deliberate use of forests as resources), efficiency (avoidance of waste), and distribution (forests for the many, not the few). Pinchot and his disciples claimed that the introduction of science and management was "breaking new ground" in North American forestry, consistent with other progressive tendencies of the era. Like John Muir, Gifford Pinchot fathered generations of loyal ideological descendants.

The ideological contest in the USA over preservation versus conservation only partly describes ideological separations elsewhere. For example, environmentalism in the USSR has not two but three distinct traditions (Weiner 1988): (1) utilitarian, (2) cultural-aesthetic-ethical, and (3) scientific.

The Soviet utilitarian tradition trusts in technology and management to bring about order and efficiency in the use and protection of natural resources. In sharp contrast are arguments for nature protection based on cultural, aesthetic, and

For John Muir, California's Sierra Nevada mountains were a sacred place of high temples. (*Photo courtesy of Forest History Society.*)

moral grounds. The early Russian experience in this context emphasized landscape protection and preservation of "monuments of nature." Looking to German and Swiss philosophy, this second group believed that love for nature fosters love of one's native land, love of beauty, and respect for life. The third Soviet tradition is a particular form of scientific ecology aimed at protection and long-term study of pristine ecological reserves called *zapovedniki*. The purpose is to guide economic land uses according to ecological carrying capacity, establishing a highly scientific basis for land management. The presence of this third tradition explains why ideology in Soviet environmentalism has been influenced to a great extent by professional scientists (Weiner 1988).

Integrating Conservation and Development   Especially since the late 1970s, environmentalism has been dominated and sometimes obsessed by a search for "sustainable development," or the integration of nature conservation with economic development for the mutual benefit of both. Many environmentalists see "sustainable development" as the new social and political arena for shifting environmental concerns to the center of economic policies (Engel and Engel 1990). As noted in Chapter 3, a rationale and policy for managing timber to produce sustainable yields can be traced back several hundred years in central Europe. However, recent ideas on sustainability identify concepts and goals much more complex than perpetual flows of wood. The Greenpeace activist, Arne Naess, charts a sequence of thinking from the idea of "progress" to that of "development" and "economic growth," and subsequently to present ideas on "sustainable development." From there conceptualization might lead to a possible future of "ecological development" and ultimately "ecosophical development" (Naess 1990).

Yet forestry lives with the fact that environment and development have remained conceptually distinct until very recently. Through the 1970s and early 1980s, environmentalist Cassandras in the industrialized countries warned of the dangerous environmental consequences of economic growth. In this category were the Club of Rome's *Limits to Growth* (Meadows et al. 1972), and the unpleasant scenarios of *Global 2000* (Council on Environmental Quality 1982). The priorities expressed in these documents were decidedly opposite those of the developing countries, whose leaders argued that environmental management was a distant concern, if not an outright brake on badly needed economic progress (Holdgate et al. 1982). Also, the prophets of doom were challenged for ignoring how social institutions emerge to confront and solve even the most daunting problems (Maddox 1972; Grayson and Shepard 1973).

The conceptual divide between environment and development gradually dissolved, and attitudes slowly became more conciliatory. For example, the World Conservation Strategy, released by IUCN in 1980, asserted that the purpose of nature conservation is to satisfy utilitarian objectives. Conservation was defined as "management of human use of the biosphere so that it may yield the greatest sustainable benefit to present generations while maintaining its potential to meet the needs and aspirations of future generations." The World Conservation Strategy advocated that each country work for environmental planning and legislation; the integration of nature conservation and economic development; and a review of research, education, and other institutions strengthening nature conservation. Additional strategies were presented at the international level, e.g., global programs to protect genetic resources and tropical forests (IUCN 1980).

Despite these positive proposals to stimulate "sustainable development," international response to the World Conservation Strategy was disappointing. By the late 1980s, only a few countries had prepared national conservation strategies along lines proposed by the World Conservation Strategy. The World Conservation Strategy was heavily weighted towards classical views of nature preservation, and was correspondingly weak on economic and social policies.

The World Commission on Environment and Development became a second forum to define and interpret issues of sustainable development at global scale. Chaired by Gro Harlem Brundtland of Norway, this independent body was created by the United Nations General Assembly in 1983. In its report *Our Common Future*, the Brundtland Commission based its diagnosis and recommendations for sustainable development upon multiple themes of interdependence (WCED 1987): (1) different environmental stresses are related to each other; (2) ecological and economic systems are highly interdependent; (3) environmental and economic problems are explained by social and political factors; and (4) environmental impacts extend across political boundaries. Sustainable development was defined broadly

> Sustainable development is best understood as a process of change in which the use of resources, the direction of investments, the orientation of technological development, and institutional change all enhance the potential to meet human needs both today and tomorrow.

In its problem analysis, the Brundtland Commission contended that existing institutions, especially those in natural resources, are too narrowly focused on short-term goals to attend to sustaining the environmental capital on which such goals depend. The Commission lamented the fragmentation of agencies and policies across economic sectors and political subdivisions, and the separation of environmental policies from policies in other domains of decisionmaking.

The Brundtland Commission's work has attracted considerable world attention, sparking numerous debates about its assumptions and recommendations. For the deep ecology faction, *Our Common Future* is seriously compromised by not taking a firm stance to substantially reduce global population (Naess 1990). A completely different perspective argues that the scope of *Our Common Future* is too ambitious and expensive for countries to be able to act upon its conclusions (Redclift 1987). A third view maintains that the Brundtland Commission was wise to avoid specificity in its definition of "sustainable development," since the unstated consequences of putting the definition into action would have been too radical for consensus (Daly and Cobb 1989).

Is it possible to integrate nature conservation and economic development without reducing global population? The "deep ecology" ideology argues for reduced human numbers. This poor and densely populated neighborhood in Guayaquil, Ecuador, is unable to provide its own water. (*Photo courtesy of World Bank.*)

Implications for Forestry

The recent ascendancy of environmentalism presents new and complex issues for forest management in virtually all countries. Although struggles about the uses and purposes of forests have always occurred, they seem particularly frequent and strident in the current era. In part, this is due to perceived scarcity of wild places as world population grows. This means that commodity and non-commodity claims on forests increasingly come into competition. Additionally, social concerns about forests have shifted and broadened. Long-standing worries about the supply of particular forest products (e.g., timber and game) have expanded into a much more complex agenda which now includes forests in relation to global climate change and conservation of the world's biological diversity. Particularly striking is the number and influence of persons who feel that they have a legitimate stake in forests far away. Where once forestry was mainly about satisfying local and regional needs, many contemporary issues in forestry are truly international or global because of environmental linkages.

The prominence of environmentalism brings to forestry a number of revised assumptions, attitudes, and symbols. Forestry is caught in ideological battles over forest use, conservation, and preservation. These battles span an entire spectrum of rival doctrines fervently defended like so many different theologies. The ethical issues of preserving or manipulating wild nature are not about right versus wrong, but rather about one moral right pitted against another. The forestry profession is prodded to manage forests sustainably, but the rubric of "sustainable development" typically lacks operational content other than to imply an unspecified commitment to future generations. More generally, many current views on forests and sustainability require extensive exploration and testing:

• *Do trees have rights?*—A strong preservationist view contends that nonhuman life is valued independently of human life, and that nature should be protected for its own sake. Consequently, it is wrong for humans to interfere with forests, and to make judgments about managing them. This philosophy is related to changing cultural values, presenting an obvious dilemma for forestry.

• *Nature conservation to benefit the poor?*—The hypothesis that nature conservation and economic development can be harmonized is inconsistent with most of history. Traditionally, it has been the world's rich and aristocratic who have championed wildlife reserves, amenity areas, and other nature reserves. Very often, this has been at the expense of displaced tribal groups and rural peasantries. Skeptics legitimately ask what factors make this conflict any different in the 1990s than in previous decades and centuries, even if everyone agrees that old patterns must be avoided.

• *What is forest sustainability?*—The economist's concern to sustain forests by managing them as a form of land-based capital differs in both concept and prescription from the ecologist's concern to sustain ecosystems. Moreover, sustaining a particular state of forest "naturalness" often requires considerable human intervention. Conversely, leaving forest ecosystems without human intervention alters their composition and character. From an ecological standpoint, a given forest cannot simultaneously remain a preagricultural wilderness, remain truly undisturbed, and still function to conserve endangered species and biological diversity (Botkin 1990). This is contrary to what many environmentalists want and expect.

• *Anything but timber*—Environmentalists across a wide spectrum of philosophies regard logging of industrial timber as a major cause of forest damage. Especially in the context of forestry in the developing countries, this now motivates a search for non-timber goods and services which can generate commercial returns, thereby displacing logging. This raises numerous questions on identifying such alternatives, and on evaluating their technical and economic feasibility.

In summary, a common thread running through many facets of environmentalism is commitment to experimentation and activism. The world's educated and affluent are anxious to push ahead with new initiatives to protect forests. Their frequent questioning of the human costs of a technological society—and their parallel embrace of wild nature—is a continuation and expansion of the romanticism which gripped European intellectuals starting about 200 years ago. Equally significant is that it is through advances in modern science that the world's environmentalists recognize the central importance of forests in the life-support functions of Mother Earth. These two forces combine to produce a very rapidly changing social milieu for forestry.

MANAGEMENT STRATEGIES AND ISSUES

That forests should be managed in ways that favor environmental protection is practically indisputable as a principle for right action. The truly substantive issues focus on how this should be done in terms of strategies and tradeoffs. One response is to more adequately quantify tradeoffs among forest uses by valuing the forest's protective, ecological, and amenity attributes.

Secondly, the environmental agenda generates a range of ideas on how to manage forests for minimal disturbance. Some of these approaches are "new," while others are being rediscovered from the past.

Valuation Questions

As observed in Chapter 3, a classic problem in forestry is the simultaneous production of market and nonmarket outputs. There are no prices for most of a forest's environmental services, ecological functions, and psychophysiological values. Many of these are produced as public goods and externalities (i.e., benefits and costs external to forest owners). Secondly, methods of national income accounting fail to show that depleting or adding to a country's forests also changes national wealth and productive capacity.

Forests and Unpriced Values   The conspicuousness of externalities and unpriced values in forestry attests to the incomplete reach of the market. Also, the abstractions through which economists regard "land" and "natural resources" in a production process do not represent the multidimensional meanings of land and nature in actual human experience (Daley and Cobb 1989). Hence in forestry it might be argued that estimation of market values but not other values produces an asymmetrical view of social worth which is more obscuring than illuminating.

This problem has been recognized for a long time, leading to various method-ologies which attempt to internalize externalities and assign "correct" prices when the market does not. Thus a whole body of valuation concepts and techniques has emerged to cope with the presence of market failures and imperfections as they affect the choice of social investments (Gittinger 1982). These concepts and techniques are used to appraise billions of dollars of capital flows from the World Bank and other international development agencies to the developing countries. Methodologies attempt to adjust for externalities and nonmarket values by assign-ing "shadow prices" to correct for unpriced and mispriced inputs and outputs. This is distinct from a purely financial analysis, which focuses on cash flows computed from market prices. The derivation of shadow prices is a highly complex under-taking, and draws on extensive theoretical foundations. Applications in forestry are being tested and adapted (Gregersen and Contreras 1979). Watershed values, wildlife values, and other environmental dimensions of forestry are not well in-corporated in project analysis to date. Considerably more progress is needed and expected in the years ahead.

Especially for the developing countries, there is great interest in assigning shadow prices to subsistence production of fuelwood, forest food products, and local construction materials as these uses compete with industrial timber in a given forest or woodland (e.g., Peters et al. 1989). This is to restate the familiar propo-sition that so-called minor forest products probably would be considered major if only policymakers had reliable numbers to make assessments. Also essential is progress in quantifying the anti-erosion functions of forests and trees, such as with respect to slowing the sedimentation of reservoirs and irrigation systems. The wider application of economic analysis to evaluate agroforestry practices is badly needed, and this might help quantify the environmental impacts of trees on farms and in communities.

In both developing and industrialized countries, questions are becoming more numerous regarding the economic worth of wildlife conservation, forest recreation, nature study, and ecological preserves. In some cases, "contingent valuation" studies use carefully constructed questionnaires to estimate the willingness of individuals to pay for these mainly nonmarketed services. This is a young but promising valuation framework receiving increasing theoretical development and methodological refinement (Mitchell and Carson 1989).

A particularly challenging estimation is the existence value individuals derive by simply knowing that a forest or component ecosystem exists, even though these individuals never visit or use it. For example, individuals in the industri-alized countries may come to appreciate the existence of forests in Amazonia through television nature programs and museum exhibits. Consider, for example, the possibility that 200 million persons in the world might individually assign an existence value of US$5 per year to the existence of Amazonian forests. This aggregates to US$1 billion, or an amount sufficient to provide US$10 per hectare annually towards the protection of 100 million hectares of Amazonian forests.

Progress is needed in valuing the anti-erosion functions of trees and forests. Severe erosion impedes agricultural development in eastern Java, Indonesia. (*Photo courtesy of FAO.*)

The analytical problem is how to convert existence value into monetary demand. This has been done with modest success by private conservation organizations, which solicit contributions from persons interested in environmental issues. Hence conservation organizations in the USA raise about US$150 million annually for global environmental causes (Earhart and Shillinger 1990), a sum almost certainly far below the true existence values of the resources in question.

Forests in National Income Accounts   Measures of national income like gross domestic product (GDP) and its variants are commonly used to indicate the level and composition of a country's industrial structure, savings and investment, consumption expenditures, government expenditures, and total economic activity. For the most part, these national income accounts are designed to measure variations in short-term activity in the market economy. The accounts are less suited for gauging long-term shifts in a country's productive capacity. One reason is that they omit changes in the quantities and qualities of natural resources, or "natural capital."

National income accounting shows manmade capital like equipment and buildings depreciating as these assets lose their ability to produce future income. In most countries, natural capital—e.g., soils, forests, fisheries, water, and minerals—is not treated similarly. Hence natural capital can be depleted or degraded without any change in the national accounts, even if this drawing down of natural capital makes the country worse off in the future.

If true income is sustainable income, then most national accounts overstate true income by disregarding both the depreciation of natural capital and the defensive expenditures which ensue (Daly and Cobb 1989). Defensive expenditures are the costs of offsetting or mitigating the side effects of resource depletion, e.g., anti-sedimentation measures associated with deforestation in a watershed. More generally, defensive expenditures include most other environmental protection activities. Arguments are made that because these defensive expenditures are unwanted but "regrettably necessary" costs which provide no final products for consumption, they should be subtracted from true national income (El Serafy and Lutz 1989). In the many proposals to reform national income accounting, a country would see itself becoming poorer if it observed a rising sum of ecological damages plus defensive costs, including damages and costs in forests.

A few of the industrialized countries—Norway, France, the Netherlands, Canada, the USA, and Japan—have been experimenting with systems of environmental accounting, in some cases for many years. Each of these countries faces the conceptual problem of how to represent natural capital, and the estimation problem of how to actually measure depletion and depreciation. Norway has separate accounts for material resources (minerals and fossil fuels), biotic resources (forests and fisheries), and environmental resources (land, water, air). France uses "natural patrimony accounts" to show tradeoffs between the economic, ecological, and social functions of natural resources. The French system employs separate accounts for forests, wildlife, water, and soil. Aggregation of these accounts, and conversion of physical data into monetary measures, are among the many unresolved problems (Theys 1989).

Tropical deforestation is among the issues explaining proposals on why and how to use natural resources accounting in the developing countries (Peskin 1989; Repetto et al. 1989). An example is the work by the World Resources Institute to construct natural resources accounts for Indonesia, including an account for forestry (Table 7-1). The model includes both physical and monetary accounts, and separates forest additions and reductions into manmade versus natural sources. The account omits rattan and other non-timber products, and does not include the forest's ecological functions, carbon dioxide capture, and other nonmarket services. Yet the accounting framework provides a focal point for this discussion. According to the model builders, the framework is useful for three reasons (Repetto et al. 1989, p. 53):

• It brings to light aspects of the sustainability of a country's economic growth that are not apparent from studying conventional national income accounts.
• The efforts to improve natural resources accounts simultaneously improve the information base for better resource management.

TABLE 7-1
Timber resource accounts in Indonesia, 1981–1984

	Year			
	1981	**1982**	**1983**	**1984**
Physical units (million m^3)				
Opening stock	24, 440	24, 334	24, 238	24, 001
Additions				
Growth	52	52	52	52
Reforestation	24	26	30	35
Reductions				
Harvesting	16	13	15	16
Deforestation	120	120	120	120
Logging damage	32	27	30	32
Fire damage	14	14	154	14
Net change	−106	−96	−237	−94
Closing stock	24, 334	24, 238	24, 001	23, 906
Monetary accounts (US$ million)				
Opening stock	1, 256, 047	996, 267	1, 020, 960	601, 049
Additions				
Growth	1, 503	1, 546	920	1, 088
Reforestation	0	0	0	0
Reductions				
Harvesting	927	799	539	671
Deforestation	3, 475	3, 575	2, 126	2, 515
Logging damage	915	790	532	662
Fire damage	405	417	3, 871	293
Net change	−4, 219	−4, 034	−6, 148	−3, 054
Revaluation*	−255, 561	28, 727	−413, 763	109, 775
Closing stock	996, 267	1, 020, 960	601, 049	707, 770

* Revaluation accounts for changes in timber "rental rates" (i.e., the market value of standing timber, or stumpage value).
   Source: Adapted from Repetto et al. (1989, p. 35). Used with permission of World Resources Institute.

• Estimates in natural resources accounts can be prepared with modest expenditures of time and money, drawing mainly on data already available.

Not everyone is optimistic regarding ease of implementation. Implementation requires workable compromises on difficult conceptualization and valuation questions. Various technical approaches compete with each other for attention, producing arguments over their merits and pitfalls. If the accounting is to capture changes in the productive potential of the economy, then a measure of the changing stock of forests and other natural resources is required. However, other important productive factors also should be included, especially changes in the stock of knowledge and technology. Finally, demands to reform national income accounting originate from many interests besides those of environmentalists, so that accounting frameworks for natural capital are just one item on a much larger reform agenda.

Management Approaches

Since the 1970s, environmentalism as a social force has exerted increasing influence on the goals and practices of forest management. The implicit environmental emphasis is working with nature and working for naturalness. This motivates a search for forest management strategies which minimize disturbances from timber cutting, and which generate commercial returns from goods and services besides timber.

At the policy and managerial levels, this raises provocative questions about how to work towards these objectives in practice. Some proposals favor revitalizing and extending the practice of multiple-use forestry. Closely related to multiple-use practice is a renewed look at silvicultural and economic systems to manage and protect natural forests. Biosphere reserves, extractive reserves, and nature-oriented tourism are among other conceptual directions framing discussions on how to pursue economic development while protecting nature. To be remembered is that much of this conceptualization emerges from broad theorizing and untested assumptions. The years ahead will test the economic, social, and political feasibility of the many ideas now being debated.

Multiple Use　　Historically, forest management in Europe grew out of concerns that game, fuelwood, water, and scenic beauty had to be produced and protected . In medieval England "forest" meant a district reserved for game habitat, which at the same time provided space for grazing, fuelwood, and customary use by local communities. The presence of timber was only an incidental fact (James 1981). Towards the end of the 1700s, the French began a great movement to protect forests for their indirect values, including values for human health, recreation, and artistic inspiration (Woolsey 1920). Also in the 1700s, German scientists pioneered some of the world's first studies on how forests affect climate and waterflow (Heske 1938). The overall effect was to create a European landscape which combined hunting, agriculture, grazing, fuel, timber, and amenity.

Thus the concept of the multiple use of forests in its broad sense is by no means new. However, the contemporary context is set apart by a more deliberate planning and policy framework than in the past. Unlike the incidental or circumstantial combination of forest uses in earlier eras, contemporary social concerns necessitate a more deliberate management approach and policy rationalization. This responds to the increasing scale and complexity of demands on forests, especially demands which have environmental origins. In the industrialized countries, this is evidenced by timber harvest laws, reforestation requirements, watershed regulations, and environmental impact statements intended to ensure that timber cutting does not cause unacceptable declines in other forest outputs. In the developing countries, governments attempt to increase benefits from industrial forestry, watershed protection, habitat preservation, and other uses from what is sometimes a rapidly shrinking forest base.

Studies on how tree cover affects climate and waterflow began in the 1700s. The agricultural economy of this mountain village in Cyprus depends on careful water management. (*Photo courtesy of FAO.*)

The implementation of multiple-use management is problematic for reasons identified in Chapter 3. Physical production relationships are variable geographically and through time. Two or more forest uses can be complementary at some stages of forest development, but conflicting at other stages. Analytical techniques for multiple-use decisions are advancing, but the matter of adding and comparing benefits and costs across forest management alternatives remains complex (Bowes and Krutilla 1989). The multiple goods, services, and values of forests will continue to be expressed in incommensurable units for the foreseeable future.

Moreover, multiple use can have multiple problems for public forestry agencies. In 1989, lands managed by the USA's Forest Service sold US$910 million in timber, while receiving 260 million visitor-days of recreation. The value of recreational services is roughly double the value of timber sales (Bowes and Krutilla 1989). This comparison can be very unsettling for an agency whose historical evolution and current program structure reflect an implicit focus on timber management.

New Zealand found the conflict between timber and non-timber interests to be so sharp that it reorganized its Forest Service in the late 1980s. A new Forestry Corporation was established to manage the country's state-owned industrial timber. A new Department of Conservation was assigned responsibilities for environmental and amenity management. With respect to the long-standing issue in New Zealand of "whether integration or separation of the various state forestry functions is preferable," the country opted for separation after nearly 70 years of integration. Significantly, it was New Zealand's environmentalists who argued against retaining forest development and forest conservation in a single organizational structure (Roche 1990).

Management of Natural Forests A German concept of forests as mathematically precise timber-growing factories took hold mainly during the nineteenth century, with its emphasis on science and management in the quest for economic growth. Forests of mixed species and uneven ages gave way to uniform plantations of single species, clearcutting to harvest them, and dominance of financial calculations in forest management. Then as now, this generated controversy and counterproposals. A professor of silviculture in Munich, Karl Gayer, argued for mixed species, natural regeneration, and uneven-aged management in a "back to nature" movement within German forestry. These foundations later became the basis of *Dauerwald* ("continuous forest"), a doctrine opposing clearcutting and advocating forestry interventions so conservative "that the forest hardly notices it" (Heske 1938).

The "back to nature" doctrine has its share of admirers and opponents. Foresters continue to make rational arguments for plantation forests, exotic species, and clearcutting where such practices are biologically and economically feasible. The point to be remembered is that the perspective of managing forests for minimal disturbance has strong roots within the forestry profession itself, and is not an invention of environmental groups in the late twentieth century.

Nevertheless, contemporary environmentalism represents a few distinct breaks with the past in the scope and complexity of its ideas. The geographical scope now includes the developing countries, where the dilemma is often framed as either finding ways to generate monetary returns from natural forests, or risk almost certain loss of large areas of them to competing uses. This issue finds particular prominence in the humid tropics, with its well-known problems of pronounced species heterogeneity and fragile forested ecosystems.

Reasonable evidence is accumulating that commercial logging can be a relatively benign form of generating monetary returns from natural forests, even in the humid tropics (Poore et al. 1989). Here it is important to determine the circumstances under which monetary returns to retention of natural forests exceed returns to forest conversion for agriculture and timber plantations. The answer depends on the conclusions of economic analysis compared with purely financial analysis (Leslie 1987). It also depends on distinguishing current practices, which are more destructive than necessary, from potential practices under appropriate incentives and penalties. The thesis is that even the complex natural forests of the humid tropics can be managed for timber according to practices which are technically feasible, but that present failures occur because of social and economic reasons (Buschbacher 1990).

These reasons overlap the deforestation causes identified in Chapter 2: government policies biased against forests as a land use, insecure land tenure, poorly designed and administered logging concessions, underpricing of timber cutting rights, and inadequate benefits flowing to local communities. Much remains to be learned about the comparative silvicultural systems for managing natural forests in

Foresters continue to make rational arguments for clearcutting where the practice is biologically and economically feasible. (*Photo courtesy of Forest History Society.*)

the tropics, since many of these systems are young and experimental. However, the key elements for successful natural forest management go well beyond silviculture to rectification of the larger policy context. A recent worldwide review summarizes the conditions necessary for natural forest management to succeed (Poore et al. 1989, pp. 207–208):

• Government establishment of a permanent forest estate within which the natural forests have a guaranteed future in overall land use
• Secure tenure for the managers of the natural forest (government, corporate, community, and other managers)
• Technical standards for an annual allowable cut, cutting cycles, tree marking, harvesting methods, and environmental safeguards
• Adequate control over all aspects of harvesting and subsequent forest regeneration to avoid environmental damages
• Economic and financial policies which do not require from the forest more than it can yield sustainably
• Environmental policies which satisfy a public increasingly conscious of environmental problems

Biosphere Reserves   The search for strategies to manage natural forests is joined by a search for feasible strategies to give protection to legally declared forest reserves, national parks, wildlife sanctuaries, and other protected areas. Since 1970, the world's legally protected areas have expanded by over 80 percent, mainly in the developing countries (McNeely et al. 1990). However, the legal declaration of protected areas often implies denial of logging, mining, hunting, fishing, and even fuelwood collection. This creates obvious conflicts with local communities, which perceive many more costs than benefits.

Starting in the 1970s, the IUCN worked with the United Nations to promote the concept of "biosphere reserves" (Gregg and McGean 1985). The objective is to accommodate local human populations while maintaining the undisturbed or lightly disturbed character of legally protected areas. Conceptually, this is done through the zoning of land uses, typically featuring a strictly protected core area surrounded by a multiple-use buffer zone (Oldfield 1988).

In principle, biosphere reserves have a role for forest management in the buffer zones. Managed forests and agroforestry provide a transition between the protected core and an outer agricultural landscape (Poore and Sayer 1988). Also, forest corridors connect pairs or groups of protected areas. This allows wildlife to migrate between them, thereby reducing the risks that wildlife populations will become extinct (Harris 1984). For example, the small country of Costa Rica is working towards using forest corridors to link its national parks, forest reserves, and wildlife sanctuaries so that these individual areas do not become isolated islands in a sea of surrounding development.

Despite the intuitive appeal of buffer zones as a plan or concept, it is difficult to find working models. This is because government agencies responsible for reserve management typically have little authority outside of the legal boundaries of these reserves. Secondly, many buffer zones already are developed for commercial uses, meaning that the buffer concept offers little that is new or special to the communities. Thirdly, agreements between governments and communities over compensation for lost access depend on delicate political negotiations, with high risks that these negotiations will break down and that agreements will not be honored. In summary, the linking of core protected areas and multiple-use buffers continues to be attractive as a strategy, but future initiatives will require advances in managerial skill and policy sophistication (Wells et al. 1990).

Extractive Reserves   Emphasis on both protecting forests from disturbances and providing financial gain for local communities focuses attention on non-timber forest products. Resins, rattan, herbs, nuts, fruits, skins, and other non-timber forest products are gathered and sold by residents of a forested area, including indigenous tribes and other resident cultural groups. If sufficiently attractive from the perspective of cash income and labor feasibility, this extraction slows or prevents forest conversion to non-forest uses.

Thus "extractive reserves" have been proposed, either as independent entities or as buffer zones adjacent to legally protected areas. The extracted products are obtained as they occur naturally in the forest. Alternatively, their abundance and

If attractive from the perspective of cash income and labor feasibility, the extraction of non-timber forest products slows or prevents forest conversion to other land uses. (*Photo courtesy of FAO.*)

productivity are enhanced through means which encourage growth and reproduction of the desired plants and animals.

Conditions necessary for successful extractive reserves include (1) relatively large areas of forest per community and per person supported; (2) the presence of stable and profitable markets; and (3) security of tenure in the forested area. The first condition is explained by the extensive character of most forms of extraction which rely on products other than timber. The second reflects the frequent dilemma that profits are skewed towards product buyers, with low prices received at the level of primary harvesters. Finally, the tenure condition is absolutely essential if overharvesting is to be avoided. Presently, these conditions are simultaneously achieved only under exceptional circumstances.

Importantly, the concept of extractive reserves often links forest protection with cultural protection. Such is the case of Brazil and its extractive reserves for rubber tapping (Schwartzman 1989). In 1987, the Brazilian government began designating special forest user rights for peasant settlements which collect the latex of rubber trees growing wild in Amazonian forests. Representing these settlements was Chico Mendes, spokesperson and social activist for Brazil's National Council of Rubber Tappers. In 1988, Mendes was assassinated in a violent conflict over protecting the forests for rubber tapping versus opening them for cattle ranching.

In Brazil and much of the rest of the world, the social struggle of Chico Mendes and his rubber tappers was perceived as a fight about a way of life worth protecting. Chico Mendes became a martyr not only for forest protection, but also for the rights of the peasant groups he represented (Revkin 1990; Shoumatoff 1990). Partly because of the legacy of Chico Mendes and his allies, the Brazilian government declared the country's first four extractive reserves in 1990.

The perceived link between cultural survival and forest gathering systems goes well beyond Brazil and the rubber tappers (Goodland 1982). In Asia, tribal groups and peasant communities have been able keepers of the forest, but now face destabilizing forces as modernization comes closer (Bromley and Chapagain 1984). This can have profound consequences. For example, one perspective argues that indigenous groups are not naturally in harmony with their physical environment, but only appear to be until they obtain more powerful technologies (Guthrie 1971).

Furthermore, indigenous conservation practices may diverge from Western norms in terms of issues and priorities. In the Philippines, the Ati hunting and gathering culture is well known for extracting dozens of important non-timber products from its forest reserve (Stewart 1990). However, these include at least some plants and animals which are threatened or endangered. Where is the taking of threatened species more widespread than in this single community? In short, the matter of the land wisdom of local communities is controversial, with many issues remaining to be sorted out (Seeger 1982; Ellen 1986; Callicott 1989). These are issues fundamental to the workability of setting aside forests as extractive reserves.

Nature-oriented Tourism   Yet another option which generates incomes from forests without cutting their timber is tourism oriented to natural history. Nature-oriented tourism (i.e., ecological tourism, or "ecotourism") is a small but rapidly growing segment of the world's enormous travel industry. Affluence, education, and environmentalism combine to produce increasing numbers of visitors to forested wildlands in their own countries and abroad. This generates incomes in the form of transportation, lodging, food, guide services, souvenirs, handicrafts, and other elements of tourism expenditures.

At least some of this ecotourism is finding its way to the developing countries (Laarman and Durst 1987). Visitors include persons attracted by birdwatching, nature photography, wildlife viewing, trekking, and numerous other special interests. Some travelers are motivated by seeing the tropical forests for the first time, given their perceptions that these forests and their wildlife are disappearing. Ecotourists are a diverse socioeconomic mix, ranging from university students to high-income professionals, and including varying combinations of domestic and international participants. A widely shared characteristic of ecotourists is a high level of formal education.

A key question in ecotourism is the amount of income captured by the destination region, particularly by its low-income people who live off the land. Much of tourism's total income is retained by suppliers of goods and services who live far from the wildlands destinations. For example, tour guides and food often are imported from outside the destination regions. One study of ecotourists in Latin America and the Caribbean Basin shows significant amounts of income flowing back to supplier regions, especially for major items like air transportation and tour packages (Boo 1990).

A parallel issue is pricing policy at the destinations. The fee to see Rwanda's mountain gorillas ranges up to US$200 per person per day. This compares with very low entrance fees to visit Costa Rica's national parks, which in 1989 charged US$0.30 per person per day. In part, these extreme pricing differences are due to the relative attractiveness of the different destinations. Yet another explanation is administrative pricing, not related to market supply and demand. Typically ecotourism destinations charge too little or nothing for entry, and fail to collect even the full amount of this nominal revenue. Many forestry and park agencies are obligated to transfer revenue they collect from tourists to the national treasury rather than retain it for management of the protected areas. In a few countries, dissatisfaction over these arrangements has catalyzed reforms in fee and revenue systems.

However, improvement of revenue systems is not entirely sufficient to ensure positive benefits for resource management. Nature-oriented tourism gives market value to forest components otherwise having no such value, and educates visitors about environmental processes. Yet at the same time, visitors can "love a place to death." An example is the Galapagos Islands of Ecuador, where current visitation far exceeds planned levels (Wilson and Laarman 1988). Trekking in Nepal is the cause of depleted vegetation and trash along its main routes (Jeffries 1982), and several African game parks are seriously overcrowded (Western 1986).

Hence the national management of ecotourism demands a more disciplined approach than many countries are willing or able to implement. This forces a dilemma upon governments which badly need the foreign exchange spent by international tourists. These governments can either limit visitation and risk loss of tourism income in the short run, or permit growing visitation that risks degradation of their destination attractions. Policymakers seek intelligent ways to avoid this predicament, such as through investments in infrastructure which increases use without impairing the protected resources. Thus a recurrent theme is defining social and biological carrying capacities, and formulating policies and incentives to work within them. Yet concepts of carrying capacity can be ambiguous, and future work will have to more effectively translate theoretical principle into operational strategy.

ENVIRONMENTAL CHALLENGES IN SCIENTIFIC CONTEXT

The strategies identified in the preceding section address mainly local and regional questions of determined origin and consequence. Beyond this realm are environmental issues more difficult to explain in terms of causality, and which have physical and economic effects eluding ordinary assessment. These environmental alterations are subject to wide margins of uncertainty.

A first set of these problems is determined largely by the general limits of biogeographical features, such as disturbances in particular river basins. These disturbances have been recognized for thousands of years. A second category of impacts has much greater spatial dimensions, as when air pollution emissions in one country produce "acid rain" over lakes and forests in one or more other countries. A third class of problems has truly global consequences. In this third category are global climate change and the loss of species, germplasm, and other elements of biological diversity.

However, the geographical scope of environmental alterations is not easily delimited. The issues stemming from deforestation in the tropics elicit concerns globally, even though many of the most immediate impacts are experienced locally. Threats to species and biological diversity engender an international response, as in relation to tropical forests. Yet other issues regarding species and wildlife are confined mainly within individual countries, e.g., the debate on the spotted owl in the USA (Thomas et al. 1990). Finally, global climate change touches the entire global village, with all contributing to the problem and all subject to its effects.

Selected International Issues

Some of the most difficult challenges in managing forests for ecological functions and environmental services are those which involve "fugitive" resources. Examples are wildlife migrations, river flows, and air streams. When these movements cut across national political boundaries, management difficulties are accentuated.

Migratory Wildlife   Migratory wildlife was the subject of most of the early nature conservation which had an international focus. Numerous international wildlife treaties have been signed since 1900 (Table 7-2). Characteristically, these are exhortations to conserve nature, but impose few or no binding commitments. Thus despite noble language "to protect and preserve" in the Convention on Nature Protection and Wildlife Preservation in the western hemisphere, the convention has virtually no impact in slowing forest conversion in Central America and other regions of the Caribbean Basin. These are tropical wintering habitats for songbirds which migrate south from the USA and Canada, raising alarms that deforestation in tropical America seriously threatens the existence of migrating songbirds.

The perceived loss of songbird habitat generates a complex and volatile mix of emotions, opinions, and facts. Evidence is strong that many migrating species exhibit population declines in forest reserves of the eastern USA (Table 7-3). Yet these reserves are small and isolated patches of forest, located mainly in urban and suburban settings. This makes it difficult to distinguish population declines due to forest fragmentation in the USA from effects due to deforestation in the tropics. Adding further complexity, the removal of forests for crops and pastures alters nesting and feeding habitats to favor some migrating species, just as it displaces others (Askins et al. 1990).

TABLE 7-2
Selected international wildlife treaties since 1900

Name of Convention	Year Signed	Year Effective
Convention for the Preservation of Wild Animals, Birds, and Fish in Africa	1900	——
Convention for the Protection of Birds Useful to Agriculture	1902	1905
Convention Relative to the Preservation of Fauna and Flora in their Natural State	1933	——
Convention on Nature Protection and Wildlife Preservation in the Western Hemisphere	1940	1942
African Convention on the Conservation of Nature and Natural Resources	1968	1969
Convention on Wetlands of International Importance Especially as Waterfowl Habitat ("Ramsar" Convention)	1971	1975
Convention for the Conservation of Antarctic Seals	1972	1978
Convention Concerning the Protection of the World Cultural and Natural Heritage	1972	1975
Convention on International Trade in Endangered Species of Wild Fauna and Flora ("CITES")	1973	1975
Convention on the Conservation of Migratory Species of Wild Animals ("Bonn Convention")	1979	1983
Convention on the Conservation of European Wildlife and Natural Habitats ("Berne Convention")	1979	1982
Convention on the Conservation of Antarctic Marine Living Resources	1980	——

Source: McCormick (1989, p. 178).

Hence the postulated relation between deforestation and migrating songbirds is by no means settled (Hutto 1988). Progress in understanding the songbird problem has been thwarted by several obstacles: (1) inadequate knowledge of the rate and extent of habitat conversion in the neotropics; (2) inadequate knowledge of the habitat requirements of individual migratory species; (3) biased and inconsistent techniques to estimate bird numbers; and (4) excessive focus on academic research not related to the larger question of forest conversion (Askins et al. 1990).

TABLE 7-3
Population changes in songbirds of eastern North America which winter in Latin America and the Caribbean Basin, 1966–1978 compared with 1978–1987

Preferred habitat	Songbird populations		
	Increasing	No change	Decreasing
	(Number of bird species)		
Forest	4	2	25
Generalized	0	0	3
Open-scrub	10	0	6
Total	14	2	34

Source: Askins et al. (1990, pp. 42–43).

Does forest conversion in Central America and the Caribbean Basin reduce songbird populations in the USA and Canada? *(Photo courtesy of Forest History Society.)*

International Watersheds   Changes in a watershed's tree cover have multiple and complex implications for soil and water phenomena. Issues include the impacts of logging, grazing, and agriculture on the level of groundwater, springs, and wells. Other issues are the extent of on-site erosion, stream sedimentation, and the quantity and timing of waterflows in streams and rivers. These questions are especially pertinent in the developing countries, given widespread perceptions that deforestation causes substantial damages downstream (Eckholm 1976; Brown and Wolf 1984). However, explanations of these problems commonly are plagued by "myth, misunderstanding, misinformation, and misinterpretation" (Hamilton and King 1983, p. 131).

A particularly volatile set of controversies concerns human activities in Himalayan uplands as they relate to downstream environmental problems in India and Bangladesh. A prevailing assumption maintains that deforestation in Nepal accounts for disastrous flooding and massive siltation on the plains of the Ganges and Brahmaputra rivers. The Ganges and Brahmaputra carry very high sediment loads (Figure 7-3). Related problems are rapid siltation of reservoirs, abrupt changes in

The hydrological relationships betwen
alteration of tree cover in Himalayan
catchments and downstream flooding in
the Ganges-Brahmaputra river systems are
the subject of myth and misunderstanding.
(*Photos courtesy of World Bank.*)

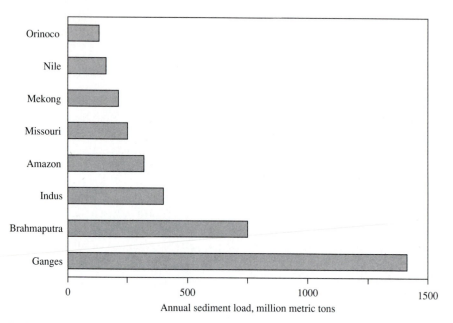

FIGURE 7-3
Sediment loads of the Ganges and Brahmaputra rivers compared with other selected major rivers. (*Source: Ives and Messerli (1989, p. 116).*)

the courses of rivers, spread of sand and gravel across rich agricultural soils, and increased incidence of diseases in the downstream areas.

As apparent victims of careless and harmful land use in Nepal, should the downstream countries seek economic, political, or military reprisals? Secondly, do downstream damages in India and Bangladesh help Nepal in its requests to obtain international aid for forestry? These are among the international issues raised by perceived watershed relationships.

Yet this Himalayan dilemma has been interpreted from a very tenuous understanding of the processes which surround it. Closer examination shows many assumptions to be founded on falsely based intuition, and not supported by facts (Hamilton 1987). For the major Gangetic rivers, hydrological records and other verifiable data indicate that sedimentation rates and waterflow fluctuations are dominated by natural causes. Important among them are rainfall amounts, rates of snow and ice melt, and occasional outbursts of upland lakes dammed by earth or ice. These are factors of weather and climate which have little connection with deforestation. Moreover, downstream flooding and sedimentation are due in large part to local land-use changes in the downstream regions themselves.

These carefully considered observations undermine much of the conventional wisdom which blames upstream deforestation for downstream disasters. Nepal's deforestation is serious in particular catchments, but this does not warrant extrapolations to regional and international scale. The earnest search for scientific validity has a crucial lesson for policy (Ives and Messerli 1989, p. 144):

> Considering the enormous costs and energy requirements needed for forestation of large areas in the mountains, if such were undertaken with the major objective of modifying conditions on the plains, an expensive disappointment is a likely result.

Transboundary Acid Rain   The term "acid rain" was first used to describe a relation between coal burning, wind direction, and vegetation damage near Manchester, England (Cowling 1982). In the current context, acid rain refers to the phenomenon that rain and snow are much more acidic (measured by pH values) than in "natural" precipitation. During the 1970s, parts of Scotland, Norway, and the eastern USA recorded rainfall more acidic than vinegar. Some scientists maintain that rain over many areas of Europe and North America is probably 10 to 100 times more acidic than rain before the Industrial Revolution. This leads to complicated environmental repercussions regarding damage or alleged damage to crops, drinking water, buildings, statuary, and the ecological functioning of lakes and forests. Policy responses to acid rain are frustrated by highly inadequate information on the true causes, pathways, and extent of its impacts (Park 1987; Regens and Rycroft 1988; Tomlinson 1990).

The acidity problem is attributed to sulfuric and nitric acids in the atmosphere. These acids are produced from emissions of sulfur dioxide and nitrogen oxides put into the atmosphere by both natural and manmade sources. The largest share of total emissions in the industrialized countries is from power plants, motor vehicles, and industrial smelters. These emissions are carried high into the atmosphere where they frequently travel long distances, often changing chemically in the process, before precipitating back to earth as acids and acid-forming compounds. Some of these deposits are "dry," while others are mixed with rain and snow.

The acid rain phenomenon has become a prominent international problem pitting upwind polluters against downwind countries fearing environmental damage. According to computer models of long-distance pollutant travel, eastern Canada receives significant deposits of sulfur compounds from the midwestern USA, just as the Nordic countries receive most of their sulfur deposition from other regions of Europe (Figure 7-4).

The effects of acid rain on forests and forest soils emerged as a very puzzling issue beginning in the early 1980s. Reports from Europe indicated extensive forest damage from air pollutants, including half a million hectares of forest affected in both Czechoslovakia and Germany. At the same time, studies in the eastern USA revealed greatly reduced growth rates and seedling reproduction in certain coniferous forests at high elevations.

In Germany, forest damage was first observed near major emission sources of sulfur dioxide. However, a survey in 1984 indicated that about half of West Germany's total forested area showed signs of *Waldsterben*, or "forest death" (Schutt and Cowling 1985). Yet the extent and seriousness of the damage are fiercely debated. Some of Germany's affected forests of Norway spruce (*Picea*

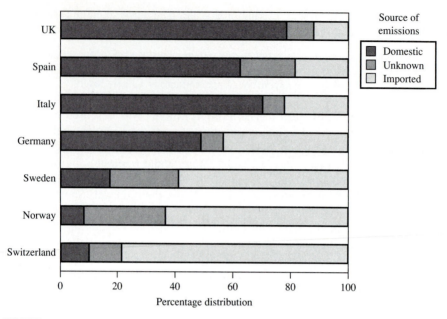

FIGURE 7-4
Sulfur depositions from domestic and imported emissions, selected European countries in the early 1980s. *(Source: Wetstone and Rosencranz (1983, p. 20).)*

abies) have recovered, and decline of other forests now appears to be explained by simple nutrient deficiency rather than *Waldsterben*.

In North America, forest problems because of air pollutants have been suspected for a variety of forest types. In southern California, local impacts of air pollutants on trees are clearly established. Yet unlike Europe, North America has no widespread decline of forests over broad areas. The hypothesis that acid rain is linked to forest damage has been difficult to prove or disprove. Hence evidence shows that sugar maples (*Acer saccharum*) in Canada are suffering some form of environmental stress, especially near emission sources. However, field surveys have not found symptoms or correlations supporting linkages between maple decline and acidic deposition (NAPAP 1990). Likewise, natural pine forests in the southern USA experienced reduced growth rates from the 1940s through the 1980s (Binkley et al. 1989), but explanations for this are highly speculative (Sheffield et al. 1985).

These various facets of current knowledge, all of them subject to continuing reformulation, produce an exasperatingly complex scientific problem (Woodman 1987). Knowledge of where and how air pollutants affect forests is highly tentative. Even when negative trends or events in forest growth are detected, they are difficult to relate to specific causes. The difficulty of attributing causality is complicated by the lack of baseline data on forest behavior over long periods of time.

The effects of acid rain on forests and forest soils emerged as a puzzling issue beginning in the early 1980s. Much remains to be understood about tree physiology when trees are under stress. (*Photo courtesy of Jonas Palm.*)

The causes and consequences of transboundary air pollutants provoke sharp conflicts in national and international politics. In Germany, the fear of *Waldsterben* strengthened the Green Party and other environmentalists in their arguments for stricter pollution controls. By 1983, the government of West Germany came out in favor of stricter emission controls for European countries, reversing its earlier position. On the other hand, Britain has opposed international agreements on reducing emissions of sulfur dioxide, such as those favored by the Nordic countries. Britain is western Europe's largest emitter of sulfur dioxide, exporting most of its emissions and importing only a modest share of its depositions (Postel 1984).

In North America, the acid rain controversy has been politically charged for both Canada and the USA. Since the early 1980s, Canada's government has asked for greatly reduced emissions of sulfur dioxide on both sides of the border. The USA has insisted upon more research to identify causes and estimate economic impacts before abatement action is taken. The various political disputes on acid rain raise the concern as to "whether nations are responding intelligently to the scientific uncertainty which pervades the issue" (Wetstone and Rosencranz 1983, p. 4).

Selected Global Issues

Among contemporary environmental problems, perhaps few seem more consequential at a global level than the disappearance of species and the warming of the atmosphere. The first issue is part of the larger concern to conserve the world's biological diversity. The second is a question of how to prepare for living on an increasingly warmer planet, and how to slow the warming to a manageable rate.

Loss of Species and Germplasm   Biological diversity refers to the variety of the world's organisms at different levels of aggregation: ecosystems, species, and genes. Because of deforestation in the tropics and other environmental disturbances, biological diversity is being reduced at rates considerably greater than in previous eras. The problem is sometimes stated in terms of depleting biological capital, or narrowing and reducing habitats, species, and germplasm. Issues for social policy turn on the consequences of these losses. Issues for biological science are to identify what is being depleted or altered, and to define intervention strategies to slow or offset these changes.

Strategies to conserve biological diversity include both *in situ* and *ex situ* approaches. *In situ* strategies leave species where they are found in nature, protecting them in their natural setting. The designation of protected cores in biosphere reserves exemplifies the *in situ* approach. *Ex situ* methods remove species from their natural habitats for preservation and propagation in zoos, botanical gardens, seed collections, and other permanent collections. For example, about 40 germplasm banks around the world are part of the International Board of Plant Genetic Resources, which stores over one million varieties of plants. In any particular case, the combination of *in situ* and *ex situ* approaches depends on purpose, operational feasibility, and numerous other decision factors.

The reasons for conserving biological diversity tend to divide into utilitarian and nonutilitarian arguments. The utilitarian framework stresses the role of wild relatives of domesticated food and animal crops as stocks of genetic resources useful now or in the future for breeding purposes. Here objectives are to develop new varieties, and to diversify production as a means to manage risk. This same rationale applies to wild relatives of trees for timber and other purposes. Thus the heterogenous forests of Central America and Mexico are the original sources of species and varieties of *Leucaena leucocephala* for tree breeding in agroforestry, and several tropical pines for selection and breeding in commercial plantations. Important medicinal compounds are based on natural or synthesized substances discovered in wild plants, animals, and microorganisms. Finally, the preservation of undisturbed ecosystems has scientific utility for the study of evolutionary processes and ecological relationships.

A key concept is that ecosystems and organisms which currently have little or no human value may acquire such value in the future as they become better known. "Option value" is satisfied by human capability to respond to an uncertain future of changing and unpredictable biological, social, and economic events. The short phrase "extinction is forever" succinctly expresses what is to be avoided.

However, the utilitarian framework is only one part of the rationalization for protecting biological resources. The nonutilitarian premise goes beyond attempting to price nature in terms that have economic or even scientific meaning. This third dimension focuses on intangible and usually philosophical dimensions that all species have inherent rights. The more extreme adherents of this viewpoint doubt that a utilitarian account is even worth pursuing, relying instead on reasoning which is almost totally biocentric, e.g., "the biosphere will miss extinct species" (Ehrenfeld 1988).

The determination of extinction rates and causes poses difficult challenges for science, and ultimately for policy. It is generally agreed that the greatest numbers of species and gene pools at risk are found in tropical regions, particularly in zones where human activity is expanding. Losses are potentially greatest where there are high concentrations of species in small areas, high levels of endemism (i.e., species restricted to a particular region or locality), and strong human pressures for forest conversion. Even if these are agreed upon as appropriate criteria for defining critical areas, application of the criteria can lead to diverging views on where to concentrate protection efforts (Figure 7-5). These differences are explained by gross inadequacies of the field data, and by variations in how the criteria are weighted.

Additionally, attention to the tropics can leave out key temperate regions. An example is the temperate region of southern Africa, where species richness (ratio of species to land area) is the world's highest, and where a large proportion of plant species are both endemic and threatened (McNeely et al. 1990). In summary, the matter of choosing protection priorities is not straightforward.

Estimation of past and pending extinction rates is subject to a considerable amount of guessing. Numbers of species by regions and habitats are only crude approximations, especially for the tropics. Species-area curves model how the number of species decreases in relation to decreasing areas of habitat (Simberloff 1986), but this provides only rough rules of thumb for particular places and times. Additionally, data on current deforestation are crude, and projections of future deforestation rates and locations are speculative.

Another issue is scientific objectivity. Skeptics imply that biologists exaggerate losses of species and germplasm in order to make a more convincing case for protection, and possibly to increase their research budgets (Simon and Wildavsky 1984).

Finally, the protection of biological diversity requires a number of value judgments on distinctiveness, utility, and threat (Reid and Miller 1989). Which habitats and species should be given priority, and for what reasons? Do utilitarian arguments prevail, and is taxonomic rank important? Alternatively, is all biological life to be accorded equal protection status? It would seem that utility measures can hardly be avoided, and that protection strategies must account for human usefulness, even if such measures are exceedingly difficult to agree upon.

Global Warming   Global warming refers to the observation that average global temperatures appear to be about one-half degree Celsius higher than a

FIGURE 7-5

Priority regions for protection of biological diversity, 1980s. *(Sources: Reid and Miller (1989, p. 73); McNeely et al. (1990, pp 86–87).)*

	Source of recommendation		
	USA National Academy of Sciences	IUCN/UNEP	N. Myers
Asia			
Eastern Himalayas		X	X
Philippines		X	X
Sri Lanka	X	X	
Kalimantan (Indonesia)	X		
Sarawak (Malaysia)			X
Sulawesi (Indonesia)	X		
Peninsular Malaysia			X
Indo-China		X	
Bangladesh/Bhutan/Nepal		X	
Vietnam/Kampuchea/Thailand		X	
Southeast China		X	
Africa			
Madagascar	X	X	X
Mountainous East Africa	X	X	
Cameroon	X		
Equatorial West Africa		X	
Latin America			
Coastal Ecuador	X		X
Brazilian Atlantic Coast	X		X
Eastern and southern Amazon	X		
Uplands of western Amazon			X
Chocó region of Colombia			X
Oceania			
Hawaii	X		X
New Caledonia	X		X
Queensland, Australia			X

century ago, and the theory that this is explained in large part by a "greenhouse effect" (Schneider 1989). The greenhouse theory postulates increasing atmospheric concentrations of carbon dioxide, chlorofluorocarbons (CFCs), methane, and nitrous oxides. These greenhouse gases allow sunlight to penetrate the atmosphere, but trap the resulting heat. Already in 1896, the Swedish chemist Svante Arrhenius postulated greenhouse warming on the basis of Europe's coal combustion. Yet the greenhouse issue received little attention until very recently. In part this is because no one was able to establish whether carbon dioxide was in fact building up in the atmosphere, as Arrhenius had predicted.

Since Arrhenius, atmospheric measurements and computer climate models have provided considerable evidence that the greenhouse phenomenon is real. Since 1958, continuous observations of atmospheric carbon dioxide on the Mauna Loa mountaintop in Hawaii have shown that carbon dioxide concentrations have been steadily increasing. Also, data from polar ice cores suggest that concentrations of atmospheric carbon dioxide have been rising for at least a century. During the 1980s, scientists added CFCs, methane, and nitrous oxide to the list of greenhouse gases, and empirically verified that they trap heat. Studies of Mars and Venus show correlations between concentrations of these gases and planetary surface temperatures. Also, research of climatic history reveals that the Earth's ice ages occurred during periods of low atmospheric carbon dioxide, and its warm periods occurred when carbon dioxide was high (Flavin 1989).

Even if greenhouse gases are building up, the data with respect to global temperatures are much less conclusive. Some data indicate a temperature rise of 0.5 degree Celsius since 1880 (Jones et al. 1986), but the matter is far from settled (Abelson 1990). The disagreement over temperature change is explained by the difficulties of separating short-term from long-term movements, and of isolating causal factors. Among such factors are variations in the sun's radiation to Earth, volcanic eruptions, and changes in the movements of ocean currents.

Another confounding detail is incomplete understanding of future cloud cover as the global warming augments ocean evaporation. Cirrus clouds at high altitudes add to the greenhouse effect, while stratocumulus clouds over oceans have a cooling effect by reflecting sunlight back towards space. A further complication stems from increased emissions of sulfur dioxide. These emissions produce not only acid rain, but also modifications of clouding in ways that conceivably cool the atmosphere. Finally, most present climate models suffer from poor knowledge of the planet's sources and sinks of carbon, including how carbon passes in and out of oceans and forests.

Deforestation is among the many sources of greenhouse gases (Table 7-4). For the aggregate of the developing countries, forest cutting and burning appear to be a main source of carbon emissions (Table 7-5). To this must be added the combustion of fuelwood in hundreds of millions of households. Yet it is the industrialized countries which are responsible for the bulk of greenhouse gases, mainly through their massive combustion of fossil fuels for energy production.

TABLE 7-4
Principal sources of greenhouse gases in global climate change

Gas	Principal sources	Estimated greenhouse contribution (percent)
Carbon dioxide	Fossil fuels	44
	Deforestation	13
Chlorofluorocarbons	Foams, aerosols, refrigerants, solvents	25
Methane	Wetlands, rice, fossil fuels, livestock	12
Nitrous oxide	Fossils fuels, fertilizers, deforestation	6

Source: Adapted from Flavin (1989, p. 13).

TABLE 7-5
Deforestation as a factor in carbon emissions for
selected developing countries, 1980s

Country	Deforestation*	Fossil fuels†	Sum
	(emissions, million tons)		
Brazil	336	53	389
Indonesia	192	28	220
Colombia	123	14	137
Thailand	95	16	111
Ivory Coast	101	1	102
Laos	85	< 1	85
Nigeria	60	9	69
Philippines	57	10	67
Malaysia	50	11	61
Myanmar	51	2	53
Others (64 countries)	514	181	690

*Deforestation emissions estimated for 1980.
†Fossil fuel emissions estimated for 1987.
Source: Flavin (1989, p. 29). Used with permission of Worldwatch
Institute.

Global warming has complex and largely unforeseeable consequences for the
amount, distribution, and composition of the world's forest vegetation. Forest
ecosystems are adapted to particular ranges of temperature and moisture. A large-
scale warming alters these conditions, and initiates or accelerates changes in vegetation zones. Thus a warming might shift the northern hemisphere's temperate
forests northward, even as the southern hemisphere's forests expand southward.
This suggests a greater total area of forests in the world, but that prospect is
constrained by the possible dieback of forests where adaptation will not keep pace
with climate change. Thus a pessimistic scenario envisages large areas of dead
and dying forests, combined with only minimal immigration of forest types appropriate for the modified climate. The realism of such a scenario depends on
both the rate of climate change and the rate of forest migration. Given sufficient
time, forests exhibit an ability to migrate and adapt to numerous environmental
changes, including climate. At the moment, the impact of global warming on
forests is necessarily speculative (Sedjo and Solomon 1989).

Just as climate affects forests, forests are able to affect climate. If deforestation puts carbon into the atmosphere, reforestation takes it out. The process of
plant growth through photosynthesis combines water and carbon dioxide to make
oxygen and plant carbon. Thus the growing of forests sequesters carbon from
the atmosphere, and the maintenance of standing forests holds that carbon in the
biomass (Detwiler and Hall 1988). This prompts investigation of using forests
as a vehicle for slowing global warming, and advances new arguments for tree
planting.

Recent estimates consider the amount of tree planting that would be required
to capture the approximately three billion tons of "excess" carbon currently as-

Fuelwood burning in hundreds of millions of households releases carbon emissions into the atmospere. Yet an even more important source of carbon emissions is combustion of fossil fuels in the industrialized countries. (*Photo courtesy of FAO.*)

The use of forests as a vehicle for slowing global warming advances new arguments for tree planting. These workers weed a government tree nursery in Ecuador. (*Photo courtesy of FAO.*)

277

similated by the atmosphere each year (Sedjo 1989). The result is about 465 million hectares of fairly rapidly growing forest, or nearly five times the existing global area of forest plantations. Even then, massive establishment of more forests merely postpones a more fundamental solution, such as dramatic adjustments in energy production and consumption. This is because the new forests capture excess carbon only during the years of their active growth, and because continued expansion of forest area could conflict with other land uses. Moreover, the severity of climatic disruptions in extreme scenarios of global warming leaves many unanswered questions about what types of new forests to establish, and where to locate them. Here, too, are legitimate scientific issues which need careful attention in the face of enormous uncertainty.

When Do We Know Enough to Make Decisions?

The commanding environmental issues of this era are difficult to act upon because of limited understanding of cause and impact. Examples briefly introduced here are songbird populations in the Americas, waterflows from Himalayan mountains to the plains below, acid rain in Europe and North America, impacts of deforestation on species and germplasm, and links between forests and global warming. Each of these complex problems is defined internationally or globally, blending politics with science to produce a truly explosive mix.

Decisions on these environmental issues must proceed from present ignorance. Within the framework of hypothesis testing in statistics, two types of errors occur (Figure 7-6). The first is reacting to a perceived problem when none exists, or the Type I error. The Type II error is not responding to a problem which is real. Efforts to minimize one kind of error increase the likelihood of making the other error. It is impossible to minimize both kinds of errors simultaneously.

FIGURE 7-6
Decision errors in hypotheses on perceived environmental risks.

State of the world	Decision	
	Accept null hypothesis	**Reject null hypothesis**
Environmental situation "X" is not a problem (Null hypothesis)	Correct decision	Type I error
Environmental situation "X" is a problem	Type II error	Correct decision

X1 = alteration of songbird habitat in tropics
X2 = effect of upstream deforestation on downstream flooding
X3 = effect of acidic deposition on forest growth
X4 = effect of forest conversion on biological diversity
X5 = effect of global climate change on forests
XM...XN = other likely or conceivable impacts

This decision structure is present in each of the issues from migrating song-birds to global warming. Governments and industries opposed to intervention on a given environmental question cite inconsistent and incomplete scientific data as the reason for not taking action. Their scientific position asserts the absence of an environmental problem until the presence of the problem can be proven conclusively. In a formal statistical sense, this makes them unlikely to make a Type I error, but vulnerable to a Type II error. Conversely, environmentalists are impressed by arguments to avert a Type II error, but in so doing they are likely to respond to perceived problems which in fact may not be real. Here the scientific position is that environmental disturbances are occurring, and it is unsafe to assume absence of the problems until proven otherwise. This contest of basic assumptions dominates environmental policy, since classical hypothesis tests using statistics are virtually ruled out by problem complexity.

The case of global warming illustrates the decision dilemma under uncertainty. Suppose that the governments of the world's most influential countries agree that global warming is occurring, and further regard this to be threatening. They reach an international agreement to radically reduce carbon emissions, build sea walls to keep back anticipated rising of the oceans, and establish vast new areas of forest plantations. However, suppose that the rising concentrations of greenhouse gases do not translate into the expected warming, e.g., because increased atmospheric clouding generates feedback which offsets the warming. The world has reacted to a problem which did not materialize, spending billions of dollars for prevention and mitigation which proved unnecessary in the end.

Suppose, instead, that the world fails to attempt adaptive and mitigative strategies, but the warming does occur. The warming comes more rapidly than if preparatory measures had been undertaken. The world spent few resources to avert the problem, but perhaps truly massive resources to cope with the damages.

Reflection on the policy framework suggests gradations in the scale and timing of decisions more varied than the two possibilities of responding or failing to respond. For example, in forestry it might be prudent to commit increased funding to the silviculture and management of forests which grow in warmer and drier climates. Other redirections of efforts might favor redoubled initiatives to slow tropical deforestation, and to define sensible strategies for using forests to capture atmospheric carbon dioxide. These initiatives can be combined in various ways, and adjustments in strategy can be incremental with successive advances in information and understanding.

However, each redirection has opportunity costs in terms of not being able to pursue alternative programs. These alternatives are foregone because of losing funds now reallocated to the fight against global warming, or because of incompatible objectives with that goal. Each threat of environmental crisis competes with all others—and with the totality of societal needs—for favor and funding.

Finally, global warming has both winners and losers. Some of the northerly countries might anticipate a warming with at least some degree of enthusiasm. Moreover, a low-income country like China may regard global warming as an acceptable price to pay if China is allowed to use its vast coal deposits for national economic development. More generally, the majority of the developing countries could be expected to resist limits on their use of fossil fuels, arguing that their struggles for economic growth should not be burdened by still more constraints. Likewise, the forested developing countries will not easily agree to curtailing deforestation unless appropriate financial transfers compensate them for their sacrifice of land development. These and other international differences stand in the way of decisions regarding what to do about global warming, even if countries readily agree on the consequences at stake.

SYNTHESIS

The rationale for protecting the environmental services and ecological functions of forests rests on a wide set of arguments which are economic, scientific, cultural, and philosophical in their assumptions and origins. On the one hand, environmentalism is propelled by perceptions of grave environmental threats and only modest scientific comprehension of explanations and consequences. On the other, environmentalism moves ahead as a social force through the spread of attitudes that wild nature must be protected on an otherwise crowded and despoiled planet.

In Western societies, environmentalism sprouted from European roots in the 1700s. A few nature essayists convinced the reading public that factory systems and large cities were separating people from the pleasantries of wooded landscapes. Thus emerged the Arcadian vision of a better world in which man and nature live peacefully together in a beautiful garden. At about the same time, a scientific world view insisted that man vigorously pursue his control over nature in order to use it productively for the expansion of noble human purposes. It was from these separate outlooks that "two roads diverged" (Worster 1977). One road led to the wisdom of preservation, and the other to the wisdom of managed use. In the late twentieth century, the Brundtland Commission's urging to integrate conservation with economic growth in a single framework attests to the persistence of separation, but a preference for convergence.

Perhaps the most significant facet of environmentalism is the challenge it poses to orthodox policies of economic growth. Material needs are ensured for the majority of persons in affluent societies, but wild nature is perceived to be scarce. The rationale to protect nature extends beyond utilitarian logic to a so-called "deep ecology" faction, which values nature preservation for its own sake.

Grim scenarios of tropical deforestation, disappearing species, acid rain, and climate warming refocus many environmental issues at a higher level. These apocalyptic visions transform forest protection from a practical or even ethical act into an imperative for planetary survival. When these different preoccupations are added up, it is little wonder that the current age is above all an environmental age.

Until quite recently, the developing countries argued that protection of nature and the environment was an unaffordable luxury. This view has turned around dramatically. A revised perspective sees environmental degradation and material poverty as two sides of the same coin. Land productivity is threatened through deforestation and associated pressures, and poor persons become poorer as this natural capital is depleted. In the fierce battle of competing theories about how the world works, this revisionist model has gained wide recognition and acceptance.

Yet the new understanding of the positive role of nature conservation in economic development is an understanding (or hope?) mainly among the world's affluent. No one has reliable evidence of the extent to which nature conservation in fact serves the needs of the poor. Objective information on this linkage is desperately needed. That the relation can be mainly synergistic is an article of faith, and an implicit pledge that historical patterns of conflict will be broken.

To move from policy rhetoric to implementation turns attention from goals to means. Several elements constitute what might be construed as an environmental strategy, with direct applications for forest protection. First is improved measurement of environmental, ecological, and amenity benefits. This finds tangible expression in a highly creative branch of economics to correct for unpriced values, and to incorporate the depletion of natural capital in measures of national income. Major gaps still divide theory from practice in both areas. Perhaps even more important is whether economic rationalization is worth the effort. Through the present, policy positions on environmental matters are won less often with good economic data than with impassioned presentations of images and symbols (Arnold 1987). Improved valuation moves environmentalism in the direction it seeks, but cannot be relied upon as a main vehicle.

In forestry, environmentalism invigorates old debates about the virtues and problems of multiple-use management, and about why and how to manage natural forests sustainably. These are familiar questions in forestry, but questions without easy resolutions. It is conceivable that systems of multiple use and all-natural forests may in the end leave environmentalists with less undisturbed forests than zones of highly productive, even-aged forest plantations. In this debate, the range of forest management strategies is too broad to simplify into particular doctrines.

A considerable amount of conceptualizing addresses ways to add commercial value to forests without cutting their timber. Extractive reserves and nature-oriented tourism are among the possibilities. The concept of biosphere reserves permits limited commercial development to occur around a protected core. The genesis of most of these ideas is relatively recent, with concepts running far ahead of implementation. This implies the likelihood of many corrections as experience is evaluated for lessons learned.

Many of the world's most challenging scientific and managerial issues are reserved for forests in relation to the environment at an international and global scale. Some issues are regional (e.g., songbird migration, international watersheds, acid rain), while others affect the world as a whole (e.g., species loss, global climate change). These problems are characterized by incomplete and disputed scientific understanding of causes and consequences, and by a wide variety of perspectives on what to do about them. The decision framework is complicated by conflicting cross-country interests, so that each of these issues is ultimately one of international politics.

In the final analysis, environmentalism redefines forestry in relation to dramatically shifting social values. In this environmental age, good forestry is that which protects the diversity of plant and animal life, and the diversity of human cultures. The forest is not just a timber factory, but also a link with climate regulation, water flow, scientific knowledge, and cultural survival. The premise of environmentalism is that forests should be nurtured to promote health, beauty, inspiration, discovery, and a sense of permanence (Hays 1987). There is nothing novel in reciting what forests are able to do, since these attributes have been known for centuries. More consequential is that today's environmentalism prods forestry to produce these results directly rather than as incidental and uncertain side effects of other objectives.

ISSUES FOR DISCUSSION AND INVESTIGATION

1 From origins in upper-class gatherings of nature lovers in Europe and North America during the late 1800s, environmentalism has expanded to become a worldwide mass movement a century later. True or false? Explain and defend.

2 John Muir's Sierra Club of the late 1800s was mainly a hiking club of affluent males who lived near San Francisco, California. By 1970, it had been transformed into an organization with thousands of members and an activist environmental lobby (Cohen 1988). By the 1990s, the Sierra Club was lobbying on issues which affect forests well outside of California and the USA. What factors explain changes in the membership, objectives, and geographical context of the Sierra Club?

3 Environmentalism is the last stage in a series of successive human understandings about the biophysical world: fear, understanding, use, abuse, and worry (Bowman 1975). Explain and illustrate with examples relevant to forestry.

4 Investigate Sir Philip Sidney's *Arcadia* as an inspiration influencing subsequent thought on man and nature.

5 In Western societies, beliefs and attitudes about man's role in the natural world began diverging in the 1700s (Worster 1977). One tradition went the direction of Gilbert White, Henry Thoreau, and John Muir. The other included Linnaeus, G.H. Hartig and Heinrich Cotta (co-founders of German scientific forestry), and Gifford Pinchot. (i) Trace how these lineages explain forestry's aims and practices in the contemporary era. (ii) Identify other individuals in the historical development of environmental thought, and describe their role and contributions.

6 (i) Compare the following terms as they are understood in English-speaking North America: conservationist, preservationist, and environmentalist. (ii) Are these terms useful across cultures and languages? If not, how does this affect the conceptual framework of forest protection at the international level?

7 In the 1940s, Aldo Leopold (1949) lamented, "Your true modern is separated from the land by many middlemen, and by innumerable physical gadgets. He has no vital relation to it." (i) Discuss how and why this separation has increased through the years in urbanized Western societies. (ii) What does this separation mean for the struggle between forest use versus forest preservation?

8 (i) What is nature religion, and how does it contrast in form and function between tribal societies and modern industrialized societies (Albanese 1990)? (ii) How does nature religion affect forest management?

9 Leaders of movements for social transformation always understand that in order to change a situation, they must appeal explicitly or implicitly to moral considerations (Engel and Engel 1990). What are the critical issues in weighing and choosing one claim of morally superior behavior (e.g., all nature is sacred and must be protected) against another (e.g., natural resources should be used to serve the masses, particularly the poor)?

10 "Save the rainforest" is a rallying cry for politicians, actors and singers, peace groups, and wildlife associations. What common and separate reasons motivate these diverse persons to want to save the rainforest? To what extent can the beliefs and actions of these disparate elements be described as a social movement? As a political alliance?

11 Simon and Wildavsky (1984) contend that there should be a presumption in favor of statements that lead to the facts as best we know them, especially in a scientific context. Regarding estimates on species losses because of deforestation, suppose that biologists implicitly favor high numbers over low numbers. (i) Is this bad science or simply prudent science? (ii) Is possible exaggeration justified if the goal of protecting forest habitats and species is an ethical act?

12 Economics has developed a number of tools to estimate "shadow prices" for forest goods and services which are not exchanged in markets. (i) How will more accurate and comprehensive valuation of the forest's goods and services meet the aims of environmentalists? (ii) Is it possible that improved valuation could instead stifle these aims? Explain.

13 (i) What is the connection between environmentalism, forests, and national income accounting? (ii) Simon Kuznets was a pioneer in national income accounting. In the 1940s, Kuznets recommended that measurements of national income consider some of the adjustments and corrections still being discussed today (Kuznets 1948). Why is it difficult to change systems of national income accounting?

14 Environmentalists welcome multiple-use management because it obliges public forestry agencies to coordinate and harmonize forest uses. True or false? Explain and defend.

15 In the humid tropics, the management of natural forests is "demonstrably feasible on technical grounds, but has generally failed for social and economic reasons" (Buschbacher 1990). What are these reasons?

16 What are biosphere reserves, and what are their objectives?

17 What are extractive reserves, and what are the conditions for their success?

18 In 1988, Chico Mendes was murdered for defending the interests of Brazilian rubber tappers in Amazonian forests against competing interests of cattle ranchers (Revkin 1990; Shoumatoff 1990). How, if at all, has the murder of Chico Mendes affected environmentalism in Brazil and the world?

19 Tourism is both friend and enemy of wildlands protection. (i) Explain and illustrate. (ii) Who or what is an ecotourist? (iii) What determines carrying capacity for ecotourism?

20 In 1990, the incoming director of the national parks agency in Peru said: "Our plans for ecologically sensitive jungle tourism and sustained harvests of Brazil nuts and other products from intact forest help solve many of our resource management problems simultaneously: it produces employment, safeguards biological diversity, protects steep tropical watersheds, attracts domestic and foreign tourism, and allows us to show off our rainforest to the world." (i) Is this wishful thinking, or a practical development strategy? (ii) What questions will have to be answered if the strategy is to be feasible?

21 Science does not have adequate explanations for several complex environmental alterations. Identify knowledge gaps with respect to the following: (i) decreased songbird populations in eastern North America; (ii) downstream flooding and sedimentation on the Ganges-Brahmaputra rivers; (iii) impacts of acid rain on forests in central Europe; (iv) rates and causes of species extinctions in the tropics; and (v) future rates of global climate change.

22 Summarize the decision risks in formulating a policy response to any of the planet's poorly understood environmental phenomena perceived to have negative effects for human welfare.

23 May (1978) and Arnold (1987) portray environmentalists in an unfavorable light. In excessively favoring birds and ferns over desperately poor people, environmentalism is cruelly amoral, the opposite of the ethical doctrine it purports to be. Moreover, environmentalists include too many vain and selfish individuals whose motives are less to protect nature than to attain personal profit, prestige, and power. (i) Are these negative characterizations widespread, or are they the ranting of a bitter minority? (ii) How do environmentalists reply?

24 Michael Frome (1988) contends that foresters today are technical people, focused mostly on timber production, and without the missionary zeal of earlier generations of foresters who fought to save the Earth. Is this an accurate portrayal? If accurate, what challenges face the profession? Consider where and how forestry students are recruited, the formal university education they receive, and the professional assignments they accept.

REFERENCES

Abelson, Philip H. 1990. "Uncertainties about global warming," *Science* 247:1529.

Albanese, Catherine L. 1990. *Nature Religion in America: From the Algonkian Indians to the New Age*. University of Chicago Press, Chicago.

Arnold, Ron. 1987. *Ecology Wars: Environmentalism as if People Mattered*. Free Enterprise Press, Bellevue, WA.

Askins, Robert A., James F. Lynch, and Russell Greenberg. 1990. "Population declines in migratory birds in eastern North America," pp. 1–57 in Dennis M. Power (ed.), *Current Ornithology*, Volume 7. Plenum Press, New York.

Binkley, D., C. T. Driscoll, H. L. Allen, P. Schoeneberger, and D. McAvoy. 1989. *Acidic Deposition and Forest Soils: Context and Case Studies in the Southeastern United States*. Springer-Verlag, New York.

Boo, Elizabeth. 1990. *Ecotourism: The Potentials and Pitfalls*. World Wildlife Fund, Washington, DC.

Botkin, Daniel B. 1990. *Discordant Harmonies: A New Ecology for the Twenty-First Century*. Oxford University Press, New York.

Bowes, Michael D. and John V. Krutilla. 1989. *Multiple-Use Management: The Economics of Public Forestlands*. Resources for the Future, Washington, DC.

Bowman, James S. 1975. "The ecology movement: A viewpoint," *International Journal of Environmental Studies* 8(2):91–97.

Bromley, Daniel and Davendra P. Chapagain. 1984. "The village against the center: Resource depletion in South Asia," *American Journal of Agricultural Economics* 66(5):869–873.

Brown, Lester R. and Edward C. Wolf. 1984. *Soil Erosion: Quiet Crisis in the World Economy*. Worldwatch Paper 60, Worldwatch Institute, Washington, DC.

Buschbacher, Robert J. 1990. "Natural forest management in the humid tropics: Ecological, social, and economic considerations," *Ambio* 19(5):253–258.

Callicott, J. Baird. 1989. *In Defense of the Land Ethic: Essays in Environmental Philosophy*. State University of New York Press, Albany.

Callicott, J. Baird and Roger T. Ames (eds.). 1989. *Nature in Asian Traditions and Thought: Essays in Environmental Philosophy*. State University of New York Press, Albany.

Cohen, Michael P. 1988. *History of the Sierra Club, 1892–1970*. Sierra Club Books, San Francisco.

Council on Environmental Quality (of USA). 1982. *The Global 2000 Report to the President: Entering the Twenty-First Century*. Penguin Books, Harmondsworth, England.

Cowling, Ellis. 1982. "An historical resume of progress in scientific and public understanding of acid precipitation and its biological consequences," pp. 43–83 in F. M. D'itri (ed.), *Acid Precipitation: Effects on Ecological Systems*. Ann Arbor Science, Ann Arbor, MI.

Daly, Herman E. and John B. Cobb, Jr. 1989. *For the Common Good: Redirecting the Economy Toward Community, the Environment, and a Sustainable Future*. Beacon Press, Boston.

Detwiler, R. P. and Charles A. S. Hall. 1988. "Tropical forests and the global carbon cycle," *Science* 239:42–47.

Earhart, J. E. and G. Shillinger. 1990. "A summary of the U.S.-based private sector response to global conservation issues," International Forestry Working Group, Society of American Foresters, SAF National Convention, Washington, DC.

Eckholm, Eric. 1976. *Losing Ground*. W W Norton and Company, New York.

Ehrenfeld, David. 1988. "Why put a value on biodiversity?" pp. 212–216 in E. O. Wilson and Francis M. Peter (eds.), *Biodiversity*. National Academy Press, Washington, DC.

Ellen, R. F. 1986. "What Black Elk left unsaid: On the illusory images of Green primitivism," *Anthropology Today* 2(6):8–12.

El Serafy, Salah and Ernst Lutz. 1989. "Environmental and resource accounting: An overview," pp. 1–7 in Y. J. Ahmad, S. El Serafy, and E. Lutz (eds.), *Environmental Accounting for Sustainable Development*. World Bank, Washington, DC.

Engel, J. Ronald and Joan G. Engel (eds.). 1990. *Ethics of Environment and Development: Global Challenge and International Response*. University of Arizona Press, Tucson.

Flavin, Christopher. 1989. *Slowing Global Warming: A Worldwide Strategy*. Worldwatch Paper 91, Worldwatch Institute, Washington, DC.

Fox, Stephen R. 1981. *John Muir and His Legacy: The American Conservation Movement*. Little-Brown, Boston.

Frome, Michael. 1988. "Heal the earth, heal the soul," pp. 247–255 in P. Borrelli (ed.), *Crossroads: Environmental Priorities for the Future*. Island Press, Washington, DC.

Gittinger, J. Price. 1982. *Economic Analysis of Agricultural Projects*, 2nd edition. Johns Hopkins University Press, Baltimore and London, England.

Goodland, R. 1982. *Tribal Peoples and Economic Development*. World Bank, Washington, DC.

Grayson, Melvin J. and Thomas R. Shepard, Jr. 1973. *The Disaster Lobby: Prophets of Ecological Doom and Other Absurdities*. Follet, Chicago.

Gregersen, Hans M. and Arnoldo H. Contreras. 1979. *Economic Analysis of Forestry Projects*. FAO Forestry Paper 17, FAO, Rome.

Gregg, William P., Jr., and Betsy Ann McGean. 1985. "Biosphere reserves: Their history and purpose," *Orion* 4(3):40–51.

Guha, Ramachandra. 1990. *The Unquiet Woods: Ecological Change and Peasant Resistance in the Himalaya*. University of California Press, Berkeley.

Guthrie, Daniel. 1971. "Primitive man's relationship to nature," *Bioscience* 21:721–723.

Hamilton, Lawrence S. 1987. "What are the impacts of Himalayan deforestation on the Ganges-Brahmaputra lowlands and delta?" *Mountain Research and Development* 7(3):256–263.

Hamilton, Lawrence S., and Peter N. King. 1983. *Tropical Forested Watersheds: Hydrological and Soils Response to Major Uses or Conversions*. Westview Press, Boulder, CO.

Harris, Larry D. 1984. *The Fragmented Forest: Island Biogeographical Theory and the Preservation of Biotic Diversity*. University of Chicago Press, Chicago.

Hays, Samuel P. 1987. *Beauty, Health, and Permanence: Environmental Politics in the United States, 1955–1985*. Cambridge University Press, New York.

Heske, Franz. 1938. *German Forestry*. Yale University Press, New Haven.

Holdgate, Martin, Mohammed Kassas, and Gilbert White. 1982. *The World Environment, 1972–1982*. Tycooly Press, Dublin, Ireland.

Hutto, R. L. 1988. "Is tropical deforestation responsible for the reported declines in neotropical migrant populations?" *American Birds* 42:375–379.

Inglehart, Ronald. 1977. *The Silent Revolution: Changing Values and Political Styles Among Western Publics*. Princeton University Press, Princeton.

IUCN (International Union for the Conservation of Nature and Natural Resources). 1980. *World Conservation Strategy*. IUCN, Gland, Switzerland.

Ives, Jack D. and Bruno Messerli. 1989. *The Himalayan Dilemma: Reconciling Development and Conservation*. Routledge, New York.

James, N. D. G. 1981. *A History of English Forestry*. Basil Blackwell, Oxford, England.

Jeffries, Bruce E. 1982. "Sagarmatha National Park: The impact of tourism in the Himalayas," *Ambio* 11(5):274–281.

Jones, P. D., T. M. L. Wigley, and P. B. Wright. 1986. "Global temperature variations between 1861 and 1984," *Nature* 322:430–434.

Kuznets, Simon. 1948. "On the valuation of social income," *Economica* (Feb./May):1–16, 116–131.

Laarman, Jan G. and Patrick B. Durst. 1987. "Nature travel and tropical forests," *Journal of Forestry* 85(5):43–46.

Leopold, Aldo. 1949. *Sand County Almanac*. Oxford University Press, New York.

Leslie, A. J. 1987. "A second look at the economics of natural management systems in tropical mixed forests," *Unasylva* 39(155):46–58.

Lovelock, James E. 1979. *Gaia: A New Look at Life on Earth*. Oxford University Press, New York.

Maddox, John. 1972. *The Doomsday Syndrome*. Macmillan, London, England.

May, Allan. 1978. *Voice in the Wilderness*. Nelson-Hall, Chicago.

McCormick, John. 1989. *Reclaiming Paradise: The Global Environmental Movement*. Indiana University Press, Bloomington and Indianapolis.

McNeely, Jeffrey A., Kenton R. Miller, Walter V. Reid, Russell A. Mittermeier, and Timothy B. Werner. 1990. *Conserving the World's Biological Diversity*. International Union for the Conservation of Nature and Natural Resources (IUCN), Conservation International, World Wildlife Fund-U.S., and the World Bank. Gland, Switzerland, and Washington, DC.

Meadows, Donella H., Dennis L. Meadows, Jorgen Randers, and William W. Behrens III. 1972. *The Limits to Growth*. Universe Books, New York.

Milbrath, Lester W. 1984. *Environmentalists: Vanguard for a New Society*. State University of New York Press, Albany.

Mitchell, Robert C. and Richard T. Carson. 1989. *Using Surveys to Value Public Goods: The Contingent Valuation Method*. Resources for the Future, Washington, DC.

Naess, Arne. 1990. "Sustainable development and deep ecology," pp. 87-96 in J. R. Engel and J. G. Engel (eds.), *Ethics of Environment and Development: Global Challenge, International Response*. University of Arizona Press, Tucson.

NAPAP (National Acid Precipitation Assessment Program, USA). 1990. *Annual Report of the President and Congress, 1989*. Government Printing Office, Washington, DC.

Nash, Roderick. 1973. *Wilderness and the American Mind*. Yale University Press, New Haven.

Oldfield, Sara. 1988. *Buffer Zone Management in Tropical Moist Forests*. IUCN Tropical Forest Paper 5, International Union for the Conservation of Nature and Natural Resources, Gland, Switzerland.

Ophuls, William. 1977. *Ecology and the Politics of Scarcity*. W. H. Freeman, San Francisco.

Park, Chris C. 1987. *Acid Rain: Rhetoric and Reality*. Methuen Company, London, England.

Peskin, Henry M. 1989. *Accounting for Natural Resource Depletion and Degradation in Developing Countries*. World Bank Environment Department Working Paper No. 13, Washington, DC.

Peters, Charles M., Alwyn H. Gentry, and Robert O. Mendelsohn. 1989. "Valuation of an Amazonian rainforest," *Nature* 339(29):655–656.

Poore, D. and J. Sayer. 1988. *The Management of Tropical Moist Forest Lands: Ecological Guidelines*. International Union for the Conservation of Nature and Natural Resourcs (IUCN), Gland, Switzerland.

Poore, Duncan, Peter Burgess, John Palmer, Simon Rietbergen, and Timothy Synott. 1989. *No Timber Without Trees: Sustainability in the Tropical Forest*. Earthscan Publications, London, England.

Postel, Sandra. 1984. *Air Pollution, Acid Rain, and the Future of Forests*. Worldwatch Paper 58, Worldwatch Institute, Washington, DC.

Redclift, Michael. 1987. *Sustainable Development: Exploring the Contradictions*. Methuen, London, England.

Regens, James L. and Robert W. Rycroft. 1988. *The Acid Rain Controversy*. University of Pittsburgh Press, Pittsburgh, PA.

Reid, Walter V. and Kenton R. Miller. 1989. *Keeping Options Alive: The Scientific Basis for Conserving Biodiversity*. World Resources Institute, Washington, DC.

Repetto, Robert, William Magrath, Michael Wells, Christine Beer, and Fabrizio Rossini. 1989. *Wasting Assets: Natural Resources in the National Income Accounts*. World Resources Institute, Washington, DC.

Revkin, Andrew. 1990. *The Burning Season: The Murder of Chico Mendes and the Fight for the Amazon Rain Forest*. Houghton Mifflin, Boston.

Roche, Michael. 1990. *History of New Zealand Forestry*. New Zealand Forestry Corporation and G.P. Publications, Wellington, New Zealand.

Russell, Dick. 1988. "The monkeywrenchers," pp. 27–48 in P. Borrelli (ed.), *Crossroads: Environmental Priorities for the Future*. Island Press, Washington, DC.

Schneider, Stephen H. 1989. "The greenhouse effect: Science and policy," *Science* 243:771–781.

Schutt, P. and E. B. Cowling. 1985. "Waldsterben, a general decline of forests in central Europe: Symptoms, development, and possible causes," *Plant Diseases* 69:548–558.

Schwartzman, S. 1989. "Extractive reserves: The rubber tappers' strategy for sustainable use of the Amazon rainforest," pp. 150–165 in J. O. Browder (ed.), *Fragile Lands of Latin America: Strategies for Sustainable Development*. Westview Press, Boulder, CO.

Sedjo, Roger A. 1989. "Forests to offset the greenhouse effect," *Journal of Forestry* 87(7):12–15.

Sedjo, Roger A. and Allen M. Solomon. 1989. "Climate and forests," pp. 105–119 in N. J. Rosenberg, W. E. Easterling, P. R. Crosson, and J. Darmstadter (eds.), *Greenhouse Warming: Abatement and Adaptation*. Resources for the Future, Washington, DC.

Seeger, A. 1982. "Native Americans and the conservation of flora and fauna in Brazil," pp. 177–190 in E. G. Hallsworth (ed.), *Socio-Economic Effects and Constraints in Tropical Forest Management*. John Wiley and Sons, New York.

Sheffield, R. M., N. D. Cost, W. A. Bechtold, and J. P. McClure. 1985. *Pine Growth Reductions in the Southeast*. USDA Forest Service Resource Bulletin SE-83, Asheville, NC.

Shoumatoff, Alex. 1990. *The World is Burning: Murder in the Rainforest*. Little Brown, Waltham, MA.

Simberloff, Daniel. 1986. "Are we on the verge of a mass extinction in tropical rain forests?" pp. 165–180 in D. K. Elliott (ed.), *Dynamics of Extinction*. John Wiley and Sons, New York.

Simon, Julian L. and Aaron Wildavsky. 1984. "On species loss, the absence of data, and risks to humanity," pp. 171–183 in J. L. Simon and H. Kahn (eds.), *The Resourceful Earth: A Response to Global 2000*. Basil Blackwell, Oxford, England.

Stewart, Timothy P. 1990. *Economic Analysis of Land-Use Options to Encourage Forest Conservation of the Ati Tribal Reservation in Nagpana, Iloilo Province, Philippines*. Unpublished M.S. thesis, North Carolina State University, Raleigh.

Theys, Jacques. 1989. "Environmental accounting in development policy: The French experience," pp. 40–53 in Y. J. Ahmad, S. El Serafy, and Ernst Lutz, *Environmental Accounting for Sustainable Development*. World Bank, Washington, DC.

Thomas, J. W., E. D. Forsman, J. B. Lint, E. C. Meslow, B. R. Noon, and J. Verner. 1990. *A Conservation Strategy for the Northern Spotted Owl*. U.S. Forest Service, U.S. Bureau of Land Management, U.S. Fish and Wildlife Service, and U.S. National Park Service. Washington, DC.

Tomlinson, George H., II (ed.). 1990. *Effects of Acid Deposition on the Forests of Europe and North America*. CRC Press, Boca Raton, FL.

WCED (World Commission on Environment and Development). 1987. *Our Common Future*. Oxford University Press, Oxford.

Weiner, Douglas R. 1988. *Models of Nature: Ecology, Conservation, and Cultural Revolution in Soviet Russia*. University of Indiana Press, Bloomington.

Wells, Michael, Katrina Brandon, and Lee Hannah. 1990. *People and Parks: An Analysis of Projects Linking Protected Area Management with Local Communities*. World Bank, Washington, DC.

Western, David. 1986. "Tourist capacity in East African parks," *Industry and Development* 9(1):14–16.

Wetstone, Gregory S. and Armin Rosencranz. 1983. *Acid Rain in Europe and North America*. Environmental Law Institute, Washington, DC.

White, Lynn. 1967. "The historical roots of our ecological crisis," *Science* 155(3767): 48–56.

Wilson, Mystie A. and Jan G. Laarman. 1988. "Nature tourism and enterprise development in Ecuador," *World Leisure and Recreation* 19(1):22–27.

Woodman, James. 1987. "Pollution-induced injury in North American forests: Facts and suspicions," *Tree Physiology* 3:1–15.

Woolsey, Theodore S., Jr. 1920. *Studies in French Forestry*. John Wiley and Sons, New York.

World Wildlife Fund. 1989. *World Wildlife Fund 1989 Annual Report*. Washington, DC.

Worster, Donald. 1977. *Nature's Economy: The Roots of Ecology*. Sierra Club Books, San Francisco.

INTERNATIONAL COOPERATION

The preceding chapters indicate that the one world of forests is increasingly small and interconnected. To recognize these connections, and to act upon them through international cooperation, is to work towards a comprehensive sense of reality and priority in forestry.

International cooperation takes a number of forms. Development assistance ("foreign aid") is intended to strengthen the economies of recipient countries. This assistance flows through a donor country's own programs (bilateral assistance), and through its participation in international organizations (multilateral assistance). Additionally, countries collaborate internationally in forest science and technology for reasons of perceived mutual gain. Thirdly, governments enter into international conventions and agreements, including covenants affecting the protection and management of forests.

In forestry, international cooperation faces relatively few political impediments. Differences in political systems are of only minor importance for forest protection and management, and forestry has few government or commercial secrets. Moreover, the prominence of regional and global environmental issues heightens a sense of shared international responsibility in forestry. Additionally, the felt need to advance forest protection and management in the developing countries unites individuals and organizations from around the world in a common cause.

DEVELOPMENT ASSISTANCE

Development assistance took hold at the end of the Second World War when the USA's Marshall Plan helped revive the economies of western Europe. This unquestionable success persuaded Western governments that development assistance should be applied to spur economic growth in the poor countries of Africa, Asia, and Latin America. Optimism about the possibilities of development assistance reached its peak in the 1960s, a period of unusually rapid economic growth in the developing world. Subsequent views on development assistance have been decidedly more cautious.

The institutional network for development assistance emerged in the 1940s. The World Bank (originally the International Bank for Reconstruction and Development) was conceived in 1944 to rebuild war-torn Europe. As attention subsequently turned to what are today's developing countries, the World Bank was joined by the Inter-American Development Bank, the African Development Bank, the Asian Development Bank, and other regional development banks. The United Nations system began in 1945, and with it were created the Food and Agriculture Organization and other specialized international organizations (FAO 1985). This structure of development banks and United Nations agencies remains the primary conduit for multilateral development assistance.

Additionally, a number of international NGOs provide assistance to forestry. Examples are CARE International, the Pan American Development Foundation, and the World Wildlife Fund. Forestry funding by these NGOs totals several million dollars each year. Other NGOs, such as IUCN and IIED, receive most of their forestry funding from multilateral and bilateral donors.

Tropical deforestation, acid rain, and global climate change place forests at the center of various initiatives for development assistance in the 1990s. Yet the development banks, United Nations agencies, and bilateral programs are under attack for many and often contradictory reasons. They are criticized for trying to do too much, and for apparently doing too little (WCED 1987, p. 313). This means that forestry commands a higher status in development assistance than ever before, but at a time coinciding with "aid fatigue" in key donor countries (Krueger et al. 1989).

Composition and Trends in Forestry

Development assistance to forestry has been growing rapidly. By the end of the 1980s, this assistance exceeded US$1 billion annually. Well over half of this is bilateral, with the development banks and the United Nations agencies each contributing smaller proportions (Table 8-1). Data compiled by FAO indicate that Africa and Asia receive over three-fourths of total development assistance to forestry. Latin America, the Caribbean Basin, and the Middle East are smaller recipients.

Funding for forestry is likely to increase considerably into the 1990s. The World Bank's forestry loans and grants are about US$400 million for 1992, compared with US$193 million in 1988. Australia, Canada, Denmark, Italy, Japan, the Netherlands, and the UK each foresee their bilateral forestry assistance increasing by at least 10 percent annually. An analysis by FAO suggests that overall increases in development assistance to forestry could equal 7.5 percent per year during the first half of the 1990s (FAO 1989).

TABLE 8-1
Estimated bilateral and multilateral development assistance to forestry, 1988

Bilateral assistance		Multilateral assistance	
	Million US$		Million US$
Germany	147	World Food Program	131
USA	83	World Bank	130
Canada	75	Asian Development Bank	75
Sweden	58	UNDP	25
France	43	UNSO	12
EEC	35	FAO	12
Netherlands	32	Inter-American Development Bank	7
Denmark	29	UNIDO	3
Japan	26	ILO	2
UK	23	UNESCO	2
Switzerland	23	UNEP	2
Finland	22	African Development Bank	1
Norway	13		
Italy	11		
Australia	5		
New Zealand	4		
Belgium	1		
Spain	1		
Ireland	< 1		
Austria	< 1		
Portugal	< 1		

Source: FAO (1989, pp. 10–12).

While growth in forestry assistance is impressive, it comes on a modest base. Despite the emergence of tropical deforestation on the global agenda, forestry captures only a small fraction (about 1–2 percent) of the world's development assistance.

Examples of Multilateral Programs

Several multilateral organizations fund programs to strengthen forestry in the developing countries. This institutional framework is still evolving. Programs are proposed and modified in response to constantly changing perceptions of need, priority, and political advantage.

Food and Agriculture Organization   FAO is an autonomous organization within the United Nations group of specialized agencies. Its broad objectives are to help countries improve their agriculture, fisheries, and forestry. Headquarters are in Rome, and liaison and regional offices are located in North America, Latin America, Africa, and Asia. Membership includes over 150 countries. Within the United Nations system, FAO is the dominant and most traditional agency for development assistance to forestry. Although FAO's Forestry Department is the smallest of the agency's functional departments, FAO nevertheless has the largest forestry staff of any international organization.

Activities at FAO's Rome headquarters are mainly the collection, analysis, and diffusion of information on all aspects of forestry, emphasizing the developing countries. Information is disseminated through technical publications and through training courses, study tours, seminars, and technical meetings. Additionally, headquarters staff provides administrative and technical support to FAO's field program.

This field program is active in approximately 90 developing countries. FAO's forestry field projects are coordinated by some 250 professional staff, principally in Africa and Asia. These forestry projects typically function as partnerships among host governments, FAO, and external funding agencies such as UNDP and bilateral aid agencies. Projects emphasize land use planning and forest management; forestry for rural development; fuelwood and energy; desertification control; watershed management; wildlife management; forest industries development; and forestry education, research, and training (Pardo 1990).

The headquarters building of the Food and Agriculture Organization is situated near the heart of ancient Rome. The FAO has the largest forestry staff of any international organization. *(Photo courtesy of FAO.)*

FAO's forestry assistance has evolved through different contextual phases, reflecting changing priorities and concepts in forestry at a worldwide level (FAO 1985; Pardo 1990):

• *Institution building*—The period after the Second World War (1945-1950s) required that FAO organize itself and define its institutional role in relation to its member countries. Activities in forestry concentrated on building or strengthening forest services, forestry schools, forest laws, national forest policies, and global forest statistics.

• *Expansion*—The 1960s and early 1970s witnessed FAO's extension into newly independent countries following their decolonization, the expansion of FAO's forestry field projects into these countries, and emphasis on forest industries as a vehicle for economic development.

• *New directions*—The period from the late 1970s to the present has broadened FAO's work in forestry. Efforts have shifted from the former centrality of forest industries to new programs and projects linking forestry with agriculture, watershed management, wildlife management, energy supply, and other sectors. Increased support for community forestry, as distinct from national forestry, is another of the leading conceptual revisions in FAO's forestry portfolio.

World Bank and Regional Development Banks   The World Bank rapidly increased its lending to forestry following release of a forestry policy paper in the late 1970s (World Bank 1978). The World Bank has been joined by the regional development banks, particularly the Asian Development Bank and Inter-American Development Bank, in extending loans and grants for forestry assistance.

Similar to the changing priorities at FAO, forestry assistance in the development banks has undergone considerable transformation. This is nowhere clearer than in the World Bank, where forestry funding increased from an average of US$20 million a year in the 1970s to an average of US$130 million a year in the 1980s. In the 1970s, the bulk of World Bank funding was for sawmills, pulp mills, and industrial forest plantations. In the 1980s, the bulk of funding shifted to farm and community forestry, watershed rehabilitation, and forestry components of agricultural projects (World Bank 1986). This was a deliberate step to strengthen linkages between forestry and agriculture, to tackle policies contributing to deforestation, and to make forestry more central in poverty alleviation (Spears 1987).

This redefinition of forestry has helped place the sector in closer alignment with current development priorities. However, forestry remains a small component in total bank lending. The long time horizons in forestry, and the unquantifiable and external character of many of forestry's benefits, contribute to the challenge of making forestry projects financially attractive. Thus the future of forestry lending in the development banks depends on improved valuation of benefits, strategies to hasten project returns, and strategies to lengthen grace periods (i.e., the time before loan repayment commences). In many cases, bank lending for forestry is not viable without accompanying reforms of prices, subsidies, taxes, and market competition (McGaughey 1986).

United Nations Environment Program   The UNEP was established in 1972 by the United Nations Conference on the Human Environment. It works with national governments, agencies of the United Nations, and NGOs to attempt to monitor the state of the global environment. This is done with a staff of 200 scientists, administrators, and information specialists. Headquarters are in Nairobi, and UNEP also maintains several regional offices elsewhere. UNEP's activities are decided by a governing council of representatives elected from among UNEP's member countries.

UNEP collaborated with FAO to produce the global assessments of forest resources for 1980 and 1990 (Chapter 2). It helped introduce the International Tropical Timber Agreement (Chapter 5), and was a partner with IUCN and WWF in the World Conservation Strategy (Chapter 7). UNEP furnishes the secretariat for the Convention on International Trade in Endangered Species of Wild Fauna and Flora (CITES), and for the Convention on the Conservation of Migratory Species of Wild Animals.

United Nations Development Program   Based in New York, the UNDP was established in 1965. It has a significant role in the United Nations system as a main provider of project funding. In the early 1990s, UNDP's portfolio included over 5,300 projects in more than 150 developing countries, representing a total investment of US$7.5 billion. UNDP is a principal funder of FAO's field projects, and also carries out its own UNDP projects affecting forests and environmental management.

World Food Program   When measured in dollar amounts, the WFP is one of the largest multilateral contributors of development assistance to forestry. WFP headquarters are in Rome, and field projects are spread across most of the developing countries. The bulk of WFP's aid goes to the very poorest countries, and Africa receives most of it.

Since it began in 1963, the WFP has distributed grains and other food products from donor countries to feed the hungry during emergencies. The original relief orientation of food assistance has been joined by a more controversial program in which food is exchanged for work on long-term development projects. The controversy is explained by numerous inefficiencies in using food as a form of payment, and by a basic inconsistency between food aid and attainment of self-reliance in agriculture (Singer et al. 1987).

Many food-for-work projects include tree nurseries, tree planting on farms and public lands, hillside terraces, watershed rehabilitation, and other activities broadly defined as forestry and soil and water management. Despite the substantial magnitude of food aid in forestry assistance, evaluations of successes and failures in food-aided forestry are surprisingly few and incomplete (Kramer 1987).

Tropical Forestry Action Plan

The TFAP is perhaps the nearest approximation to a global strategy for protecting and managing the world's tropical forests. The TFAP was launched in 1985 by

The World Food Program is one of the largest contributors of development assistance to forestry. Workers receive food rations in exchange for their labor in tree planting, terracing, and other activities broadly defined as forestry and soil and water management. *(Photo courtesy of FAO)*

the FAO, World Bank, UNDP, and the World Resources Institute to provide a "common framework for action" in tropical forestry. The TFAP framework defined the following objectives: (1) to increase awareness of the need to conserve and manage tropical forests, (2) to increase the amount of donor assistance to tropical forestry, and (3) to improve the coordination of this assistance.

By 1990, 70 developing countries had started or completed TFAP activities (Figure 8-1). In each country, TFAP begins with a sectoral review to identify and justify funding priorities for forestry in its multiple connections with land use, forest industries, fuelwood and energy, conservation of forest ecosystems, and institution building (e.g, policy reform, research, training, and extension).

However, several NGOs have complained that TFAP recommendations give too little attention to forest preservation, indigenous groups living in forests, and environmental and social issues in general. These critics contend that TFAP makes no serious attempt to reform the content and direction of forestry, harmonize forestry within the national economy, or analyze trade-offs and balance conflicting demands on forest lands (Winterbottom 1990).

In many respects, the TFAP represents most of the hopes and frustrations of development assistance to forestry. The TFAP has very successfully brought together the major world players with the political influence and financial resources to make a difference in tropical forestry. Forestry has achieved a certain preeminence under

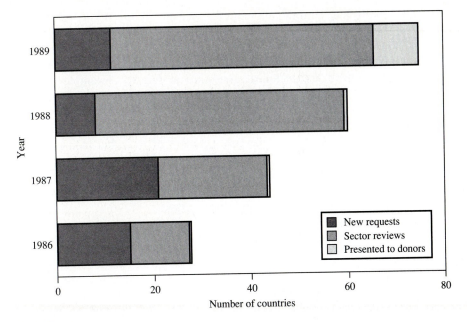

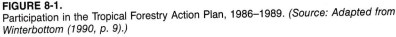

FIGURE 8-1.
Participation in the Tropical Forestry Action Plan, 1986–1989. *(Source: Adapted from Winterbottom (1990, p. 9).)*

TFAP. International funding for forestry assistance has increased remarkably, as has the frequency and quality of the discussions among donor agencies (Ullsten et al. 1990). At the same time, some of the TFAP players are unhappy with others, even if the collaboration process has been underway for only a few years. The TFAP suggests that, while world concern to protect and manage tropical forests has never been greater, international cooperation to do this is still in an early stage of adjustment and groping for solutions.

Forestry Assistance in Context

The list of organizations directly or indirectly providing development assistance to forestry is long and not easily summarized. As noted, FAO and WFP are among the major players, but UNEP and UNDP illustrate organizations having important support functions. The forestry portfolios of the World Bank, Asian Development Bank, and Inter-American Development Bank have been growing rapidly. To these organizations can be added the International Labor Organization (ILO) for its decades of work on employment and labor conditions in forestry and the forest industries, and the United Nations Industrial Development Organization (UNIDO) for its work on forest industries.

In the private voluntary sector are hundreds of organizations with some bearing on land management, tree planting, and forest conservation. As noted, a few of the better-known entities at the international level include CARE, WWF, IUCN, and IIED. Yet there are many more. Several countries sponsor "Peace Corps" or equivalent organizations of volunteers to provide development assistance on the ground. Finally, the bilateral programs of individual donor governments direct a substantial volume of financial and technical assistance to forestry. Examples are the USA's Agency for International Development (AID), Canada's CIDA, Germany's GTZ, France's CCCE, Britain's ODA, Japan's JICA, Sweden's SIDA, Finland's FINNIDA, Denmark's DANIDA, and several others.

Indeed, development assistance has many aspects of a sizable industry when considering the magnitude of its capital transfers, consulting services, and administrative machinery. Development assistance to forestry cannot be examined apart from this broader context. This is a context of frequent and sharp criticism of the development establishment and its conduct, as follows:

• *Criticisms from the political right*—The political right argues that development assistance expands government bureaucracies and supports government interventions at the expense of private economic activity. Development assistance masks and often worsens economic inefficiencies, and distorts local production incentives. According to this perspective, countries which do not receive external aid turn out to be more resourceful and prosperous than countries which welcome massive doses of outside assistance (Bauer 1972).

• *Criticisms from the political left*—The political left often sees development assistance as an instrument of conspiracy to reward the economic and political elites of the developing countries, while the poor masses continue to suffer squalor and neglect. The benefits of development assistance are skimmed off at the top, and nothing remains for the bottom. The political left maintains that acceptance of outside aid puts governments deeper in debt, increases their dependency on continued inflows of foreign capital, and seriously compromises their political autonomy (Hayter 1971).

• *Politics masquerading as economics*—While development assistance supposedly is about economic growth and humanitarian issues, in practice the giving of development assistance is heavily dominated by politics. In important cases, the patterns of bilateral development assistance show that donor governments are primarily attempting to win and retain political alliances. Thus Britain sends most of its development assistance to its former colonies, e.g., India, Pakistan, Bangladesh, and Kenya. Other examples are the USA's disproportionate aid to Israel and Egypt, and the USSR's many years of massive aid to Cuba.

• *The development assistance which stays at home*—The question of who benefits from development assistance is controversial, and no different in forestry than in any other sector. "Tied aid" refers to the frequent condition that the recipient country is expected to purchase goods and services from the donor country. This means that the primary beneficiaries of aid are companies in the donor countries which export study teams, consulting services, equipment, and the like. Many consulting firms charge high overheads, most of which pays staffs in the home countries. Foreign advisors sent to developing countries usually cost the equivalent of US$250 thousand per year for salary, airfares, and housing and education allowances. Only a part of this is captured by the recipient country.

• *Lack of coordination*—Development banks and assistance agencies sometimes duplicate efforts, or even work at cross-purposes. There is "donor competition" to have the best project, to recruit the best local staff, and to have the most influence with a forestry agency. One external team may advocate a particular policy direction for forestry which is inconsistent with the advice and project of another donor. An objective of TFAP is to improve donor coordination, but a small sector like forestry is inherently vulnerable to too many advisors.

• *Attacks by environmentalists*—Beginning in the 1980s, the World Bank, Inter-American Development Bank, and other development agencies have been assailed for financing projects which environmentalists assert are environmentally unsound. The charges include destructive impacts on forests because of road building, hydroelectric dams, cattle ranching, agricultural resettlement, and wood-processing industries. In response to these criticisms, the development banks are working

Foreign advisors to developing countries usually cost the equivalent of US$250 thousand per year for salary, airfares, and housing and education allowances. *(Photo courtesy of FAO.)*

diligently to show that they are indeed aware of the environmental consequences of their activities, and are acting upon them. However, many of the recent environmental demands placed on development assistance are unrealistic in relation to current institutional capabilities. This produces frustrations and contradictions within the development agencies (Le Prestre 1989).

• *Impatience*—In a long-term undertaking like forestry, most real progress takes decades to materialize and become visible. Yet accountability in the development banks and agencies is measured in annual cycles of committing new funds and getting new projects approved. Short time frames often mean that a forestry project is evaluated after 5–10 years, when in fact decades are needed to correct early mistakes and bring the project to fruition. Moreover, short time frames make the development banks and agencies susceptible to "fads and fancies." Contributing to this are constantly shifting perspectives and ideologies about how to increase the effectiveness of development assistance, and how to define assistance priorities. The result is a development landscape littered with policies and projects scrapped prematurely because of impatience and discontinuities.

Despite steady attacks on development assistance, it continues to be requested and provided. Many in the development establishment see the problems of aid as inadequate management rather than failed policy. Improved management requires internal reforms and revised institutional arrangements, but does not imply abandonment of the assistance effort.

Skeptical taxpayers in the donor countries are not as convinced. Surveys of public opinion in countries like the USA and UK show that voters have critical and often erroneous views about the size, purpose, and nature of aid programs. Most believe that aid programs are larger than they are, that aid is provided mainly in the form of free gifts, and that most aid is embezzled by corrupt politicians (Wall 1973; Rielly 1983). When confronted by these opinions, governments and multilateral organizations typically issue new studies showing the benefits of aid (e.g., Cassen 1986; Riddell 1987) in order to blunt the more extreme critics of assistance policy. While forestry may be one of the new rising stars in the development banks and agencies, it cannot rise higher than permitted by the unsettled debates on the whole of development assistance.

COLLABORATION IN SCIENCE AND TECHNOLOGY

International collaboration in forest science and technology assumes numerous organizational forms, both formal and informal. Some arrangements are strictly bilateral, while others are regional or global. The usual purposes of collaboration are to take advantage of pioneer research and technology in other countries, to enhance professional expertise through international contacts, to exchange genetic material internationally, to save research costs by combining budgets and staff from multiple countries, and to expedite technology transfer from one country to others. Seldom stated but usually implicit is the desire to build international friendships and good will.

Twinning refers to agreements between two institutions to share or exchange personnel, equipment, and funding—often with the goal of strengthening the weaker of these institutions. For example, several institutions in the industrialized countries have been sending scientists and professors to strengthen forestry research and education in China. Networking extends the twinning concept to bring together several institutions which pool expertise and resources for work on problems of shared interest. Thus several networks test and exchange tree seed from worldwide sources in order to identify the best species and strains of plant material for each network member.

Selected Organizations and Networks

Two organizations that provide important support to forestry research at the global level are the International Union of Forestry Research Organizations (IUFRO) and the Man and the Biosphere Program (MAB). The special role of bodies like IUFRO and MAB is to initiate and coordinate research on a multidisciplinary, global basis. Both IUFRO and MAB are briefly profiled. This is followed by short descriptions of the Multipurpose Tree Species (MPTS) Research Network and the Central America and Mexico Coniferous Resources Cooperative (CAMCORE). MPTS and CAMCORE illustrate international research cooperation organized around species and regions.

International Union of Forestry Research Organizations   Begun in 1892 among seven European countries, IUFRO is one of the world's oldest international scientific organizations. One century later, IUFRO represents 106 countries, 700 affiliated institutions, and 15,000 individual forest researchers. A small secretariat is located in Vienna, Austria.

The goal of IUFRO is to encourage and facilitate cross-country research on forestry themes of both topical and perennial interest. Participating researchers are organized into broad divisions, each of which contains numerous working groups. The more active working groups convene meetings, symposia, and field visits. Through the activities of its working groups, IUFRO publishes numerous proceedings each year. At roughly 5-year intervals, IUFRO holds world congresses to unite all of its divisions and working groups at a single site.

In recent years, IUFRO has aimed to build forestry research capacity in the developing countries. Expenditures for forestry research are far less in developing than in industrialized regions (Figure 8-2), even though research needs are in many ways subjectively greater in the former. Stronger research capacity in the developing countries requires greater scientific and technical training of researchers, stability of research funding from year to year, and improved library and information services (Bengston and Gregersen 1988). Also needed are institutional changes to focus research more sharply on current social and economic problems, fortify technology transfer through forestry extension, and make research relevant within a framework of reformed forest policies (Buckman 1987).

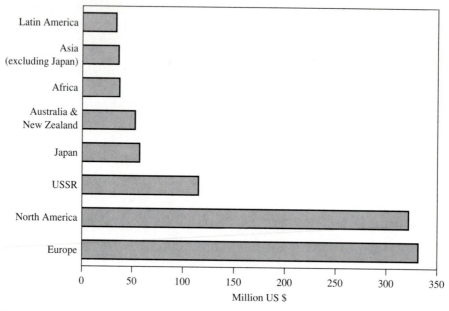

FIGURE 8-2.
Expenditures for forestry research by major world regions, 1981. *(Source: Mergen et al. (1988, pp. 158-159).)*

Man and the Biosphere Program The MAB is coordinated through the United Nations Educational, Scientific, and Cultural Organization (UNESCO), with its main office in Paris. Beginning in the 1970s, MAB was set up to be an intergovernmental and interdisciplinary research program focusing on the world's different ecological systems. MAB's overall aim is international scientific cooperation organized around a number of key research themes linking man and the environment.

Membership in MAB has grown to include over 110 countries. Each country has a national committee which defines and organizes research, training, and information dissemination under MAB's aegis. MAB pioneered the concept of biosphere reserves (Chapter 7), of which there are more than 260 worldwide. MAB's research includes projects on biological diversity, soil conservation in arid and semiarid regions, restoration of forested ecosystems, monitoring of global climate change, and numerous other subjects within an ecosystems framework.

Multipurpose Tree Species Research Network The MPTS is designed to coordinate research, communication, and training on the production and use of multipurpose trees for farm forestry in Asia. Begun in the mid-1980s, the MPTS network comprises forestry and agroforestry researchers in about a dozen developing countries. External funding of US$2–3 million annually is provided mainly through bilateral assistance from the USA. Member countries in the MPTS network provide co-financing and logistical support for staff and facilities.

Figure 8-3 shows the organizational structure of MPTS. Most network activities are coordinated through a central secretariat at the Faculty of Forestry in Bangkok, Thailand. This secretariat interacts with national MPTS networks in member countries. The ideal national network brings together universities, forest research institutes, government agencies, and nongovernmental and private organizations. Through extension and outreach programs, these national networks are expected to interact with small farmers as the MPTS clients.

Activities within the MPTS network include scientific and organizational meetings, cooperative research projects, training sessions, travel grants, publications, and small research grants. A network newsletter is distributed internationally. Additionally, the MPTS network has developed computer software to standardize methods for recording and analyzing MPTS data (MacDicken et al. 1990).

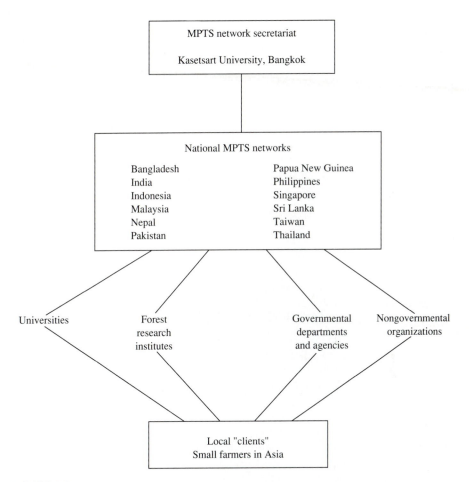

FIGURE 8-3.
Organizational structure of the Multipurpose Tree Species Research Network, 1990. *(Source: Adapted from Fui (1990, p. 3).)*

Central America and Mexico Coniferous Resources Cooperative CAM-
CORE is an international cooperative to conserve the genetic base of threatened
forest trees in Central America and Mexico (Dvorak and Laarman 1986). Begun
in 1980, CAMCORE was founded because of concern for the genetic degradation
of several Central American and Mexican pine species. Some of these pines from
Middle America are in widespread use over the tropics and subtropics for industrial plantations and farm and community forestry. Other species presently have
no industrial use, but may someday prove important as their physical properties,
growth rates, and adaptability are better understood. Degradation of the resource
is explained by increasing pressures on forests in many parts of the region as a
result of shifting agriculture, fuelwood cutting, and illegal logging.

The CAMCORE program began by collecting the seed of endangered species
and provenances of conifers. It later diversified to include several Central Ameri-

CAMCORE is an international
cooperative to conserve the genetic
base of threatened forest trees in
Central America and Mexico. Here a
CAMCORE tree climber collects seed
from *Pinus chiapensis* in southern
Mexico. *(Photo courtesy of CAMCORE.)*

can and Mexican hardwoods. This seed has been collected from several thousand mother trees. With respect to worldwide scientific attention on maintaining biological diversity, CAMCORE preserves races of a number of species which almost certainly would be lost in future years if not for deliberate intervention.

CAMCORE is distinguished from most other international networks in that much of its membership comprises private companies (Figure 8-4). Each company contributes annual dues, and is expected to establish gene conservation banks and genetic tests recommended by CAMCORE's international advisory board. On an annual basis, seed collected from Central America and Mexico is sent for processing to North Carolina State University in the USA. From there, the seed is sorted and distributed to CAMCORE members. A standardized research protocol governs international coordination of gene banks and genetic tests. Reports on these tests are shared among members, and genetic material is exchanged in order to provide the best matches for local growing conditions. In this way, CAMCORE strives to simultaneously manage for *ex situ* genetic conservation and improved plantation productivity.

FIGURE 8-4
Membership in the CAMCORE cooperative, 1990. *(Source: CAMCORE Cooperative.)*

Private companies

- Indústrias Klabin de Papel e Celulose S.A. (Brazil, active)*
- Manville Productos Florestais (Brazil, active)*
- Pisa Florestal (Brazil, active)*
- Companhia Florestal Monte Dourado (Brazil, contributing)†
- Smurfit Cartón de Colombia (Colombia, active)*
- Pizano/Monterrey Forestal (Colombia, active)*
- Smurfit Cartón de Venezuela (Venezuela, active)*
- CVG-PROFORCA (Venezuela, active)*
- Deforsa S.A. (Venezuela, active)
- Mondi Paper Company Ltd. (South Africa, active)*
- Sappi Forests (Pty) Ltd. (South Africa, active)*
- Weyerhaeuser Co. Foundation (USA, contributing)†

Governmental or other publicly funded organizations

- Centro Agronómico Tropical de Investigación y Enseñanza (Central America, active)*
- Empresa Brasileira de Pesquisa Agropecuária (Brazil, active)*
- South African Forestry Research Institute (South Africa, active)*
- Universidad Austral de Chile (Chile, active)*
- Centro de Genética Forestal (Mexico, honorary)‡
- Instituto Nacional de Investigaciones Forestal y Agropecuarias (Mexico, honorary)‡
- Dirección General de Bosques y Vida Silvestre (Guatemala, honorary)‡
- Escuela Nacional de Ciencias Forestales; Corporación Hondureña de Desarrollo Forestal (Honduras, honorary)‡
- Instituto Nicaragüense de Recursos Naturales y del Ambiente (Nicaragua, honorary)‡

* Active members contribute annual dues for membership.
†Contributing members are patrons of the program, but do not receive seed.
‡Honorary members are governmental institutions in countries where seed collections are made.

Others   IUFRO, MAB, MPTS, and CAMCORE illustrate cooperative structures at global and regional levels. Other examples include

• *Joint FAO/ECE/ILO Committee on Forest Technology, Management, and Training*—The Joint Committee is a forum on forest working techniques, forest planning and management, and training of forest workers. Participants represent research institutes, training institutes, universities, and forest enterprises in 34 countries of Europe and North America.

• *Nitrogen-Fixing Tree Association*—Based in Hawaii, the NFTA produces and exchanges publications and newsletters for interested members, mainly in the Asia-Pacific region.

• *Organization for Tropical Studies*—The OTS is a consortium of approximately 50 universities and natural history organizations in the USA which collaborate with similar institutions in Costa Rica. The purpose is to advance tropical science, especially research and training in tropical biology and ecology.

• *International networks for germplasm conservation and tree breeding*—To the examples of MPTS and CAMCORE can be added other networks organized around species and regions. Among them are international projects coordinated by the Oxford Forestry Institute in tropical pines and hardwoods; by the Commonwealth Scientific and Industrial Research Organization in *Acacia*, *Casuarina*, and *Eucalyptus*; by the Centre Technique Forestier Tropical in African hardwoods and Pacific eucalypts; by CATIE in farm and fuelwood trees in Central America; by the Danish Tree Seed Center in tropical pines, teak, and *Gmelina*; by the Canadian International Development Research Center in bamboo and rattan; and by the International Poplar Commission in the genus *Populus*.

Within FAO are six regional forestry commissions for Europe, North America, Latin America, Asia-Pacific, the Middle East, and Africa. These commissions identify and debate issues of regional importance, including issues in forestry science and technology. A similar role is played by Silva Mediterranea, an FAO committee on Mediterranean forestry. Under the Nordic Council and other institutional arrangements, Finland and the Scandinavian countries convene periodic activities in forestry research and related matters of regional interest.

Principles for Successful Collaboration

International cooperation in forestry science and technology demands extensive communication among interested organizations and individuals. Efforts to build and maintain viable networks can be time-consuming and sometimes expensive in outlays for travel and meetings. Disagreements commonly arise over leadership, priorities, and budgets. Successful collaboration depends on the following conditions (Plucknett and Smith 1984; Burley 1987; Gregersen et al. 1989):

• *Clear and shared interests*—International networks work best when they focus on well-defined issues of genuine mutual interest across two or more countries.

• *Able leadership*—Successful networks are managed by individuals commanding respect and confidence among their professional colleagues at an international level. Leaders must be able to negotiate conflicting interests, and find satisfactory compromises where differences exist.

• *Capable and active participants*—Scientific and technical expertise is a determining factor when networks depend on sharing or exchanging contributions among collaborators. Network effectiveness is limited by the weakest and least active of its members.

• *Assured financial support*—Budgets have to be adequate and predictable not only for the birth of a network, but also for its long-term functioning and growth.

• *Good communications*—Network participants must actively communicate with each other through meetings, technical publications, newsletters, and other means. This builds the identity of the network, enhances a sense of commitment to work within it, and fulfills the central purpose of information exchange.

• *Client orientation*—Many international networks in forestry have forest landowners, small farmers, forest industries, forest workers, or other clients as beneficiaries. Collaboration in forestry science and technology must anticipate how results will be transferred to these clients. Collaboration which does not begin with a client bias will in the long run struggle to make itself relevant.

These principles are easily understood, and yet much remains to be learned about effective international collaboration in forestry. Forestry networks like IUFRO have a century of experience, but others are new or still emerging. International networks may be futile to establish without first elevating scientific and professional capacity at national levels. To be remembered is that dozens of developing countries have only a few professionals working in forestry and natural resources. Even fewer of these individuals have the facilities and advanced education to work in forestry science and technology at an international level.

This implies that the creation and expansion of forestry networks, particularly in the developing countries, must proceed cautiously. Also, internal coordination of research and technology within countries is an important prerequisite for participation in international networks. All of this is broadly defined as "institution building" (Buckman 1987). Finally, forestry may learn from agriculture that productive international collaboration rests on careful ranking of topics and priorities, and that success is determined by the presence of clearly defined and highly visible goals which orient everyone in a common direction (MacDicken et al. 1990).

INTERNATIONAL AGREEMENTS AND CONVENTIONS

Various proposals to cooperatively protect and manage forests are reflected in international declarations, resolutions, protocols, pacts, conventions, and treaties. The totality of these agreements constitutes what might be called "international policy" affecting forestry. These agreements may partially limit national sovereignty in order to achieve some perceived collective good at regional or global levels. Few international agreements exist for forests alone, but forests are implicit in numerous conventions aimed at regional or global environmental management.

Various proposals to cooperatively protect and manage forests are reflected in international declarations, resolutions, protocols, pacts, conventions, and treaties. *(Photo courtesy of Forest History Society.)*

Regional Agreements

The European Community (EC) is the world's leading experiment in coordinating economic and social policies across sovereign countries, including policies on agriculture and forestry. Within the European Community, forestry authorities of the twelve member countries meet several times a year. Likewise, the EC's forestry research directors meet frequently. The EC's policy body has asked for coordinated regional action on (1) forestry in the economically poorest subregions of the Community; (2) afforestation of lands no longer needed for agriculture; (3) research in forestry and wood technology; (4) legislation to ensure quality standards in forest planting stock, and (5) economic assistance to forestry in developing countries. Also important are supranational agreements on wildlife, such as the Convention on the Conservation of European Wildlife and Natural Habitats.

Significantly, the EC has decided not to impose a common forestry policy. For forestry, the EC's member governments have opted for voluntary cooperation rather than legally binding constraints. This responds to the real difficulty of defining a common policy suitable for the variety of forestry situations among the EC's members. Secondly, it reflects the absence of a strong rationale for adherence to a single framework (Hummel and Hilmi 1989).

Within North America, the USA has agreements with Canada and Mexico for forestry cooperation. Goals are international sharing of forest inventories and other data bases; joint action in emergency situations such as fire suppression and pest control, particularly near international borders; and cross-country consultation on policy, planning, and administrative matters affecting forestry.

A number of regional agreements with forestry implications relate to international rivers and lakes. Thus Canada and the USA have an International Joint Council (IJC) to oversee provisions of their Boundary Waters Treaty. The work of the IJC has grown enormously to encompass issues regarding management of all lands surrounding the Great Lakes, as well as lands in other watersheds straddling the Canada-USA border. Other agreements on international watersheds include those for the Rhine and Danube rivers in Europe, the Indus and Mekong rivers in Asia, and the Niger River and Lake Chad in Africa. Several of these arrangements operate on the politics of "antagonistic cooperation," or cooperation because of social and economic necessity among governments which in most respects are politically unfriendly with each other (Caldwell 1984).

On the other hand, international cooperation can be a focal point to attempt to improve political relationships. Thus the governments of Costa Rica and Panama are jointly entrusted with the protection and management of La Amistad ("friendship") Biosphere Reserve. On its northern border, Costa Rica shares forests of the San Juan River Basin with Nicaragua. Genuine international management of these forests is not now a reality. Yet Costa Ricans refer to "peace parks" and "peace forests" to verbalize hopes of what might someday be possible as these separate countries pursue shared objectives.

Global Conventions

The world is too divided economically, socially, and politically to act as a global society. However, a spirit of global community is increasingly apparent in many issues of widespread concern, especially environmental issues of world proportions (Chapter 7).

Much of the desire for world community centers on problems of the global commons—the oceans, atmosphere, and outer space—owned by the world collectively. Forests have not been a part of this scheme until recently. The increasing awareness of connections between forests and climate change, and between forests and species habitats, is changing this.

Quite conceivably, the next several years will generate new global arrangements with implications for forests. Through the decades, national governments have agreed to numerous global conventions having the character of international law. In this category are treaties on international trade in endangered species, international migration of wildlife, and wetlands of international importance. Dozens of other treaties include those on oil pollution in oceans, regulation of whaling, protection of ocean fisheries, protection of Antarctic seals, exploration of minerals on the ocean floor, and exploration and use of outer space. In 1987, 56 countries agreed to limit and later reduce their consumption of the most common types of chlorofluorocarbons in response to reports that the planet's ozone layer is thinning. In preparation are proposals for global conventions to protect the world's biological diversity, and to mitigate global warming.

Of course, intent leads action by a wide margin. Such conventions are little more than symbolic declarations unless accompanied by adequate research, monitoring, systems of rewards and sanctions, and public education. Most of these programmatic efforts have been severely underfunded (Caldwell 1984).

Hence various proposals identify new or revitalized financing strategies. For example, some proposals recommend taxing fossil fuels and other sources of emissions which contribute to atmospheric warming. Most of this revenue would be raised in the industrialized countries. The revenues could finance a global trust fund with objectives to slow the accumulation of greenhouse gases, and to mitigate expected environmental disruptions. Financing from the trust fund could be directed to reforestation and afforestation, stabilization of shifting agriculture, and other measures which help curb or offset tropical deforestation (WRI 1989).

Also on the horizon of possibilities are concessions for conservation of biological diversity. The concept is that environmental NGOs or other entities could pay rent to national governments for contractual rights to manage protected wildlands, such as tropical forests of global importance. A variation of the conservation concession is to transfer property rights for protected wildlands to environmental NGOs or agencies of the United Nations, with appropriate payments being made to host governments (McNeely 1989).

Yet another arrangement takes the form of an "International Environmental Facility" to coordinate external assistance for environmental management in the developing countries. Undoubtedly, forests would receive considerable attention in such an arrangement. The facility could seek financing in the form of grants, loans, endowments, and equity. Potential partners in the facility would be the multilateral development banks, bilateral development agencies, relevant United Nations agencies, environmental NGOs, and governments of the developing countries. A single facility could be established with global responsibility, or separate facilities could represent different regions of the developing world (WRI 1989).

Several proposals key on the existence of substantial debts owed to external lenders by governments and private companies in many developing countries. A "debt-for-nature" agreement refers to an arrangement in which some of a country's debt is purchased by a third party, such as an environmental NGO, in exchange for that country's commitment to strengthen wildlands protection (Prestemon and Lampman 1990). This approach is recent, dating from the late 1980s. Since then, countries participating in debt-for-nature agreements include Bolivia, Costa Rica, Ecuador, the Philippines, and Madagascar. These agreements can be set up in numerous ways. Figure 8-5 illustrates an agreement worked out among WWF, a commercial bank, the government of Ecuador, and Ecuador's Fundación Natura (an environmental NGO).

Impacts of debt-for-nature swaps have been small in relation to the overall debt burden, but options based on debt relief are far from exhausted. It is conceivable that debt relief could be coordinated on a global basis, and that this would release financial resources of direct and indirect benefit to forest protection and management in several indebted countries.

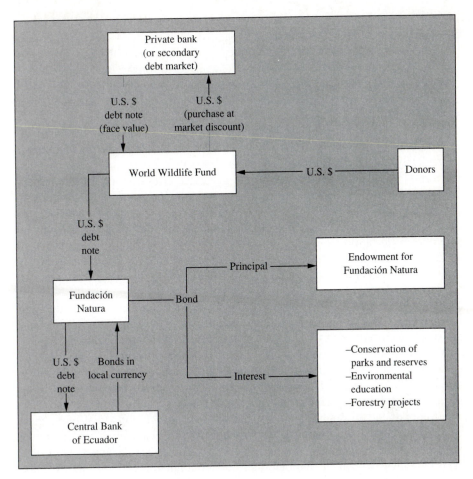

FIGURE 8-5.
Structure of a debt-for-nature agreement in Ecuador, late 1980s. *(Sources: WWF (1988) and Prestemon and Lampman (1990, p. 14).)* Reprinted from *Journal of Forestry,* published by the Society of American Foresters, 5400 Grosvenor Lane, Bethesda, MD 20814–2198.

SYNTHESIS

Development assistance emerged in its present institutional form at the end of the Second World War. With it has evolved a stream of constantly revised doctrines, approaches, and priorities. Forestry—broadly defined to encompass farm and community forestry, food-aided tree planting, watershed management, and protected wildlands—enjoys a relatively respectable status in today's programs of development assistance. Worldwide preoccupation with tropical deforestation and other environmental threats explains forestry's rising position in the international development banks and agencies. Forest industries, while never entirely disappearing from the development agenda, have lost ground in relation to forestry's "new directions." This redefinition of forestry explains why development assistance to the sector attracts broader and deeper financial support than ever before. This support promises to continue to grow into the 1990s.

Bilateral and multilateral assistance is channeled to forestry through dozens of programs and hundreds of projects too numerous to cite individually. The development assistance of virtually all major industrialized countries includes at least some projects in forestry. Among the larger multilateral efforts are forestry projects of the World Bank, World Food Program, and FAO. Coordinated mainly through FAO, the Tropical Forestry Action Plan is the world's single largest program to strategically tackle the problems of protecting and managing the planet's tropical forests. Yet like the WFP, the TFAP generates criticisms of ineffectiveness. Because the TFAP has been operating for only a few years, evaluations of its performance must allow adequate time for internal adjustments to take place. On the other hand, critics argue that the TFAP is too smothered in bureaucracy for true reforms to be possible.

In this respect, the whole of development assistance—including assistance to forestry—has to contend with attacks from the political right, the political left, and environmentalists. Many of these attacks are founded on legitimate grievances. Yet negative attitudes about development assistance also reflect misunderstandings by voters in some of the industrialized countries. In the long run, development assistance to forestry rises or falls on this wider social and political debate.

Aside from development assistance, international cooperation in forestry builds upon cross-country collaboration in science and technology. This can be traced through IUFRO's growth from a small group of forest researchers in Europe about a century ago into a system of working groups now spread across 106 countries. The Man and the Biosphere Program likewise numbers thousands of researchers, and international coordination is central to MAB's organization and planning. At regional levels are networks and cooperatives like MPTS and CAMCORE, both of which depend on international collaboration for germplasm collection, provenance testing, and other cross-country activities to achieve goals set by members collectively. Other cooperative arrangements include universities which share facilities for tropical research, networks besides MPTS and CAMCORE for germplasm conservation and tree breeding, and numerous committees and associations which attempt to transfer forestry research and technology at regional or global levels.

The principles for success in these collaborative endeavors are well known. They emphasize well-articulated interests shared by all members, able leadership, capable and active participants, assured financial support, good communications, and client orientation. Forestry networks are held back to the extent that these conditions are presently unmet in numerous practical cases. A great deal of institution building remains for the future, particularly in the developing countries, if networks in forest science and technology are to become truly effective.

Several international agreements and conventions directly or indirectly affect forestry, particularly through environmental issues of widespread impact. Few of these issues can be defined and managed by individual countries or small groups of countries. Rather, they require a collective response by the world's governments acting in unison. This explains a redefinition of many issues from national to international levels, a proliferation of statements on the rationale for global cooperation, and the debate of conceptual proposals for global organization.

Regional agreements affecting forestry include attempts to harmonize forestry actions within the European Community and within North America, councils and commissions to manage international rivers and lakes, and arrangements to manage binational forest reserves. As this book goes to press, there are no global conventions on forests. However, several conventions take up issues of indirect consequence to forests, and proposals are being drafted for global conventions on biological diversity and atmospheric warming.

A number of ideas suggest how global initiatives could be funded, e.g., in relation to taking control of deforestation in the developing countries. Proposals include taxes on carbon emissions and other sources of greenhouse gases, international rent payments to the governments of developing countries for conservation concessions, establishment of an international environmental facility to coordinate environmental management in the developing countries, and coordination of debt relief on a global basis.

Hence potential strategies are many and often creative. To be overcome is the inertia of past generations of working separately, and of past political indifference to pluralistic approaches. Realistically, effective global coordination of forest protection and management will not happen with the signing of a few documents. Global conventions demand extraordinary commitment and exceptional human energy to translate noble declarations of purpose into programs that produce practical results. However, the broadening of social and political concern about forests in so many parts of the world suggests that incremental movement towards global arrangements is virtually inevitable, even if progress is measured in decades rather than years.

ISSUES FOR DISCUSSION AND INVESTIGATION

1 Enlightened self-interest is the most reliable basis for international cooperation in forestry (Hummel and Hilmi 1989, p. 97). Explain.

2 There is entirely too little external development assistance to forestry in the developing countries. True or false? Defend.

3 A few years after its inception, critical judgments were made about the effectiveness of the Tropical Forestry Action Plan (Winterbottom 1990). (i) What were those judgments? (ii) In what ways is it useful and necessary to evaluate TFAP after its first few years? In what ways is it premature?

4 The golden rule in development assistance is that "those who have the gold make the rules." Explain, and discuss in the context of forestry projects funded by the development banks and the bilateral assistance agencies.

5 Beginning in the late 1970s, the World Bank claimed to have dramatically shifted its forestry portfolio away from industrial forestry. (i) What factors — political, philosophical, environmental, and economic — explain this shift? (ii) Was the shift genuine, or was it mainly cosmetic to show accord with the demands of environmentalists? (iii) Is the shift permanent? Why or why not?

6 The Philippines receives considerable external assistance to forestry. In the early 1990s, donors and potential donors to Philippine forestry include the Asian Development Bank, the World Bank, the Australian government, the German government, the Japanese government, the USA government, and the World Wildlife Fund. From the standpoint of the Philippine government, what are the advantages and disadvantages of having this array of foreign assistance to forestry?

7 The title of a book about Australian forestry aid to Nepal is *Innocents Abroad in the Forests of Nepal* (Griffen 1988). The author relates that the Nepal-Australia Forestry Project "stumbled forward" since its beginnings 20 years earlier, and expresses the hope that perhaps something beneficial will emerge from it twenty years into the future. (i) Discuss the acceptability of this 40-year time frame from the viewpoints of Australia's taxpayers and politicians, Nepal's forestry officials, and Nepal's rural residents as project beneficiaries. (ii) Why does it take so long for development projects to achieve accomplishments?

8 Through the years, the banks and agencies which administer development assistance are given new mandates to be factored into their programs and projects. The series of revolving issues includes integrated rural development, appropriate technology, basic needs, women in development, private enterprise, and now environment and sustainability. (i) Investigate the extent to which this succession of emphases has influenced the content of development assistance in forestry. (ii) Comment on the coming and going of these fashions in development assistance as a source of frustration for the development banks and agencies.

9 IUFRO is the largest coordinating body for international cooperation in forestry research, but it works with a modest budget. What strategies should IUFRO's leaders embrace to most effectively advance the international "union" of forestry research?

10 The USA has formal scientific exchange programs in forestry with more than 20 countries. For example, the USA and USSR have established a Forestry Working Group to encourage joint research projects, scientific conferences, and professional publications. From the standpoint of the USA and its exchange partners, what should be expected from these programs? That is, what constitutes success in bilateral scientific cooperation?

11 An international forestry research network is intended to reduce costs, minimize duplication, boost efficiency, and lead towards national self-sufficiency in research capability and management (Burley 1987). What obstacles have to be overcome in order to achieve these benefits?

12 The CAMCORE cooperative is an international research network drawing mainly on private funding. (i) What factors explain mainly private funding in CAMCORE, and mainly public funding in most other international forestry networks? (ii) How might the matter of private or public funding determine a network's goals and organization?

13 "Careful consideration must be given to the focus of new or expanded [international] forestry research networks to ensure they are both relevant and manageable" (MacDicken et al. 1990, p. 2). What is the concern here?

14 During most of the 1980s, the government of the USA failed to endorse new international agreements on matters pertaining to the global environment, and reduced its commitment to international programs it previously supported. Investigate the reasons for this position, together with its political and psychological impacts, both positive and negative.

15 Various international agreements to protect the world's forests, atmosphere, and oceans are declarations of principle rather than binding legal treaties. These declarations often outreach current implementation capacity. Instead, many describe an idealistic world of "should" and "shall" in advance of current possibilities. This raises the challenging question (Caldwell 1984, p. 80): "Is the cause of world environmental protection more likely to be harmed than helped by declarations of principle to which signatories have neither the intention nor ability to observe?"

16 Identify possible strategies to finance global conventions aimed at slowing tropical deforestation. What will be required to make these strategies politically acceptable and administratively effective?

REFERENCES

Bauer, Peter T. 1972. *Dissent on Development*. Harvard University Press, Cambridge.

Bengston, David N. and Hans M. Gregersen. 1988. "What influences forestry research capacity in developed and less-developed countries?" *Journal of Forestry* 86(2):41–43.

Buckman, Robert E. 1987. "Strengthening forestry institutions in the developing world," *Ambio* 16:120–121.

Burley, J. 1987. "International forestry research networks—objectives, problems, and management," *Unasylva* 39(157/158):67–73.

Caldwell, Lynton K. 1984. *International Environmental Policy: Emergence and Dimensions*. Duke University Press, Durham, NC.

Cassen, Robert and Associates. 1986. *Does Aid Work?* Report to an Intergovernmental Task Force. Oxford University Press, Oxford.

Dvorak, William S. and Jan G. Laarman. 1986. "Conserving the genes of tropical conifers," *Journal of Forestry* 84(1):43–45.

FAO (Food and Agriculture Organization). 1985. *FAO: The First Forty Years, 1945–85*. FAO, Rome, Italy.

FAO. 1989. *Review of International Cooperation in Tropical Forestry*. Committee on Forest Development in the Tropics, Report FO:FDT/89/3, FAO, Rome, Italy.

Fui, Lim Hin. 1990. "Importance of MPTS information exchange to network success," *Farm Forestry News* 4(1):3, 10.

Gregersen, Hans, Ronnie de Camino, Philip Kio, and Peter Oram. 1989. *International and Regional Organizations and Networks Involved in Tropical Forestry Research*. Technical Advisory Committee, Consultative Group for International Agricultural Research.

Griffin, D. M. 1988. *Innocents Abroad in the Forests of Nepal: An Account of Australian Aid to Nepalese Forestry*. Anutech Pty Ltd., Canberra, Australia.

Hayter, Teresa. 1971. *Aid as Imperialism*. Penguin Books, New York.

Hummel, F. C. and H. A. Hilmi. 1989. *Forestry Policies in Europe*. FAO Forestry Paper 92, Food and Agriculture Organization, Rome, Italy.

Kramer, John Michael. 1987. "Food aid support for international forestry," pp. 292–296 in *National Convention of Society of American Foresters*. Minneapolis, MN.

Krueger, Anne O., Constantine Michalopoulos, and Vernon W. Ruttan. 1989. *Aid and Development*. Johns Hopkins University Press, Baltimore and London, England.

Le Prestre, Philippe G. 1989. *The World Bank and the Environmental Challenge*. Associated University Presses, Cranbury, NJ.

MacDicken, Kenneth G., Sathit Wacharakitti, and Celso B. Lantican. 1990. "Research networks: What they are, what they can do," *Farm Forestry News* 4(1):10–3.

McGaughey, Stephen E. 1986. "International financing for forestry," *Unasylva* 38(1):2–11.

McNeely, Jeffrey A. 1989. "How to pay for conserving biological diversity," *Ambio* 18(6):308–313.

Mergen, Francois, Robert E. Evenson, M. Ann Judd, and Jonathan Putnam. 1988. "Forestry research: A provisional global inventory," *Economic Development and Cultural Change* 37:149–171.

Pardo, Richard D. 1990. "The institutional response: Multilateral technical assistance agencies," pp. 399–406 in *National Convention of Society of American Foresters,* Washington, DC.

Plucknett, D. L. and N. J. H. Smith. 1984. "Networking in international agricultural research," *Science* 225:989–993.

Prestemon, Jeffrey P. and Scott E. Lampman. 1990. "Third World debt: Are there opportunities for forestry?" *Journal of Forestry* 88(2):12–16.

Riddell, Roger C. 1987. *Foreign Aid Reconsidered*. Johns Hopkins University Press, Baltimore.

Rielly, John E. 1983. *American Public Opinion and United States Foreign Policy*. Chicago Council on Foreign Relations, Chicago.

Singer, H., J. Wood, and T. Jennings. 1987. *Food Aid: The Challenge and the Opportunity*. Clarendon Press, Oxford, England.

Spears, John. 1987. *Tropical Deforestation: A Suggested Policy Research and Development Agenda for the Bank in the 1990s*. World Bank, Washington, DC.

Ullsten, Ola, Salleh Mohd. Nor, and Montague Yudelman. 1990. *Tropical Forestry Action Plan: Report of the Independent Review*. Kuala Lumpur, Malaysia.

Wall, D. 1973. *The Charity of Nations: The Political Economy of Foreign Aid*. Basic Books, New York.

WCED (World Commission on Environment and Development). 1987. *Our Common Future*. Oxford University Press, Oxford.

Winterbottom, Robert. 1990. *Taking Stock: The Tropical Forest Action Plan After Five Years*. World Resources Institute, Washington, DC.

World Bank. 1978. *Forestry Sector Policy Paper*. Washington, DC.

World Bank. 1986. *World Bank Financed Forestry Activity in the Decade 1977-86: A Review of Key Policy Issues and Implications of Past Experience to Future Project Design*. World Bank, Washington, DC.

WRI (World Resources Institute). 1989. *Natural Endowments: Financing Resource Conservation for Development*. World Resources Institute, Washington, DC.

WWF (World Wildlife Fund). 1988. "Debt-for-nature swaps: A new conservation tool," *World Wildlife Fund Letter* 1:1–9.

PROGRESS THROUGH LEARNING

This book identified factors complicating forest management for development. They begin with ambiguities about the meaning of development, and questions about certain aspects of Western industrial development as a model. To the often changing messages coming from development theory must be added constraints in forest management. Among them are long production periods, complex production relationships, unresolved sustainability issues, and the central importance of unpriced values and off-site impacts.

Forestry faces a reconstruction in advancing its science and technology, rationalizing its policies, and building public support. Very crucial will be fresh and intensified efforts to examine the adequacy of long-accepted doctrines. Most essential of all is learning how to answer the double question of "forests for whom and for what" in a context of social expectations remarkably different than even one or two decades ago.

FORESTRY IN THE REMAKING

The theme of forests for human development demands a close look at the perceptual environment. Perceptions of forestry's role are changing rapidly, as would be expected for a relatively young professional endeavor. To be remembered always is the youth of forestry in relation to biological time. Widespread policy interest in forests has a history of only 200–300 years in Europe, 100–150 years in North America, and only 20–30 years (or less) in many regions of the developing world.

Forestry and Unmade Connections

The still experimental character of development theory and practice, combined with just a few generations of forest management, produces an immature field of knowledge and practice. This has several manifestations. Key among them is weak integration of forestry and forests in the larger economy and social setting. This is explained by generally insufficient attention to forces outside the sector which dominate what happens inside it. Among these forces are land tenure, rural-urban migration (and its reverse in some industrialized regions), expansion of rural infrastructure, housing policies, social welfare policies, and fiscal and trade policies.

A second and closely related factor is forestry's traditionally understated linkages with agriculture, water supply, energy supply, and leisure pursuits. These linkages exist, but past priorities frequently have been directed elsewhere. Funding and other inputs for forest management will continue to be low as long as these broader connections are ignored or underestimated.

Other unmade connections can be cited for farm and community forestry. Early projects in farm and community forestry in developing countries often failed because they ignored experience already accumulated in agriculture. Efforts to organize tree growing at the local level repeated some of agriculture's mistakes, partly for reasons of forestry's past isolation (Blair and Olpadwala 1988). Nor is it clear that outside intervention to assist small-scale tree growing in the tropics is making an effort to learn from centuries of farm and community forestry in temperate regions. The shared context of small-scale tree growers from one country to another is often obscured behind hundreds of local studies, few of which are compared with each other.

Evidence of immaturity also shows in the post-1970s alarm about tropical deforestation. Wildly divergent estimates of rates of deforestation—and assessments of its consequences—attest to inadequate knowledge. Ignoring all historical perspectives, many persons fail to see that contemporary deforestation in the tropics relates to centuries of shifting land frontiers in temperate zones.

Formal Models Versus Learning-by-Doing

Forest management makes extensive use of formal models in planning, budgeting, and optimization. Yet even so-called comprehensive models are inadequate tools for evaluating the redesign of forest policies (King 1975), the social efficiency of forest ownership (Stewart 1985), and the restructuring of public agencies to administer forests (Velay 1975). Benefit-cost studies are of little help in debates about the relative amount of forest that should be allotted for amenity values, or methods to encourage forest cooperatives. In general, formal models simply cannot handle these poorly defined issues. Hence most policy analysis in inexact fields like forestry emerges from ordinary knowledge, social learning, and interactive problem solving (Lindblom and Cohen 1979).

It might be thought that sectoral planning plays a major part in learning and subsequent redesign of forestry. This is questionable. Comprehensive planning is notoriously bad and expensive in developing countries. Data requirements frequently are too demanding, and analytical skills too limiting, for planning to lead to learning. Frequently, learning is better accomplished through sensible politics and sound public administration than through planning exercises (Caiden and Wildavsky 1974).

In a different context, public forest planning in the industrialized countries is heavily burdened with political content and legislative requirements. Planning can be costly, time-consuming, and highly controversial (Binkley et al. 1988). This is the high price paid for previous gaps in mutual education between forest managers and the public. Planning has led to learning on both sides, but with future progress dependent on greater rationality. Presently, the costs of planning may well exceed the benefits (Fox et al. 1989).

In contrast to these synoptic thinking-through approaches are those which stress learning-by-doing. The problems of forest management are turned over to local people to solve on the basis of their needs, knowledge, skills, and constraints. Learning takes place in an acting-out strategy, and frequently works. Yet in its most extreme forms, this approach misses the benefit of experience gained elsewhere, and forgoes technologies which no amount of local effort can duplicate without external inputs. Moreover, local time and labor invested in tree growing and forestry have opportunity costs, so that goals like "maximizing local participation" become a dubious objective (Johnston and Clark 1982).

Furthermore, a people's forestry has three distinct problems not characteristic of a people's agriculture. First is widespread and discouraging apathy to forestry and tree growing in more countries than forestry proponents like to admit (Westoby 1985). The second problem concerns the vague and often infeasible ideas people have about their needs from forests, and their inadequate thought about how one goal is traded for another (Baskerville 1988). The third problem is the comparatively long time period for acting-out strategies in forestry to produce learning experiences.

ESTABLISHING AN IMPROVED LEARNING PROCESS

In a young practice like forestry, no learning takes place without open and honest self-appraisal, coupled with positive attitudes towards changing things for the better (Korten 1980). Learning also means recognizing the falsity of uniquely correct approaches and absolute priorities (Hirschman 1971). Thus policymakers should be planning to fail—but constructively (Michael 1973).

Allowing for Surprise and Discontinuous Change

For the most part, forest management in both theory and practice has been considered a continuous practice in which change is gradual and predictable. However, this thinking can be challenged in light of newer and alternative conceptual frameworks calling attention to surprises, discontinuities, and crises which arise unexpectedly and dramatically.

The usual focus on annual averages, annual budgets, and other short-term cycles is rendered less relevant in the historical long run by extreme cases, abrupt reversals, nonlinearities, and catastrophes. These rare occurrences are recognized in fire management, forest hydrology, forest pathology, and other technical disciplines. However, a more encompassing perspective would see the entirety of forest management in a past and especially a future of multiple and shocking surprises.

Several factors explain why forestry is particularly vulnerable to surprises and discontinuities. The first is orientation to a biological system in which nature rather than man often has the last word, no matter how much man struggles to dominate. The second and related factor is great scientific uncertainty regarding rates and patterns of species extinctions, productivity changes under multiple harvests of plantation forests, the relation of forests to climate change, and a long and growing list of other questions on environmental management. The third and highly volatile factor is explosion of public interest in forests and their uses, but an interest founded in many cases on incomplete, confused, and often distorted

FIGURE 9-1
Illustrations of surprises and discontinuities affecting forest planning, policy, and management. *(Source: Framework adapted from Brooks (1986, p. 326).)*

Unexpected discrete events:

- Calamitous forest fires in Kalimantan (Indonesia) and China, hurricanes in Nicaragua and USA, wind storms in France and UK, and other unexpected natural disasters
- Destructive population explosions of insect pests (*Leucaena* psyllid in Philippines, spruce budworm in eastern Canada)
- Political upheavals leading to abrupt changes or losses of most key forestry officials (many countries)

Discontinuities in long-term trends:

- Sudden increase in fuelwood demand following rapid petroleum price escalation in 1970s
- Falling demand for sawnwood and wood panels in industrialized countries due to profound economic and social changes affecting housing (USA, some parts of Europe)
- Sharp economic downturn in early 1980s leading to collapse and restructuring of forest industries (west coast of North America)
- Major adjustments in wood-processing industries of Japan, Taiwan, and Korea following Indonesia's ban on log exports
- Relatively short period for nontraditional exporters of forest products to achieve significant market shares (Chile, Brazil)
- Dramatic ownership changes in large forest products corporations affecting strategies on forestlands (USA)
- Relatively quick emergence of thousands of nongovernmental and voluntary organizations on issues of environment and economic development (starting 1970s)
- Emergence of Japan as a major giver of international assistance to developing countries (starting 1980s)

Sudden emergence of new information in public and political consciousness:

- Discovery of a fuelwood crisis (late 1970s)
- Discovery of tropical deforestation (early 1980s)
- Discovery of forest decline in Europe (early 1980s)
- Discovery of global warming (late 1980s)

information. This spreading but frequently uninformed social interest leads to the fourth factor, which is the elevated political attention to forests at a global level. Unpredictable nature, limited science, exploding social interest, and increased political stakes are potent ingredients for surprises in forestry (Figure 9-1).

Often a dramatic surprise raises intense concern for a short period, but not for a sufficient length of time to permanently alter the direction of policy. This is perhaps the situation of many programs and projects in wood energy begun after petroleum prices escalated sharply in the late 1970s. On the one hand, petroleum prices stabilized thereafter. On the other, efforts faltered as political and professional attention was pulled away by still newer issues. Many other examples could be cited of short-term initiatives in forestry which unceremoniously die for lack of continuing interest.

Often the "discovery" of new information is the result of long-term trends always present but recognized by only a few prophets and silent or inarticulate scientists. Aspects of acid rain, tropical deforestation, and global climate change fit these descriptions. Much of this information could have been obtained earlier if only news media, professional mainstreams, and political leaders knew where and how to look for it. Instead, it remained submerged and disputed among a few scattered individuals.

The discontinuities, then, often include those of communication. The latent information emerges quickly once a perceptual threshold is bridged. This threshold is crossed only in the presence of articulate writers and speakers, capable of presenting powerful conclusions from previously isolated observations. Quite suddenly, a larger audience perceives the correctness of the new doctrine, and they in turn spread the revised understanding to still wider audiences. A chain reaction takes place, and within just a short time an entire new paradigm is in place.

If surprises and discontinuities are prominent in forestry, how should that affect learning strategies? A first response is to recognize that the improbable happens, and that more surprises are on the way. These surprises will be both negative and positive, and will occur in science, technology, nature, and social organization (Brooks 1986).

Beyond the necessary act of surprise recognition, Figure 9-2 sketches a few strategies emerging from systems theory. Most important is to broaden the response base in forestry in order to anticipate surprises and interpret problems from

FIGURE 9-2

Strategies to contend with surprises and discontinuities in forestry. *(Sources: Brooks (1986); Timmerman (1986).)*

- Seek wide range of experience, ages, backgrounds, and viewpoints in human systems
- Encourage organizational self-knowledge, diversity, dissent, and criticism
- Use pilot studies to experiment with actual systems, but at levels below the catastrophic
- Invest in research and development, especially in R&D of human systems and social organization
- Conduct detailed retrospective studies on "what might have been"
- Prolong the experimentation of pre-solution periods

perspectives not otherwise possible. In this context can be judged the rationale for recruiting professionals from nontraditional backgrounds, and for encouraging NGOs and other grass-roots organizations to participate in formulating forest policy. The assumption is that diversity of the response base reduces the risks of unwelcome surprises.

CREATING A POSITIVE IMAGE OF THE FUTURE

In the West, thinking increasingly emphasizes the possibility of choice over the inevitability of fate (Berting 1988). The future can be managed. The challenge is moving beyond merely good intentions to workable strategies and policies. Fortunately, human ingenuity often comes to the rescue in dramatic ways. These are the positive surprises, and the bias for hope (Hirschman 1971).

A positive image of the future is helped by studying the leading accomplishments already completed or underway in various parts of the world. The worldwide search for success stories has applicability in forest research (Spears 1988), case studies of saving tropical forests (Green and Barborak 1987), and environmental management very broadly (Repetto 1985). The gap between the leading edge and the average provides clues for learning, inspires images of the possible, and implicitly sets targets (Repetto 1986).

Perhaps no indicator of progress is more encouraging than the growing awareness of forestry issues among the world's political leaders and educated public. Although this is a relatively small and elite body of persons, it embraces the planet's opinion makers. From this level diffuses a recognition of problems and opportunities into broader social and political strata. The upsurge of environmentalism in the industrialized countries during the 1960s and 1970s led almost inevitably to a more global outlook there, and to the spread of environmental consciousness to intellectual and professional leaders in the developing countries.

Meanwhile, institutions have not been standing still. The 1970s gave birth to the United Nations Environmental Program and the International Council for Research in Agroforestry. The World Bank, with negligible lending other than for conventional forest industries, quickly shifted its project portfolio during the late 1970s to favor farm and community forestry, fuelwood, and watershed management. Regional development banks for Asia and Latin America expanded forestry lending from practically nothing before 1980 to levels which now include significant forestry projects. The 1980s saw the inception of the Tropical Forestry Action Plan, the International Tropical Timber Organization, and the redirection of efforts begun in the 1970s. While still immature and failing in many respects, the creation and growth of this institutional framework marks a significant historical achievement.

Over the last few decades, forestry has benefited from an impressive stream of innovations. Malaysia increased the number of tropical hardwood species in common use from less than 100 in 1950 to over 600 in 1985. The use of wood-saving technologies has enabled industrialized countries to greatly improve recovery of waste wood in just a short time. Remote sensing technologies have advanced very far in a few decades. The advent of small computers and the software to use them offer data management capabilities not even imagined before 1980. These few examples illustrate the breadth and depth of recent technical progress. They suggest that potentially large gains can result from wider application of technologies already known, not to mention those still to be developed.

Innovations in economic, social, and institutional spheres are less tangible but no less significant. Since the 1970s, economists have made considerable experimental progress in the valuation of unpriced goods and services, even if applications in forestry are still too few. It could be expected that analytical techniques and professional consensus will lead to ever increasing acceptability and use. Moreover, forestry appears in key studies to recognize depletion of natural resources in national income accounts.

Social and institutional progress since 1980 includes developments in farm and community forestry in Asia, Central America, and elsewhere. It also includes a series of concepts on buffer zones around protected areas, certification of imported tropical timbers, declaration of extractive reserves, and other innovative proposals to protect forests. Not all of these concepts will stand the test of time in application. Yet they demonstrate the intellectual power of an imaginative force which did not exist until recently. In this force lies the creative problem-solving capability for the future.

Finally, slow but steady evolution of new ideas and issues can be inferred by following the themes of World Forestry Congresses. Coordinated between FAO and its member states, these congresses summon world forestry expertise to exchange views and redefine priorities. Just after the Second World War, the forestry congress in Finland (1949) addressed how forests could supply industries with more raw material. The principal debate was whether this meant timber quality or quantity. The theme in India (1954) examined a few problems of tropical forestry, especially soil and water conservation, which may have been the main meaning of environmental protection at the time. The forestry congress in the USA (1960) focused on multiple use, particularly to accommodate recreation and leisure. In Spain (1966), the issues were about the role of forestry in the changing world economy.

In the 1970s and after, the themes turned social. Thus the forestry congress in Argentina (1972) focused on forests for socioeconomic development; in Indonesia (1978), on forests for people; and in Mexico (1985), on forests for the integral development of society. Influenced by social concern for forest sustainability, the congress in Paris (1991) explored forests as a natural and cultural heritage to be passed along to the world of the future.

Themes, speeches, and declarations lead action by a wide margin. Yet the rhetoric is a barometer of opinions at high levels. This rhetoric reveals an unquestionable evolution of main ideas over a few decades. While forestry practice is necessarily conservative, the perceptions and philosophies which surround it are shifting profoundly.

ISSUES FOR DISCUSSION AND INVESTIGATION

1 Identify indications of immaturity ("unmade connections") in forestry, and explain why this immaturity exists. What will be needed to advance forestry's maturity in the years ahead?
2 What are the limitations of formal models in linking forests with development? What are the limitations of learning-by-doing?
3 Surprises and discontinuities are prominent in forestry. Illustrate with examples of discrete events, breaks in long-term trends, and discovery of new information. What are the strategies to cope with surprises and discontinuities?
4 Worldwide support for doing something about forest problems, while far from being a popular groundswell, gives cause for considerable optimism (Saouma 1985). Explain and illustrate.
5 Although forestry appears to be a highly conservative undertaking, it has been evolving rapidly and dramatically. True or false? Explain and defend.

REFERENCES

Baskerville, Gordon. 1988. "Management of publicly owned forests," *Forestry Chronicle* 64:193–198.

Berting, Jan. 1988. "The goals of development in developed countries," pp. 141–181 in UNESCO (United Nations Educational and Scientific Organization), *Goals of Development*. UNESCO, Paris.

Binkley, C. S., G. D. Brewer, and V. A. Sample (eds.). 1988. *Redirecting the RPA: Proceedings of the 1987 Airlie House Conference on the Resources Planning Act*. Yale University School of Forestry and Environmental Studies Bulletin 95, New Haven.

Blair, Harry W. and Porus D. Olpadwala. 1988. "Planning for appropriate forestry enterprises: Lessons from rural development experience in Third World countries," *New Forests* 2:41–64.

Brooks, H. 1986. "The typology of surprises in technology, institutions, and development," pp. 325–350 in W. C. Clark and R. E. Munn (eds.), *Sustainable Development of the Biosphere*. International Institute for Applied Systems Analysis, Cambridge University Press, Cambridge.

Caiden, Naomi and A. Wildavsky. 1974. *Planning and Budgeting in Poor Countries*. John Wiley and Sons, New York.

Fox, B., M. A. Keller, A. J. Schlosberg, and J. E. Vlahovich. 1989. "Opportunity costs of implementing forest plans," *Environmental Management* 13(1):75–84.

Green, G. C. and J. Barborak. 1987. "Conservation for development: Success stories from Central America," *Commonwealth Forestry Review* 66(1):91–102.

Hirschman, Albert O. 1971. *A Bias for Hope*. Yale University Press, New Haven.

Johnston, Bruce F. and William C. Clark. 1982. *Redesigning Rural Development*. Johns Hopkins University Press, Baltimore.

King, K. F. S. 1975. "Forest policies and national development," *Unasylva* 27(107):9–13.

Korten, D. C. 1980. "Community organization and rural development: A learning process approach," *Public Administration Review* 40(5):480–511.

Lindblom, C. E. and D. K. Cohen. 1979. *Usable Knowledge: Social Science and Social Problem Solving*. Yale University Press, New Haven.

Michael, D. N. 1973. *On Learning to Plan and Planning to Learn*. Jossey-Bass Publishers, San Francisco.

Repetto, Robert (ed.). 1985. *The Global Possible*. World Resources Institute, Yale University Press, New Haven.

Repetto, Robert (ed.). 1986. *World Enough and Time*. World Resources Institute, Yale University Press, New Haven.

Saouma, Edouard. 1985. "Forestry: Essential for development," *Unasylva* 37(147):2–6.

Spears, John. 1988. *Containing Tropical Deforestation: A Review of Priority Areas for Technological and Policy Research*. World Bank Environment Department Working Paper 10, World Bank, Washington, DC.

Stewart, P. J. 1985. "The dubious case for state control," *Ceres* 18(2):10–14.

Timmerman, P. 1986. "Mythology and surprise in the sustainable development of the biosphere," pp. 435–454 in W. C. Clark and R. E. Munn (eds.), *Sustainable Development of the Biosphere*. International Institute for Applied Systems Analysis, Cambridge University Press, Cambridge.

Velay, Louis H. 1975. "Designing forest services to suit the country," *Unasylva* 27(109):17–23.

Westoby, Jack C. 1985. "Foresters and politics," *Commonwealth Forestry Review* 64(2):105–116.

INDEX